THE AUTHORITY OF THE GOSPEL

The Authority of the Gospel

Explorations in Moral and Political Theology
in Honor of
OLIVER O'DONOVAN

Edited by

Robert Song and Brent Waters

WILLIAM B. EERDMANS PUBLISHING COMPANY
GRAND RAPIDS, MICHIGAN / CAMBRIDGE, U.K.

© 2015 Robert Song and Brent Waters

Published 2015 by
Wm. B. Eerdmans Publishing Co.
2140 Oak Industrial Drive N.E., Grand Rapids, Michigan 49505 /
P.O. Box 163, Cambridge CB3 9PU U.K.

Printed in the United States of America

21 20 19 18 17 16 15   7 6 5 4 3 2 1

Library of Congress Cataloging-in-Publication Data

The authority of the gospel: explorations in moral and political theology in honor of
    Oliver O'Donovan / edited by Robert Song and Brent Waters.
        pages   cm
    Includes bibliographical references and index.
    ISBN 978-0-8028-7254-8 (cloth: alk. paper)
    1. Theology.   2. Christian ethics.   3. Political theology.
    4. Christianity and politics.   5. O'Donovan, Oliver.
    I. O'Donovan, Oliver.   II. Song, Robert.   III. Waters, Brent.

    BR118.A94   2015
    241 — dc23

                                                                    2014039161

www.eerdmans.com

Contents

CONTENTS

Foreword

Oliver O'Donovan once described a friend and colleague's ventures into political theology and social ethics as a series of guerrilla raids rather than a constructive project. The last thing that could be said of Oliver's work is that it is 'occasional' in the bad sense — reactive or piecemeal. Throughout his colossally distinguished career, his work has been marked by the patient, coherent assemblage of a viewpoint thoroughly permeated by primary theological convictions. It is why he is so hard to characterise as a thinker of 'left' or 'right' — and why therefore he is so hard to dismiss and so necessary a presence. From my own first encounters with his work, some thirty-five years ago, I have been aware of the way in which he succeeds in radically reframing questions by connecting them steadily with these theological fundamentals. And those fundamentals amount to what is surely one of the most eloquent and compelling restatements in the modern age of a classical Reformed divinity which, like Calvin's own thinking, is imbued with the insights of the patristic age as well as the results of painstaking scriptural exegesis.

In accord with this tradition, Oliver is profoundly concerned with that most unfashionable of subjects, *authority*, more specifically the nature of political authority in relation to the universal Lordship of the risen Christ. In one of his most magisterial and brilliant works, *The Ways of Judgment*, he succeeds in connecting that living in the presence of judgment that is the heart of faithful discipleship with the constant call to exercise judgement in public affairs. Because we live under authority and thus have that to which we must hold ourselves accountable, we cannot avoid the task of discerning in the transactions of human society what is and is not truly lawful and right. But this is at the same time an abstention from any claim to ultimate judgement: the fellowship of believers exists as witness to judgement, not, in the present age, agent of judgement. It points to what Oliver calls the 'post-political', the ultimate condition of free fellowship with God on the part of human creatures. The Church is the context in which the political subject is both fulfilled and surpassed; and in that connection it is the indispensable presence which keeps alive argument about what is just in a society, what does and does not assure the human flourishing willed by the creator, what does and does not shape a sustainable 'tradition of purposes and goals' in a society. And behind all of this lies the conviction that what has been revealed in Jesus Christ crucified and risen is justice — the answer to the cry of God's people for judgement to be given and enacted, for just or equitable or orderly or perhaps 'apt' relation to be at last established between God and the world and between human agents.

In this as in all his books, Oliver is developing a full-blooded doctrine of Church, ministry, and sacraments in the course of discussing what we might mistakenly have thought at first to be issues quite alien to this agenda. Equally, the sustained and often complex arguments about theory repeatedly issue in extraordinarily acute judgements on specific questions of the day. Oliver's comment on current concerns is always illuminating precisely because he never begins from a package-deal of current orthodoxies; many have found his reflections on the debates in the Anglican Communion over sexual ethics uniquely helpful because they cut across the conventional tribal divides — and repeatedly help you see what the underlying, non-journalistic questions are for any Church that seeks to be theologically honest. The issue for him is always how to approach any question from the centre of Christian conviction concerning the calling of the Church and the believer as baptised into Christ's resurrection.

Oliver is a difficult, enriching writer, the stimulus of whose work is exceptional for all those who have engaged with it. Even the guerrilla (whose identity the reader may have guessed) will need to sit and ponder whether or not he is thinking in a properly theological mode about this or that issue — war, abortion, racism, whatever it may be. The present volume is a worthy tribute to one of the most serious thinkers the Anglican family has nurtured in the last century or so; a learned, subtle, compassionate voice, ambitious for truthfulness and obedient to grace. It is a joy to salute him and wish him many years.

ROWAN WILLIAMS
Cambridge, Lent 2014

Contributors

NIGEL BIGGAR is Regius Professor of Moral and Pastoral Theology, and Director of the McDonald Centre for Theology, Ethics, and Public Life, at the University of Oxford.

BRIAN BROCK is Reader in Moral and Pastoral Theology at the University of Aberdeen.

JONATHAN CHAPLIN is Director of the Kirby Laing Institute for Christian Ethics, Cambridge.

ERIC GREGORY is Professor of Religion at Princeton University.

SHINJI KAYAMA is Pastor, Rokkakubashi Church (Yokohama), the United Church of Christ in Japan.

JEAN-YVES LACOSTE is a Life Member of Clare Hall, University of Cambridge, and an Honorary Fellow of the Australian Catholic University.

JOAN O'DONOVAN is Honorary Fellow at the University of Edinburgh.

OLIVER O'DONOVAN is Emeritus Professor of Christian Ethics and Practical Theology at the University of Edinburgh, and Emeritus Student and Canon of Christ Church, Oxford.

ROBERT SONG is Professor of Theological Ethics at Durham University.

HANS ULRICH was until his retirement Universitätsprofessor at the Theological Faculty of the University of Erlangen-Nürnberg, Chair for Systematic Theology and Theological Ethics.

BERND WANNENWETSCH has held chairs in systematic theology and ethics at the Universities of Oxford and Aberdeen.

BRENT WATERS is the Jerre and Mary Joy Stead Professor of Christian Social Ethics and Director of the Jerre and Mary Joy Stead Center for Ethics and Values at Garrett-Evangelical Theological Seminary.

JOHN WEBSTER is Professor of Divinity at the University of St Andrews.

ROWAN WILLIAMS served as the 104th Archbishop of Canterbury from 2002 to 2012 and is now Master of Magdalene College, University of Cambridge.

JOHN WITTE, JR. is Jonas Robitscher Professor of Law, Alonzo L. McDonald Distinguished Service Professor, and Director of the Center for the Study of Law and Religion at Emory University.

HOLGER ZABOROWSKI is Professor of the History of Philosophy and of Philosophical Ethics at the Catholic University in Vallendar, Germany.

Introduction

Robert Song and Brent Waters

Oliver O'Donovan is widely regarded as one of the pre-eminent Protestant Christian ethicists of the present time. In a career which has spanned over four decades and included appointments at Wycliffe Hall, Oxford, Wycliffe College, Toronto, the University of Oxford, and the University of Edinburgh, his teaching and scholarship has exerted a conspicuous influence on a generation of moral theologians. The breadth of his intellectual interests within Christian ethics, the formidable range of theological, philosophical, and historical learning he brings to his writing, the imagination and profundity of insight he displays, as well as the elegance, poise, and wit of his prose, are all familiar to students of the discipline, and many of his works have become standard reference-points in their area.

It may be difficult to recall, looking back, how the scene looked in Christian ethics when O'Donovan entered it. The dominant analytical style of moral philosophy was dedicated to the meta-ethical study of the language of morals, and was wedded to a seemingly impassible division between descriptive and prescriptive moral claims; it had yet to learn that it might have practical responsibilities, and even when it did eventually learn this, its repertoire was almost entirely limited to one or another variety of utilitarian or Kantian analysis. Protestant ethics was absorbed in disputes about the meaning of love, whether this implied discerning value in or bestowing value on the object of love, whether one was liberated from moral norms by the situational context or, more promisingly, required to qualify norms to give substance to love. Christian political engagement was dominated by political realism, while liberation and political theologies were only just beginning to make their presence felt. In Britain, Anglican social ethics had devised middle axioms to lubricate the gap between the Church of England's theological commitments and its continuing social responsibilities as purveyor of moral values to the nation; but it was only dimly aware of the tortuous and increasingly awkward path ahead of it, indicating that in important ways it no longer spoke for the country of which it was the established church. British evangelicals held fast to the Bible, but disputed whether Christian ethics should be cast fundamentally as creation ethics or kingdom ethics, and in general had very little understanding of the classical theological tradition.

The contours of Christian ethics as it has come to be known in the decades since then were hardly in sight, in other words. The recovery of the virtues and of eudaemonist thinking for Protestant ethics, the role of the church in ethical deliberation, the thick engagement with the theological tradition, and in particular with Augustine of Hippo, Thomas Aquinas, and Karl Barth, the rise of modernity-critique, the problematizing of liberalism, the rise of tradition-based thinking, the engagement with pluralism — all of these have advanced decisively since then. O'Donovan has not been closely associated with all of these developments, and some of them he critically engages fairly vigorously, but he has made distinctive contributions to many of them. Perhaps no other of his contemporaries has managed to combine so effectively a deep familiarity and love of Scripture, an extraordinary knowledge of the magisterial tradition of doctrinal and moral theology, and a commitment to the illumination of both the concepts and application of Christian ethics.

O'Donovan's recent retirement affords an opportunity to acknowledge and honour his formative contributions to Christian ethics. The primary purpose of this book, however, is not to assess his work; that is a task that may be entrusted to a future generation of doctoral students in search of theses to write. Rather each of the essays is an attempt to show how each of the contributors have been enabled to develop their own thinking through serious engagement with his work. Or to change the metaphor, the objective of this book is to build upon, expand, and perhaps even correct a few lines of an agenda for Christian ethics that he has been instrumental in building. To genuinely honour O'Donovan, one cannot remain content with reciting but must risk one's own exposition.

The first essay in the volume, by Bernd Wannenwetsch, addresses themes related to the subject of O'Donovan's Oxford doctoral thesis and first book, *The Problem of Self-Love in Augustine* (1980). Augustine's understanding of love and its relation to faith appears on the face of it flatly to contradict that of

Luther: the one appears to make the response of love primary, the other the receptivity of faith. Schematically, one might be characterised as faith formed by love, the other as love formed by faith. Yet, so Wannenwetsch argues, the two are finally much closer conceptually than this analysis might suggest. Criticising the Lutheran–Roman Catholic Joint Declaration on the Doctrine of Justification (1999) for some mechanistic formulations of the relation of faith and love, he shows how both thinkers integrate the priority of divine action with the unity of justification and sanctification; for neither of them is love made external to or independent of a receptivity to grace. For Luther faith is active, using love as a tool; it is conceptualised as affection, and not just as cognition. For Augustine, love is always responsive to God's prior love; it is never a formless or arbitrary love, but always ordered to the good. This is not to say that both agree on all matters, and in a postscript Wannenwetsch draws out a major residual difference between the two of them.

O'Donovan's second major volume was his remarkable *summa* of moral theology, *Resurrection and Moral Order: An Outline for Evangelical Ethics* (1986), a work which combined wide biblical and theological reading to show forth the possibilities for a reshaped and renewed evangelical and Anglican ethics. A central theme of this book was the recapitulation of creation in the resurrection of Christ: the resurrection affirms the goodness of creation, but also points it forward to its eschatological fulfilment. Jean-Yves Lacoste finds in this interrelation of eschatology and protology the key to unlock a problematic faced by the philosophies of Martin Heidegger and Emmanuel Levinas. For Heidegger, Lacoste argues, although he takes intersubjectivity for granted, any kind of relationship with other people remains unthematised — the other remains curiously faceless. For Levinas, by contrast, the other is constantly present, and appears to me, speaking; yet even as he does, he holds me hostage without any possibility of dialogue. However, in both cases the relationship with the other is always a private rather than a public matter; in both cases the city is absent. The world of politics is divorced from the world of morality, and for neither Heidegger nor Levinas is there any possibility of moral negotiation of disputes between hostile political entities at a public level. For Christianity, however, it is possible to talk of a city which echoes the created order and prefigures the eschatological city, and which is therefore inherently related to the good. Violence is therefore not primordial, nor is it ultimate, as is witnessed by the Christian doctrine of just war, which bridges the gap between public and private morality and dares to speak about the moral use of violence because of its confidence in the coming messianic age.

Nigel Biggar also approaches the ethics of war, but with a rather different range of questions in mind. O'Donovan's inaugural lecture at Oxford, delivered in 1983 and published as *Principles in the Public Realm: The Dilemma of Christian Moral Witness* (1984), addressed the evergreen topic of the nature of the Church's interventions in matters of public policy. Although this took divorce rather than war as its case study, O'Donovan has dedicated two books to the ethics of war (*Peace and Certainty: A Theological Essay on Deterrence* [1989] — a book on nuclear deterrence published just as the Berlin Wall was about to fall, as he later ruefully observed — and *The Just War Revisited* [2003]), as well as several articles. Biggar takes up O'Donovan's claim that Christian ethicists should be cautious about making detailed pronouncements on policy, arguing instead that while churches may do well to be more circumspect, individual ethicists should have the courage to stand with those who bear the weight of making decisions on behalf of the public. Putting his money where his mouth is, Biggar gives a detailed defence of the justice of the 2003 invasion of Iraq, an argument all the more striking in that it is written in full knowledge of the consequences of the war.

The presenting issue of the church's role in politics has compelled O'Donovan to probe the specifically theological nature of political authority, and turned him to the thematic of the significance of ecclesiology for political theology. This is the preoccupation which has formed what are arguably O'Donovan's pre-eminent constructive achievements to date, his twin works on political theology and ethics (*The Desire of the Nations: Rediscovering the Roots of Political Theology* [1996] and *The Ways of Judgment* [2005]). Drawing on a formidable knowledge of the mediaeval tradition of political theology, exemplified in *From Irenaeus to Grotius: A Sourcebook in Christian Political Thought* (1999), the massive reader which he co-edited with Joan O'Donovan, and expounded in essays such as those collected alongside several of Joan's in *Bonds of Imperfection: Christian Politics, Past and Present* (2004), he has opened out the language and practice of political theology from the Hegelian and Marxisant tendencies with which it had become associated. In its stead he has restored a continuity with the classical tradition of Christian political thinking, drawing on a rich and detailed engagement not only with those conventionally regarded as the highest peaks in the range — Augustine, Thomas Aquinas, the magisterial Reformers — but with a host of lesser known and often unknown figures as well (who can forget their first encounter with Norman Anonymous or Nikephoros Blemmydes?). And all of this has been grounded in an extraordinarily fertile and perceptive reading of Scripture, notable both for its grand scope across the range of both Old and New Testaments, and for its grasp of the most unlikely detail.

The result is an unashamedly theological vision of the political realm. The Old Testament establishes that 'the Lord is king' (Psalm 93.1), ruling over both Israel and the nations of the world. Although a duality between the claims of political authority and the claims of God has been inserted into human political experience, a duality that was first evident in the exile in Babylon, Jesus Christ proclaims anew that unitary kingship in his preaching of the Kingdom of God, and decisively establishes it in his death and triumphant resurrection. While the claiming of the Great City as the Holy City promised in the book of Revelation has yet to be manifested in this time between the times, the political structures of the old age are given licence to continue their rule, but only within the eschatological context of Christ's reign. The church therefore also finds itself as a political authority, ruled by another king, with a Christological and eschatological orientation that can never allow it to become merely a provider of spiritual services to an autonomous political realm. Secular political authority now finds itself divested of any ultimate claim on its subjects' identity, the sole justification of government now being found in the rendering of judgement. Rulers are to renounce their sovereignty, a truth that they came to realize in the period known as Christendom, which O'Donovan interprets not as a bid for secular power by the church, but as secular power's recognising the command of Christ represented in the church. Political acts are finally authorised as analogies of divinely authorised acts, something increasingly forgotten in the liberal social orders which have succeeded Christendom and which assume that political order is ultimately founded in human corporate will.

Exploration of various themes within O'Donovan's political theology occupies nearly half of the essays in this collection. The picture is of course broadly Augustinian in its general shape, and a number of these essays investigate the relation of his discussions of moral and political matters to those found in Augustine. Eric Gregory, for example, accepts O'Donovan's Augustinian distinction of saving history from political history, and his emphases on the impotence of political action to achieve eschatological fulfilment and the need for this-worldly patience, and on the centrality of practical reasonableness rather than prophecy as the primary mode of political theology. He rejects the idea that an Augustinian posture in politics requires what he calls an 'atmospheric Augustinianism' that extols the regrettable necessity of dirty hands. There is in O'Donovan not just a realism about sin but also an openness to the good: there is what is presumably an analogy of participation of human acts in divine acts, even if the human mirroring is always through broken glass. But he wonders whether O'Donovan's rightful rejection of his-

toricist efforts to find salvation in every act of providence or to render pro-
phetically legible every historical moment leads him to fall short of his commitment to the gracedness of creation and to neglect the possibility of Karl
Barth's 'secular parables'. Just as Biggar would like ethicists to be free to venture specific prudential judgements, might there not also be a place for venturing specific prophetic judgements?

The possibilities of moral action are also treated in Shinji Kayama's discussion of Augustine's preaching. Relatively little has been written on the
moral aspects of Augustine's preaching. While he is always intensely aware of
human fallenness, his sermons entertained greater openness to hints of human
transformation than his treatises, Kayama suggests. Preaching is a means of
moral pedagogy, both as the preacher expounds the text of Scripture and as
he edifies the congregation, explaining the reality of sin and directing them to
the amendment of life. In preference to looking to neighbour-love, Kayama
draws out the theme in relation to *pax,* one of the central ordering concepts
in Augustine's social and political thought. By the time of the *City of God, pax*
has become related to the providential ordering of society, used for different
ends by both the city of God and the earthly city. However, on its way it has
become a complex and multivalent term, simultaneously protological, Christological, historical, and eschatological, and, in the context of the Donatist
schism, decisive for ecclesiastical ordering. Peacemaking in a church setting
may require *correctio,* in this case the coercion of the Donatists, an action
which Kayama faults for failing to separate two spheres of judgement.

The task of expounding Scripture was also central to the Reformers' understanding of the church, as Joan O'Donovan notes in her chapter on the
political significance of Cranmer's Prayer Book reforms. Oliver O'Donovan's
work in the area found expression in one of his lesser-known works, *On the
Thirty-Nine Articles: A Conversation with Tudor Christianity* (1986, 2011), and
Joan O'Donovan takes up the apologetic task of explaining the legacy of the
English Reformation to a Church of England that has fallen out of sympathy
with its liturgical heritage and to a political establishment that sees the Church
as one amongst many interest groups of private individuals. This liberal pluralist construction of religion, she argues, cannot be owned by a Church whose
public worship defines and empowers the secular practices of government
through the public reading of Scripture. Because freedom comes from the
believer's justification by faith, not from the juridical assignment of rights, the
Church's primary allegiance is always its conformity to true worship, not to
secular jurisdiction. Its responsibility is to proclamation in the context of eschatological judgement, leaving the civil authority with the task of political

judgement in the context of history, operating with a derived authority which is always subject to the judgement and mercy of God.

The secular liberal response to religious plurality is the subject of Jonathan Chaplin's chapter. Addressing O'Donovan's Kuyper Prize lecture, 'Reflections on Pluralism', Chaplin, who writes as a Kuyperian neo-Calvinist, endorses O'Donovan's rejection of the conventional pluralist paradigm which proclaims neutrality between different comprehensive doctrines, sharing with him the concern that its requirement for public reasons silences citizens and forbids them from letting their deepest commitments have any public significance. He also concurs in finding no reason to endorse a normative pluralism of ideologies: 'secularity', as O'Donovan puts it, 'is a stance of patience in the face of plurality, made sense of by eschatological hope'. However, Chaplin writes to correct what he sees as some of O'Donovan's misreadings of the neo-Calvinist version of pluralism: Christian pluralists, he maintains, do not have a secular liberal conception of public reason, nor are their accounts of practial reasoning incompatible with the norms O'Donovan lays out. Their favoured notion of 'consociational democracy' — a system that confers reasonable accommodation of religions not only in practical reasoning but also in the procedural side of policy-making and in certain substantive outcomes — is also one that he argues is hospitable to O'Donovan's notion of public judgement.

The theme of what holds a people together is also central to Brent Waters's chapter. The focus here is on communication in its broadest sense, that is, that which constitutes individuals as a shared community, a 'we'. Waters shows how members of a society in their differentiated but overlapping social spheres are for O'Donovan united through communication, the sharing of their common objects of love. Central to this is the concept of a particular people in a particular place: a people which is composed of a variety of associations that precede the state and have to be respected by it, and which is attached to a physical location that is geographically identifiable and is not simply 'borderless space'. Internet technologies and modern transport have of course complicated the significance of place, but while they may have diminished space for the online shopper at his or her keyboard, they assuredly have not done so for the delivery driver who has to haul the sofa up the stairs. The connection between communication and the market is also taken up by Waters: if we are moving from the primacy of the nation-state to the primacy of the 'market-state', it is important that we attend to some tensions he observes in O'Donovan's understanding of the market.

The last of the chapters specifically devoted to political theology is Brian Brock's discussion of the nature of the public realm, responding to O'Donovan's account in *Common Objects of Love: Moral Reflection and the Shaping of Community* (2002). Like Gregory, Brock wonders whether a more positive account of the possibilities of politics can be given. Augustine, he points out, has two emphases, maintaining on the one hand that societies are formed out of the shared loves of their members, and on the other that the earthly city is no real city. O'Donovan primarily expounds the former, but Brock argues that in doing so he joins with modern contractarian political theories in seeing societies as constituted by the need for people to collaborate so that they may achieve certain shared secular goods. Drawing on Bernd Wannenwetsch and Dietrich Bonhoeffer, Brock enquires how political societies can be sustained in ways that are not formalist or proceduralist. This requires a vision of society not just as locked in an irremediable conflict occasionally mitigated by court rulings, but as freed to be reconciled: people are united not by shared objects of love, but by shared love of each other. Such a city is no earthly city, of course, and it is to the church that we are to look as the place where reconciliation under the Word and a waiting for consensus is made possible.

Although Hans Ulrich's chapter is directed towards thinking theologically about modern technological science, the conceptual resources he draws on are taken from ruminations on O'Donovan's understanding of the ways of judgement. Just as O'Donovan elaborates the theological context of acts of moral and political judgement, and so enables apologetically an opening to the horizon against which they finally become intelligible, so Ulrich explores the ways of discernment which the sciences need to undertake. On the basis of detailed Biblical word studies he shows that reality is that which is given in the acts of God in creating, judging, reconciling, and so on, and that any more limited context is theologically arbitrary. Nature therefore has to be seen in the context of creation: we need to seek not just knowledge, but knowledge which improves our understanding of the *conditio humana*. Understanding an individual human being, for example, requires knowing not just about their biological development, but also about the story within which their life is situated. Scientific disciplines should not be left to pass unexamined, but should be interrogated to learn about the question of their meaning. Learning wisdom in the context of the sciences involves the integration of different experiences, and the discernment of appropriate distinctions.

Holger Zaborowski also appraises the project of scientific naturalism, finding some solutions in Robert Spaemann's philosophy. Zaborowski argues that Spaemann, whose major work of moral ontology, *Personen* (1996), was translated by O'Donovan as *Persons: The Difference between 'Someone' and 'Something'* (2006), makes philosophically intelligible the possibility of a non-naturalist account of human beings. Jürgen Habermas's celebrated efforts to 'complete the project of modernity' have sought to recognize the reality of human freedom in the face of reductive physicalisms, but to date have foundered on the question of the human person. In particular, Habermas has not yet been able to render effectively in non-religious terms the theological conception of human beings made in the image of God, which leaves him exposed to the worry that only theology and not philosophy may be able to overcome naturalism. Zaborowski finds in Spaemann the basis for a richer philosophical anthropology that unites nature and freedom in the human person, and makes room for religious commitment not in a foundational role but as a postulate in a Kantian sense: he provides a philosophical theology which eases Habermas's concerns, but is still happy to entertain metaphysical commitments.

The chapters by John Witte, Jr., and Robert Song take up themes in sexual ethics and bioethics, two areas of ethics to which O'Donovan has regularly contributed, not least through a variety of Church of England working parties. In addition to his early Grove booklets on marriage and divorce, transsexualism, and abortion, O'Donovan has published a stream of articles in the area, as well as the books *Begotten or Made?* (1984), written in response to the British government's Warnock Report on then new fertility and embryology techniques, and *Church in Crisis: The Gay Controversy and the Anglican Communion* (2008) (published in the UK as *A Conversation Waiting to Begin: The Churches and the Gay Controversy* [2009]), an eirenic contribution to the continuing Anglican dispute over same-sex relationships. He has always sought to trace presenting issues back through their history, and John Witte, Jr.'s piece — chosen in part in recognition of O'Donovan's move from Oxford to Edinburgh — is an intriguing account of Scottish Enlightenment views of the family. This introduces to contemporary discussion an almost entirely forgotten strand of thought on marriage, an alternative Enlightenment, which argues firmly in favour of traditional understandings, but appeals to natural law argumentation rather than to Biblical or theological premises. There may be tensions between O'Donovan's approach and that of Henry Home, Francis Hutcheson, William Paley, and others, but the centrality of nature in their thought may give substance to O'Donovan's understanding of marriage as a natural good, and may have additional value at a time when theological modes of thought are given short shrift in public debate.

Song's piece is bioethical in focus, and examines the rare phenomenon of body integrity identity disorder, in which a person desires the surgical amputation of a healthy limb. In addition to its significance in its own right, investigation of this enables another angle to be opened on the question of sex reassignment surgery in cases of gender dysphoria, a topic on which O'Donovan was one of the earliest theological contributors; but it does so without needing to enter the morally fraught arenas of sexuality and gender. Resorting to surgery in such circumstances invokes the question whether it should be understood as an implicitly docetic triumph of the will over the body, or as a potentially justifiable intervention which recognises that the body has been affected by the fall but does not deny its fundamental goodness. Paying detailed attention to the ethics of mutilation and of surgery for psychiatric disorders, but rejecting the primacy of autonomy often found in philosophical bioethics, Song concludes by drawing on some themes on the nature of the believer's identity in Christ which have figured in O'Donovan's writings on homosexuality.

The final chapter of the volume, by John Webster, turns to the relation of moral and pastoral theology to Biblical exegesis and dogmatic theology, a theme which has engaged O'Donovan throughout his career, but which has emerged as a central consideration of his most recent work, *Self, World, and Time* (2013), the first part of a trilogy, *Ethics as Theology*. Moral theology is subordinate to exegesis and dogmatics as action follows being, Webster argues, but this posteriority in the order of being does not preclude a mutually responsive interrelation between them: ethics can inform dogmatics as it displays theological science in the creaturely realm of practice. The importance for pastoral theology of referring back to its fundamental doctrinal orientation is illustrated through a haunting meditation on the nature of sorrow. This emotion, so vividly familiar, is too readily addressed in pastoral and clinical practice without an understanding of its theological significance. Webster expounds Augustine's and Aquinas's teaching that sorrow and pain can only exist in good natures, since their presence demonstrates a creature's refusal of that which harms it, and therefore its holding fast to the good. There is a fundamental asymmetry between good and evil; sorrow is flight from evil, and so points to the goodness of God. For Christians, therefore, it teaches a way of responding to the question of suffering: they are called not to the elimination of sorrow, but to the disciplined cultivation of it in accordance with their new nature in Christ.

Each of the authors has been a beneficiary of Oliver O'Donovan's teaching, either in the classroom or as a faculty colleague or academic peer, and all have been taught through his writing. The essays are offered as tokens of appreciation, and given in the anticipation that further tuition lies ahead. Oliver's own postscript to the volume provides a first taste of precisely that, elaborating on the injunction: 'Know Thyself!'

Many of the chapters in this volume were originally presented at a conference entitled 'The Authority of the Gospel: A Symposium in Honour of Oliver O'Donovan', held at St John's College, Durham University, on 8-11 January 2011. We are grateful to the Stead Center and to the Faculty of Arts and Humanities, and the Department of Theology and Religion, Durham University, for funding which made the conference possible; and also to Nathaniel Warne for his editorial assistance on the volume.

A Love Formed by Faith:
Relating Theological Virtues in Augustine and Luther

Bernd Wannenwetsch

A Personal Preface

Amongst the many stimuli I am grateful to have received from Oliver O'Donovan over the years, his work had the welcome effect of prompting me, a confirmed Lutheran, towards Augustine's writings. (Should our theological conversations over time have, in turn, intensified Oliver's interest in reading Luther, I would happily accept the blame.) An early fruit of this expansion of my theological horizon was a German essay entitled *Caritas fide formata* (love formed through faith), the translation of which is the basis for this present contribution.[1] I recall discussing this essay with Oliver over a Bavarian beer back in Erlangen during his visit in 1999. Our conversation, which diversified over the ensuing years we spent as colleagues at Oxford, recently returned to the intertwined theme of faith and love as we respectively revisited this connection for our current writing projects, both of which include reflections on Paul's theological hymn on love and its fellow virtues of faith and hope in 1 Corinthians 13.[2] As this essay occupies a place in our mutual enquiry, I have decided to leave my original treatment of

---

1. Bernd Wannenwetsch, 'Caritas fide formata. "Herz und Affekte" als Schlüssel zu "Glaube und Liebe"', *Kerygma und Dogma* 45 (2000): 205-224. Andrew Genzler, Martin Scheidegger, Tina Bruns (Oxford), Andrew Keuer, Michael Laffin, and David Robinson (Aberdeen) all contributed in various ways to the production of the present English version.

2. Oliver O'Donovan, *Self, World, and Time: Ethics as Theology I — An Induction* (Grand Rapids: Eerdmans, 2013), in a chapter titled 'The Trajectory of Faith, Love, and Hope', and a forthcoming commentary of mine on 1 Corinthians, coauthored with Brian Brock.

Augustine and Luther mostly intact, extending its implications largely through the footnote section as to how individual aspects of my interpretation relate to Oliver's developing account of Augustine, the Reformers, and the broader subject matter.

The main thrust of this essay is to demonstrate that Luther's employment of the concept of faith can be understood as 'grammatically' congenial to Augustine's use of the concept of love, if we set the affective dimension in the Reformer's account of faith alongside the substantive, ordered portrayal of love in Augustine. While I remain confident that this analysis stands, a deeper engagement with O'Donovan's work on Augustine, including some newer, unpublished material, has prompted me to consider how the remaining difference from the Wittenberg Reformer can be accounted for. In an extended paragraph at the end of this contribution, then, I will investigate how *caritas ordinata* (reasonable love, as O'Donovan has portrayed Augustine's account) relates to *caritas fide formata* (faith-formed love, as I have portrayed the Wittenberg account). The suggestion I will put forward in this section is that the Wittenberg Reformers (Melanchthon included) conceived of love in terms of 'the affect of faith' as ultimately qualified from the subject, not — as Augustine did — from the object of love. In making this distinction, however, I will go on to delineate that this account is worlds apart from dominant accounts of modern 'subjectivity' in that, for the Reformers, the new heart of the believer is endowed with Christ's own affections.

The Greatest of These?

While the question of preeminence appears to have been decided already in 1 Corinthians 13:13 ('. . . but the greatest of these is love'), a theological argument remains to be made regarding the *relational ordering* of faith and love. Our enquiry must lead beyond the question of preeminence to investigate in what respect and on which occasions we ought to speak first of faith or first of love. For this purpose, the scholastic formula *fides caritate formata* (faith formed by love) and its inverse, *caritas fide formata* (love formed by faith, which I will use to paraphrase the Reformers' position), will set the terms of our discussion. Tracing the respective historical and argumentative contexts of both interpretive formulae will help us to shed light on current ecumenical and ethical discussions. Moreover, by taking this investigative route we will find that a frequently neglected issue will be attributed a key function — the role that the transformation of the affections[3] is to play in the doctrines of grace and of good works. What needs to be demonstrated is how the affections serve as a transmission line between the character of the person as determined through faith on the one hand, and the character of her action as determined through love on the other. In order to elucidate this connection, we will investigate the contributions of Augustine, Luther, and Melanchthon. First, however, a look at two contemporary examples will help us see how significant the theologically sensitive relation between faith and love remains today.

a. 'Cause and Effect' or 'Act and Actor'?

Some of the most controversial discussions (especially in Germany) surrounding the 'Joint Declaration on the Doctrine of Justification', issued by the Lutheran World Federation and the Papal Office for the Furthering of Christian Unity,[4] turned on the question of how love relates to justification by faith alone. The Declaration presents the following as a matter of consensus: 'When persons come by faith to share in Christ, God no longer imputes to them their sin and through the Holy Spirit effects in them an active love. These two aspects of God's gracious action are not to be separated' (Nr. 22). The challenge here arises precisely in *how* this inseparability of the 'two aspects of God's gracious action' is to be conceived without constructing a relationship in which the parts condition one another in a problematic way. Faith and love must be related as tightly as possible, yet without their distinctiveness being obscured. If they are not held in close proximity, 'justification by faith alone' faces dangers in two directions: faith can disappear into love, thereby losing its receptive character, insofar as love can more easily than faith be understood by reference to its active side as a human work or virtue; but love can also be absorbed into faith, when the pure receptivity of faith is emphasized to the point of losing sight of the unity of justification and sanctification. In either case, ethics is left in the dark or, more likely, will be sent off in search of a secondary connection to compensate for the deficit.

---

3. The term 'affections' does not indicate simple spontaneous expressions of emotion, but refers to what Aristotle called 'conditions of the soul' (fear and hope, joy and pain, and so forth), which are excited by external triggers and correspond with specific physical movements.

4. http://www.vatican.va/roman_curia/pontifical_councils/chrstuni/documents/rc_pc _chrstuni_doc_31101999_cath-luth-joint-declaration_en.html. http://www.lutheranworld.org/ Special_Events/OfficialDocuments/jd97.EN.html. The Joint Declaration was issued in 1997 and signed in 1999.

Several familiar frameworks commend themselves for a construal of the relation between faith and love. A certain type, represented by the schemes of 'ground and consequence' and 'cause and effect',[5] predominates in the Joint Declaration — and in the formulations employed by both sides. Where the Protestant side speaks of justification by faith as 'the basis . . . from which the renewal of life proceeds' (Nr. 26), the Roman Catholic side speaks of the spiritual gift of grace that becomes 'effective . . . in active love' (Nr. 24). The same logic crops up in other phrases, such as in the portrayal of justification as the 'basis' (*Fundament* in the German version) for sanctification (Nr. 25) and articulates itself even in those passages where attempts are made to differentiate the doctrinal traditions, such as in the Lutheran reference to the perfection of justification by faith, which, according to the document, is aimed at 'growth in its effects in Christian living' (Nr. 39).

Such a shared manner of speaking about 'ground and consequence' and 'cause and effect' might appear plausible and unproblematic on first glance. Protestants associate the mentioning of 'basis' (Nr. 25) or 'cause' with the priority of justification, while Catholics, on the other hand, are pleased with the same language as it implies the necessity with which a particular cause *must* have an effect. Despite its initial plausibility, though, this ecumenical consensus on language turns out to be questionable. As we will see, it falls short of the standard of reflection represented by two major theological authorities, Augustine and Luther. Irrespective of their differing emphases, both Augustine and Luther articulated the connection of faith and love by presuming an *organic* relation such as between actor and act, rather than a mechanistic logic such as that of cause and effect. As Luther put it: 'Therefore faith remains the actor and love remains the act.'[6] Emphasis on organic relation becomes mandatory once it is realized that 'effect' and 'act' are rooted in two distinct spheres — 'act' in the personal, and 'effect' in the impersonal. Whereas the act always remains the action of an actor, for which she remains liable, an effect is freed from its cause in the very moment of its occurrence, released into the sovereign sphere of effects, in which each individual 'effect' is destined to become a cause of yet further 'effects'.

In the main parts of this essay, we will investigate the theological reasons why the relationship of faith and love needs to be understood in terms of such

---

5. The fine philosophical distinction between the two pairs is neglected in the Joint Declaration, which uses both side by side and also, in part, mixes them.

6. Martin Luther, *Werke*, Weimar edition *(WA)*, Weimar, 1883-1929, 17 II, 98, 25, translation mine.

a close and quasi-'personal' relationship, and why this cannot be translated without incapacitating loss into an impersonal framework such as 'cause and effect', 'ground and consequence', or 'possibility and realization'. The issue of the type of relationship that prevails between faith and love leads us right into the central questions of justification theology: Must faith be formed through love in order to justify, as the scholastic formula *fides caritate formata* would have it? Or must we presume the relation to be the reverse, love finding its form through justifying faith: *caritas fide formata?*

b. Creative Love — Deposit of Faith?

Along with addressing these worthwhile questions in justification theology, clarifying the way in which faith and love depend on one another will also be of paramount importance for moral theology, as this relationship affects several contested issues in contemporary ethical debates. For example, as regards the question of recognizing non-marital or same-sex relationships in the Church, it makes a decisive difference whether love is understood as a potentially independent *effect (Wirkung)* of faith, or, alternatively, as a *work-form (Wirkform)* of faith, that is, the active dimension of faith itself. Again and again in these discussions one comes across the argument that if love is the basic principle of Christian ethics, it is to be understood as bestowing on human practice its ethically qualifying form. Thus the conclusion, echoed in various types of agapeism that have flourished since the 1960s, that whatever is open to love must be acceptable, irrespective of a potential 'tension' with individual components of the *depositum fidei* ('deposit of faith').

This argument can be found, among many other places, in the document *Mit Spannungen Leben* ('Living with Tensions') that the Evangelical Churches in Germany (EKD) issued on the topic of homosexuality in the church.[7] This statement, of a status somewhere in between a 'Green' and a 'White' Paper, presupposes that it is possible for there to be tension between faith and love, in which love must have the last word. First, the statement holds that according to biblical evidence 'homosexual practice contradicts the will of God'. Then it continues: 'at the same time however the question about living a homosexual relationship, which is ethically responsible in light of the love command, is not dealt with in these scriptural passages.' So the statement

---

7. *Mit Spannungen Leben. Eine Orientierungshilfe des Rates der EKD zum Thema 'Homosexualität und Kirche'*, ed. Kirchenamt der EKD (Hannover, 1996).

concludes, 'that it is decisive for a homosexual relationship whether it is lived . . . in love'.[8]

Here we are obviously dealing with a similar logic that we found in the dogmatic formulations of the Joint Declaration, making faith a (mere) foundation for love. It is in this vein that the EKD statement accounts for the biblical evidence as a kind of deposit of faith, on the 'basis' of which love, it is assumed, can then unfold in its own dynamic and 'ethical design', even if it may entail legitimating a practice that stands in contradictory relationship to the deposit of faith. There are other, potentially stronger arguments, which might endorse accepting homosexuality in the church, but what interests us here is merely the *kind* of argument that the EKD paper represents, as it concerns the relationship of love and faith in the context of an argumentative strategy that has gained a good deal of prominence in moral debates of our time. It is with the various forms of agapeism, old and new, in view, that our investigation of faith and love in Luther and Augustine will attempt to demonstrate that the very idea that love may 'trump' faith, even if only in exceptional circumstances, rests on the basis of a theological mistake.

The Soteriological Precedence of Faith over Love: Luther

> *All Christian teaching, work, and life, is understood in a nutshell, clearly and perfectly in the two parts of faith and love, through which the person is placed between God and his neighbour as a means that receives from above and gives again below and becomes so to speak a vessel or a pipe, through which the spring of divine goodness flows without a letup to other people.*[9]

For Luther, faith and love function first as ushers, as it were, guiding the Christian into her correct place. The believer is not a person grounded in herself as to reach out in various directions — towards 'a relationship with God' on the one hand, and a 'relationship with the world' on the other; rather the human person experiences herself from the start as one who is placed between God and the neighbour and thus is continually claimed by both sides. This '*ek-static*' way of living corresponds to Luther's famous phrase at the end of his *Treatise on Christian Liberty*: 'We conclude, therefore, that a Christian lives

---

8. *Mit Spannungen Leben*, p. 21, translation mine.
9. *WA* 10 I/1, 100, 8-13, translation mine.

not in himself, but in Christ and in his neighbor. . . . He lives in Christ through faith, in his neighbor through love'.[10] Already in this depiction of a stance 'in-between', Luther rules out the possibility of what we may call the 'autonomy of love', in which the relationship with God (faith) would be seen as laying down a mere foundation for the relationship with the world (love). In contrast to the idea of God's work being to lay the foundation (the possibility), with human work being construction upon this through ensuing action, Luther's idea of 'standing between' indicates rather that *both* faith *and* love are rooted in divine activity. God's action overflows toward people (faith) and through these people to others (love).

Because Luther's intention is to prevent faith and love from being distributed either in two separate realities or in two separate subjects, it is not surprising to find the language of the organic prevailing in his account: 'For as faith brings you blessedness *(Seligkeit)* and eternal life, so it also brings you good works and it cannot be obstructed. For just as a living person cannot abstain from acting, but must move, eat and drink, and work . . ?', so it is, the Reformer concludes, with a living faith: 'Just have faith, and every work will flow from you naturally'.[11] As he puts it in the famous passage from the *Preface to Paul's Letter to the Romans:* 'Oh it is a living, busy, active, mighty thing, this faith. It is impossible for it not to be doing good works incessantly'. Thus, as Luther concludes, if the right works were lacking, it would not indicate a 'mere faith' *(bloßer Glaube)*, lacking the right formation through love. Rather, according to the Reformer, 'Whoever does not do such works . . . is an unbeliever'.[12] While it ought to have become clear by now that for Luther faith and love belong together in an organic way, the question remains about their respective weightings.

a. Works of Faith or Works of Love?

At stake in this question is a proper understanding of Galatians 5:6: 'For in Christ Jesus, neither circumcision nor un-circumcision is of any avail, but faith working through love' (RSV).[13] In his interpretation of this passage in the Commentary on Galatians, Luther articulates his position over against the 'Sophists' of the scholastic tradition:

10. *Luther's Works: The American Edition (LW)* (Saint Louis: Concordia; Philadelphia: Fortress Press, 1955-1986), 31, 371.

11. *WADB* 7, 10, 12-3, translation mine.

12. *LW* 35, 370.

13. *Pistis di' agapes energoumene.*

For they say that even when faith has been divinely infused . . . , it does not justify, unless it has been formed by love. They call love "the grace which makes one acceptable," namely, that justifies . . . and they say that love is acquired by our merit of congruity, etc. In fact, they even declare that an infused faith can coexist with mortal sin.[14] In this manner they completely transfer justification from faith and attribute it solely to love as thus defined. And they claim that this is proved by St. Paul in this passage — "faith working through love" — as though Paul wanted to say: "You see, faith does not justify; in fact, it is nothing unless love the worker is added, which forms faith."[15]

In Luther's judgment, such interpreters prove themselves 'unrefined students of grammar' by confusing subject and object as well as the active and passive voice. In contrast, he offers this vivid distinction:

Furthermore, Paul does not make faith unformed here, as though it were a shapeless chaos without the power to be or to do anything; but he attributes the working itself to faith rather than to love . . . but he declares that it is an effective and active something, a kind of substance or, as they call it, a "substantial form." . . . He does not say: "Love works." No, he says: "Faith works." He makes love the tool through which faith works.[16]

Luther thus essentially reverses the scholastic conception: Love is not the groundwork (forma) of an otherwise 'rough' and unformed faith. Because faith is inescapably active, the formula must not be fides caritate formata, but, as we might put it in terms of a precise inversion of the scholastic formula, caritas fide formata: love formed through faith. Or, once again in Lu-

---

14. Here Luther is referring to the scholastic idea that was later dogmatised at the Council of Trent, according to which 'the received grace of Justification is lost, not only by infidelity whereby even faith itself is lost, but also by any other mortal sin whatever, though faith be not lost.' Trid. Session 6, 15, in: The Council of Trent. The canons and decrees of the sacred and ecumenical Council of Trent, trans. J. Waterworth (London: Dolman, 1848), pp. 30-53, here: p. 42.

For the Tridentine teaching, faith justifies only insofar as it is the initial impulse for the wider grace event (Trid. 6:8); taken by itself, i.e. without the formation through love, faith remains 'vain confidence' (Trid. 6:9), which neither justifies nor takes part in sanctification (Trid. 6:10). It is only because the Council of Trent operates with such a reductive (from the viewpoint of the Reformers) cognitive-only notion of faith that it can assume the continuance of such a faith in humans even with the loss of grace.

15. Luther, Lectures on Galatians, in: LW 27, 28.

16. LW 27, 29.

ther's own succinct formula: 'Therefore faith remains the actor, and love remains the act'.[17]

b. From Meritorious Love to Receptive Faith

Why is Luther acting as a pedantic grammarian, instead of contenting himself with the scholastic dialectic? Why emphasize love in terms of works, as *act,* and allow only faith to be the *actor?* The immediate answer is that Luther, like Paul, is concerned that on behalf of salvation and the believer's assuredness of it, justification must be understood solely as God's act towards the human person. Faith, having come from hearing (Rom. 10:17), is something entirely receptive and as such stands at much less risk than love of being construed as an immanent human power that contributes to justification. Here Luther is reacting to a development in theology growing since the twelfth century in which faith and love had been increasingly held in tension by construing the former in intellectualist terms[18] and the latter in affectual ones.

The reason why Luther propelled faith to the center of his theology must be understood against the backdrop of the peculiar blandness that this trend had lent to this concept in the High Middle Ages. On the one hand, the Reformer reacted against the narrowing of faith to a mere *cognitio incepta;* on the other, the relative insipidity of the concept of faith in his time allowed Luther to make it the central category in his early-Reformation theology, as this theology centred around faith's invisibility and receptivity.

It was the enthroning of love, understood as psychological potency, as the central theological category that caused Luther's worry. Love so defined had come to play the decisive role in High Mediaeval accounts of the human preparation for the reception of grace, and it was this capacity-oriented understand-

---

17. *WA* 17 II, 98, 25, translation mine.

18. Thomas Aquinas, in applying the Aristotelian distinction between intellectual and practical virtues, placed faith among the former type, conceiving of it as that which precedes love and hope, by providing these other virtues with cognition of their object. 'Without first apprehending its object by sense or intellect, the appetite cannot move towards it in hope or love. Faith is how the intellect apprehends the object of its hope and love'. Thomas Aquinas, *Summa Theologiae* 2-2.4.2-5; 2-1.62.4. *(Non enim potest in aliquid motus appetitivus tendere vel sperando vel amando, nisi quod est apprehensum sensu aut intellectu. Per fidem autem apprehendit intellectus et quae sperat et amat.)* Whereas Thomas categorised faith as a *medium apprehensivum* of a specific prerogative to the grace moment, the Reformers later described it as the means to apprehending saving grace itself.

ing that earned love its privileged position amongst the 'infused virtues' (faith, love, and hope) within the justification event. In the *preparatio ad justificationem,* the process of human preparation for the justification by God, 'initial love of God' was regarded as a criterion for the authenticity of repentance, in the form of a demonstration of genuine contrition *(vera contritio).* In this, humanity's natural capability to love was seen to be co-operating with divine grace.[19] And in the justifying bestowal of supernatural virtues, love was understood as that which first lent faith its form and outward palpability, in that it oriented human beings for good works.[20] Thus, the entire grace event came to be seen as embedded in love that exclusively granted this event its experimental affective reality.

The Reformers broke with exactly this critical function of love on both sides of the grace event. In Luther's account, love must not be regarded as already meriting forgiveness due to the affective intensity of contrition, because forgiveness is freely granted by God on the sole basis of the *fides absolutionis* that existentially clings to the promise of grace. As later stated in the Formula

19. It had become standard among scholastic theologians of the twelfth and thirteenth centuries to identify the intensely felt pain of contrition with justifying love, as the 'true contrition of love', which was seen as being subsequently merely expressed in outward acts of repentance. The following sentence from a combination of Ezekiel 33:12 and 18:21f functioned as a legitimating reference: *In quacumque hora peccator ingemuerit, non recordabor iniquitatum eius* (At this hour, in which the sinner sighs, I will consider his offense no more); cf. Decretum Gratiani: De poenitentia, dist. 1, ch. 32, *Corpus Iuris Canonici,* revised by A. Friedberg, Vol. 1, L 1879², 1165; cf. Berndt Hamm, 'Von der Gottesliebe des Mittelalters zum Glauben Luthers. Ein Beitrag zur Bußgeschichte', in: *Lutherjahrbuch 1998* (Göttingen: Vandenhoeck & Ruprecht, 1998), pp. 19-44.

20. The defining of love as a *'habit'* (as the Latin translation of the Aristotelian notion of *arête* which literally means the 'holding' of a certain disposition to act), which allowed love to appear as a psychological potential, was reflected in a shift in interpretation of Romans 5:5. While Peter Lombard in the twelfth century had identified love with the Holy Spirit arriving in the heart (*'quod spiritus sanctus est caritas, qua diligimus Deum et proximum',* Sententiae in IV libris distinctae, lib. 1 dist. 17, chap. 1), love was understood in the late Middle Ages as a *gift* of the Spirit to then become manifest in the heart. Irrespective of whether this newer interpretation would prevail as it did amongst Ockhamists such as Gabriel Biel, who maintained that the person, in his freedom, could achieve by himself true acts of love of God and contrite love, or whether this interpretation was sharply challenged, as in Luther's order of Augustinian Eremites, where Johann Staupitz would only concede a naturally precipitated 'gallows remorse' that must first be assisted by Christ's suffering — the discussion remained stuck on the question of the *satis esse,* the 'doing enough' in terms of the requirement of *facere quod in se est* (to do what is humanly possible) towards the reception of justifying grace. This soteriological impasse was broken open by the Reformers. Cf. Hamm, 'Von der Gottesliebe des Mittelalters zum Glauben Luthers', pp. 28-44.

of Concord on the so-called *particulae exclusivae,* faith alone is to be regarded as the *means* of receiving saving grace: 'that neither renewal, sanctification, virtues, nor other good works are our righteousness before God, nor are they to be made and posited to be a part or a cause of our justification [*tamquam forma aut pars aut causa iustificationis*], nor under any kind of pretense, title, or name are they to be mingled with the article of justification as pertinent or necessary to it'.[21]

In summary, with regard to justification, Luther broke with accounts of the active, meritorious function of love in favor of faith[22] as receptive and empirically ungraspable. For the moral life of a Christian, however, he was more than happy to maintain love as the central concept.[23] As we will see, the key for a sound understanding of the relatedness of faith and love, as it becomes visible when brought into the light of the doctrine of sanctification, lies

21. Formula of Concord, Solid Declaration Art. III, in: *The Book of Concord: The Confessions of the Evangelical Lutheran Church,* trans. and ed. Th. G. Tappert (Philadelphia: Fortress Press, 1959), p. 546.

22. This puts the question addressed in 1 Corinthians 13:3 about precedence in the indivisible relationship of faith and love into perspective. Regarding the Pauline statement in that epistle, Luther raises the following consideration: Although it appears as if Paul reckoned that there could be such a thing as a 'pure faith' (1 Cor. 13:2 '. . . and if it has not love'), it is, however, an *'impossible* example' that the Apostle expresses here; something that is as impossible as for a human to speak with the tongue of an angel (*Luthers Epistelauslegung,* Vol. 2, ed. E. Ellwein [Göttingen: Vandenhoeck & Ruprecht, 1968], 176f, translation mine, emphasis added). Luther comments on 1 Corinthians 13:13 that whereas faith is the greater in the here and now but will one day be transformed into seeing, love is the greater in that it will have existence in eternity (loc. cit. 181), although in the here and now it is only the fruit of faith. Along similar lines, Augustine states: 'If, through faith, we love what we cannot yet see, how much greater will our love be when we have begun to see' (*On Christian Teaching,* 1.38.42, trans. R. P. H. Green [Oxford: Oxford University Press, 1997], p. 28)!

23. On the basis of this distinction, Luther rejected the attempt made in the 'Book of Regensburg' to reconcile this matter. In this Melanchthon, Bucer, and Pistorius from the Protestant side, and Eck, Pflug, Gropper, and Contarini from the Catholic side, made the attempt to harmonize, with reference to Galatians 5:6, the scholastic formula *fides caritate formata* with Melanchthon's forensic emphasis in the concept of justification by faith. Over against such a 'double understanding of justification', Luther insisted that Galatians 5:6 does not speak of a *'iustum fieri'* (someone who becomes justified), but of an already justified sinner. For him, the necessary distinction of 'becoming something' and 'doing something' corresponded to that between faith and love (*WA* Br. 9, Nr. 3616 40-50). Cf. Simon Peura, 'Christus als Gunst und Gabe. Luthers Verständnis der Rechtfertigung als Herausforderung an den ökumenischen Dialog mit der Römisch-katholischen Kirche', in: O. Bayer et al., eds., *Caritas Dei. Beiträge zum Verständnis Luthers und der gegenwärtigen Ökumene,* FS T. Mannermaa (Helsinki: Luther-Agricola-Gesellschaft, 1997), pp. 358ff.

in the role played by the affections. In order to understand this connection better, however, we need to turn first to the Church father to whom Luther was especially indebted.

The Order of Love: Augustine

In a cursory reading, Augustine may seem to flat-out contradict Luther on the relation between faith and love. 'Our root is our charity', we read in Augustine; 'our fruits are our deeds. What matters is that your deeds spring from charity. . . .'[24] Furthermore, where Luther stresses that faith is never empty, but always effective, we read in Augustine: 'This deliberate love cannot remain idle'[25] and 'All love either descends or ascends.'[26] But what sort of love does the great North African bishop have in mind when he speaks of it in such a way? Only if we analyze his use of language in these contexts more thoroughly will an assessment become possible as to whether there really is disagreement with Luther.

a. Formal Love: Amor

As we will see in the following, Augustine's theology of love is only intelligible as coherent when we pay attention to a duality in his use of the concept 'love'. What we render equivocally as 'love' in the English language refers to two distinct ways in which the bishop of Hippo addresses the phenomenon: on the one hand, he speaks of love as a universal human potency that cannot remain 'empty' in that it necessitates enactment of any sort; on the other hand, he speaks of love as enacted — in the respective forms of human agency that cannot but 'tell' from what sort of love each individual act originated. Although Augustine is not always consistent in his application of terms, he tends to use *amor* in the former, and *caritas/concupiscentia* in the latter case.

Amor (or sometimes *appetitus*) depicts the elemental human capacity to desire as a formal category that reflects the teleological character of the human

24. Augustine, *Expositions of the Psalms 51–72*, Exposition of Psalm 51, 12, trans. Maria Boulding (Hyde Park, NY: New City Press, 2001), p. 23.
25. Augustine, *Expositions of the Psalms 51–72*, Exposition 2 of Psalm 31, 5, p. 367.
26. Augustine, *Expositions of the Psalms 121–150*, Exposition of Psalm 122, 1, trans. Edmund Hill (Hyde Park, NY: New City Press, 2004), p. 29.

existence, its *Aus-Sein* of something, its movement towards that which draws it — the respective object of love. As such potency, love is always in motion and 'cannot rest', but is yet to be given direction in each moment of enactment in concrete human action. Just as *amor* is able to stretch itself upward, so it can just as well reach downward: 'After all, what is it in any one of us that prompts action, if not some kind of love? . . . Shameful deeds, adulteries, villainies, murders, all kinds of lust — aren't they the work of some sort of love? Purify this love, then, divert onto your garden the water that is going down the drain. . . .'[27]

It is disquietingly easy to illustrate Augustine's logic of love and its perversion with contemporary examples. Who in the Balkan War would not have acted 'out of love' for their own people? Who would wish to condemn a married man who walks out on his wife and children to live with another woman when the irresistible power of love has struck again? And who would be so cruel as to not cover up lies that are told on the bedstead of a terminally ill patient — out of love? Today's paraphrase of Paul's statement that love bears all things (1 Cor. 13:7) seems to be: love excuses everything; love does whatever seems pleasing to the one who loves. This 'worldly religion of love', as sociologists Ulrich Beck and Elisabeth Beck-Gernsheim have termed it,[28] has come to define the instinctive patterns of reaction in contemporary moral debates in Western societies.

But was it not Augustine himself who taught such a 'worldly religion' to his contemporaries and us moderns? After all, he is famously reported to have said, 'Love, and do what you want.'[29] Are the variants of a 'Situation Ethic'[30]

---

27. Augustine, *Expositions of the Psalms 1–32*, Exposition 2 of Psalm 31, 5, p. 367.

28. Ulrich Beck and Elisabeth Beck-Gernsheim, *The Normal Chaos of Love*, trans. Mark Ritter and Jane Wiebel (Cambridge, UK: Polity Press, 1995). 'While a religion which lacks firm teaching usually vanishes, love is a religion without churches and without priests, and its continued existence is as certain as the tremendous force of sexual needs now freed of social disapproval' (p. 177). According to Beck and Beck-Gernsheim, this 'post-traditional religion' is characterised by '. . . a kind of positivism making norms out of individual preferences and values' (p. 177), and as 'lover-love', it is essentially different from love of neighbour: Lover-love stands under the perennial threat of its opposite. 'Faith in love means you love your lover but not your neighbour, and your loving feelings are always in danger of turning into hate. Ex-lovers lose their home and even their residence permits; they have no right to asylum' (p. 180).

29. Augustine, *Homilies on the First Epistle of John*, 7.8, trans. Boniface Ramsey (Hyde Park, NY: New City Press, 2008), p. 110.

30. The irony here is that the tag 'dated', with which 'Situation Ethics' tends to be introduced to students in today's classrooms as a somewhat simplistic, easily refutable moral theory

the essence of which have survived so well in the default moral instincts of our time not entitled to borrow authority directly from the great African bishop in making ethical praxis dependent on whatever an un-predetermined love will decide in each situation? Yet a delicate but decisive difference lies precisely in *how* Augustine's formula is rendered — whether one renders it as Rudolf Bultmann did as *ama et fac quod vis*,[31] or as it actually reads in the original wording: '*dilige et quod vis fac*'.[32] Whereas *amare* is (mostly) applied neutrally by Augustine, *diligere* already includes the moment of discernment, the close reading of the formula thus being: 'Love as much as you like, but take care what you love.'[33] With this in mind, we can understand why Augustine arrives at the following categorical distinction: 'Love of God and love of your neighbor are called charity [*caritas*]; but the love of the world . . . is called concupiscence [*concupiscentia*].'[34]

b. *Categorical Love:* Caritas *and* Concupiscentia

In the state of enactment, Augustine holds, love is inescapably related to its objects[35] and receives its qualification from them. Thus he summons his read-

---

that was popular in the 1960s — only demonstrates the lack of interest in what *actually* shapes people's minds and hearts and hence their moral disposition to act. Perhaps we should say that once a moral idea has become so deeply ingrained in the fabric of moral instincts as to become a sort of 'religion' in the way Beck and Beck-Gernsheim have described, it can comfortably vanish from the discussion of 'moral theories'.

31. Rudolf Bultmann, 'Das christliche Gebot der Nächstenliebe', in: *Glauben und Verstehen I* (Tübingen: J. C. B. Mohr, 1933), p. 239. This shortened reference to Augustine, taken on its own, does not yet make Bultmann the father of 'agapism'. On the one hand, he left no doubt that love is made possible by faith: 'Liebe wird unsere Existenzmöglichkeit nur dadurch, daß wir unsere Existenz als durch Christus in Gott gegründete bzw. neugegründete erfassen ('Love becomes a possibility of our existence only when we grasp our existence as one that has been grounded and newly grounded through Christ in God') (ibid., p. 243; translation mine); on the other hand, this dependence of love on faith remained in the sphere of an existential-theological logic of 'possibility' and thus insulated the formative moment. It was for this reason that Bultmann eventually arrived at a maxim not dissimilar to Situation Ethics: that love is not in any way pre-determined in its scope of viable options by, say, a tradition of faith, but is able to recognise itself only in the act of deciding.

32. Augustine, *In Epistolam Joannis ad Parthos tractatus* 7.8.

33. Augustine, *Expositions of the Psalms 1–32*, Exposition 2 of Psalm 31, 5, p. 367.

34. Augustine, *Expositions of the Psalms 1–32*, Exposition 2 of Psalm 31, 5, p. 367.

35. Although Augustine's theology of love developed over the course of his lifetime to eventually allow for a greater number of *appropriate* objects of human love (including the

ers: '. . . let the current that drove you into the arms of the world be directed to the world's Maker.'[36] This leads us to read the quoted formula for the 'love ethic' with a clear emphasis: *Dilige et* quod vis *fac*, 'love in such a way that you love God above all; what you *then* will, you can be safe in doing.' If anything, this construal of love is critically directed against any sort of voluntarism by which one does what one wills, thereby simply following one's natural inclination. Since *amor* is primarily qualified through the objects toward which it directs itself, Augustine comes up against a categorical difference here. Irrespective of how one wishes to distinguish the various kinds, intensities, and emotional surroundings of love, the ultimate test in each case is the question of whether it directs itself toward worldly things or to the one who made these things in the first place. The appropriate consideration of created things lies in their being 'used' *(uti)* for other ends, while love always means the 'enjoyment' *(frui)* of an object or a creature *for its own sake*. This latter form of affection can, strictly speaking, be directed only to God[37] because ultimately, as there is no fear in love (1 John 4:18), only the eternal, ever abundant God can be loved without the fear of loss that necessarily attaches to every love of transitory goods.

Because love towards transitory goods can never be completely free from this fear of loss, such a love *makes* un-free as well. It holds people in its spell, both through the fear of loss itself and through the resulting attempt to secure oneself against that loss. Such love eventually isolates its agent from her fellow human beings, who in this light will appear, above all, as threatening rivals, meant to be shut out in some way or other.[38] The political form of such a love is the *civitas terrena*, in which the law must keep the clashing interests that result from this love of worldly things forcefully and temporarily in control. Each of the two categorical loves has its own political form: 'The two cities were created by two kinds of love,'[39] as the famous passage in *De civitate Dei*

---

neighbour and the self) than he had first envisioned, throughout his career as a Christian thinker he held on to the claim that the distinction of loves is determined by their respective objects: '. . . anything which is not loved for its own sake is not really loved' (*Soliloquies: Augustine's Inner Dialogue*, 1.13.22, trans. Kim Paffenroth [Hyde Park, NY: New City Press, 2000], p. 44). Since love cannot be sufficiently differentiated by referring to whether it loves an object as an end or a means (for 'utility love' is no love at all), the difference between love and love remains grounded solely in the objects of each love.

36. Augustine, *Expositions of the Psalms 1–32*, Exposition 2 of Psalm 31, 5, p. 367.
37. Augustine, *De civitate Dei* 15.7.
38. Augustine, *De libero arbitrio* 1.4.10.
39. Augustine, *City of God* 14.28, trans. Henry Bettenson (London: Penguin Books, 1972), p. 593.

(14.28) reads. Social formation and ethical praxis are, ultimately, referents to a distinct type of love: 'each man is conformed to the thing he loves'.[40]

Just as love of things rubs off on the person and her social interactions in such a way as to render the relationships she has with others instrumental to this pursuit of worldly things, setting the focus of one's love on God, in turn, sets free a healthy worldliness. For Augustine, this is valid, first of all, in view of all the material world: 'Through this love of the Creator everyone uses even creatures well.'[41] But the point is also valid more specifically with regard to the love of neighbour and the self. As the mature Augustine realizes, the enjoyment of God in the first place (which in his early years was understood as excluding any other object) allows and makes possible the right enjoyment of the neighbour and self-enjoyment. Because once loved 'in God', that is, according to what God has called them to be, both the self and the other person are neither merely 'used' nor set up as an idol. 'Let us then enjoy ourselves and our brothers *in* the Lord. . . .'[42] Augustine's entire *ordo amoris* finds a precise summary in the following definition: 'By love [*caritas*] I mean the impulse of one's mind to enjoy God on his own account and to enjoy oneself and one's neighbor on account of God; and by lust [*concupiscentia*] I mean the impulse of one's mind to enjoy oneself and one's neighbor and any corporeal thing not on account of God.'[43]

As we have seen, for Augustine love is clearly in the center of his theology. What occupies this place is, however, not love 'as such', which indeed is able to tend toward evil, but 'true love':[44] love towards God, self, and neighbour, as

40. Augustine, 'The Catholic Way of Life and the Manichean Ways of Life', 21.39, trans. Donald A. Gallagher and Idella J. Gallagher, in: *The Fathers of the Church*, Vol. 65 (Washington, DC: The Catholic University Press of America, 2008), p. 33.

41. Augustine, *Against Julian* 4.3.33, trans. Matthew A. Schumacher (The Catholic University Press of America, 1957), p. 198.

42. Augustine, *The Trinity* 9.8.13, trans. Edmund Hill (Hyde Park, NY: New City Press, 1991), p. 280, emphasis added.

43. Augustine, *On Christian Teaching* 3.10.16, trans. R. P. H. Green (Oxford: Oxford University Press, 1997), p. 76.

44. 'True' love here means not only 'love in an actual or complete sense', but more specifically refers to the formative role of truth for love. 'True love then is that we should live justly by cleaving to the truth . . .' (Augustine, *The Trinity* 8.7.10, 253.) In such cases in which the demands of truth appear to be in tension with the demands of love (should one lie for the benefit of a loved one?), priority must be given to truth over (what appears as the imperative of) 'love'. True love is always love *in* the truth (Augustine, *Contra Mendacium* 18). This inter-relation of truth and love, which prompted Frederick S. Carney ('The Structure of Augustine's Ethics', in: W. S. Babcock, ed., *The Ethics of Augustine*, JRE Studies in Religion 3 [Atlanta: Scholars Press, 1991], p. 28) to speak of a 'double matrix' in Augustine's ethics, is

according to the order of love.[45] When love is thus conceived as having a form, from which it cannot free itself without becoming some other thing, any 'religion of love' is demystified.

c. Radical Love: The Transformed Eros

Having paid attention to the complexity of Augustine's use of 'love' language should have prepared us for a requalification of the earlier observation that his views appear diametrically opposed to Luther's on the relation between faith and love. Indeed, Augustine comes very close to Luther when he says, 'In terms of precept, the love of God comes first; but, in terms of practice, the love of neighbor comes first.'[46] Luther would express the same thing thus: Faith rules the *vita passiva,* and love the *vita activa.* We recall that Luther's principal reason for distinguishing between faith and love in this way was with justification in view, in which it was crucial to emphasize the action of God alone by laying the stress on the invisibility of this act and the corresponding pure receptivity on the part of the human being.

Yet Augustine also understands *caritas,* the love of God, as something essentially *receptive* and not — as in the tendency of later scholastic theologians — as something effective in itself or as a psychological capacity. Instead he conceives love first as that which is excitable in the human being through external impulses. The beauty and goodness of God are qualities that attract lovers and seduce them into love. The famous 'conversion passage' in the tenth book of the *Confessions* aptly describes this moment of erotic love. First Augustine confesses, 'Late have I loved you, Beauty so ancient and so new. . . . Lo, you were within, but I outside, seeking there for you, and upon the shapely things you have made I rushed headlong. . . .' The statement recapitulates the entire winding journey of his soul to its ultimate destination

---

grounded in the divine Trinity, in which typically the Son is symbolized as Truth and the Spirit as Love. 'Now we are human beings, created in our Creator's image, whose eternity is true, whose truth is eternal, whose love is eternal and true, who is a Trinity of eternity, truth, and love . . .' (Augustine, *City of God,* p. 463).

45. 'We must, in fact, observe the right order even in our love for the very love with which we love what is deserving of love. . . . Hence, as it seems to me, a brief and true definition of virtue is "rightly ordered love". That is why in the holy Song of Songs Christ's bride, the City of God, sings, "Set love in order in me"' (Augustine, *City of God,* p. 637).

46. Augustine, *Homilies on the Gospel of John (1–40)* 17.8, trans. Edmund Hill (Hyde Park, NY: New City Press, 2009), p. 312.

in God, but then Augustine goes on to describe the decisive twist: 'You called, shouted, broke through my deafness; you flared, blazed, banished my blindness; you lavished your fragrance, I gasped, and now I pant for you; I tasted you, and I hunger and thirst; you touched me, and I burned for your peace.'[47]

There lies a significant gap between Augustine's *eros,* the quest for the end of his soul's journey, the attempt of a gradual ascent utilizing all the dimensions of his physical and mental powers (10.6-26), on the one hand, and his eventual arrival in God, on the other. Instead of fluid transition, Augustine recalls a moment of rupture. God's voice does not rise out of the swelling sounds of nature. Rather, it rings out unexpectedly and suddenly, it breaks forth with intensity irresistible to the ear, a 'destroying deafness'. Even as a searcher, it dawned on Augustine that he was actually the one sought by God and eventually found.[48] It reflects this order, when, in this passage, hearing is named first in the order of sensations, whereas in the earlier 'senses-song' (10.6), sight came first. While the sense of sight contains a dimension that is more actively orienting, capable of approaching the sensory object by looking in its direction and fixing the gaze on it, the sense of hearing is the quintessential receptive sense that is always 'awoken' by an urgent sound that hits the ear.

This consideration throws the quotation mentioned at the beginning of our engagement with Augustine into a new light: 'Our root is our charity, and our fruits are our deeds. What matters is that your deeds spring from charity. . . .'[49] Having first assumed a tension with Luther's concept of faith as the doer of works, we can now recognize in the background of Augustine's reflection an image of the root with reference to its biological connotations.[50] A root constitutes, so to speak, the 'basic part' of a tree. However, it is not, in itself, the ground on which the tree stands. A tree receives its life force not *from* the root, but *through* the root. The root forms, as it were, the 'pipe' (recalling the statement of Luther cited on page 6, above) through which the life forces flow

---

47. Augustine, *Confessions* 10.27.38, trans. Maria Boulding (Hyde Park, NY: New City Press, 1997), p. 262.

48. Thus it is understandable why, already at the beginning of Book Ten, Augustine cites 1 Corinthians 13:12. This reference makes the decisive experience a motto of the account of his soul's journey to God: 'I will know fully, even as I have been fully known' (NRSV).

49. Augustine, *Expositions of the Psalms 51–72,* Exposition of Psalm 51, 12, p. 23.

50. For this I am indebted to my wife, Elisabeth Wannenwetsch, whose biologically trained perspective helped that of the theologian when he could not see the forest for the trees.

from the ground to the trunk in order to find their essential expression of life in the fruit eventually. Seen in this way, the root is truly a 'receptive organ': it stretches itself out toward the life force; its growth, its entire 'activity' is dedicated to this receptivity.

It is precisely in this receptive sense that love forms the *radix* of Christian life in Augustine's account. And it was with such 'radical love' in view that Augustine introduced his famous dictum *dilige et quod vis fac* with the following example, whose offensiveness to today's pedagogical standards should not make us overlook the principled point it intends to make:

> A father beats a boy and a slave dealer flatters him. If you set forth the two things, blows and flattery, who would not choose the flattery and avoid the blows? If you pay heed to the persons, it is charity that beats and wickedness that flatters . . . people's deeds are indistinguishable apart from the root of charity. For there are many things which can come about that have a good appearance and don't proceed from the root of charity. . . . Love, and do what you want. . . . The root of love must be within; nothing but good can come forth from this root.[51]

From this characterization of radical love as the pinnacle expression of Augustine's *ordo amoris*[52] we look back again to the account of his conversion in order to emphasize two mutually connected facts. First, Augustine is not concerned with an 'un-moved mover' (Aristotle) but with an active God who is searching for and addressing (*tolle, lege*: 'take and read') the human person. Therefore, love towards God cannot *simply* be an aesthetic *eros* enflamed by the perception of the so-being of the object desired. Second, because the love of the actively *pursuing* God can only be thought of as causative, and human love as receptive towards the one who 'has loved first' (1 John 4:19), there is no

51. Augustine, *Homilies on the First Epistle of John* 7.8, trans. Boniface Ramsey (Hyde Park, NY: New City Press, 2008), p. 110.
52. The analytic distinction between formal, categorical, and radical love that I have proposed here yields a dramaturgical slant that corresponds to the inner drama of discovery in Augustine's theology of love. Oliver O'Donovan has presented a more structuralizing description of Augustine's *ordo amoris*. He distinguishes between 'cosmic love', which finds the objects of love with a compelling teleological attraction in the natural order, 'positive love', which itself constitutes the objects of love, 'rational love', which perceives the externally set order of the Good with awe, yet remains at a certain interior distance from it, and 'benevolent love', which willingly affirms each objective order of things, inserts itself, and takes others in. Oliver O'Donovan, *The Problem of Self-Love in Augustine* (New Haven and London: Yale University Press, 1980), pp. 10-36.

reason or necessity to deprive the love of God of its affective, erotic moments.[53] For how could the active God be loved except by also loving what he does, and what he effects in those who love him?[54] It was for this reason that Augustine was bound to describe his personal justification as the overwhelming and awakening of the senses. Once the causative character of the love of God[55] has

---

53. 'Does anyone live without enjoyment? And do you suppose, my brothers and sisters, that people who fear God, worship God, love God, get no enjoyment out of it?' Augustine, *Expositions of the Psalms 73-98*, Exposition of Psalm 76, 14, trans. Maria Boulding (Hyde Park, NY: New City Press, 2002), p. 83. 'If these emotions and feelings that spring from love of the good and from holy charity are to be called faults, then let us allow that real faults should be called virtues' (Augustine, *City of God*, 14.9, p. 563). The transforming of *eros*, grounded in God's in-breaking activity, was missed by Karl Holl and Anders Nygren in their respective interpretations of Augustine, which read in his lines an unbroken eudaimonism. K. Holl, 'Augustins innere Entwicklung', in: *Gesammelte Werke zur Kirchengeschichte* 3 (Tübingen: J. C. B. Mohr, 1928), pp. 54-116. Nygren's interpretation of Augustine's 'synthesis' of *eros* and *agape* portrays *eros* as Augustine's determining logic that experiences merely some 'disturbance' from *agape*. So, in Nygren's view of Augustine, 'fellowship with God retains the character of a choice on man's part. . . . thus by rational calculation and an act of preference, man chooses God: for that is what Eros demands' (Anders Nygren, *Agape and Eros*, trans. Philip S. Watson [London: S.P.C.K., 1953], p. 556).

54. 'Love of good, too, is a relation to the good. What I find, in admiration, to be good, I find to be good *for me*.' Thus is Oliver O'Donovan's summary of Augustine's argument in his essay *On the Nature of the Good*, which opens with the declaration, 'The supreme good, than which none is greater, is God. As such it is the immutable good, which means it is truly eternal and truly immortal. All other goods are *from* this good, but not *of* this good . . .' (*De natura boni* 1). O. O'Donovan, *Self, World, and Time*, p. 109. This same insight is mirrored in Melanchthon's often-misunderstood formula in the introduction to his *Loci Communes*, 'This is to know Christ: to know his benefits' (*hoc est Christum cognoscere beneficia eius cognoscere*, MWA 2.1.7.). A soteriological narrowing of the doctrine of Christ, as some meant to perceive as prevailing in this formula, can only be assumed, if the divine object of cognition is first seen in abstraction from its efficacy, and hence from the specific creaturely vantage point of cognition: as a sinner, in need of the peculiar benefits that Christ's life is to the faithful.

55. In this respect, Augustine's interpretation of Romans 5:5 has often been misunderstood, if one sees him as comprehending the 'love of God' as an objective genitive rather than as a subjective genitive. However, in accordance with Augustine's intention, we should rather speak of a causative genitive with respect to the justification of God: *'caritas quippe Dei dicta est diffundi in cordibus nostris, non qua nos ipse diligit, sed qua nos facit dilectores suos: sicut iustitia Dei . . . qua nos fideles facit'* ('For this charity or love of God which is said to be shed abroad in our hearts is not his own love for us but that by which he makes us his lovers: like the righteousness of God by which we are made righteous through his gift . . .'). Augustine, *The Spirit and the Letter* 32.56, in: *Augustine: Later Works*, trans. John Burnaby (London: SCM Press, 1955), p. 241. On this connection O'Donovan aptly remarks: 'For Augustine, "love" is not a *nomen actionis* for which the distinction between subjective and objective genitive is

first been clarified, it can then be described unreservedly and compellingly in its affective, sensual dimensions.

As we have seen, however, by Luther's time the theological use of the word 'love' had assumed an overly strong association with the immanent human power to desire. For this reason the Reformer had to regain the radical receptivity that inhered within the Augustinian theology of love through a liberating shift in the use of concepts. Paying less attention to vocabulary, and reflecting instead on the ways in which the respective terms were actually used by the two great theologians, it dawns on us that what Luther named 'faith' serves a theological function not at all dissimilar to Augustine's radical 'love', the causative love of God in humankind.[56] This observation allows us to see in turn that the more strongly emphasized epistemological dimension that accompanies the notion of 'faith' actually lies within the horizon of Augustine's understanding of love. Thus, according to the bishop of Hippo, 'no one can love a thing that is quite unknown'.[57] And the reverse also holds true: what one loves, one will know that much more.[58] True love is knowing and passionate at the same time; to know means to love, and to love means to know.

---

relevant; it is a *nomen personae*, and the "love of God" shed abroad in our hearts is nothing other than the Holy Spirit who sheds it'. *The Problem of Self-Love in Augustine*, p. 130.

56. Although Luther felt the need to make a distinction between faith and love in the way he did on the aforementioned grounds, insight of their close connection permeates many of his remarks. So we read in his *Treatise on Christian Liberty*: '. . . by faith the soul is cleansed and made to love God' (*The Freedom of a Christian*, LW 31:359, trans. W. A. Lambert, rev. Harold J. Grimm [Philadelphia: Muhlenberg Press, 1957]; WA 7, 30, 36-31); or already in his Interpretation of the Psalms from 1513-16 he writes: 'For this reason we rejoice, because we believe the divine promises, and we hope for and love the things which He promises' (*ideo enim gaudemus, quia promissionibus divinus credimus, et que promittit, speramus atque diligimus*) (LW 11:518, trans. Herbert J. A. Bouman [Saint Louis: Concordia Publishing House, 1976]; WA 4, 380, 35-37).

Briefly stated, Luther's concept of faith took up the affectivity of love but insisted that its character of agency be ruled by receptivity. In this way the Reformer reunited what had been separated in the course of the medieval development into an intellectualized faith on the one hand, and an emotionalized love on the other: *qua unitur spiritualiter spiritui nostro per fidem et caritatem* ('. . . by which He is united spiritually with our spirit through faith and love'). Psalm 85, LW 11:158, trans. Herbert J. A. Bouman (Saint Louis: Concordia Publishing House, 1976), WA 4, 8, 10 f. Cf. also B. Hamm, 'Warum wurde für Luther der Glaube zum Zentralbegriff des christlichen Lebens?'; cf. also Peter Manns/Rainer Vinke, 'Martin Luther als Theologe der Liebe'; in: O. Bayer et al., eds., *Caritas Dei*, pp. 265-286.

57. Augustine, *The Trinity* 10.1.1, trans. Edmund Hill (Hyde Park, NY: New City Press, 1991), p. 287.

58. *De Trinitate* 9.5.8.

Love as the Affect of Faith

In view of this essential commonality between Luther and Augustine, it is little surprise to realize that the affective dimension also plays an essential role in the Reformation understanding of faith and love — a fact that has been notoriously overlooked in modern Protestantism. The Apology of the Augsburg Confession IV puts it this way: 'Faith is not only cognition . . . but also obedience to God . . . [it is] no less an active worship than it is enjoying love.'[59] In this context, it is of particular significance that the Reformers described faith and the process of justification as a renewal of the *heart*. Thus, Luther comments on 1 Corinthians 13: 'but love is pure goodness, a condition in the soul. Such a heart is to be produced by faith.'[60] Article XX of the Augsburg Confession *de fides et bonis operibus* (Faith and Good Works) describes this association in more detail (particularly in the Latin version), laying out how the heart becomes 'apt' for good works. Through the Spirit taken in through faith, it states, '. . . hearts are so renewed and endowed with new affections as to be able to bring forth good works'.[61] The triple spiritual occurrence — renewal of the heart, new affects, good works — is not to be understood as a sequence in time. Rather, the creation of the new affections occurs simultaneously with the creation of the new heart. For the heart is, as Melanchthon puts it, the 'seat of all affections',[62] the orienting center of the senses and affections.[63] This connection between the heart and the affections forms the anthropological hinge, so to speak, between justification and sanctification. In compressed form, the con-

---

59. '. . . *fides non tantum notitia est . . . sed oboedientia erga Deum, . . . non minus latreia quam dilecto*'. *Die Bekenntnisschriften der Evangelisch-Lutherischen Kirche* (BSLK) (Göttingen: Vandenhoeck & Ruprecht, 1979), p. 203.

60. *Luthers Epistelauslegung*, Vol. 2, ed. E. Ellwein (Göttingen, 1968), p. 184, translation mine.

61. *Book of Concord*, p. 45. '. . . *corda renovantur et induunt novos affectus, ut parere bona opera possint*.' BSLK, p. 80.

62. '. . . *sedem omnium affectuum*'. Philipp Melanchthon, *Loci Communes* 1521 Lateinisch-Deutsch, ed. H. G. Pöhlmann, 2nd ed. (Gütersloh: Gütersloher Verlagshaus, 1997), p. 94 (de peccato).

63. As Hans Walter Wolff (*Anthropology of the Old Testament*, trans. Margaret Kohl [London: SCM Press, 1974]) has pointed out, the Hebrew term for 'heart', *leb(ab)*, does not refer to the biological organ only but also denotes the *state* of the heart, and above all the potency of orienting oneself through desire and will (44ff). In this sense the heart is directed to recognition (Prov. 15:15) and as such enjoys a particularly strong nervous connection with the sense of hearing. In this way, the 'hearing heart', which Solomon asks for (1 Kings 3:9-12), can be seen as paradigmatic. The heart as the orienting centre of human sensitivity and affectivity is itself of a sensory quality. Cf. B. Wannenwetsch, 'Plurale Sinnlichkeit. Glaubenswahrnehmung im Zeitalter virtueller Realität', *NZSTh* 42 (2000): 299-315.

nection reads as follows: justification is the creation of a new heart — the heart governs the affections — the affections govern the will and action.

In order to understand this sequence more properly, we need to look at what is precisely signified by the dashes between the individual occurrences in the triplet. (i) In order that justification is not segregated from sanctification, that the unity of divine acts are not torn apart, and that a person's faith remains *this* person's faith, the act of justification itself must already bear an affective dimension for the justified one: precisely as the renewal of the *heart*. (ii) However, in order for this affective dimension not to become a meritorious criterion for justification, the term 'heart'[64] is sufficiently wide and general so that it cannot be identified with a single, observable human faculty that can be exercised meritoriously well, or even with one particular affect that could be

---

64. Already in the Old Testament, the heart is regarded as the center of the human person — a non-spatial locus within a man or woman which, albeit deprived of empirical access, is known as the place wherein occurs the decisive movement and which is also the privileged 'point of connection' for God: 'Man looks at the outward appearance, but the LORD looks on the heart' (1 Sam. 16:7, RSV).

This dialectic comes to expression in Melanchthon's work, when he speaks of 'heart' in a pointed double sense. Thus, at the end of his anatomic-theological work, 'The Parts and Movements of the Heart', he expresses the wish that God 'may live always in our hearts and in this, his dwelling place, to lead the hearts, the spirits of life and the soul . . . with his Spirit' ('er möge immer in unseren Herzen wohnen und in dieser seiner Wohnstatt die Herzen, die Lebensgeister und das Gemüt . . . mit seinem Geist lenken') (cited from: *Melanchthon Deutsch;* ed. M. Beyer et al., Vol. I [Leipzig: Evangelische Verlagsanstalt, 1997], p. 121, translation mine). In the chapter 'de hominis viribus' (of human powers) in the *Loci Communes*, Melanchthon challenges the idea that the will is capable of ruling the affections. Rather, he argues, *affectus affectu vincitur* (cited from the Latin-German edition, p. 36): the confused and reluctant affections of humanity can only be overcome by another 'spiritual affect'. This rapture is identified with the renewal of the heart, 'when the will was pulled away by love to the object of its faith' ('wenn der Wille durch die Liebe weggerissen wurde zu seinem Glaubensgegenstand', St. A. I 24, 26f).

Melanchthon is keen to emphasize the affective moment of faith in the climactic triad that characterizes distinct though inseparable aspects of faith *notitia — assensus — fiducia,* when certainty *(fiducia)* is portrayed as a motion *(motus)* of the heart and will, in which alone the frightened conscience is able to come to peace. This is to be understood, as Friedrich Mildenberger pointed out, as a refraction of time. It is the *remembered* faith that ascribes in retrospect a constitutive moment to its affective motion. Cf. F. Mildenberger, 'Gesetz, Vernunft und Freiheit. Zum Verhältnis von Religion und Sinnlichkeit bei Melanchthon'; unpublished manuscript, quoted with permission of the author. Augustine also knows of this theologically necessary dialectic between the visible and the invisible, as is evident in his comment on the root metaphor for love that we mentioned above: 'Now a root is hidden. The fruits of a tree can be seen, but not its root. Our root is our charity, and our fruits are our deeds'. *Expositions of the Psalms 51–72,* Exposition of Psalm 51, 12, p. 23.

seen as supremely important in this process. Instead, the 'heart' describes the orientation *(das Woraufhin)* of all human affects, which is in itself not empirically accessible — just as we found it to be the case with Augustine's 'radical love'. (iii) However, attention must be directed toward individual affections in view of sanctification, when the eye wanders ahead in the course of meditating on the grace event as a whole. Sanctification is the doctrine that deals with the concrete formation of the will and its disposition to act. *'Fides bonae voluntatis et iustae actionis genitrix est.'* Faith is the root of a good will and of right action, as it coincides with a transformation of the affects from the 'impious affects' (BSLK 80) to the new affects as fruits of the Spirit.

Thus far we have become aware of the key role of the affections in the relationship of faith and love. Space does not allow us a deeper analysis of the aforementioned examples of the Joint Declaration on Justification and a liberal love ethic in light of this finding. However, we should briefly point to a few implications, beginning with those on the subject of justification.

Investigating the role of the affective in justification without paying attention to the relation in which the affections stand to the heart as their organizing centre will leave us with a highly unsatisfactory alternative. The lack of discrimination in this vein will likely end up with a conception of the 'affect' of love as an innate human capacity that can and should be exercised to meritorious effect (the Roman Catholic temptation); alternately, a perspective intending to avoid this problem of meritoriousness, but also failing to pay attention to the heart-affections relation, will likely conceive of faith as coldly distant from anything affective (the Protestant temptation). Without examining the key role of the heart-affects connection, we cannot even hope to measure the extent to which the traditional Catholic and Lutheran ways of reflecting on the event of grace can be harmonized. However, if we understand faith as the categorical transformation of the heart, and love as transformed affectivity that comes with it, it becomes evident that the transformation itself must be so invisible as to remind us of Adam's deep slumber during the crucial operation performed on him that resulted in the creation of Eve. Sleep entails the cessation of all intellectual and intuitive capacity in time and space, as God goes about forming new life. But the invisibly transformed heart orients the perceptible affections, an orientation from which flows human action.

For the understanding of the Christian life and its reflective form in theological ethics, we should highlight two points in particular resulting from our analysis. First, modernity's tendency to emancipate ethics from affectivity — a tendency that has its reference point in Kant's moral philosophy and still has a stronghold in Protestant ethics — is to be resisted. As we have seen, at the core of the disposition to act is not the will or any other human faculty, but *caritas fide formata* — love formed by faith as the 'central affect' or the *genitrix* — the root through which the forces of divine life flow into all human capacities that comprise agency. The opposition of a stone-sober 'love towards action', on the one hand, and an enthusiastic *eros,* on the other, is also misleading. Unlike a tense love of neighbour that is anxiously concerned with its own purity by not seeking anything for itself, love formed by faith aims at seeing the beauty of God's creatures in those to whom the loving action is directed. This love is both like and unlike *eros.* It is like *eros* in that it is beauty that attracts and entices action, but is it unlike *eros* in that it perceives the beauty in the other person by way of a borrowed gaze *de divino. Caritas fide formata* represents a specific eschatological aesthetic that learns to see the other with the eyes of God and to love her according to whom she is destined to become in God's singular view. Only an eschatologically (trans)formed *eros* is capable of saving love, and its objects, from the condescending nature of a 'pure' *agape.*

Second, we have seen that the recognition of the affectivity of faith helps us understand the connection between faith and love, and hence of justification and sanctification, more organically than this is possible through common formulae such as 'cause and effect', 'gift and task', 'indicative and imperative', and so forth. If we allow for this affective dimension of faith, then the aspect of transformation must certainly be emphasized all the more over and against gradualist concepts. Christian ethics cannot articulate a pure 'ethic of love', but must rather articulate an ethic of love as both transformed and ever transforming. What it needs to represent and commend is love towards God and his commands, a love that, along with God and the neighbor, loves the *ordo amoris* itself, in which the faithful are oriented towards God and the neighbour in a distinct manner. The criterion, then, is not any kind of natural love, however theologically elevated, but love transformed into the obedience of faith: *caritas fide formata.*

Postscript: Ordered Love and/or Formed Love

A deep communality between the two great theologians has become apparent in that we have seen that 'faith' functions in Luther's theology in much the same way as 'love' functions in Augustine's, considering the affective quality of Luther's 'faith' on the one hand, and the substantial, ordered quality of 'love' in Augustine on the other. Yet, the emphases remain different, and while we have allowed that the respective historical contexts have prompted, to a certain degree, a particular articulation of the relationship of faith and love in either case, the question remains as to what degree the difference in articulation is due to theological rather than contextual considerations. For all the commonality of perspective demonstrated above, is there a more substantial sense in which Augustine's *caritas ordinata* differs from the Reformers' *caritas fide formata*?

a. Love Defined by Its Object Relation (Augustine)

The key to answering this question comes from taking a closer look at what structurally defines the *ordo amoris* for Augustine, *viz.* a sense of 'appropriateness', when rational love is defined (and limited) by the respective objects to which it turns. Oliver O'Donovan has described this Augustinian tradition as one in which love is characterized by wisdom as 'the intellectual apprehension of the order of things which discloses how each being stands in relation to each other'.[65] In a chapter entitled 'the ordering of love', he characterizes Augustine's account of love as depending on the intelligibility of respective objects in an ordered cosmos, when love in its pursuit 'grasps' its objects together with their respective nature and assigned place in that cosmos. 'True human love, conformed to the image of God's love, must always involve an integration of will and reason in a rational and comprehending affection which accords with the truth of its object. Love cannot be love in a vacuum of intelligibility; the human soul loves only on the basis of an understanding of its object.'[66]

Love's task of 'understanding its object' entails a twofold aspect: towards the one understanding and towards the understood. The appropriateness of each act of love presumes an existing, objective order of creation, within which individual objects of love can be assessed with respect to what befits human life according to teleologically oriented reason. Love is to be reasonable, insofar as it concerns the agent's capacity to grasp the level of fittingness of each object within a consideration of the agent's own reality (as a human being, a creature, and more specifically her concrete standing in the world), and of the potential object's reality as ordered by God and ordained to specific purposes. *Caritas ordinata,* therefore, means differentiating love: loving any legitimate object according to its own being, as it affects the agent's being. Hence, for

65. Oliver O'Donovan, *Resurrection and Moral Order: An Outline for Evangelical Ethics,* 2nd ed. (Leicester: Apollos; Grand Rapids: Eerdmans, 1994), p. 26.
66. O'Donovan, *Resurrection and Moral Order,* p. 236.

Augustine, the challenge of love is to 'love God as God' and 'neighbour as neighbour'.[67] Below, we will see how Luther's terminological shift towards the language of faith can be understood as positively responding to this challenge. Before we turn to this, however, it is worth considering whether the other shift that we identified in the Reformer's concept — towards emphasizing the crucial role of the heart as seat of affections — has any parallel in Augustine.

An observation that O'Donovan makes in the context of contrasting Augustine's theology of love with the classical Greek account of virtues in Plato (*Republic* 435a-441e) will point the way. Whereas Plato's account was based on the tripartite hierarchical understanding of the human soul, in which the intellect acts as sovereign, for Augustine true virtue is love for God which finds its manifestations in the cardinal virtues that are now qualified in terms of their responsiveness to love's capacity to theologize the *telos* of each virtue. As O'Donovan summarizes Augustine's concept: 'Temperance is the loving subject preserving himself unspoiled for God; fortitude is his glad endurance of all for God's sake, justice is his stance of subordination before God . . . and prudence is his discrimination between that which helps and that which hinders his pilgrimage towards God.'[68] With regards to our interest in what orients love, O'Donovan sees the most striking difference in that while Plato's account rested on the assumption of a 'self contained organization and operation of a differentiated soul,' Augustine proceeded on the basis of a 'relation of an undifferentiated soul to a differentiated external reality'.[69]

Augustine's emphasis on an undifferentiated soul — in accordance with his insistence on the simultaneity of creation of form and matter (*Deus fecit utrumque simul*)[70] — forms a most interesting parallel with the Wittenberg Reformers' emphasis on the equally undifferentiated heart ('one heart', Jer. 32:39). To conceive of faith as being coterminous with the creation of a 'new heart' takes up the prophetic legacy of Ezekiel (36:26) and Jeremiah (24:7), who each articulated the promise of the messianic future in terms of the replacement of the old, sclerotic heart with an entirely new one. This prophetic tradition was key for the Reformers, as they perceived a theological difference between the classical anthropological tradition (from the Greek philosophers of the Attic period to their adoption in the theological systems of the High Mediaeval Ages) and the Hebrew understanding of the human existence.

---

67. Augustine, *Sermo de disciplina Christiana* 3.3.
68. O'Donovan, *Resurrection and Moral Order*, p. 223.
69. O'Donovan, *Resurrection and Moral Order*, p. 223.
70. Augustine, *De Gen. ad. litt.*, I.15.29.

b. Love Defined by Its Subject (Luther)

The latter tradition attributed the orienting function in the human person not to reason but to the 'heart', and, most significantly, did this in such a way as to altogether avoid the impression that the heart was one of several human faculties, only designed as a controlling function for the others. Whereas the place and function of reason can and must be specified with precision within a system of human faculties, the heart according to the biblical tradition is a mysterious place that is only ever fully known by God. To the human eye, the operations of the heart are obscure, in sharp difference from the 'light' associated with reason. The features that we associate with rationality, the operations that reason performs on other human faculties — bringing to light, revealing, uncovering, clarifying (with regards to the affections), probing, convicting, orienting (with regard to the will as geared towards action) — are here specifically designated as God's operations *in* the heart (the orienting center of the human being), not *on* the heart (as a distinct organ).

For the Reformers, the renewal of the heart as shorthand for the renewal of the whole human person is, as we saw it stated in the *Apologia Confessionis,* associated with the heart's endowment with 'new affections'. What is new about the affections is, however, not described (as in Augustine) as creaturely 'fittingness' restored through the wholesome re-qualification of each affect through (eventually) appropriate objects, but rather in terms of a personal re-qualification: as the putting on of Christ's own affections — not affection *for* Christ, but affective life *in* Christ: to love with Christ's own love, fear with Christ's own fear, and so forth.[71] Along these lines, we might well say that the Reformers conceived of love as being qualified not through its respective objects, but through the subject of the loving agent. To point out this distinction is reminiscent of the work of Pierre Rousselot, which O'Donovan credits with having traced 'with great insight the distinction between what he has called the "ecstatic" school, which interpreted love subjectively, and the ontological school which runs from Augustine to Thomas Aquinas.'[72]

The decisive point to bear in mind in this context is that the Wittenberg

---

71. For a fascinating account of Luther's concept of transformed affectivity as rooted in his account of psalmody, an activity in which the stormy chaos waters of human affections are overcome through Christ's own affection, see Günter Bader, *Psalterium affectuum palaestra: Prolegomena zu einer Theologie des Psalters* (Tübingen: Mohr, 1996).

72. O'Donovan, *Resurrection and Moral Order,* p. 251. Cf. Pierre Rousselot, *The Problem of Love in the Middle Ages: A Historical Contribution* (Milwaukee: Marquette University Press, 2002).

Reformers' focus on the subject of love can in no way be considered prototypical of a modern subjectivity that ends up endorsing an individualized, arbitrary love ethics. Rather, the Reformers bound up this love with an arguably even higher form of objectivity than any *ordo amoris* could achieve in its careful balancing of a hierarchy of objects, in that they strictly associated the quality of love with (not mere emulation of, but) *participation in* Christ's, the new Adam's, own loving. For Luther, this transformed affectivity of faith that becomes palpable in acts of love was part of the *admirabile commercium,* the happy exchange in which everything that is Christ's becomes mine, and everything that is mine becomes Christ's. It would seem only fitting that Luther couched his portrayal of this extension of the Christological concept of the *communicatio idiomatum,* the exchange of attributes, from an inner occurrence within the two natures of Christ towards the outward relation of Christ with the believing soul, in a bridal metaphor, with its particular proximity to the affective life.[73]

While the varying weight given to the object-relation marks a notable difference in the way in which Augustine and Luther portrayed the appropriateness of love, we should be cautioned against overstretching the conceptual significance of this difference by our previous discovery of a striking grammatical convergence in their accounts. The Wittenberg Reformers had their own way of stressing the 'order' moment in their account of sanctification, in that they portrayed it not only within the framework of faith and love but more specifically and comprehensively as a matter of *faith exercised in love within the divinely assigned spheres of social life, politia, economia, and ecclesia.*[74] Luther conceived of these 'estates' — elementary forms of social life — as 'fellow-creatures' of humankind,[75] created together with the first human beings, in order to provide the social spheres that are necessary for a flourishing and obedient life.

73. Luther speaks of that 'happy exchange, in which the rich, noble, righteous bridegroom Christ takes as spouse the poor, shamed, evil little whore [cf. Hos. 1–3] and acquits her of all evil, decorating her with all good things.' LW 31:352. Cf. on the significance of the concept of *communicatio idiomatum* for Luther: Oswald Bayer, *Martin Luther's Theology: A Contemporary Interpretation,* trans. Thomas H. Trapp (Grand Rapids: Eerdmans, 2008), pp. 225-238.

74. '. . . *in talibus ordinationibus exercere caritatem',* Confessio Augustana, Article 16 on Civil Government ('. . . that everyone, each according to his own calling, manifest Christian love and genuine good works in his station of life.' *Book of Concord,* p. 38); cf. Bernd Wannenwetsch, 'Luther's Moral Theology', in: *Cambridge Companion to Martin Luther,* ed. Donald K. McKim (Cambridge: Cambridge University Press, 2002), pp. 120-135.

75. '. . . *concreatae sint . . .',* WA 40 III, 222, 35. For Luther's teaching on the Three Estates, cf. Bayer, *Martin Luther's Theology,* pp. 120-153.

As we found Luther responsive to the idea of ordered love, so we find Augustine not insensitive to the theological reasoning that drove the Reformers' 'subjective' account of love. Irrespective of his general tendency to focus on the object of love for determining its appropriateness within the *ordo amoris*, the tone must necessarily change when the 'object' at stake is God who is to be understood as the subject of all love before he can be considered a possible object of human love. As O'Donovan puts it in an attempt to interpret Augustine's famous *ipse praemium* ('he himself is the reward') expression: 'In giving himself, the subject of love, to be the object of our love, he has given us also the love with which it is appropriate to love him.'[76] Here the appropriateness of love is not defined immediately in terms of its object relation but via the 'detour' of considering the subjectivity of the one who has loved first. When it comes to God, the appropriateness of love is not something that arises from reasonable assessment of this potential or compelling object, but is received together with the love of God shown towards humankind. Before love can be reasonable, it must be revelatory. As we will see below, the order of love cannot be a mere ordering of objects, but must be, first of all, an appropriate ordering of loves according to their categorical differences.

c. Categorical Love Revisited

If, as the Reformers held, a sufficiently affective account of 'faith' is appropriately circumscribing the love of God, we need to bear in mind that this use of a term distinct from love correlates with the unique object-relation of love, when it is due to God alone. What those do, who *love* God in this exclusive way, is to not put their *faith* in any created objects. Stressing this theological exclusivity was the moment of truth in the early Augustine's insistence that God alone can be loved properly. The fact that his insistence suffered from an insufficient conceptual framework (of differentiating love as fruition from 'using' as the appropriate mode of dealing with all other objects) should not distract us from its theological premise that remains valid: that God is deserving of a different kind of love than any other object. Later in his career, Augustine came to acknowledge the aporia in which any such undifferentiated concept of love (understood as one and the same capacity, qualified solely through its respective objects) must lead, and he sought to overcome it by speaking of loving created things 'in God'.

---

76. O'Donovan, *Resurrection and Moral Order*, p. 250.

While this attempt, as necessary a step as it was, remained somewhat formulaic, it is worth considering whether the Reformers' construal of 'faith' as a term for love of God exclusively can be understood as a further step in the direction that the mature Augustine pointed. In this vein, love can be seen as not merely *qualified* through its respective objects (whilst in itself remaining the same thing under each qualification), but *classified,* when it comes to God as an object categorically different from any other. Faith, when understood according to the affective and existential breadth that the Reformers attributed to it, represents a distinct category of love, not one merely quantitatively distinct from other loves. In God's case, loving in the object-specific way that Augustine stressed as the general principle of appropriateness does not mean to love him more than anything else, but to love him in such a way as to altogether defy comparison.

To distinguish faith (as love of God) and love (of created things, including the order in which they have been created) in such a categorical way, instead of speaking of one *ordo amoris* that includes God (albeit as prime) amongst the totality of possible objects of love, does by no means suggest severing (such) love from (such) faith. These categorically different ways of loving are kept together as one in Israel's central summons (Dtr. 6:5): to love God (*unlike* any other object) with 'all your heart, all your soul, and all your strength', and the neighbour (*like* other objects, such as the self). As Oliver O'Donovan puts it: 'Love of God is affirmed in and through our other loves, structuring them and ordering them, so that with each new discovery of good that world and time lay open to us, the question of the love of God is put again, its sovereignty over other loves reasserted or forgotten.'[77]

77. O'Donovan, *Self, World, and Time,* p. 110.

In War and in Peace: Heidegger, Levinas, O'Donovan

Jean-Yves Lacoste

I

If the essence of existence is care; if existence is actually lived as coexistence; if coexistence reflects that care in the shape of care for the other man, in the form of concern[1] — then the primary intersubjective phenomenon, to use a word foreign to Heidegger, is an unrestricted peace. The other man, says the philosopher, is my "double" ('a duplicate of the Self').[2] And in saying this, Heidegger eliminates any possibility of asymmetric and dialectic relations (master/slave, etc.). The other man is the one for whom I care by offering him something to eat and drink, or more modestly by stepping aside on the pavement, or in an extreme way by presenting him with the liberating experience of anxiety — but it is not important who occupies here the position of the Self and that of the Other, which are completely interchangeable, and where no-

---

1. We are following the translation of *Fürsorge* by Joan Stambaugh in her edition of Martin Heidegger's *Being and Time* (Albany: SUNY Press, 1996) rather than that of John Macquarrie and Edward Robinson (San Francisco: HarperCollins, 1962), who opt for "solicitude": the word *sollicitudo* actually appears later in the text, §42 note 2, when Heidegger refers to the Vulgate's translation of the Greek μέριμνα but does not there mean *Fürsorge*. One will note that the Italian translation of Pietro Chiodi (Milan: Longanesi, 1966) contents itself, quite justifiably, simply to use "to care" and "care of the other man".
2. Robinson-Macquarrie, p. 162.

This essay was translated by Kenneth Jason Wardley, who wishes to express his thanks to Oliver O'Donovan for his comments on an earlier version of the text.

one is ever so removed that it precludes occupying the place of the other man. I am the other as well as myself. The other occupies my place as much as I can occupy his. And the equipoise between one and the other is therefore perfectly peaceful. Any violence is absent from Heidegger. The text certainly goes no further. As regards the other man, about whom we are concerned, nothing suggests that he is loved, and the other man is not really addressed personally: he is almost faceless.

Existence, according to Heidegger, has no history: he will only concede one, much later on, to being. Peace, therefore, is one of the first phenomena (at least, in order of their discovery [*in ordine inventionis*]), and it is certainly not a peace that is won. Being-in-peace is purely and simply a property of being-in-the-world understood in terms of its elementary features. Prior to care and to peace, there is (obviously) nothing to describe, because that would be to describe lived "phenomena" prior to existence and of which there is no mention in the text other than to deny that they take place — thus we are "thrown" into the world but come from nowhere, and thus there is a "fall", albeit one that does not refer to any supralapsarian state whatsoever.[3] A question must be asked, one which still no one has really asked: might the *existentiell* analytic, insofar as it is concerned with the fact of existence and it alone, nevertheless still have its counter-factual moment? One possible answer may be to relegate violence, contempt of the other man, war, everything that is obviously opposed to the logic of care, to the realm of the existential or more precisely the ontic-existential: all that would exist (and how could one deny that?), but it would not bear any *existentiell* weight. A second possible answer may be to observe that in violence, war, etc., we are still "taking care" of the other man. But since that answer is not offered by the text can we make do with the first answer? Does the fact of existence not conceal these omnipresent phenomena — despising the other man, not seeing in them this *alter ego* that, to once again use a lexicon that is not that of Heidegger, I should love as myself — in spite of the examples of kindness offered by the philosopher? And might it conceal them as barely significant, like the small print at the bottom of the page? The two answers are mutually dependent. The primacy of concern, indeed, does not negate the ways in which we do not care about other people, but simply relegates them to the background, where the work of description can be uninterested in these phenomena. That they exist is not disputed (one need only have eyes to see). We are dealing, however, with something of no interest to us or which can only interest us under the heading of behavior in

3. See Robinson-Macquarrie, p. 220.

which we do not lay hold of what belongs to us. The logic of concern, and of concern for the other man, is *existentiell.*

The logic of contempt or indifference towards the other man is so only in a paradoxical way: it is written into existence as something that need not appear in order that we understand amongst ourselves what existence means. The reasons why peace and war are not named in the text are clear. Peace does not need to be negotiated and concluded: to be in peace, it is enough just to exist. (As for someone who refuses to let peace prevail between himself and the other man, it is enough to say that he lives a diminished life, less revealing of the way of being the being that we are, or that he commits an implicit contradiction of his being-in-the-world.) War does not need to be named: the other person never appears either in the guise of the unfriendly neighbor [*inimicus*] or — *a fortiori,* in a text that devalues "public" life and affords existence no political horizon — that of a public enemy [*hostis*].

Is this description of existence rather Utopian? Can it be the case, after all, that violence and war are at once real and yet without philosophical interest? Existence has its horizon, the world, and within this, it would seem naïve to universalise the peaceable, more or less friendly encounter with the other man. Concerning the other man, I take the initiative, or am meant to take the initiative, to will and to do what is good (a term absent from the text . . .), in small or large ways. The other man takes — or is meant to take — the same initiative towards me, reciprocally and in total symmetry. Now, who guarantees us this reciprocity? The other man is my double, which means that I am or that I act towards him as he is or acts towards me. The description, however, is only as good as the assumption it rests upon, which we can state in partially Heideggerian terms: that of universal concern. This assumption never appears in the text, although it underpins it. Since he and I are doubles of one another, the description of what I am teaches us everything there is to know about the other man as well as about myself. On the other hand, after the section dedicated to concern, very little will reappear in the text about the other man — we will be forced to meet him, in fact, only in the study of speech, which is necessarily speech addressed to another man, or the study of gossip, which is necessarily gossip with others. There will be nothing more. Its almost primary thesis — the "thesis of concern" — is plainly stated, and something to which the book will not return; any such critical return has neither possibility nor opportunity. It is for this reason, then, that we have to use the adjective "Utopian" in order to talk about a phenomenon that is not absent from the world (there is concern, in abundance). But neither is it omnipresent; it could be so only in some other world. At the beginning of the book peace reigns, and it reigns still more so at the end, where the highest experiences take place in the absence of the other man, therefore in the absence of any possible intimacy. Now, who will maintain without batting an eyelid that the care which qualifies all that I do — all of my activities — inevitably blossoms into concern as soon as we have anything at all to do with the other man, however that might be? Care is pre-ethical. Concern, to judge by the few examples provided by Heidegger, is not; and the transition from a pre-ethical care to a concern which has unmistakably ethical aspects is thus not really a transition but transition and break. There is a place for concern in the logic of existence. But when we go on from that to say, or try to say, that existence, in which the other man intervenes (in experience and in description), is inevitably lived as concern, we say too much, or demand too much from the fundamental structures of existence. A world where coexistence would be experienced only as concern is possible. It is, unfortunately, not the world in which we live, and in which the other person is as likely to be the recipient of our scorn or indifference as of our care.

One will argue, of course, about the subtle nature of "we" in Heidegger. The encounter between one man and another is summed up in the coexistence of more than one "I", completely interchangeable and that never achieve (and, from the Heideggerian perspective, were they even meant to?) the formation of a "we", understood in a non-nominalist way as more than simply a set with two 'I's as its members. *Dasein* speaks, he speaks to *Dasein,* but the concept of dialogue is missing from the book. "Intersubjectivity", both word and concept appeared in philosophy before Heidegger. The long investigations of the topic devoted by Husserl have the merit of seeing a problem where Heidegger sees only a "fact". In any case, the 'inter-' is completely absent from *Being and Time.* "We", therefore, cannot really establish itself in a thought where existence (not of any particular thing, but in general) takes precedence over what exists, and where existence is indiscriminately singular and plural. It is no wonder that existence reveals itself profoundly in the painful and totally individual phenomenon of anxiety, and Heidegger, in a later text, considers loneliness among the basic concepts of metaphysics.[4] What is most important happens in the absence of the other man — an absence that is not felt as a deprivation. The peace which prevails between men reigns from start to finish in the book. But once the conceptualization of concern is completed, the description of exis-

4. See Martin Heidegger, *The Fundamental Concepts of Metaphysics: World, Finitude, Solitude,* trans. William McNeill and Nicholas Walker (Bloomington: Indiana University Press, 2001) [*Die Metaphysik der Grundbegriffe, Welt-Endlichkeit-Einsamkeit,* GA 29-30]. The most important text is in fact devoted to the phenomenon of boredom, itself a solitary experience.

tence is not richer than at its beginning — far from it. Coexistence is a primitive fact. No one doubts its reality. This reality, however, soon slipped into the margins of the book. *Being and Time* was written four years later than Buber's *I and Thou*. Heidegger did not read this book and would not have known what to make of it.

II

The alternative philosophy — and phenomenology — that Levinas offers in *Totality and Infinity* evidently forms a contrast to a philosophy which does not acknowledge violence; the book was written following a war and bears its scars in its haunted, haunting preoccupation. Can we encounter one another only as warriors on a battlefield, in which case would we become the "dupes"[5] of moral discourse? Have we or can we find the means to end war? We have spoken about Utopia in regard to Heidegger; nothing, however, is more rooted in history and its catastrophes than Levinas's meditation. Can or should classical phenomenology *think* about peace? Heidegger suggested its reign without really thinking about it. Husserl never encountered the problem — and the intersubjectivity which did present him with a problem to solve was a wholly peaceful one which, as such, passed without question. Levinas, however, only ever asks this one question. And in order to ask it, he takes at once a position upstream of any definition of the other as either unfriendly neighbour [*inimicus*] or as public enemy [*hostis*] (it will be, in both cases, a question of "my" enemy, determined as such by the way that he looks at me), and we treat the other man as they appear to us, in an appearance that Levinas calls originary, as a face always liable to be violated and as a mouth that has nothing to say to us except, silently, "you shalt not kill". Before I do anything, the other man has made the first move. Before I notice or admit that he and I both have existence in common, thus before I can even try to define him as *alter ego*, his appearance — his "epiphany" in the para-theological vocabulary of Levinas — has taken possession of me: I am his "hostage".[6] Because Levinas is speaking in the aftermath of war, he knows that the other man may well not make his demands heard or that these demands may well go unnoticed (otherwise, why remind

---

5. Emmanuel Levinas, *Totality and Infinity,* trans. Alphonso Lingis (Pittsburgh: Duquesne University Press, 1969), p. 21.

6. The term is absent from *Totality and Infinity*. However, *Otherwise Than Being: Or Beyond Essence* (Pittsburgh: Duquesne University Press, 1998) makes abundant use of it.

us of them along with the conceptual violence specific to *Totality and Infinity?*). The other man may be relegated to the rank of a "specimen", or instance [*Stuck*] of humanity. Philosophers generally only practice philosophy and are not, at least in the first instance, peacemakers. Levinas certainly thinks within the city and for the benefit of the city. There, however, he thinks meta-politically or apolitically in order to demonstrate the genesis of a peaceful city for which he proposes no politics whatsoever, for the simple reason that 'politics is opposed to morality'.[7] The description of the other man's face in his *appearing* ("*apparoir*", in the idiosyncratic French[8] of the author) will therefore be extremely formal, as though he had only to appear to and take me hostage, and that I agree to be taken hostage, for all humanity to be included in it. This may, of course, be the case, but is it enough to make everyone at peace with everyone so long as they accept a fundamental experience as their own? It is possible. Existence has no more history in Levinas than in Heidegger, and nothing forbids a formal description, in addition to being valid for all, from providing us with the conditions in which a universal peace might reign, in conditions in which morality excuses us from any politics. Still, failure always remains possible, not least because it has always been present. In *Being and Time,* war and peace do not have to be named, and the peace assured by our concern remains undisturbed for the rest of the book or in the remainder of the oeuvre (nothing in the post-war texts, it must be said, was written against war). In *Totality and Infinity,* however, the threat of war is perpetual. The philosopher knows what the conditions are, and what phenomena must be given an appropriate welcome, for establishing peace. But he also knows that that establishment is fragile. Peace was not there at the beginning. If it should prevail in the end, this can only be in the messianic city, which is now Utopian. And if it happens that it now reigns, between men tacitly following the rules dictated by the philosopher, it does so precariously.

The other man, in Heidegger, does not appear to us as a pleading face — even if the first demand which is made of us, to show our concern by feeding the one who is hungry, presupposes something like an unspoken, unnamed face-to-face encounter, one which has to have taken place. In Levinas, on the other hand, it is important to note that the plea contained in the "epiphany" of the face absorbs every other meaning that this appearance contains. There

---

7. *Totality and Infinity,* p. 21.

8. Translator's note: Levinas's stylistic choices in French reflect a somewhat eccentric commitment to language considered old-fashioned or even archaic. For example, words such as "apparoir" might well seem odd to modern French-speakers, giving Levinas's texts what Lacoste considers a slightly "precious" air.

is no room for dialogue and discussion in Heidegger, there is no room for interlocution in Levinas, since only the other man speaks, and in silence. Heidegger knows of no other "ethical" phenomenon than that which exists in an act of concern[9] (and of a concern that one must assume is reciprocal), Levinas knows of no other than that of the other man whose appearance takes us hostage. What is there to say except that violence and war should be avoided at all costs? And to whom may this be said, if not him that can only exhibit violence toward us, who was already potentially more a private [*inimicus*] than a public enemy [*hostis*]? Any exchange of words, then, becomes secondary: words are at the service of the accusation, whether uttered or not. You are the one who can kill me — nothing else. The other man — or I as the other of the other — thus occupies only one position, that of the accuser, easily converted into that of the accused. It hardly puts a strain on the exposition of the text (though it strains its exegesis a little . . .) to conclude that the fundamental tone of the relationship between *ego* and *alter ego* is that of fear. I appear to the other man as a potential enemy. The other man strikes me as a potential enemy. Levinas's tactic aims to lead us to an experience of the possibility of peace. It does so, however, by insisting upon an experience of the abiding possibility of war. Ethics does not want the good. It wants to end violence.

There is no objection to Levinas's robust realism. He wrote following a war, but this would be almost anecdotal *(sit venia verbo)* if one forgot that we still think with wars going on all around us, and that a philosophy that would bracket out war entirely would be a philosophy written somewhere other than earth, in a *Nephelokokkygia,* a "cloud-cuckoo-land".[10] Thinking about violence, therefore, leads one to also think that thought can itself be violence — violence to the truth almost inevitably leads to violence to the other man, through whatever intermediate steps. Beyond all the theoretical abysses that separate them, a reading of Levinas must lead, paradoxically, onto the same ground as a reading of Hegel. Hegel wants to reach an eschatology that is the triumph of peace. He wants, however, to reach that destination without the slightest illusion about the time of history, which is to say, about the empire of violence. Peace — and peace is desired by all, regardless of the ways in which it is said to be attained — is not, in Hegel's view, the driving force of history but an absolute *telos.* These things are well known. However, it re-

---

9. A second phenomenon can receive the qualification of "ethical", that of the "voice of conscience" (*Being and Time,* §46). This appeal, however, is content-less. And it does not intersect the logic of the good. We refer to our essay, 'Ethique et Phénoménologie', in *Présence et parousie* (Genève: Ad Solem, 2006), pp. 231-256.

10. Aristophanes, *The Birds,* 819.

mains, and this is not insignificant, that the author of *Totality and Infinity* writes (violently) against Hegel on the ground that peace is an ever-present possibility. Hearing the silent supplication of the other man and refusing to use violence against him, this is nothing less than to suspend, if only temporarily, the dialectics which make up history. Violence dominates history and drives it forward. History, however, can be bracketed out. Yet that is always *my* task and *my* task in a pre-political mode: the task of a man who is not yet a citizen. Levinas wrote against war, but what he proposes against war is not a Kantian project of perpetual peace, but a demand rooted in an experience, private to two people, myself and the other man. The end of war begins with the relationship that I choose to maintain with my neighbor. Well then, who is my neighbor?

One distinction is missing from Levinas, or rather it would be useless to him, that of the private and public enemy *(inimicus* and *hostis),* a distinction which Schmitt, in particular, underscores strongly.[11] The public enemy [*hostis*] can, for reasons given by Schmitt, escape our attention: because he is faceless, because we would probably never speak to one another, because his "hostility" is determined independently of him and of me. The enemy constituted by personal unfriendliness [i.e. as *inimicus*], however, has a face. He probably lives in the same city as me. What Levinas, curiously, calls the "humanism" of the other man is understood as everyone's right — no human has less humanity than any other. Levinas's 'other man', however, appears, as such, to me in the private experience of a face-to-face encounter, and not like the public enemy [*hostis*], who simply appears in the plural, nor like the citizen (still in the plural) of a state with which our country has signed a peace treaty. Every man is my neighbour: it is, of course, his right. "Perpetual peace" should be willed, and can ideally be achieved. But it will still be, and this is where an Hegelian critique of Levinas will always have its two pennies' worth to offer,

---

11. See Carl Schmitt, *The Concept of the Political,* trans. George Schwab (Chicago: University of Chicago Press, 1996), pp. 29-33. Translator's note: the relevant passage in Schmidt reads, 'As German and other languages do not distinguish between the private and political enemy, many misconceptions and falsifications are possible. The often quoted "Love your enemies" (Matt. 5:44; Luke 6:27) reads "diligite inimicos vestros", ἀγαπᾶτε τοὺς ἐχθροὺς ὑμῶν, and not *diligite hostes vestros*. No mention is made of the political enemy. [. . .] The enemy in the political sense need not be hated personally, and in the private sphere only does it make sense to love one's enemy, i.e., one's adversary. The Bible quotation touches the political antithesis even less than it intends to dissolve, for example, the antithesis of good and evil or beautiful and ugly. It certainly does not mean that one should love and support the enemies of one's own people.'

at the level of a relationship between man and man (or at the level of a fraternal community), a relationship that may or may not transcend the boundaries of the city, but which does nothing to prevent that the duty of my fellow man, within his city, may be to confront me as a *hostis*. It is here, evidently, that Levinas is right to criticize politics in the name of morality. Is the neighbour thus not defined in apolitical terms, independent of our equal status as citizens, also independent of the role which we play in the same city or of the relationships that we forge across the border which separates our two cities? The meeting with the other man as Levinas conceives it is an eschatological experience, or an eschatological promise. This experience, however, is always and inevitably a micro-experience: a small-scale experience of a universal closeness that we would certainly not be able to achieve. This experience has nothing in its fabric that prevents it from being universalized. But under what conditions?

Because the concepts used by Levinas inaugurate a heuristics of private life, they seem, at first glance, unable to do anything except subvert (or deny) political existence. Is there really a hiatus between private and political life? The question is easier to ask than to answer.

However, everything happens, both in Levinas and in Heidegger, as if public life was, in Heidegger's words, an "inauthentic" or "improper" [*uneigentlich*] life. The traditional definition of man is as a political animal. He is obviously not that in Heidegger. No more is he that in Levinas, whose response to the highly public threat of war is to interpret phenomena which are hardly public at all, whether we think of the caress or the epiphany of the face. The idea that we universalize the richest experiences that we perform in private deserves to be taken seriously, however little it may be done in practice. To take it seriously is thus to dispense with a rhetorical treatment. Why can't the achievements of private life be shared more widely? Why can't relations of brotherhood be enlarged beyond the circle of brothers? Why can't they be enlarged even to the scale of cities or nations?

The incremental steps taken above show that there is a break somewhere. The monastic community (the community where one wants to live an "angelic" life) is intended to be a community of brothers in which no one has to fear the threat of any other man. But who will deny that it also represents the most risky model of human community, one that will leave the widest scope for hostility if the community is not kept under close oversight — if the brothers do not enjoy the protection of an abbot? War and violence are not phenomena which we could ever be finished with once and for all. War, moreover, may prevail within the smallest community. To bring an end to war — any kind of war — is one of the most venerable projects of any political — and to which it should be added, political and moral — philosophy. It does not follow, however, that any concept capable of describing a pacified or peaceful intersubjectivity can describe political experience adequately, and that concepts able to account for political experience are also capable of reporting the non-public life. The city is absent from Heidegger. It is almost absent from Levinas. We can certainly make universal judgements: every man, as such, is the object of our care, every man appears before me with the justified demand that we live in peace — and if all were at peace with one another, every state would be at peace with every other one. But if we read Levinas, or §26 of *Being and Time,* as though they offered us a prescription for world peace, then it is a safe bet that we would be taking leave of their clearest intentions. There is no need to belabour Heidegger's intentions, of course. But it is true of Levinas's intentions, too, and more so. The game played according to him is a game for two players. This game is not limited to myself and the other man: in order to respect the ambitions of philosophy, it is necessary that anyone can play. Can it, however, be played in the city and by someone who wishes to act the part of the citizen? The city is missing from Heidegger, as it is from Levinas as well. The existing subject that we face in *Totality and Infinity,* and elsewhere, is not defined by membership of a city, even remotely: whoever talks about politics talks about the threat of war, and we cannot reject the rule of politics without refusing to be defined as citizens. No more is he defined by membership of the *oikoumene;* the idea of cosmopolitanism is absent. In both places, either in the initial analysis of *Being and Time* or in the work of Levinas, the phenomenon of the world eclipses that of the city. According to Heidegger, the highest decisions are taken alone, the highest experiences are solitary, and "co-being-there" vanishes when it is a matter of resolutely facing finitude. Levinas is certainly anything but a thinker of solitary experience, and above all of that supreme experience of solitude. It takes two to exist (as Levinas taught us somewhat better than Buber and Ebner), and Heidegger concedes the point without realising its full consequences. Levinas never thinks about the phenomenon of solitude, which is either pre-moral, or a deliberate refusal of the silent call of the other man. But one way or the other, real life (the phenomenon of existence, if you will) is private, more or less. Levinas thinks under the threat of war, but proposes no negotiated solution to the problem of war. His theme is peace and being-in-peace, and what he proposes is an elaborate theory of intersubjectivity that works well, avoiding the reduction of the other man to the status of an object, avoiding the master-slave dialectic, avoiding, more generally, the narrow representation of the relationship between one man and another which the term "intersubjectivity" (even one that works well) can evoke.

Can we really do without a philosophy able to think coexistence within a city? According to Heidegger and Levinas, it passes without comment that we are inhabitants of a city, but that nonetheless deserves to be said; in not saying so, we might conceal a lack of thinking. So let us, with other conceptual landmarks, attempt to say so.

III

The initial landmarks will be theological. This is not to give theologians undue ambitions. It will, however, be in order to use resources where there is no alternative lying to hand. What then does theology — Christian theology — tell us about our co-existence in private experience, and our co-existence in public or political experience? A first point should be obvious: the traditional theological distinction between "individual" morality and "social" morality. This distinction, it should be noted, is assumed in discussions with wider interests. Thomas Aquinas (if we agree to regard him as the greatest moral theologian of his time) devoted a booklet to the political art (the *De regimine principum*), but one would be hard pressed to find a clear distinction, in his *Summa Theologiae,* between what a friend has the right to require of us and what the city also has the right to demand of us: the unity of the moral act weighs heaviest on its subdivisions, the unity of action comes before the spheres of action. These spheres clearly exist: we do not behave towards a friend (either in the experience of *amor* or that of *caritas*) as we behave in relation to a homeland. The demands that the friend and the country make upon us are different, and our responses to these demands will necessarily be different. There is no split, however, between those demands. No split, certainly, but a clear distinction. We always say (how can we not?) that our neighbour is our neighbour even when he or she is not known to us by sight. My duties towards my fellow citizen, however, do not completely overlap with what I owe my brother or my friend, far from it. Again, the problem of the ideal city, where all are brothers of all, is never far away. But again, this city — the monastery, the Beguine convent — appears as ideal: it is not enough merely to establish it for enmity to be outlawed once and for all. Moreover is it not always a worthwhile exercise to distinguish between "individual" morality and "social" morality, noting that on the one side there are rights and duties unknown on the other, and vice versa? At least it would enable us to say that political experience can be moral.

One example here comes to mind, as an objection addressed to Levinas, the theory of just war. Every private war is unjust because it is completely immoral. Even if the "humanity" of the other man is hard to recognize in the *inimicus,* it can and ought to be recognised, for someone who insults or defames me is still my neighbour in spite of everything and it needs only a little heroism on my part to treat him as a brother. War, however, in the literal sense, is fought less between individuals than between nations or equivalent entities. Could we therefore bring about a universal peace? The difficulty we have mentioned of keeping the peace within the enclosure of the monastery is a clear warning to us: the peace of all with all will never prevail, at best, other than in the form of an universal armistice (assuming that it is possible), and hostility — at least, the presence of the *hostis* — can never be abolished. That would be the abolition of politics. Peace must be willed. Just war theory even specifies that there is a right to war only if all means to reach a peaceful settlement of disputes between cities and nations have been tried and failed. Is the consequence of describing war as "just", however, not only to guarantee a (limited) right to violence, but more brutally, to guarantee the rights of violence? That is, alas, what it must be. The description proposed by Levinas, whatever its elegance, suffers unfortunately from the absence of one point of reference, the law. There is no law to step in and prevent my meeting with the other man being violent. The game played by two in *Totality and Infinity* and (differently) in *Otherwise Than Being* obeys no rule other than that which theory has lain down. The description, of course, carries implicit requirements: the appearance of the other man does not require me to have done with violence except insofar as his appearance is such as I have a duty to let appear. And it is as this duty is fulfilled that peace will be able to prevail between us. However does the prescription (and one should never neglect the prescriptive force of phenomenological descriptions) possess the means of enforcement? It comes to the fore in the field of reason. If I recognize in myself the "hostage" of the other man, then I shall have standards capable of governing my behaviour towards him. It does not intrude — of course — in a world where violence demands of us that we should fight against it, where we know that rooting it up would be Utopian, and where we know that we can justly bring violence to bear against. The peace of all with all — whether we are speaking about individuals or about cities — must be desired and hoped for, but this hope is strictly eschatological. War is simply absent from Heidegger; Levinas, by contrast, writes against war, but the logic of what he writes is that of a messianic age. If theology, at least in mainstream Christianity, dares to talk about just war it is because it speaks in advance of this messianic age, and in knowing that the continued presence of war, private or public, tells us that this age has not arrived.

Mentioning just war requires a reference to a second, and connected, classic case, that of self-defence. The other man appears (discreetly) in Heidegger as one who begs for bread; in Levinas he appears to me as one who begs me to spare his life. Levinas tells us therefore that we occupy the position of aggressor or potential murderer. Now, if I am the one who can kill, whatever murder may be in question, the other man is *alter ego,* whether or not we call him that in so many words, and therefore occupies the same position of potential murderer towards me. Do I have the right to defend myself against the murderer? Common sense grants me this right without restriction. Here again, messianic requirements may be opposed to common sense: "if someone strikes you on the right cheek, turn to him the left one also" (Matt. 5:39). Common sense, in this case finds itself properly disoriented or confused. Theological tradition, if it admits self-defence, thus certainly speaks in terms of this common sense. Is it restricted to these terms? We suggest an answer: the language that it preserves for us offers the means to survive in times that are not exactly the "last". No one in the philosophical tradition has ever denied the right to self-defence. As "self" defence it is therefore compliant with the moral law as well as the law of the city. On this point, it is not important to which moral law philosophy refers. Unanimity is enough, and with it a loyalty to the *logos,* to the word held by the masters of rationality, whose opinion does not raise any major objection against it. I am free — unmistakably — to refuse to defend myself. I am, by the same token, free to refuse to enter into what can be a deadly circle of offence and retaliation. But I am also free, with no affront to morality, to defend myself against violence and injustice. The rejection of all violence anticipates on a small scale the messianic age. Whoever is violent towards me, however, proves that these times have not yet arrived.

The problem we have encountered here has a name: supererogation. Why should one do more than is required by the law? Why should one not? The answer inevitably comes back: which law? In response, theology (and biblical exegesis) propose a binary law, that of the (Mosaic) Torah and the messianic law, from the *torah messianica.*[12] Two laws, therefore. Both are laws, and both have the guarantee of a divine word.

Yet the law of Moses, the Torah, has an irrevocable character, while the law of "messiah" — and this is the problem presented by the parallel — demands more than does the Mosaic law. Does it "demand"? It certainly has the

---

12. I might mention that the theme of the Torah of Jesus was brilliantly illustrated in its time by William D. Davies, *The Setting of the Sermon on the Mount* (Cambridge: Cambridge University Press, 1964).

character of prescription: "and I tell you". Does the prescription, however, extend to all mankind, as the great centre of the mosaic Torah, the Decalogue, can be extended to all mankind? Or is it beyond the logic of what we usually call a law? In speaking of the *torah messianica*, we run the risk of deceiving ourselves. On the mount, Jesus commands. However, he commands his disciples and only his disciples — the "Sermon on the Mount" is not addressed to the crowds who have already received his teaching. The Mosaic Torah, meanwhile, addresses itself to the Elect (even though it is easy to find it being applied universally in the hands of those who see in the Decalogue the hard nucleus of a "natural law"). However, these other "Elect" ones, the disciples of Jesus, do not receive easily universalizable commandments.

One central tenet is certainly addressed to everyone beyond the circle of disciples, that of the love of enemy — a moral philosophy could make that its own. Not all the commands are. And concerning those who are not, we must say that they go beyond the scope of what can be demanded. The order of the supererogatory is not "meta-moral". Jesus, a possible candidate for messianic dignity, indeed proposes a law to his disciples that they can take or leave, as a whole. But if the *torah messianica* (accepting the term with every reservation) forms a whole, then it is valid or compulsory, only in a paradoxical way, as a law demanding more than the entirety of required obligations. This last clause seems self-contradictory. "The due" is defined as something which is required of all (in the case of a moral law), or simply of all members of a community, which is to say, all the inhabitants of a city. Can we include in a code of law what is *not* due? Can the legislator — can the Supreme Legislator, above all — demand more than what is due? In the face of the difficulty raised by these issues, theology has traditionally responded by appealing to a distinction between precept and counsel. We could connect this to another distinction, that of "being" and "well-being". Merely to be — to be a human being who lives a human life — it is, clearly, enough to fulfill the precepts of the law. The verb "to be enough", however, can only make us uncomfortable. What else is there to do, and why do it, when we have done enough? "Enough", on the other hand, corresponds to "necessary". Immediately the question turns around. Fulfilling the Ten Words transmitted by the law of Moses has all the appearances of the necessary, without which we would be failing to be human. Yet what is necessary is not, as such, enough. The necessary must be done. But to return to our questions, we can reply that the supererogatory (not demanded but, as we are told, "counselled") is, perhaps, at home in the realm of "enough", that "more than necessary" which complements the necessary. When supererogatory benevolence has been shown to the enemy, when the standard of every relationship between man and man has been honored in the form of mercy in the image of the divine mercy, then we can say that that is "enough". No one does what is enough unless he agrees to do (beforehand and simultaneously) the necessary. He has in any case a good reason to do that which is enough: it is here that the secrets of "well-being" lie.

Still, it is necessary to agree that the "more-than-necessary" does not contradict the necessary. Thielicke, who attracted a legitimate criticism from Oliver O'Donovan, speaks of New Testament ethics as made of an 'extra-planetary material'.[13] Now if anything is quite certain and put most clearly by O'Donovan, it is that no Christian ethic is possible without a vigorous theology of creation, and without rooting eschatological "well-being" within a "moral order" as old as the world. Thielicke's rigorous Lutheranism required him to establish a caesura between New Testament ethics and everything else, above all the Mosaic law; and the parallelism of the Mosaic Torah (and of its "ten words") and the *torah messianica* on that basis therefore results in a divorce. This divorce must be rejected. The Mosaic law or natural law on the one hand, and on the other the messianic law, both have equally the essential character of the "given", of that which we have not found but received. We must speak of a "natural" law as a received law insofar as it bears witness to our condition as creatures. But precisely because we cannot speak of moral law without mentioning creation and covenant, we cannot say that the law supervenes or is supplementary, nor give messianic law the quality of an "extra-planetary material". An eschatology without protology — an order of salvation independent of the order of creation — is a shaky eschatology. And the supererogatory, the "more than necessary" which exceeds the necessary without cancelling or tossing it into the dustbin of history, is anything but the first word of a theological ethic. Theology will not use the language of resurrection without first having used that of creation, and that of the messianic law without first having used that of the created order.

IV

The confrontation of reasons between philosophical ethics and theological ethics should thus be understood as a confrontation between illuminations rooted in the same work of elucidation. And elucidation is needed because the

13. See Oliver O'Donovan, *Resurrection and Moral Order* (Leicester: IVP, 1986), pp. 144-146.

requirements of ethics are neither obvious nor known to us in a timeless fashion, even if we know them to be inscribed in the created order. That which is "moral" in the fact of existence, such as Heidegger talks about in his analysis of concern, is not so much illuminated [*mis en lumière*] but rather pointed out: this is how we exist in the world. The "morality" of concern, moreover, is an inconclusive phenomenon, because we can clearly have the experience of solitude, and because the refusal (or inability) to enter the logic of concern is also equally a matter of fact, without any duty whatsoever intervening to lead us to forbid this fact. No description, however, is as good as an image in a good mirror, where the real appears to us as it is and without distortion. The fact of existence requires a hermeneutic and an unveiling. Philosophy, even if it means to be descriptive, does not *let* things appear without simultaneously *making* them appear — and if it did not make them appear, they would remain unknown or poorly understood. To describe is also to discover, in the sense that one can speak, for example, of a "discovery of the self".[14] Ethics was discovered long ago — theology tells us that it was discovered at the same time as the relationship of man to God. What was discovered one day, however, runs the risk of being forgotten the next. For this reason, despite the absence of any moral "duty" or of any moral "value" in Heidegger's text, the minimal reality of an ethics woven into the fact of existence cannot go unnoticed. The task of interpreting the fact of existence is therefore, no one will be surprised to learn, as much philosophical as theological. If a clarification needs to be made — if the law is not inscribed upon our hearts and must be taught to us — it will be so, trivially, because our duties and our values, our relationship to good or our relationship to evil, do not appear to us simply by virtue of the fact that we exist. We would not need to hang on to the language of morality if we were fully moral. And the blessing pronounced upon the peacemakers may be addressed to the philosopher and theologian who tell us the conditions of peace. . . .

The point of moral language is not at all obvious. This language tells us that something "is" good or bad, that there is "worth" in something, that we "ought to" do something, that it is a "matter of conscience" — but it matters little what direction it takes, because we everywhere stumble over the same problem (why morality?) that we cannot resolve without projecting something that is not evident, that of the good, of duty, etc. As soon as we admit the problem and the proposed solution, one conclusion, just as much theological as philosophical, is inevitable; being in the world does not predestine us to

14. So in Vincent Carraud, *L'invention du moi* (Paris: PUF, 2010).

loyalty to the good. All Levinas's thought tends to dictate to us our duties to the other man, and especially to tell us that we cannot escape from experiences that impose these duties upon us. Levinas, however, is writing after evil has done its work, and therefore presupposes that we can refuse to make our own the experiences he describes as he describes them. He proposes, or rather imposes, a certain way of looking at the other man which, if all were to make it theirs, would bring an end to the reign of violence and war. And if, from a thinker who tries to give ethics the status of first philosophy, we return to Heidegger, whose theoretical ambitions are different, but who, in interpreting the phenomenon of concern, cannot avoid encountering behavior which will properly be called "moral", here again the deliberate neutrality of description cannot completely hide the fact that here, too, we cannot describe without prescribing. And if we prescribe, it is because it is necessary to prescribe. We are told that patterns of concern, in their most elementary form, deserve to be called back to mind. But if, even for a moment, they need recollection, does that not mean there is something running counter to the recollection, an ever-present threat of immorality? Reinventing ethics, rediscovering it, is the concern of every thought interested in existence at its most proper, most "authentic". We would not have to rediscover it if we cared constantly and spontaneously about the other man. But we do most certainly have to rediscover it, which means that we are able to do good (morality is not a hopeless enterprise . . .) but also able not to do it. The good is what we are always able to forget.

Theology is well aware of this, in speaking to us the language of creation and covenant, since they are essentially inseparable, in order to tell us that the covenant is asymmetrical, the covenant of a faithful God with an unfaithful man. The "created order", what does that mean? It means, first of all, the rejection of any Marcionite or Gnostic ethic separating what was done in the beginning, the creation, from what was given at the end, salvation. The "created order" is thus to inscribe morality in the "nature" of man. As to that, one must agree. O'Donovan's short critique of Thielicke provides us with all the means to do so. If that which produces the "messianic law" is "extra-planetary material", from which planet do the basic commandments that require us to seek good and love kindness come from? As there is an excess of evil, so there is surely an excess of good. Love of the enemy demonstrates it perfectly! The "messianic law" certainly contains antitheses ('but I tell you'), however, this excess and these antitheses appear in a discourse that does not mean to "abolish" but to "fulfill". Theology commonly speaks of old and new covenants. But in speaking like this, it does not refer to an old God and a new God. There is discontinuity, but it is set within an even greater continuity, which cannot be forgotten. The "material" of New Testament ethics is a biblical material, addressed to a sinner, but to whom was prescribed, since Leviticus, a "law of holiness". We can always allow that the "perfection" demanded by Jesus of his disciples exceeds that law of holiness. In order to allow it, however, one must first admit that creation, covenant, the breaking of and restoration of the covenant are inseparable. The first words of the covenant are interpreted by O'Donovan as they should be, from an end-point — an accomplishment — which is the real beginning. The created order is seen from the experience upon which every theology stands or falls, the experience of the resurrection. Whoever talks about resurrection is talking, as is suggested by the episode of the Transfiguration (the description of which is perhaps a first version of the Easter narratives), about "transformation" (Matt. 17:2). Nothing is transformed where its transformation does not preserve their essential identity. That is the key to the relationship between Old Testament ethics and New Testament ethics. Whoever speaks of a moral experience transformed by the "Christ event", therefore, cannot do that without also preserving the discourse of creation and of a covenantal economy as old as creation.

What is undeniable is that the Jewish and Christian Scriptures talk about a covenant with men who will always be able to break it, and that, like the discourse of moral philosophy, moral theology proceeds to a constant and realistic *memento* of what Kant calls "radical evil". Would morality be necessary if man did not fundamentally compromise with evil? We can describe ideal societies, pre-Adamic so to speak, from which evil and hence the idea of evil would be absent, for instance, that of C. S. Lewis's *Out of the Silent Planet*. How could it not be that these descriptions preserve an element of truth with the irrealism which belongs to any Utopia? In those cities that have no place (or *topos*), no moral law is necessary, neither as practical direction, nor as doctrines of duty and value. Moral teaching will no longer be necessary, according to the prophetic text (Jer. 31:33-34), on the day when the law will be written on the heart of man — the messianic day that will be the end of radical evil, and the end of all moral teaching. The law, however, is not written on our hearts (which forces us to speak of a promise still not yet fulfilled). If theology requires us to speak of the "messianic age" in connection with the preaching (or, more widely, the "event") of Jesus, these do not involve either a total patency of the good or an intuitive knowledge of the law on the part of all, or of all believers. We must therefore resign ourselves, in any description of our own times, to their pre-messianic character. It is therefore necessary to recall, to shed light, and therefore to make it appear.

What this amounts to is that a concept must enter the scene, that of truth.

We need to put in play the concept of truth as "unveiling" or "unconcealment" that we find in Heidegger from 1930 onward. Philosophy and theology are both needed because in daily moral experience, or experience inviting moral reflection, we deal with what is hidden as much as with what is plain. Must we talk about duty and values as veiled realities that call mournfully upon us to be brought out into the light? Evidently we know nothing about the first moralist, the first to teach a community or tribe about doing good. For us, the moralist is, in any case, a necessity. The theologian will always point out that if the law is not written on our hearts, then "consciousness" and "synderesis" remain in every man as witnesses of his creatureliness. Morality, philosophical and theological, obviously has no eschatological destiny: the day when the prophecy of Jeremiah will be fulfilled will see the end of moral discourse. We use moral language, of course, because we have the ability to do so, as rational animals: if we were completely deprived of moral reason, the distinction between good and evil would be for us a sealed book. We use moral language, however, in a world that one should not identify too quickly with creation, or, if you will, in a history that does not offer a clear and distinct testimony to the ethical order bound to creation. Creation is accessible to us only in a mix of creation and de-creation. Theology can point us to the created order directly. Philosophy does not speak of creation, but it wants — often, but not always — to put us in a situation where our being-in-the-world involves kindness and concern for the other man. In the one case as in the other, therefore, the message that we pick up is the same: not only is ethics necessary, but it is even possible to reveal what is *de facto* hidden from us or only indirectly known by us. Neither philosophy nor theology lays a foundation for good and evil. They discern them, and as long as their work of discernment can be shared with us, they provide evidence of what has no evidence in the world. The evidence is the experience of truth. This is why wars cannot cease unless man is revealed to himself as ordered to the good and summoned to do good. Both the order underlying the created community and the order underlying the saved community have their package of good news: we were not condemned from the beginning to violence and injustice. It was necessary to unwrap it. It will remain necessary to protect it against being forgotten: the truth which the philosopher speaks and the truth which the theologian speaks (and both can agree to tell the truth) are essentially forgettable. Since it will remain necessary never to forget that war can be just and defence legitimate, because the other man, himself or his city, instead of taking us "hostage" or being the obvious recipient of our concern may well appear to us wielding unjust violence — we will need, finally, a moral language to teach us that lesson and to tear us away from the foolish logic of vengeance. . . .

The idea of a world which has forgotten all that it knew of good or our moral duty, the idea of a world that has succumbed to barbarism, is not absurd. To make a case for truth — an ethical case, that is, which, where necessary, cuts short any discussion of being, will always be necessary, within the conditions of history, to remind us that the *eschaton* has not yet arrived. The world, bearing as it does the traces of its creation, is not doomed to immoralism, though, accidentally or occasionally, it may fall victim to it. This is the possibility that preoccupies Levinas, perhaps the first philosopher to have meditated on the threats posed by war. Looking for a philosophical consensus — or an agreement between philosophers and theologians — on war would obviously be a waste of time. The possibility of war never entered into Heidegger's thinking; whatever he had to say about our duties towards the other man was only a preamble to the question of being, which wholly obscured the question of the good. But theology, finally, speaks to us about the good — above all, about what it is good to do — and is in a position to argue for an earthly city that connects the traces of a created order to an anticipation of the city of God. It does so in what it knows to be pre-messianic times, in which war can be just and self-defence "legitimate". The three sets of problems that have here engaged us, the phenomenology of Heidegger and Levinas and the theology of O'Donovan (with which his teacher Paul Ramsey should be associated) are not redundant. They would not be important if they were not open to challenge. The philosophy and theology of war and peace, at any rate, have the means to act as objective allies, and — who knows? — even to enter into a willing covenant.

Regime Change in Iraq:
A Christian Reading of the Morals of the Story

Nigel Biggar

To Judge or Not to Judge? The Public Role of the Christian Ethicist

It seems that I am one of a minority of people who have not decided that the invasion of Iraq was immoral. Initially I did oppose it on the ground that Washington's claim of a link between the regime of Saddam Hussein and al-Qaeda had been discredited; and in the autumn of 2002 I said as much in an article published by the *Church Times*.[1] In the opening months of the following year, however, I took to reading Kenneth M. Pollack's book, *The Threatening Storm: The Case for Invading Iraq*.[2] Its review in the *TLS* described Pollack as "one of the foremost American authorities on the Middle East", and considered his book to be "a beacon of reason and responsibility".[3] *The New York Review of Books* confirmed this judgement, writing that Pollack, "a respected expert on the Gulf region both in and out of government, provides a meticulous account of . . . the pros and cons of different options in the current controversy over Iraq".[4] *Prima facie,* then, *The Threatening Storm* seemed to carry authority, and in reading it I found it circumspect and judicious and its argument in favour of invasion seemed very largely cogent. So I changed my mind, and in early March I wrote an article for the

---

1. Nigel Biggar, "We Cannot Hide Behind the UN", *Church Times,* 8 November 2002.
2. Kenneth M. Pollack, *The Threatening Storm: The Case for Invading Iraq* (New York: Random House, 2002).
3. Peter Baehr, "The Critical Path", *Times Literary Supplement,* 31 January 2002, pp. 3-5.
4. Brian Urquhart, "The Prospect of War", *The New York Review of* Books, 19 December 2002, pp. 16-22.

Guardian, arguing that, although Tony Blair's moral case for war lacked a plausible account of how Iraq's possession of weapons of mass destruction would amount to an intolerable threat, one could nevertheless be provided. Perhaps it was fortunate for my reputation that the *Guardian* declined to publish my submission.

Now it seems that I was mistaken on an important point. Now it seems that Saddam Hussein did not in fact possess the weapons of mass destruction that he was supposed to have, and that he did not pose the imminent kind of threat that he was alleged to. First of all, this moves me to think again about what role a Christian ethicist — indeed, any academic ethicist — should, and should not, play in public deliberation; and it brings to mind Oliver O'Donovan's warning that ethicists should beware of making precise judgements on policy. "Any private contribution to a current political debate", he writes, ". . . is not . . . in a position to offer precise recommendations".[5] I appreciate the problem, but I cannot embrace the proposed solution. The problem is that of the ethicist overreaching his competence, speaking with greater confidence than he has a right to, and thereby damaging his own moral authority. The solution proposed is that he should withhold himself from making precise, definite judgements. One reason for my dissent is that, if an informed ethicist is not in a position to offer precise, albeit fallible judgements, then I do not know who else is. What the ethicist lacks in expertise about Iraq, for example, the Iraq pundit in the Foreign & Commonwealth Office is likely to lack in just war doctrine. So if moral judgements are to be made at all, then any judge will have to shoulder risks in making them, by entering territory where he is not entirely at home. Moreover, it seems to me that every evangelical judge has a pastoral responsibility not to count ethical purity a thing to be grasped, but instead to come down from the realm of general principle and take the form of a servant to those who are burdened with the responsibility of *deciding*. People in positions of governmental leadership carry responsibility (often onerous) for making decisions (sometimes momentous) on our behalf under pressure of very limited time. It is therefore incumbent on those of us who have ethical expertise, it seems to me, to take moral principles and to show what they might amount to concretely. This then furnishes "the burden-bearers of the world"

---

5. Oliver O'Donovan, *The Just War Revisited* (Cambridge: Cambridge University Press, 2003), p. 127. I note that O'Donovan's view here is the reverse of the position taken by William Temple, who in *Christianity and the Social Order* (New York: Penguin, 1942), argued that whereas the church as a corporate body should deal only in the currency of general principles, individual churchmen may offer casuistic counsel in a private capacity (pp. 18-19).

— to use Reinhold Niebuhr's sympathetic phrase[6] — with a model of moral reasoning against which to hone their own deliberation efficiently in the light of the actual circumstances in which they find themselves. Not to venture a definite judgement is to leave the ethical task only half done; and I think it unreasonable to expect lay people to have the leisure — or superior overall competence — to finish the job.[7]

Perhaps, however, the ethicist may be definite, but only on condition that he is modestly hypothetical. Maybe, as O'Donovan puts it, "useful recommendations will tend to be introduced by the useful word 'if' ".[8] The rationale for this seems sensible. Any judgement about policy that a Christian ethicist reaches will depend on what he knows about the facts of the case; and that will be certainly limited and probably inexpert. Ethicists who reflect on medical practice, the social responsibility of the media, and foreign policy will have some knowledge of medicine, journalism, and international relations; but they will not have the same level of expertise as physicians, journalists, and diplomats. What is more, since the facts or their interpretation may well be in dispute, ethicists should furnish policy-makers with definite judgements on a *range* of hypothetical cases, so that they have several models of moral reasoning against which to prove their own thinking. This is the line that Ronald Preston took, when he observed that the Church of England's 1982 report on the ethics of nuclear weapons, *The Church and the Bomb*,[9] would have been better, if, rather than proposing only one course of action, it had "listed other feasible ones, with arguments for and against each".[10] So maybe in future I should be more circumspect, and more generous in my deployment of the word 'if', when presuming to judge policy.

I confess, however, that I am not yet wholly persuaded. I am not wholly persuaded that an alternative, less cautious strategy is not equally appropriate: namely, that of crafting a definite judgement, laying out one's reasons for it as thoroughly as possible, dealing with objections as carefully and charitably as

6. See, e.g., Reinhold Niebuhr, *An Interpretation of Christian Ethics* (New York: Seabury, 1979), p. 15.

7. I concur here with Ronald Preston, who held that the church should sometimes take the risk of making precise judgements about policy ("Appendix 2: Middle Axioms in Christian Social Ethics", in *Church and Society in the Late Twentieth Century: The Economic and Political Task* [London: S.C.M., 1983], pp. 153-154).

8. O'Donovan, *The Just War Revisited*, p. 127.

9. *The Church and the Bomb: Nuclear Weapons and the Christian Conscience* (London: Hodder & Stoughton, 1982).

10. Preston, *Church and Society in the Late Twentieth Century*, "Appendix 2", p. 151.

possible, taking for granted that any moral argument's cogency depends on its grasp of the facts, and then offering it up as a contribution to public deliberation and waiting to see how it fares. Maybe it will survive the fires of public criticism and prove to be right — or at least, as right as anyone knows. But even if it should prove to be basically mistaken, it will still have performed the good service of being a pebble in the shoe of public understanding, provoking reflection and refinement. Sometimes one can think long and hard and carefully — and still turn out to be wrong. But where is the shame in that? And besides, if the truth wins out, then who loses? To adapt Luther, perhaps we should err boldly (though considerately) that truth may abound! I am inclined to think, therefore, that the Christian ethicist may make a judgement on policy that is not hypothetical, provided that he thinks of himself as making a creaturely contribution to public deliberation and not as pontificating — and provided that the manner of his expression makes that self-understanding quite clear.

It may be, of course, that what is prudent for an individual ethicist is not prudent for a body that represents an ecclesial community as a whole. Maybe a church's public statement needs to be more cautious than a single ethicist's newspaper article. Maybe it needs to distinguish more clearly certain norms from their uncertain application, so as to preserve the authority of the former from any lapses in the latter. Yet surely this is also a concern that the individual ethicist should share. Perhaps, then, a church needs to be especially cautious in a different way. Perhaps it does need to conclude with a *range* of hypothetical judgements. Why? Because, except in rare cases, its own members, even if agreed on the relevant norms, will disagree about their policy implications. A statement issued on behalf of a church, therefore, needs to reflect that church's own internal plurality.

Iraq and Simplistic Public Discourse

Let us leave method there and return to the matter. I was mistaken about the gravity of the threat posed by Iraq. Have I then changed my mind a second time and concluded that the invasion itself was a mistake, even a sin? No. Why not? One reason is political. Whether or not the view that now dominates is correct in its conclusion, its supporting arguments I find too partisan, too unfair, too insufficient, and too simplistic to be persuasive; and so I think it fitting to put up some corrective resistance. The other, non-reactionary reason is that I think that wars in general are often morally complex, and I think that of Iraq in particular. Here I warmly applaud the main thrust of O'Donovan's statement that "major historical events cannot be justified or criticised in one mouthful; they are concatenations and agglomerations of many separate actions and many varied results. . . . [W]ars as such, like most large-scale historical phenomena, present only a great question mark, a continual invitation to reflect further on which decisions were, and which were not, justified at the time and in the circumstances. Such reflective questioning has a certain inconclusiveness about it."[11] This does need qualification, I think, since some wars can be conclusively determined as fundamentally unjust because they lack just cause and involve wrong intention. It seems to me that once one knows that Hitler invaded Poland in 1939 on the pretext of an act of Polish aggression that had in fact been engineered by German troops, and in order, not just to recover German territory ceded at the Treaty of Versailles, but to carve up the whole country with Stalin, then one can safely conclude that it was basically wrong. Nonetheless, large-scale wars, even ones that most people reckon just, are often morally complex and ambiguous. The Allies' just prosecution of the war against Hitler, for example, involved the vengeful hatred of 'Bomber' Harris and his carpet-bombing of Dresden; and judging by Antony Beevor's account of the invasion of Normandy, it often involved the cold-blooded killing of German prisoners by American troops.[12] Moreover, while it achieved regime change in Berlin, which was very good, it also delivered up most of Eastern Europe to the tender mercies of Stalin, which was very bad. Even just wars can be morally complex and ambiguous.

The fact that the invasion of Iraq in 2003 involved error, vice, and evil consequences, therefore, does not decide the case. The main charges leveled against it, and commonly reckoned to be sufficient to establish its immorality, are these: that the just cause was fabricated; that it was illegal; that there was gross negligence with regard to the task of securing just peace after the invasion; and that the consequences have been overwhelmingly evil and insupportable. The first I think is false. The second and third are indecisive. And the fourth is uncertain.

Lie or Error? Iraq's Possession of WMD

I do not think that the claim that Iraq possessed WMD was a lie. Rather, it was an error, and one on the part of the intelligence services, not just of the UK

11. O'Donovan, *The Just War Revisited*, p. 13.
12. Antony Beevor, *D-Day: The Battle for Normandy* (London: Viking, 2009), pp. 24, 106, 121, 153, 158, 438.

and the USA, but also of all other Western countries and of Russia. German intelligence believed it, holding since 2001 that Iraq was only two to three years away from having at least one nuclear weapon.[13] The President of France believed it: in February 2003, two months before his government threatened to veto UNSC authorization of military action against Iraq, Jacques Chirac told *Time* magazine, "There is a problem — the probable possession of weapons of mass destruction by an uncontrollable country, Iraq. The international community is right . . . in having decided Iraq should be disarmed".[14] Even the head of the 2003 UN weapons-inspection team, Hans Blix, believed it: writing in 2004 of his views on the eve of the invasion, he confessed that "[m]y gut feelings . . . suggested to me that Iraq still engaged in prohibited activities and retained prohibited items, and that he had the documents to prove it".[15] The belief that Iraq possessed WMD has since proven to be erroneous, but before April 2003 it was widespread.

Why was this? There are four persuasive reasons. First, the shocking revelation in the mid-1990s that before the 1991 Gulf war Iraq had managed to enrich uranium without being detected, and that it had been only six to twenty-four months away from having a nuclear weapon. Second, the regime's constant resistance — right up until the very eve of war in 2003 — to the UN's attempts to ensure disarmament. Third, the lack of any good reason to give the Saddam regime the benefit of doubt. And, fourth, the problem of what the Butler Report called 'mirror-imaging', that is, of reading and predicting others' behaviour according to one's own canons of prudential rationality. In retrospect it seems that Saddam Hussein's obstructiveness was a symptom, not of his actually having weapons to hide, but of his overriding need to *pretend* so for domestic and regional political purposes. To shoulder the risks of such pretence might seem crazy to Western democrats, but not to an Arab despot. This is why so many experts in so many countries believed that Iraq possessed WMD. The claim was a reasonable and widespread error, not a lie fabricated by George Bush and Tony Blair.

13. William Shawcross, *Allies: The U.S., Britain, Europe, and the War in Iraq* (New York: Public Affairs, 2004), p. 151.

14. Kenneth Pollack, "Spies, Lies, and Weapons", *The Atlantic Monthly,* January/February 2004, (online) p. 3.

15. Hans Blix, *Disarming Iraq: The Search for Weapons of Mass Destruction* (London: Bloomsbury, 2004), p. 112.

Illegality Need Not Amount to Immorality

It is true that London and Washington failed to secure the Security Council's explicit authorization for military intervention in Iraq, and that most legal opinion reckons that such authorization was necessary for the invasion's legality. As a Christian ethicist, however, I cannot regard the verdict of positive law as the final word, since positive law itself lies subject to the judgement of moral law. If that were not the case, then the plot to kill Hitler in July 1944, which was certainly illegal, would also have been immoral. I do believe that there is a strong reason to obey the law, even when the law protects criminals. There are good moral reasons of a prudential sort why we should be loath to transgress positive law even for the noblest of motives. The effective social authority of law — that is, its power to order a society, whether national or international, and to safeguard the rights of its members — depends upon the willingness to obey of those whom it commands; and the willingness of each to obey depends partly on the law's being generally observed. It is reasonable for one party to obey the law so long as others generally do so too. It is reasonable for one to suffer the constraints of law, so long as others suffer them as well. If one party were to take the law into his own hands, even for motives that seem noble in his own eyes, then why shouldn't others do likewise? Well-intentioned vigilantism can pave the road to anarchy quite as much as malicious law-breaking.

That is true. But the following is also true. Voluntary obedience will only be forthcoming so long as those who remain subject to the law are confident that those who break it will not retain the unfair advantages they have thereby seized — that is, so long as they are confident that the law will be enforced against law-breakers. If the law is not so enforced, and if law-breakers are seen to secure unfair advantage relative to the law-abiding, then the respect of the latter for the law will be shaken and its authority diminished. If this diminution proceeds far enough, then the rule of law will disintegrate and society will dissolve into anarchy. There are, then, *two* ways in which the law's authority can be undermined: first, by persons or states taking the law into their own hands; and second, by the failure of public authorities to enforce the law against law-breakers. And sometimes, of course, the two are causally related. Sometimes, it is *because* public authorities have failed to enforce the law that individuals or states are moved to enforce it themselves.

It is reasonable, it is in everyone's interests — it is in the interests of general peace — that individuals and individual states should delegate the enforcement of law and order to a body that will actually perform it. The problem with international law as it now stands, however, is that it denies the right of member states to use military force unilaterally except in self-defence, while reserving the enforcement of international law to a body (the Security Council) whose capacity to act is hamstrung by international politics and by the right of veto.

To illustrate the problem, take this analogy. Suppose that a neighbour a few houses away is beating his own children to death. Suppose that it is against the law for you to intervene directly. Suppose that you call the police to ask them to intervene instead. Suppose that before they can intervene, the police have to get authorization from a committee. Suppose that any member of the committee can prevent authorization by issuing a veto. Suppose that in this case a member of the committee is related to the neighbour, or has investments in their business, or is allied to them in some other way. Suppose that he therefore vetoes any authorization for the police to intervene to save your neighbour's children. What will you do? Will you break the law and intervene yourself? Or will you stand by and watch the children being done to death?

That is roughly the situation that we have with international law at the moment. Individual nations are forbidden to intervene militarily in the affairs of another sovereign state, unless authorized by the Security Council of the UN to do so; but the power of the Security Council to issue authorization depends upon the political interests of its members. This was the case of Kosovo in 1999, when Russia made it clear that it would veto any intervention by NATO to save the Kosovar Albanians from Serb troops, partly because of its cultural links with Serbia and partly because it did not want to set a precedent that might tie its hands in dealing with insurgents in Chechnya. It seems to me to be a grave problem with the current international legal system that it outlaws unauthorised intervention to stop mass atrocities or to topple a regime widely acknowledged as being grossly and chronically atrocious, while being unable to guarantee that authorisation will be forthcoming at all.

Given this situation it seems to me that there could be sufficiently strong moral reasons for breaking international law under certain conditions. While the authority of positive and customary law is very important, the authority of moral law is superior. While morality in some cases obliges us to obey the law even when wicked people appear to be getting away with murder, lest in the rash pursuit of justice we knock all the laws flat, in other cases it permits or obliges us to break the law in order to rescue victims from wicked oppressors, lest in our chronic failure to do justice we subject standing laws to justified contempt. While we should be very loath to break the letter of international law, there may be cases where we are morally obliged to do so. So the fact that the 2003 invasion was illegal does not, to my mind, settle its moral status. An overall judgement of the morality of the invasion must wait upon the evaluation of several other considerations. My purpose at this point is to get the reader past the notion that positive illegality settles the matter.

If I understand him correctly, this view of humanitarian intervention in relation to international law concurs with O'Donovan's. As he puts it, "courts . . . may lose authority all together, whether by constant malfunction or by inability to enact their judgements"[16] or by prohibiting humanitarian action

> which people in general are inclined to think not only justifiable, but even morally obligatory. There may well be dangers attached to . . . humanitarian intervention . . . , but they need to be overwhelmingly conspicuous if they are to provide support for a universal prohibition running counter to the humanitarian instincts of civilized peoples. To turn one's back while a neighbouring community is being slaughtered is not an easy thing to recommend; and international law should not demand it without reasons so strong as to seem, when pointed out, morally irresistible.[17]

Post-Bellum Vices

It is beyond dispute that planning for the reconstruction of Iraq after the invasion was grossly inadequate. One of the most fundamental mistakes was Donald Rumsfeld's underestimation of the number of troops necessary to secure law and order, which is the precondition of any social and political flourishing and development. This miscalculation was maintained in defiance of widespread expert opinion. Why? Three main reasons present themselves: an American form of Rousseauian romanticism, according to which political liberty naturally springs up — or should spring up — wherever the stone of tyranny is lifted;[18] neo-liberal contempt for the cultures of dependency to which the postwar reconstructions of the 1990s were supposed to have given rise;[19] and the overoptimistic assurances given by Iraqi exiles of their people's political maturity.

16. O'Donovan, *Just War Revisited*, p. 24.

17. Ibid., p. 29.

18. Thus Donald Rumsfeld's spokesman, Larry Di Rita, dismissed the claim that the invasion needed to show early benefits to the Iraqi people by saying, "We don't owe the people of Iraq anything. We're giving them their freedom. That's enough" (George Packer, *The Assassins' Gate: America in Iraq* [New York: Farrar, Straus, Giroux, 2005], p. 133). And according to George Packer, "In his [Rumsfeld's] view and that of others in the administration, but above all the president, freedom was the absence of constraint" (ibid., p. 136).

19. Ibid., p. 114.

A second fundamental error in post-bellum government was the decision of Paul Bremer, chief of the Coalition Provisional Authority, to disband the Iraqi army and purge the civil service of Ba'athists. Immediately this turned lots of young men, many of them still armed, out onto the streets with no legitimate way of earning an income. The intention (to free the new Iraqi regime of all taint by the old one) was good, but the effect (to fuel the flames of insurgency) was dire. This consequence had been predicted, and the prediction had been ignored.

The occupation of Iraq, therefore, was vitiated partly by an absence of empathy for, and patience with, 'the poor' — in this case, a society demoralized by decades of ruthless tyranny. Let us call this 'callousness'. A cognate vice appears to have infected the decision to disband the army and purge the civil service. Paul Bremer has been characterized as "a demanding corporate executive, insisting on fast and quantifiable results from his staff, hating surprises and setbacks".[20] If this is fair, then the finger points (as Rory Stewart has already hinted it should)[21] at a managerial mentality that has no patience with problems that do not admit of definite and unambiguous solutions, and adamantly repudiates the claim that the 'poor' will be with us, if not always then at least for a very long time.

The occupation of Iraq, therefore, suffered grievously from the operation of at least two vices, callousness and impatience, which generated a third: imprudence. But then, since all wars are waged by sinners, even just ones give rise to vice. The war against Hitler provided a stage for Montgomery's conceit and Patton's vainglory; and the liberation and occupation of eastern Germany in 1945 involved vengeful incontinence on a massive scale, as an estimated two million German women were raped by Soviet troops.[22] Vice alone does not an unjust war make.

Civilian Casualties: How Many Are Too Much?

The fruit of Donald Rumsfeld's callousness and Paul Bremer's impatience was civil disorder, resulting in a massive number of civilian casualties. On viewing the figures, many people conclude that the decision to invade Iraq was funda-

---

20. Ibid., p. 190.

21. Rory Stewart, "Afghanistan: Ambition and Reality" and "The Rhetoric of War", The Leonard Stein Lectures, Balliol College, Oxford, May 2010 (unpublished).

22. Antony Beevor, *Berlin: The Downfall 1945* (London: Viking, 2002), p. 410.

mentally in error. Some reckon the number of civilian losses (during the period March 2003 to June 2006) at more than 650,000.[23] More sober estimates reckon it somewhere between 100,000 and 150,000, and most discussions cite a figure in this region.[24] Even according to the lower estimates, of course, the cost has been terrible. Yet the liberation of Europe from Nazi domination cost the lives of 70,000 French civilians and about 600,000 German ones through Allied bombing.[25] And whereas these deaths were the direct responsibility of the British and Americans, the vast majority of Iraqi civilian deaths are directly attributable to foreign or native insurgents. Yes, the occupying powers had an obligation to maintain law and order, in which they failed initially. But the insurgents also had a moral obligation not to send suicide bombers into crowded marketplaces; and that is one in which they have failed persistently. The main point here is not that Saddam Hussein was a tyrant as wicked as Adolf Hitler — although he probably was as wicked in kind, if not in scale. The point is rather that the prosecution of the war against Hitler, which is very widely regarded as just, nevertheless involved massive civilian casualties. Therefore massive civilian casualties in Iraq do not *by themselves* suffice to render the 2003 invasion unjust.[26]

A Decisive Issue: Was the Cause Sufficient?

In my judgement, the reasons commonly supposed to establish the immorality of the invasion and occupation of Iraq are either false, indecisive, or uncertain. The belief that Saddam possessed WMD was an honest and reasonable error, not a lie. The illegality of the invasion, and the callousness and impatience that

23. G. Burnham, R. Lafta, S. Doocy, and L. Roberts have given a figure of 654,965, which includes deaths caused indirectly by increased lawlessness, degraded infrastructure, poor healthcare, etc. ("Mortality after the 2003 invasion of Iraq: a cross-sectional cluster sample survey", *The Lancet*, 11 October 2006).

24. For example, the Iraq Family Health Survey Study Group has given an estimate of 151,000 ("Violence-Related Mortality in Iraq from 2002 to 2006", *New England Journal of Medicine*, 31 January 2008).

25. Beevor, *D-Day*, p. 519; Patrick Bishop, *Bomber Boys: Fighting Back 1940-1945* (London: Harper, 2007), p. 356.

26. Naturally, the American and British publics have been greatly distressed by the number of Coalition military casualties. From 2003 to 2010 these amounted to 4,430 U.S., 179 U.K., and 139 'other' fatalities, giving a total of 4,748. Each of these deaths is a personal and familial tragedy, of course. Nevertheless, they need to be kept in proportion: the total number of deaths suffered by the Coalition forces over seven years in Iraq is less than one-quarter of those suffered by the British on the first day of the four-month Battle of the Somme.

vitiated the occupation, are insufficient to decide the case. And whether or not the massive civilian casualties are morally insupportable is uncertain. What would be decisive is a conclusive answer to the question, Was the cause sufficiently grave and real to warrant punitive and preventative war?

According to Christian doctrine, a war is just when, among other things, its cause is grave injustice, when its motive is love for the victims (primarily), and when its intention is to punish and rectify the wrong.[27] One kind of grave injustice is a state's murder of its own citizens on a massive scale. Does such atrocity have to be "actual or apprehended [that is, 'imminently likely to occur']" for intervention to be warranted, as stipulated by the report of the International Commission on Intervention and State Sovereignty, *The Responsibility to Protect?*[28] One obvious reason for such a condition is that only then could intervention claim to be about protecting victims. After the event is over, there is presumably no protecting left to do. Actually, that is not so. A state that has shown itself willing to carry out mass atrocities, and which succeeds in doing so with impunity, will have no compunction about perpetrating fresh atrocities and creating fresh victims, should it see fit to do so. This is all the more so where a state has succeeded in getting away with mass murder several times over. Such a regime is therefore liable to punishment after the fact, and not merely to hindrance *in flagrante delicto*. I note that, notwithstanding its earlier insistence on actuality or imminence, *The Responsibility to Protect* virtually confirms my view when it says that while "[o]verthrow of regimes is not, as such, a legitimate objective", "disabling that regime's capacity to harm its own people may be essential to discharging the mandate of protection — and what is necessary to achieve that disabling will vary from case to case. Occupation of territory may not be able to be avoided . . .".[29] Ideally, of course, humanitarian intervention to stop or punish an atrocious regime would be effected by an impartial international authority; but absent that, states and coalitions of states have a moral responsibility to act, prudence permitting.

Was Saddam Hussein's regime atrocious? Undoubtedly. The 1988 Anfal campaign against the Kurds saw repeated use of chemical weapons against a

27. See Nigel Biggar, *In Defence of War* (Oxford: Oxford University Press, 2013), esp. chapters 5, 6, and 7.

28. The International Commission on Intervention and State Sovereignty, *The Responsibility to Protect* (Ottawa: International Development Research Centre, 2001), p. 32, s.4.18: "actual and apprehended". The meaning of 'apprehended' in this clause is explained, I take it, in the subsequent one: "there must be serious and irreparable harm occurring to human beings, *or imminently likely to occur* . . ." (s.4.19. My emphasis).

29. Ibid., p. 35, s.4.33.

civilian population. Kurds claim 182,000 deaths — and of these the Iraqi military commander with sole responsibility for the region, 'Chemical Ali', was happy (literally) to own 100,000. Between 1991 and 2003, according to Western human rights groups, at least a further 300,000 people were victims of the state. So Saddam Hussein's regime was responsible for the murder of at least 400,000 of its own people in the fifteen years from 1988 to 2003. That certainly makes it atrocious; and according to Human Rights Watch, it also makes it genocidal.

Morality's Need of National Interest

In principle, toppling tyrants and liberating their peoples is a good thing to do. Mature and fulfilled human beings care about other people, and do not rest easy in the knowledge that others live in terror of state-sponsored persecution, arbitrary arrest, sadistic torture, and brutal killing. Therefore they will want to see an end to Adolf Hitler's oppression, or Slobodan Milosevic's, or Robert Mugabe's, or Saddam Hussein's; and they will do what they can — and what they may — to bring that about. To end atrocious tyranny is a good thing to do, provided that one can replace it with something better. What Iraq has taught us — and what Afghanistan is teaching us — is that ending a tyrannous regime by military force can be much easier than constructing something better. To introduce the forms of electoral democracy is not nearly enough, and is probably beside the main point. Much more important is to foster a public ethos that inclines public officers to abide by the law and to enforce it impartially. In some cases, however, that could be the work of a generation. The reconstruction of nations is a complicated and hazardous business in the best of circumstances, and in less optimal ones its successful completion may require the commitment of considerable resources over very long periods of time. What this implies is that military intervention for humanitarian purposes, if it is to succeed, must command the support of the interveners' electorate; and for that to be the case, the expenditure of blood and treasure over decades will have to find adequate justification in terms of national interest.

Some will infer from this the further, sobering lesson that morality's reach into foreign policy is a limited one. They will do so, because they assume a popular Kantian (or perhaps an Augustinian) view of morality, which, applied to international affairs, deems national interest to be an immoral motive.[30]

---

30. O'Donovan and I diverge over the strong distinction that he draws between self-interest and altruism, when he writes that morally legitimate humanitarian intervention "will

Accordingly, the fact that such interest motivated Britain's interventions in Kosovo and Iraq counts against their moral justification. I regard this view of morality as mistaken, and I prefer the alternative provided by the ethical tradition stemming from Thomas Aquinas. Combining the biblical notion that all of God's creatures (including human beings) are valuable, because loved by God, with Aristotle's notion that all things naturally seek their own preservation, Thomist thought does not view all self-interest as selfish and immoral.[31] Indeed, it holds that there is such a thing as morally obligatory self-love. The human individual has a duty to care for himself properly, to seek what is genuinely his own good. As with an individual, so with a national community and the organ of its cohesion and decision, namely, its government: a national government has a moral duty to look after the well-being of its own people — and in that sense to advance its genuine interests. Such a duty is not unlimited, of course. There cannot be a moral duty to pursue the interests of one's own nation by riding roughshod over the rights of others. Still, not every pursuit of national interest does perpetrate injustice, and so the fact that national interests are among the motives for military intervention does not by itself vitiate the latter's moral justification.

Besides, at least one interest is obviously moral: the concern for moral integrity. Nations usually want to believe that they are doing the right or the noble thing, and they will tolerate the costs of war — up to a point — in a just cause that looks set to succeed. I have yet to meet a Briton who is not proud of what British troops achieved in Sierra Leone in the year 2000, even though Britain had no material stake in the outcome of that country's civil war, and even though intervention there cost British taxpayers money and British families casualties (though admittedly very few). Citizens care that their country should do the right thing.

The nation's interest in its own moral integrity and nobility alone, however, will probably not underwrite military intervention that incurs very heavy costs. So other interests — such as national security — are needed to stiffen

---

be carried out by parties with a demonstrable interest in the welfare of those they propose to rescue — not *self*-interest, of course, which is, at best, irrelevant, but altruistic interest . . ." (*The Just War Revisited*, p. 29). In my view, self-interest is not the same as selfishness and need not be an alternative to altruism.

31. See, for example, Thomas Aquinas, *Summa Theologiae*, 2a2ae, q.25, a.4: "we may speak of charity in respect of its specific nature, namely as denoting man's friendship with God in the first place, and, consequently, with the things of God [the Creator], among which things is man himself who has charity. Hence, among these other things which he loves out of charity because they pertain to God, he loves also himself out of charity".

popular support for a major intervention. In the case of Kosovo, for example, Britain did have a security interest, albeit not immediate, in the stability of the Balkans, and therefore in curbing the activity of the Serbian source of recent disturbance. But note that this national interest was not private to Britain. It was shared by the other European members of NATO, and by the Balkan peoples themselves. Indeed, it was also shared by the UN, whose Security Council came to the view that the government in Belgrade had created a humanitarian emergency in Kosovo, which constituted a threat to peace and security in the Balkans.

The presence of national interest as a motive need not vitiate military intervention. Not all interests are avaricious. One of them is moral integrity itself; for nations care about being right, and not only about being secure and fat. But even a nation's interest in its own security — or more exactly, even a national government's concern for the security of millions of fellow-countrymen — need not be private; for one nation's security is often bound up with others'. As Gareth Evans puts it: "these days, good international citizenship is a matter of national self-interest".[32]

So national interest need not vitiate intervention. More than this, however, some kind of interest will be necessary to enable it. For it is not unreasonable (or immoral) for a national people to ask why they should bear the burdens of military intervention, especially in remote parts of the world. It is not unreasonable for them to ask why *they* should bear the burdens *rather than* others, why *their* sons and daughters should lose their limbs and lives. And the answer to those reasonable questions will have to present itself in terms of the nation's own interests; and it could and ought to present itself in terms of the nation's own morally legitimate interests.

Western Interests in Regime Change

As I understand it, the United States and the United Kingdom had three national interests in seeing Saddam Hussein toppled. The first was moral integrity. I think that it is quite clear that Tony Blair was heavily, perhaps predominantly motivated by the conviction that one should stop and end atrocious tyranny where one can.[33] If it was right to stop ethnic cleansing in Kosovo and

---

32. Gareth Evans, *The Responsibility to Protect: Ending Mass Atrocity Crimes Once and For All* (Washington, DC: Brookings Institution Press, 2008), p. 144.

33. See Andrew Rawnsley, *The End of the Party: The Rise and Fall of New Labour* (London:

to help dislodge Milosevic from power, and if it was right to stop diamond-greedy, drug-crazed, limb-chopping rebels from seizing control of Sierra Leone, then it would be right to rid the world of Saddam Hussein and to attempt to build a healthier political system in Iraq — if one could.

The second national interest was in preventing Iraq from acquiring nuclear weapons, as it persistently intended to do. The concern here was twofold. The first was that, once in possession of nuclear weapons, Iraq could invade its non-nuclear neighbours with impunity. Had it been a nuclear power in 1991, it is doubtful that the U.S. and its allies would have risked expelling Iraq from Kuwait by force of arms. And why did we care about the fate of the Gulf States and Saudi Arabia? Presumably, we cared because we have an interest in oil-supply. But surely this is a material, and not a moral interest? No, it is both. After all, oil is material upon which the global economy, and with it the livelihoods of hundreds of millions of people (not all of them Westerners) depend; and their well-being would not have been well served, if the Middle East's oil supply had become a political instrument in the hands of Saddam Hussein.

The other concern about Iraq acquiring weapons of mass destruction was that, sooner or later, they would be conveyed to al-Qaeda or its like. The story, as Philip Bobbitt tells it, is this. First, unlike previous terrorist groups such as the IRA, al-Qaeda has an interest in maximizing civilian casualties, since its intention is to terrorise Western electorates, not win their support; and had the perpetrators of 9/11 had access to WMD, they would have used them.[34] Second, al-Qaeda is intent on acquiring WMD, including nuclear ones, and may already have constructed a 'dirty' bomb.[35] Third, there is an active black market in WMD components, which has enabled Pakistan and North Korea to arm themselves with nuclear weapons, and would have enabled Libya, had the U.K. and the U.S. not frustrated it.[36] Fourth, there is therefore a risk that states supporting terrorist groups — such as Iran now and Iraq before April 2003 — will acquire WMD and secretly transfer them to terrorist groups such as al-Qaeda, in order to wage covert war by proxy. Fifth — and here I add to Bobbitt — while it is true that Ba'athist Saddam Hussein and Wahhabi Osama bin Laden were ideological opponents, it is also true that ideological opposition does not always hinder tactical alliance, since my enemy's enemy can

---

Viking, 2010), pp. 43, 91, 155, 275; Tony Blair, *A Journey* (London: Hutchinson, 2010), pp. 229, 248-249.

34. Philip Bobbitt, *Terror and Consent: The Wars for the Twenty-first Century* (London: Allen Lane, 2008), pp. 45-49.

35. Ibid., pp. 100, 119.

36. Ibid., pp. 59, 105-122.

come to look like very much like my friend. Who could have been more unlikely bedfellows than Stalin and Hitler? Nevertheless, discovery of their common interest in carving up Poland and buying time propelled them across the gulf dividing Bolshevism from Nazism and into the Ribbentrop Pact.

In itself, I find this story credible. The problem arises, however, when it is used to justify the invasion of Iraq in 2003. It is true, as Bobbitt says, that the prospect of the detonation of a WMD in a Western city is very grave indeed: apart from the massive loss of human life, liberal society as we now enjoy it would vanish overnight in the subsequent clamour for security.[37] It is also true that the development of terrorist threats of such gravity is now much harder to detect than the conventional massing of troops and tanks on the other side of one's border; and that by the time such a threat is *seen* to be substantial, it may be too late to stop it. It is true, too, that there was a risk that Saddam Hussein would transfer WMD to the likes of al-Qaeda. The fact that he turned out not to possess such weapons himself reduces the risk in retrospect, although it does not eliminate it, since no one doubts that he was intent on resuming his quest the moment the UN inspectors went home.[38] Still, even at its greatest this risk was speculative rather than substantial. Contrary to early claims by the U.S. Government, there is no reliable evidence of dealings between Saddam's regime and al-Qaeda. So the most that could reasonably be claimed before the invasion is that Saddam *might* have aided al-Qaeda to acquire nuclear weapons; and the most that could be claimed afterwards is that he *might* have conveyed nuclear weapons, *if* he himself had acquired them.

What were the prospects of Saddam achieving his aim and obtaining nuclear weapons, if left in power? In other words, what were the prospects of containment being successful? Some argue that the post-invasion discovery that Iraq did not in fact possess WMD proves that containment was working, and that the invasion was unnecessary, less than a last resort, and therefore unjust. But what needs to be proven is not that containment had been effective, but that it would have continued to be so. And on that score I think that there

---

37. Ibid., pp. 100, 181.

38. The Iraq Survey Group's final report of September 2004 (commonly known as the 'Duelfer Report' after its head, Charles Duelfer) concluded that "[t]he regime [of Saddam Hussein] made a token effort to comply with the disarmament process, but the Iraqis never intended to meet the spirit of the UNSC's resolutions. Outward acts of compliance belied a covert desire to resume WMD activities. Several senior officials also either inferred or heard Saddam say that he reserved the right to resume WMD research after sanctions" (*Comprehensive Report of the Advisor to the DCI [Director of Central Intelligence] on Iraq's WMD*, 3 vols. [Washington, DC: Central Intelligence Agency, 2004], Vol. 1, p. 49).

is good reason for doubt. Writing in 2002 Kenneth Pollack argued that containment was collapsing beyond repair. Since 1997 France, Russia, and China — all members of the UNSC — had all been pressing for a relaxation of sanctions and inspections, in order to obtain oil and military contracts and to collect debts owed.[39] In particular, China had been constructing a nationwide fibre-optic communication system, which would have enabled Iraqi anti-aircraft batteries to target American and British aircraft in the No-Fly Zones.[40] In 2002 smuggling conducted by Syria, Turkey, Jordan, and Iran was reckoned to earn Iraq between $2.5b and $3b (15-22% of Iraq's total revenue).[41] Even Thomas Ricks, one of the invasion's fiercest critics, suggests that the No-Fly Zones in northern and southern Iraq could not have been enforced indefinitely, because of the strain that maintaining them was placing on the U.S. military.[42] What is true of containment generally is also true of inspections in particular. Hans Blix is frank in admitting that without the Coalition's build-up of an invasion force in the summer of 2002 "Iraq would probably not have accepted the resumption of inspections",[43] and that "the US could not keep troops idling in the area for months" in rising temperatures.[44] In sum, it seems to me that Peter Baehr spoke common sense, when he wrote that containment is at best only a short-term measure since "[t]he unanimity of interest and durability of resolve that are required to institutionalize it do not exist in the real world of geopolitics".[45] Therefore it also seems to me that the sadly famous Dr David Kelly, Britain's expert on biological weapons and a former UN weapons inspector, was correct when he wrote shortly before the invasion that "[a]fter 12 unsuccessful years of UN supervision of disarmament, military force regrettably appears to be the only way of finally and conclusively disarming Iraq. . . . The long-term threat . . . remains Iraq's development to military maturity of weapons of mass destruction — something only regime change will avert".[46]

39. Pollack, *Threatening Storm*, pp. 100-101, 216-217, 224-227.

40. Ibid., p. 216; Thomas E. Ricks, *Fiasco: The American Military Adventure in Iraq* (London: Penguin, 2006), pp. 26-27.

41. Pollack, *Threatening Storm*, pp. 214-215, 218-221.

42. Ricks, *Fiasco*, pp. 43-45.

43. Blix, *Disarming Iraq*, p. 11.

44. Ibid., pp. 130, 14.

45. Baehr, "The Critical Path", p. 3.

46. David Kelly, "Only regime change will avert the threat", *Observer*, 31 August 2003. Dr Kelly became 'sadly famous' in Britain when, faced with the prospect of exposure as the source of a journalist's controversial claim of government duplicity, he killed himself in July 2003. Although written before the invasion, the article cited here was not published until afterwards — and after its author's tragic suicide — by the *Observer*.

Towards a Conclusion

Whither have all these considerations brought me?

Saddam Hussein's regime was of such an atrocious nature that it deserved punishment in the form of regime change, provided that there was reason to hope that it could be replaced with something more devoted to the common-weal, more law-abiding, and more humane.

The US and the UK had a legitimate interest in preventing Saddam's regime from acquiring WMD, and especially nuclear ones. This interest was in staving off two kinds of threat, one of the political manipulation of oil-supply, the other of the mediation of biological, chemical, or nuclear weapons to global terrorists, such as the al-Qaeda network.

The national self-interest of Britain and America, however, was not private but public. It was shared by most, if not all, of Iraq's regional neighbours; and, judging by the seventeen binding resolutions on Iraq's disarmament that the UN issued over more than a decade, it was also shared by the international community.

Both of the threats posed by Iraq were grave, but in neither case was realization imminent — although for reasons, which we now know to be mistaken, they seemed imminent before the invasion.

I do not think, however, that the lack of imminence attaching to the threats necessarily renders the invasion of 2003 less than a 'last resort'. The just war doctrine's criterion of 'last resort' requires that every other *effective* and *available* option has been tried before war is launched. Whether or not that stipulation had been met in April 2003 depends on how likely one thinks that effective containment could have been maintained in the long-term. As I have already indicated, I am aware of several reasons to doubt that. In that case, it is arguable that no effective alternative solution was available.

Whether or not the invasion of Iraq was a last resort is one controversial issue, upon whose resolution final judgement hangs. Another is whether or not toppling an atrocious regime and averting the risks of its coming to possess nuclear weapons was worth war — that is, whether or not going to war was a disproportionate response. The cost in lives, stability, and money proved great. It proved greater than expected. It proved greater than better planning would have incurred. But was it really not worth the vindication of the victims — past, present, and future — of an atrocious state? I cannot answer that question with confidence. Therefore, with greater confidence I can say that the cost was not *manifestly* disproportionate.

Finally, a third decisive issue is whether or not post-bellum success in replacing the Saddam regime with something better was doomed by the culpably imprudent pre-war planning[47] and early occupation administration. That might turn out to be the case. It might become clear that nothing that could have been done subsequently would have compensated for the callous, impatient, and imprudent mistakes made before and immediately after the invasion. Such a deterministic reading, however, seems implausible, for history tends not to be trammeled in that way. And besides, somewhere into the story needs to be factored the role of Iraqi political leaders, and of domestic and foreign insurgents, not excluding the hostage-beheaders and the market-place suicide bombers. The fact of being invaded by foreign forces does not absolve natives of moral responsibility.

The truth is, however, that we do not know how things will turn out. We should certainly hope and pray that they turn out better. In the meantime, I take my stand on the position articulated by the spokesman of the group of young, professional Iraqis who visited me in Oxford in March 2010. At the end of our meeting, I put to them the blunt question, "Should the invasion of 2003 have happened?" Without hesitating, he responded: "It was good that it happened. It could have been done better. And it isn't over".

---

47. See Ricks, *Fiasco*, pp. 3-111.

The Boldness of Analogy:
Civic Virtues and Augustinian Eudaimonism

Eric Gregory

> *The curious thing about the two cities in the Apocalypse, Babylon and Jerusalem, is the continuity between them. . . . The community in which God and the Lamb have set their throne is one and the same with the community where Satan and the beast have set their throne. The reason why John of Patmos will not allow the church a distinct social presence is that its witnesses claim back the Great City to become the Holy City.*
>
> Oliver O'Donovan, *The Desire of the Nations*, pp. 155-156

Introduction

Oliver O'Donovan has been rightly praised for his "judiciousness."[1] By this characterization, two of his North American admirers recommend the uncommon sobriety of his disciplined way of thinking about theology, ethics, and politics. It is a sobriety born not just of erudition, but a profound knowledge of the Christian tradition which yields salient distinctions often lost in the heat of contemporary debates. O'Donovan's distinction-making has restored a model of practical reasoning in moral and political deliberation.[2]

---

1. Philip Lorish and Charles Mathewes, "Theology as Counsel: The Work of Oliver O'Donovan and Nigel Biggar," *Anglican Theological Review* 94 (2012): 717-736, at 722.

2. In a revealing interview, O'Donovan states, "if there is any programme of recovery in my work, it is the recovery of practical reasoning, which has been lost in theology, as also in philosophy and the social sciences." See "Oliver O'Donovan and Joan Lockwood O'Donovan,"

Deliberativeness is another way of identifying this judiciousness, one that marks O'Donovan's distance from the oscillation between prophetic jeremiad and secularist punditry which can be found in Anglo-American theological ethics.

His *Augustinian* judiciousness, his admirers tell us, is "attuned to the complexities and paradoxes of a sin-riddled creature, immured in this world but longing for a divine happiness that never has more than a fugitive presence here."[3] This statement nicely captures the anthropology and eschatology of an influential strand of political Augustinianism. It is governed by what O'Donovan names as a "threefold metaphysic of a good creation, an evil fall and an end of history which negates the evil and transcends the created good."[4] So understood, politics is theologically located in the flux of history in the time between the times *(in hoc saeculo),* not in created nature.

Here is the familiar train of thought. Sociality is natural. Politics is part of that slice of time which is history after Babel. Following Romans 13, it is ordered by providence after the fall to restrain the wicked with a measure of "earthly" justice and peace for the time being. It is not abandoned by the concerns of morality, but we should be grateful for whatever order might be found in our collective life. No reader of O'Donovan — or Augustine for that matter — could underestimate this cautious, non-apocalyptic realism flowing from recognition of the fallen human condition, the contingency of history, and the mystery of providence. Civic virtues have their proper ends, ones chastened by the future rather than present dimensions of salvation. In fact, judiciousness is the virtue of an eschatological patience that knows the "not yet" of any human achievement. Here we find something like an apophatic political theology, veiled in the ambiguity of exilic pilgrimage and sin-stained temporality. No civic community can be just because justice requires the true worship of God. The great temptation of politics is idolatry, thinking you can step out of time by direct reference to God's purposes or create a science of human nature that makes action transparent to itself. Our compromised judgments are not God's judgments. Our compromised politics are not the kingdom of God, the *gloriosissima civitas dei.*

Political judgments can be seen as sad necessities that will pass away in the age to come, or more positively, as powers directed by God's providence

---

in Rupert Shortt, ed., *God's Advocates: Christian Thinkers in Conversation* (Grand Rapids: Eerdmans, 2005), pp. 248-272, at 250.

3. Lorish and Mathewes, "Theology as Counsel," p. 722.

4. Oliver O'Donovan, *Resurrection and Moral Order: An Outline for Evangelical Ethics* (Grand Rapids: Eerdmans, 1986), p. 63.

for humanity before the end of history. In either case, they find their ultimate meaning in a narration that is not ours to make. As such, though politics can be in the service of the church, we do not build the kingdom of God through revolutionary action, even as we long for that promise to be fulfilled and pray for it to come. The arts of governance stand in need of the demanding virtues of humility, patience, and prudence in order to pursue the good in the midst of this contingency. In fact, relieved of the pressure to be salvific, politics is set free to pursue its provisional and relative tasks. Such politics, like our experience of grace, operates more in the modality of healing than elevation. It tempers imperfection rather than tutors perfection. In this life, we find only a diminished peace that Augustine calls "a solace for our wretchedness rather than the joy of blessedness."[5] Before the transcendent horizon, the church confesses "that it looks for the resurrection of the dead and the life of the world to come."[6] In fact, for O'Donovan, "it is not political action but the communion of the church that looks forward to the city of God."[7] Such is the received Augustinian political wisdom that defers true happiness to eternity: "there we shall rest and see, see and love, love and praise."[8]

This essay does not seek to unmask judiciousness as a splendid vice, let alone the privilege of conservatism. Various critics have queried the seemingly minimalist implications of O'Donovan's vision of politics and civic virtue.[9] Rather, I tentatively propose a complement to O'Donovan's judiciousness, perhaps pushing beyond what he would want to say in avoiding both historicism and ahistoricism. We might call it his *Augustinian boldness* that rejects both Pelagianism and Manicheism by rediscovering "politics not as a self-enclosed field of human endeavor but as the theatre of the divine self-disclosure."[10] It is a declarative and hopeful boldness found in the very attempt to bridge the modern gap between theology and politics through a salvation-historical ap-

5. Augustine, *City of God,* trans. R. W. Dyson (Cambridge: Cambridge University Press, 1998), 19.27. Daringly, Augustine suggests even Rome offered a "shadowy resemblance" of the peace of God (cf. 5.17).

6. Oliver O'Donovan, *The Desire of the Nations: Rediscovering the Roots of Political Theology* (Cambridge: Cambridge University Press, 1996), p. 288.

7. Oliver O'Donovan and Joan Lockwood O'Donovan, eds., *Bonds of Imperfection: Christian Politics, Past and Present* (Grand Rapids: Eerdmans, 2004), p. 2.

8. Augustine, *City of God,* 22.30.

9. See, for example, Nicholas Wolterstorff, "A Discussion of Oliver O'Donovan's *The Desire of the Nations,*" *Scottish Journal of Theology* 54 (2001): 87-109; and William Schweiker, "Freedom and Authority in Political Theology: A Response to Oliver O'Donovan's *The Desire of the Nations,*" *Scottish Journal of Theology* 54 (2001): 110-126.

10. O'Donovan, *The Desire of the Nations,* p. 82.

proach. The bridge is made by way of an analogy between divine and human action that respects both transcendence and historicity. This analogy taps into a *resurrection* faith in the order of nature and the purpose of history revealed in the exaltation of Christ. It is fundamental to his account of the "missionary imperative" of the church's proclamation of the Gospel that requires "a discernment of the working of the Spirit and of the Antichrist."[11] Highlighting this boldness is my effort to bring together important themes from his work in Augustine studies, Christian ethics, and political theology. In particular, I try to connect what O'Donovan has to say about eudaimonism to what he has to say about history and politics in order to pose questions about their relationship.

Here are some of the questions. How does O'Donovan's linking of creation and redemption in Augustine's ethics relate to a postlapsarian politics of "fugitive presence"? How do providence and redemption relate in political life? Can the exercise of political virtues be a part of the life of piety, even proleptically referred to those virtues perfected in heaven? In short, how are the morals of the *res publica* related to beatitude, if at all? These questions are inspired by perplexity about two central passages in O'Donovan's corpus. I do not here offer a close reading of his writings or those of Augustine. Rather, I hope to raise theological issues that might reframe contemporary political theology by honoring this Augustinian judiciousness and boldness. Familiar questions about the unity of the virtues and so-called "doctrine of the Two" remain. But my focus tries to locate them within a perhaps less travelled route at the intersection of "political history" and "saving history."[12] Pursuing their sometimes vexed temporal relation in O'Donovan's moral and political imagination might enrich current conversations away from abstract (often spatial) formulations that seem to have run their course in the disputes about church

---

11. O'Donovan, *The Desire of the Nations*, p. 214; see also pp. 193-197 and 243-244. One careful reader has suggested that *The Desire of the Nations* can be read as the completion of Karl Barth's unfinished volume IV/4 of the *Church Dogmatics* by approaching politics missiologically. See Gilbert Meilaender, "Recovering Christendom," *First Things* (November 1997): 36-42. The questions raised by my essay are meant to read as provocations for thinking about O'Donovan's relation to Barth as much as to Augustine.

12. Jeffrey Stout has argued that questions about such a relationship should be "high on the agenda of any Christian political theology that hopes to acknowledge the sovereignty of God while transcending both resentment of, and absorption into, the secular." For example, after noting Augustine's ambivalence about pagan virtue, Stout asks, "is it not possible to discern the workings of the Holy Spirit, and thus some reflection of God's redemptive activity, in modern democratic aspirations?" See Jeffrey Stout, *Democracy and Tradition* (Princeton: Princeton University Press, 2004), p. 104.

and state divorced from dogmatic theology. These disputes, despite O'Dono-van's interventions, too often rely on a kind of atmospheric Augustinianism in praise of the limits of politics and the necessity of dirty hands. Such discussions generate tropes about pessimism and optimism which in turn sponsor battles between supposedly world-affirming incarnational Constantinians and world-denying cruciform sectarians. These oppositions, however, do not capture the richness of a theological — and so Christological and pneumatological — vision of political history.

An Augustinian Boldness

An important theme in O'Donovan's work is the claim that divine grace vindicates nature and judges history, but salvation is not immanent within either nature or history. God is the ultimate authority who transcends, judges, and reconciles all communities. Redemption will be known in the fullness of time, but it is not dependent on the process of time. Christ alone brings salvation, not civilizational progress. And yet, the history of salvation is a history, unfolding from Babylon to Jerusalem, groaning toward fulfillment in the resurrected Christ. It does not float above history as if there are two worlds and two histories. As O'Donovan states, "we must not champion 'saving history' so zealously that the kingdom of God ceases to be the destiny and purpose of *all* history."[13] There is an "earthly city" and a "city of God," marked by different loves, different hopes, and different faiths. But they are entangled with one another in hidden ways throughout history. Only God knows their boundaries, and they cannot be identified with any particular human society. The Holy Spirit is at work in all things, including politics. Nothing is theologically neutral. There is no *tertium quid*.[14] It is the fictional world that imagines politics without divine purpose that is unrealistic. In fact, O'Donovan argues for a

---

13. O'Donovan, *Resurrection and Moral Order*, pp. 65-66.

14. See H. I. Marrou, "Civitas Dei, civitas terrena: num tertium quid?" *Studia Patristica* 2 (1957): 342-350. Marrou rejects the idea that there is a "third city" between, or in addition to, the earthly and the heavenly. But, he suggests there is something else, best understood as a different sort of order within empirical history, an "inextricable mixture" of the two cities "in time" and the "mystery of history." Robert Markus greatly expanded Marrou's claim in his celebrated *Saeculum: History and Society in the Theology of Saint Augustine* (Cambridge: Cambridge University Press, 1970). O'Donovan rejects aspects of this interpretation, especially the neutrality of a *tertium quid*. See Oliver O'Donovan, "The Political Thought of the *City of God* 19," in *Bonds of Imperfection*, pp. 48-72.

confessedly Christian secular political order. But as O'Donovan puts it in characteristic theological idiom, "our complaint against historicism is that it has made every act of providence by definition an act of salvation."[15] Creation, providence, and redemption must be adequately distinguished. Soteriology does not exhaust theology, and earthly politics is not messianic.

In fact, for most of the twentieth century, Augustinianism was mobilized as an austere tradition in order to expose and to reject all manner of misguided idealisms, religious and secular. Reinhold Niebuhr, principal spokesperson of this tradition, marshaled Augustine's doctrine of original sin and dramatic narrative of "two cities" in order to deflate the pretensions of would-be utopians and latter-day Pelagians and Montanists. Christian politics, for both Niebuhr and O'Donovan, is a politics of imperfectibility. It allows no unified political and theological authority other than Christ. The Christian looks to the clarity of revelation at Calvary, not the tumult and vicissitudes of political movements.

The imperfectibility and the opacity of human affairs, however, do admit witnesses to God's rule amidst the provisional undertakings of humanity. Eschatological skepticism does not extend all the way down, rendering moot the analysis of social practices. History is not simply the flat, monotonous rise and fall of empires. Augustinian faith resists complete unmasking of intelligible desires that make sense of our embodied life. Political communities reveal tendencies. Expressions of their loves can be distinguished with reference to a common good, notably distinguished in the history of empire and the church. Both O'Donovan and Niebuhr, for example, celebrate constitutional legal traditions as part of an impressive legacy of early modern Christian political thought. Realism and idealism, however, admit multiple meanings in theology and politics.

In ways that recall what Niebuhr termed the ironies of history, either view can sponsor their own kinds of self-congratulatory clarity that cut short the newness of the good news of the Gospel. In fact, recent interpretations of Augustine and Hegel have challenged the standard realist versus idealist deployment of these figures in debates about the transformative possibilities of politics and the historical revelation of a Triune God.[16] O'Donovan's own con-

---

15. O'Donovan *Resurrection and Moral Order*, p. 66.

16. On Hegel, see Thomas A. Lewis, *Religion, Modernity, and Politics in Hegel* (Oxford: Oxford University Press, 2011). Interestingly, while O'Donovan is no Hegelian, he suggests that the "eschatological character of Christendom" — expressed in Gelasius's dictum that "two there are by whom this world is ruled" — is a "curious anticipation of Hegel's view that history progresses by differentiation." See O'Donovan, *Desire of the Nations*, p. 203.

tribution to political theology is certainly resistant to progressive metanarratives that succumb to secularist and historicist ideology. However, readers of O'Donovan wisely resist an easy schematic of realism and idealism as a way of thinking *theologically* about politics.

O'Donovan avoids the bleak realism of some Augustinians by identifying political concepts authorized by the Scriptures and revealed by divine action in history that mediates our human *good,* including central aspects of the Western liberal tradition. This attempt is shaped by a realism that is more fundamental than a trope about the limits of politics or the value of religious ideals to motivate justice. His realism, perhaps unlike Niebuhr and overly Platonized philosophical readings of Augustine, is a historical realism determined by the reality of God's Kingdom made known in the history of Israel and the life, death, and resurrection of Jesus Christ. This realism, shaped by the Advent of Christ and His Spirit rather than abstract doctrine or scattered biblical wisdom, does more than puncture idealism by repeating mantras about sin and eschatology. Or, to be more judicious, it does not puncture idealism with "the imperative of universal suspicion."[17] Political theology must offer more than prophetic critique, Weberian lament, or endless genealogy.

O'Donovan's measured contributions to political ethics find their genesis in a bold conceptual effort to overcome the excesses of both liberalism and historicism. I take the opening chapters of *The Desire of The Nations* as representative of this boldness, especially in locating political discussion against "a background in the ontology of human freedom, action and the good."[18] But what kind of boldness? I focus on the boldness of *analogy.*

Resurgent interest in political theology, drawing on the influential legacies of Carl Schmitt and Leo Strauss, often trades upon analogies between political philosophy and theology in examining shared concepts likes sovereignty, authority, and law. But O'Donovan's understanding of the evangelical task of political theology envisions a more ambitious notion of analogy. It is an understanding that links his earlier treatment of an ethics that is evangelical to an understanding of politics responsive to the divine rule. Rather than rest content with familiar Augustinian themes of sin, O'Donovan proclaims the good news for politics. This good news is neither completely this-worldly nor completely other-worldly. It neither identifies nor divides the natural and the supernatural. I quote at length:

17. O'Donovan *Desire of the Nations,* p. 10.
18. Ibid., p. 30.

[Political theology] postulates an analogy — not a rhetorical metaphor only, or a poetic image, but an analogy grounded in reality — between the acts of God and human acts, both of them taking place within the one public history which is the theatre of God's saving purposes and mankind's social undertakings. . . . The point is not to reduce the semantic range of speech about God's acts to the limits of our commonplace political discussion — *that* would be reductionism indeed! — but to push back the horizon of commonplace politics and open it up to the activity of God. Earthly events of liberation, rule and community-foundation provide us with partial indications of what God is doing in human history; while correspondingly, we must look to the horizon of God's redemptive purposes if we are to grasp the full meaning of political events that pass before our eyes . . . politics may, and indeed does, serve as a source of religious imagery, part of that broken glass whose reflections the soul transcends as it moves on and up towards the divine glory.[19]

Here, politics is neither equivocally nor univocally related to divine action. The epistemology is limited: "partial indications" and "broken glass." But action does reflect the soul's orientation to the transcendent good. By grounding analogy in reality, I take this analogy to be something like an analogy of participation that distinguishes creator and creature but refuses a competitive account of their relations.[20] In fact, the language of analogy suggests to me something even stronger than Barth's language of the "parabolic" nature of the state.[21] In a sermon on eternity, for example, O'Donovan tells his listeners that the emergence of democracy in the West "springs from that new life in the midst of Western society, the life of Pentecost."[22] That is a bold vision of po-

19. Ibid., p. 2.

20. Augustinian discussions of nature and grace, recovering from the Jansenist controversy, and predicated on certain metaphysical notions of God's relation to the world, have been a subject of ongoing controversy. These discussions have been transformed in the wake of Henri de Lubac and now entered Protestant precincts through the work of John Milbank, Hans Boersma, and Kathryn Tanner. Less work, however, has been done to explicitly relate them to political Augustinianism. For recent discussion, see Sean Larsen, "The Politics of Desire: Two Readings of Henri De Lubac on Nature and Grace," *Modern Theology* (2013): 1-32. It also would be fruitful for political Augustinians to relate these issues to the recent work of David Kelsey on the integrity of different ways God relates to humanity. See David Kelsey, *Eccentric Existence: A Theological Anthropology*, 2 vols. (Louisville, KY: Westminster John Knox Press, 2009).

21. O'Donovan criticizes Barth's position by asking "how is the constitutionally pagan state, by definition of its own righteousness, 'reminded' of what it never knew?" in O'Donovan, *Desire of the Nations*, p. 214.

22. Oliver O'Donovan, "Eternal Fire," in Oliver O'Donovan, *The Word in Small Boats: Sermons from Oxford* (Grand Rapids: Eerdmans, 2010), pp. 44-49, at 47.

litical activity framed within the broader background of salvation-history and divine self-disclosure. It is bolder than the occasional spiritualized enthusiasm for specific political practices one finds among postmillennial Christian advocates of social justice. All history is read in light of the history of God's mighty acts, including political history that seems to participate through history in the eternity of God.

To be sure, O'Donovan tells a long story that limits our expectations of political *institutions* in their distinctive task. His judiciousness can be seen in his juridical conception of the purposes of government. Secular political authority does not simply mediate the rule of God; in the aftermath of the Christ-event, governments mediate penultimate judgment alone. They are reactive institutions, giving *indirect* testimony to God in humble recognition of their "secular" temporal purposes of redressing wrongs that harm the public good. But even this "opens an account of secular authority which presumes neither that the Christ-event never occurred nor that the sovereignty of Christ is now transparent and uncontested."[23] The state, on O'Donovan's view, is put in the service of the church. But it "remains under the direction of the First Person of the Trinity; it is not filled with the Holy Spirit at Pentecost."[24] The state does not have the gifts of the Spirit. But, if all historical events are marked by that one event of redemption, might political history also bear witness not only to Christ but the Spirit that testifies to Christ? Politics does not save, but does it teach us anything about the nature of salvation?

Civic Virtues and Eudaimonism

In the wake of Ander Nygren's critique of Augustinian *caritas,* many discussions of eudaimonism in Christian ethics have focused on the relationship between human desire for happiness and the perfection of love as self-denial. Such discussions fed on longstanding Protestant anxieties about the agent-centeredness and virtue language of classical eudaimonism, often leading many of Augustine's political admirers to abandon his teachings on love. But they also circulated within a modern skepticism about teleology and the specification of virtues dependent on sources external to humanity, often

---

23. O'Donovan, *Desire of the Nations,* p. 146.

24. Oliver O'Donovan, "Response to Gerrit de Kruijf," in Craig Bartholomew, Jonathan Chaplin, Robert Song, and Al Wolters, eds., *A Royal Priesthood? The Use of the Bible Ethically and Politically: A Dialogue with Oliver O'Donovan* (Grand Rapids: Zondervan, 2002), pp. 238-240, at 239.

leading many of Augustine's admirers to become critics of modern liberalism agnostic about human ends. Both features dominate contemporary moral theology, including recent efforts to bring Aquinas and Barth together in a single vision that reconciles teleology and grace through shared Augustinian commitments.[25]

Elsewhere, under O'Donovan's influence, I have tried to bridge these discussions by joining Augustinian *ordo amoris* with a Christological interpretation of political Augustinianism. I argued for a re-reading of Augustine's theme of "using and enjoying" in multiple texts as a way of getting beyond an exclusive focus on demythologized tropes about original sin and eschatology.[26] On my account, we are distracted by hyper-Augustinian contrasts between love of God and love of the world. Such contrasts rely on philosophical views which radically subordinate proximate goods by treating them as merely vehicles to an ultimate, often intellectualist and solipsistic, experience of the highest good. These dualistic theories of value are what Augustine's theology rejects. Under the pressure of his reading of the Gospels and the identification of God with the compassion of the crucified Jesus, Augustine navigated between "ethically responsible" Stoicism and "spiritual" Platonism in ways that place the twofold love commands at the heart of all human activity and manifestations of virtue. In particular, I suggested his rejection of Stoicism and Platonism was an important cultural moment that opened space for emotional investment with those who suffer injustice.

The interrelatedness of the love of God and love of neighbor parallels a positive relation between temporal and eternal goods when oriented to their perfection in God, the source of all goods. The goods acknowledged in any good are an acknowledgment of the highest good. In fact, as John Bowlin has argued, Augustine avoids dualism because when love as eternity's virtue "descends and fixes itself upon time's objects, it perfects its act only as it exercises time's many virtues."[27] I think this helps relieve possible tensions between anti-Pelagian doubts about self-transcendence and hyper-Augustinian claims

---

25. See, for example, Daniel Migliore, ed., *Commanding Grace: Studies in Karl Barth's Ethics* (Grand Rapids: Eerdmans, 2010).

26. Eric Gregory, *Politics and the Order of Love: An Augustinian Ethic of Democratic Citizenship* (Chicago: University of Chicago Press, 2008).

27. John Bowlin, "Augustine Counting Virtues," *Augustinian Studies* 41:1 (2010): 277-300, at 299. Bowlin writes, "Such is Christ's life in time, and such is ours as we follow him. Christ does not attempt to escape time and its many virtues; he does not defer the exercise of eternity's love to the eschatological horizon. . . . Christ mixes time and eternity; he mixes temporal and eternal virtues. He knows love's joys but also its sorrows" (pp. 299-300).

that eternity displaces time. But it might also allow for a deeper recognition of the plurality of moral excellences nurtured in the time that is political history. Whether or not I am right about a non-possessive divine economy, it is telling that exegetical debates about Augustine's doctrine of love seldom join interpretation of Augustinian politics given a preoccupation with Book 19 of the *City of God*.

A virtue of O'Donovan's own reading of Augustine's doctrine of love is the way he connects love to wider issues in philosophy and theology. At the end of *The Problem of Self-Love in St. Augustine*, he helpfully shows that Christian debates about *agape* and *eros* finally involve ontology as well as ethics. In particular, beyond the moral problem of egocentricity, he shows that different theological approaches to eudaimonism raise the underlying question of God's relation to Creation as both Creator and Redeemer. Does this relation allow teleology? Once again, I quote at some length:

> Augustine's picture of the universe shows us one who is the source and goal of being, value, and activity, himself in the center of the universe and at rest; and it shows us the remainder of the universe in constant movement, which, while it may tend toward or away from the center, is yet held in relation to it, so that all other beings lean, in a multiplicity of ways, toward the source and goal of being. But the force which draws these moving galaxies of souls is immanent to them, a kind of dynamic nostalgia rather than a transcendent summons from the center. Such a summons, of course, is presupposed; but it is reflected by this responsive movement which is other than itself, so that there is a real reciprocity between Creator and creature. In the last resort what is at issue is whether all movement in the universe is from the center to the circumference or whether there is also this responsive movement. Here is the nub of the agape-eros question for Nygren, who stands in a respectable Protestant theological tradition (though an extreme point of it) rejecting immanent teleology as inconsistent with the doctrine of Creation.[28]

So far, O'Donovan on Augustine and Nygren. But the final passage of the book suggests a normative stance. O'Donovan writes:

> Between that which is and that which will be there must be a line of connection, the redemptive purposes of God. . . . However dramatic a transformation redemption may involve, however opaque to man's mind the

28. Ibid., p. 157.

continuity may be, we know, and whenever we repeat the Trinitarian creed with Saint Augustine we confess that our being-as-we-are and our being-as-we-shall-be are held together as works of the One God who is both our Creator and Redeemer.[29]

This "line of connection" respects the integrity of both creation and redemption. But it also draws them together. Augustine's rejection of Platonism in his daring account of the resurrection of the body offers an example of this continuity: "what incorruptible body could be better adapted to the joy of those who rise again than the same one in which they groaned when it was corruptible?"[30] Salvation may not be internal to history, but it is also not thoroughly external. What does this mean for politics and the soteriological status of political morality? Does the "line of connection" ever pass through those activities that we call political?

In his mediating interpretation of the key passage of Augustine's redefinition of a commonwealth, O'Donovan argues that "in denying 'justice' to religiously defective societies, Augustine meant what he said; yet the 'justice' which the heavenly city embodies is not merely supramundane: it answers to 'the right' as it is generally recognized and universally desired."[31] In fact, O'Donovan suggests, despite Augustine's "deflation of moral pretension" in politics, there is "an ability to discern the shadows cast by virtue in the most surprising places."[32] There is no certain knowledge, and constant recognition of limits, but these shadows cast light in the darkness. As deferred, it seems, the heavenly city does not simply erase time's virtues, even those virtues displayed in political life. O'Donovan's lean account of political authority as postlapsarian reaction to wrongdoing puts politics in its place, both theologically and historically. But might the exercise of imperfect civic virtue — responsive to the truth of human goods — admit a connection to redemption, if the eschatological city is to be a redeemed earth? Is there only a connection through yearning and confession, or does an immanent teleology allow us to say more about politics? Civic and theological virtues, for example, typically have different purposes and ends. But might an Augustinian vision admit something like infused civic virtues in light of salvation history? Can we differentiate yet also analogize civic and theological virtues? Might some civic virtues, including justice and courage, participate in, and have as their object, some type of

29. Ibid., p. 159.
30. Augustine, *City of God*, 22.26.
31. O'Donovan, "The Political Thought of the City of God 19," p. 61.
32. Ibid., p. 64.

redemptive end? Might there be certain virtues, including love, that make persons and societies more excellent in the contingency of the political sphere? Are these virtues consummated or consumed?

Robert Dodaro has argued that Augustine's approach to politics reaches its highpoint in the ideal of a Christian lay statesman, not an ideal political order. For Dodaro, this account of the ideal statesman is also a possible bridge between *ecclesia* and *res publica*. Civic virtues, paralleling a Neo-Platonic doctrine of the gradation of virtue outlined by Porphyry, and later Macrobius and Marinus, means the statesman can bridge the gap between the two cities. Drawing from hints in Augustine's letters, Dodaro suggests true piety might elevate traditional civic virtues by orienting them toward eternal goods.[33] O'Donovan's praise of Theodosius's penance and Savonarola's courage suggests something like an example of this kind. Here, it seems, there is a Christian political conscience that harmonizes temporal and eternal goods in political history. There seems no strict division between proximate ends focused on finite ends and those virtues directed toward final ends. By grace, even politics might share in the mixing of time and eternity. Perhaps this is where O'Donovan's lean account of politics intersects with more cosmic aspirations, rising and falling in time in a world saturated with God.

Such a vision might be less alienating than Augustinian agnosticism about anything other than reconciliation beyond history. Recall O'Donovan's insistence that not every act of providence is an act of salvation. This leaves open the question of whether there any such acts. Does Augustinian secularity, for example, allow Barthian secular parables? Do we have categories that allow us to recognize certain actions and not others as part of a salvation economy? Some theologians, for example, have written about the American civil rights movement as a Christian event for both church and society.[34] Here, the world sees an embodied sign of that kingdom "from every nation, tribe, people, and language."[35]

O'Donovan's political conceptuality seems to resist such readings as enthusiastic desires to baptize the secular. Such movements are external works

---

33. Robert Dodaro, *Christ and the Just Society in the Thought of Augustine* (Cambridge: Cambridge University Press, 2004), and Robert Dodaro, "Political and Theological Virtues in Augustine, Letter 155 to Macedonius," *Augustiniana* 54 (2004): 431-474.

34. See, for example, James H. Cone, *The Cross and the Lynching Tree* (Maryknoll: Orbis Books, 2011); Charles Marsh, "The Civil Rights Movement as Theological Drama," *Modern Theology* 18:2 (April 2002): 231-250; and, relatedly, Ted A. Smith, *The New Measures: A Theological History of Democratic Practice* (Cambridge: Cambridge University Press, 2007).

35. Revelation 7:9.

of moral redress, not genuine reconciliation. But he does offer at least one contemporary example that raises questions about the strict designation of politics as providential, divorced from saving history. Of the admittedly special case of Israel, he writes, "whatever may be the symbolic significance of the events of 1949 and 1967, about which it is appropriate to remain open-minded, these events cannot possibly disclose any meaning for the salvation of the world if they yield only a defensive, exclusive, and militarily oppressive nation-state."[36] This open-mindedness suggests that his bold analogy does admit historical example, even as it remain allergic to the consolation of univocal analogy. Theological interpretation of political history is always in danger of self-deception and pneumatological excess. O'Donovan's Anglican judiciousness is a welcome balm for theology awash in the culture wars and promiscuous prophecy. But I have suggested a political Augustinianism that wants to be more than a counsel against idolatry risks saying something about the mysterious and hidden ways of God.

O'Donovan has not given us a third volume of political *history* to read alongside his political *theology* and political *ethics*. That would be a work of prophecy rather than conceptual analysis and deliberation. Judicious Augustinians have rarely ventured into prophecy, wary of eschatologizing the present and denying the gratuity of grace in the singularity of Christ. In fact, O'Donovan tell us that "it was an evil day for Christian thought when prophecy became the fashionable category for political reflection in place of practical reasonableness."[37] But O'Donovan also has told us that Christian theology "must assume the prophet's task, and, accepting history as the matrix in which politics and ethics take form, affirm that it is the history of God's action, not sheer contingency but purpose."[38] Neither nature nor history is given in vain, even for those who have another city to love. This essay has risked the suggestion that O'Donovan's bold analogy makes such a work a possibility, albeit incomplete and inconclusive until that final act of judgment closes history.

36. O'Donovan *Desire of the Nations,* p. 287.
37. Oliver O'Donovan, *The Ways of Judgment* (Grand Rapids: Eerdmans, 2005), p. xv.
38. Ibid., p. 12.

Augustine and Preaching: A Christian Moral Pedagogy

Shinji Kayama

1. The Morality of Preaching?

Talk of the "morality of preaching" may sound somewhat awkward to many modern, especially liberal, minds. Preaching is fundamentally a theological enterprise which discovers and delivers the meaning of the Word of God; it is also a spiritual experience that initiates and nurtures the faith of the congregation. But is it a moral act? Or should it be consigned to a "spiritual" and hence "personal" domain? Here we face the ambiguous relationship between preaching and morality. Liberals are especially alerted by any form of "moral preaching" as inherently dangerous, implying some kind of religious indoctrination about secular matters. In the history of Christianity, however, preaching has been an inherently ethical act, questioning the moral basis of human existence, urging the congregation to strive for moral improvement in their aspiration for the kingdom of heaven as well as in their daily life on earth. Preaching has been also ethical in a collective, communal sense: addressed to the people of Israel, both old and new, the Word of God has been shared as the bond of the community.

In this chapter I examine the morality of preaching, using Augustine as an exemplar. Augustine was a renowned preacher to his contemporaries. A large number of sermons have survived to this day, and have been examined extensively in relation to fundamental aspects of his theology, such as Trinity, soteriology, eschatology, and ecclesiology. Little scholarly attention, however, has been devoted to examining the relationship between Augustine's sermons and his moral thinking, not to mention its social and political implications.[1] To what extent was Augustine conscious of his moral task when he preached? In what manner did he convey ethical messages in his sermons? What drove him to be morally conscious in his sermons? To answer these questions, I provide a brief overview of Augustine's career as a preacher to demonstrate the fundamentally moral orientation of his preaching. I then turn to the development of Augustine's moral thinking, paying special attention to his major (yet often neglected) socio-political concept of *pax* (peace), in order to illuminate how significant a role his preaching played in that process.

2. Preaching as Moral Instruction[2]

Augustine's career as a preacher extended nearly forty years, and he produced an expansive corpus: over 200 sermons on the Psalms alone, that amount to more than the whole of *De Civitate Dei,* and the 124 exegetical sermons on St. John are twice the volume of *De Trinitate.* Having preached extensively throughout the Bible, he was especially fond of Jesus' parables and miracles, repeatedly coming back to them. Over a thousand sermons still exist in his name, although only half are believed to be genuinely Augustine's.[3]

Augustine gave his first sermon in 391 at the age of 37 just after he became a priest in Hippo Regius. In those days, preaching was the "right" of a bishop, not of an ordinary priest like the young Augustine. He was reluctant at first, but the expectation was so high that he was compelled to preach from the outset. In a matter of two years, he was chosen as the main preacher at a council held in Hippo. Augustine was well equipped as a public speaker with his former training as a rhetor, but throughout his career he was never satisfied with his sermons, always feeling that preaching was a cumbersome task.[4] For

---

1. Cf. Paul R. Kolbet, *Augustine and the Cure of Souls* (Notre Dame, IN: University of Notre Dame Press, 2010), pp. 3-4.

2. On the ethical orientation of Augustine's sermons, see Peter Brown, *Augustine of Hippo: A Biography,* 2nd ed. (Berkeley: University of California Press, 2000), esp. pp. 240-255. Kolbet describes it in terms of "psychagogy" (*Augustine and the Cure of Souls,* pp. 7-12).

3. About 8,000 sermons are allegedly left in Augustine's name. Cf. John Rist, *Augustine: Ancient Thought Baptized* (Cambridge: Cambridge University Press, 1994), p. 4. Meanwhile, new sermons continue to be discovered, most notably the "Dolbeau sermons", and their moral and political importance is emphasised by Brown, for instance, in his *Augustine,* pp. 443-445.

4. E.g., serm. 25.

one thing, he was not well versed in Hebrew like Jerome, and his exegesis of the Old Testament was inevitably constrained by the Vulgate, a late-fourth-century Latin translation of the Bible. In addition, preaching, along with many other clerical duties, was not what Augustine aspired to achieve, not only in his younger days but throughout his life: namely, a life of contemplation.[5]

The real burden of preaching, moreover, may have stemmed from what was innate in its task, that is, to explicate the truth. For Augustine, truth was the knowledge of God, something unattainable in this world due to the sinfulness of human beings. Yet, they were created in the image of God, and their original nature urged them to aspire for truth within the limitation of a fallen world. For Christians, therefore, truth was hidden in the Bible to be discovered by those who strove for it. Augustine often described this aspiration in terms of "love". It was this "love of truth"[6] which was the main engine for his incessant engagement in an agonizing effort to explain what was inexplicable.

Then how should a preacher carry out this difficult task? Augustine wrote on the method of preaching in three works, *De Magistro, De Catechizandis Rudibus,* and *De Doctrina Christiana.* The most relevant to our discussion is *De Doctrina Christiana,* a unique work written especially for educated Christians and preachers.[7]

The first three books deal with hermeneutics, demonstrating "a way to discover" (*modus inveniendi,* 1.prooem.1) the things we should understand in the Bible. Augustine presents two original exegetical principles: *res-signum* and *frui-uti.*[8] The first pair is a hermeneutical principle to distinguish what is directly comprehensible (*res,* the thing itself), such as tree and stone, from what refers indirectly to something else (*signum,* sign), such as smoke which indicates fire. Augustine is especially attracted to signs, especially those in the Bible, because they are believed to contain divine messages to be uncovered. Considering it an important tool to interpret biblical signs, Augustine is confident in his "allegorical" method, which he learned from his mentor, Ambrose, though it seems too speculative to modern readers.[9]

The second hermeneutical principle, *frui-uti* (to enjoy and to use), is more closely related to our examination, since the formula presented an important

---

5. Cf. Brown, *Augustine,* pp. 252-253.

6. Persistently so, from the earliest work (DO 1.3.6) to his mature work (DCD 19.19).

7. Brown, *Augustine,* pp. 261-262.

8. For the following discussion in this section, see my DPhil dissertation, Shinji Kayama, "From *Ordo* to *Pax:* The Formation of a Central Political Concept of Augustine" (Oxford University, 1997), pp. 114-122.

9. Cf. Brown, *Augustine,* p. 257.

key to Augustine's moral thinking.[10] Among all goods, God is the highest good, hence the thing to be enjoyed, whereas human institutions such as customs, language, and law are signs conventionally agreed upon, thus not to be enjoyed but to be used (2.25.38–26.40). The distinction between *frui* and *uti* leads to the rightly "ordered love" (*ordinata dilectio,* 1.27.28), a fundamental moral principle in Augustine's ethics. The *frui-uti* distinction was in an experimental stage at this point, because a human was not yet clearly defined as an object of enjoyment. Still, the formula enabled Augustine to explain the relevance of human institutions in terms of instrumentality as relative goods in this fallen world.

Upon these hermeneutical foundations, Augustine launched an interesting project in the fourth book of *De Doctrina Christiana:* to expound on the method of communication (*modus proferendi,* I.1.1 & IV.1.1) — a promise fulfilled nearly thirty years after the publication of the first book, and just four years before the author's death. Augustine had been convinced all along that what is understood must be communicated, or preached to be more precise, as much as possible within the human condition. He emphasises that a preacher does not have to be eloquent, but must discern things rightly, according to the rightly ordered love based on the two hermeneutical principles. To convey what he discerns, the preacher must preach clearly (III.9.23–11.26). Augustine shows three essential ways of communication: to "instruct" *(docere),* to "attract" *(delectare),* and to "persuade" *(flectere),* all of which aim to bring about an agreement amongst the congregation (12.27). Most importantly, a sermon must always be related to their eternal salvation (18.35), through which one can attain the true end of life which is "happiness". The sermon must also encourage people to "love a good life and avoid an evil life" (25.55), starting with the preacher himself as a role model (27.59–30.63).

Evident in all four books of *De Doctrina Christiana* is this eudaemonist framework and its profoundly moral orientation. To preach is to give moral instruction, to elicit the audience to lead a better life, by striving to achieve a truly happy life *(beata vita)* through the knowledge of God within the limits of a fallen world. Augustine was convinced of the morality of preaching throughout his life, as seen vividly in a short sermon (serm. 17) delivered in the last years of his life. He points out a double task of a preacher: to "explain" and to "edify". He first introduces two passages of Psalm 50, "God will come

10. For a detailed analysis, see Oliver O'Donovan, "Usus and Fruitio", *Journal of Theological Studies* 33 (1980): 361-397, and *The Problem of Self-Love in St. Augustine* (New Haven: Yale University Press, 1982).

openly, our God, and *he will not keep silent*" (verse 3) and "These things you have done, and I kept quiet" (verse 21), asking whether God is silent or not. To solve this apparent contradiction, Augustine starts with a general statement that Christ is speaking through the scriptures, not only in the gospels, but also through the patriarchs and the prophets. The first task of a preacher, therefore, is this: "[t]he preacher explains the text; if he says what is true, it is Christ speaking" (17.1). The two passages in question must now be rightly related to mean: God is silent now, but not on the Day of Judgement.

Once the text is thus explicated, the preacher moves on to the second part of his task: to "edify" his people. He urges them to face themselves, especially their sins, all of which God sees but keeps quiet about (17.2, 3). The time left until the last judgement is "the time of mercy, for us to correct ourselves", and Augustine continues, "the time for judgement has not yet come. There is space, there's room; we have sinned, let us correct ourselves". The church is like a doctor who prescribes "a daily medicine", such as the Lord's Prayer among others. At the end of the sermon, Augustine concludes: "[d]on't make me sad with your vicious habits, because the only pleasure I have in this life is your good life" (17.7). To preach is to explain the truth as written in the scriptures, but that is not enough. It needs to instruct people to amend their lives — to be morally better by striving for the *beata vita*. Such a positive tone of voice about human morality could be heard in Augustine's sermon in his 70s.

3. Preaching to Build a Community

Through his experience in the pulpit, Augustine gradually came to understand preaching as part of the solemn task of "faith seeking understanding"[11] — a fundamental concept of his theology. Still, preaching played a crucially different role from his theological writings, which were aimed at those who were educated in the liberal arts and/or trained to be priests and bishops. Preaching was a more immediate experience, a conversation *(sermo)* with his congregation, many of whom were uneducated and illiterate. In this dialogue, Augustine's former career gave him a tremendous advantage, as John Cavadini insists: "as a professional rhetor he [Augustine] had a keen sense of his audience", and was able to adapt his own discourse to the educational level of the audi-

---

11. Cf. serm. 43.7, 9.

ence.[12] According to Cavadini, "'faith seeking understanding' is as much a homiletic principle in Augustine as it is a theological principle":[13]

> What emerges from a comparison of the homilies with *De Trinitate* is not that Augustine is popularizing, or 'exotericizing', the *result* of inquiry when he preaches, but that he recontextualizes inquiry itself for the people.[14]

Sermons produced a new method, "the dialectic of faith seeking understanding, available to all".[15] In short, preaching opened a new channel for Augustine to communicate with — and especially to edify — those who otherwise may have been overlooked, as was the case in his earliest philosophical treatises.

In late antiquity, a bishop was the leader of his flock, composed of various strands of people, men and women, young and old, rich and poor, masters and slaves, the righteous and the sinful. Augustine's community in Hippo was an intricate mixture of Roman and the African cultures, of Christian and pagan beliefs. These people found in Augustine a moral authority who gave inspiration and instruction to their fragile, unpredictable lives in the late Roman world.

In *Augustine of Hippo*, Peter Brown describes how Augustine exercised this authority over his people: "[a] bishop could approach his flock armed with many sanctions," using biblical concepts such as the last judgement and eternal punishment to evoke the fear of God. Augustine would use this fear himself, but he rarely stood "outside his flock and threaten[ed] them" in an authoritarian way. He "always thought of himself as living among a new 'people' — the *populus Dei*, the 'people of God'". For Augustine, therefore, "it was his first duty to look after his own, to maintain the identity and the morale of his 'people', the Catholic congregation".[16] Such pastoral care involved not only the spiritual health of the flock, but also entailed the moral task of building a new community according to the authority of the scriptures. In other words, "the Christian churches in the Empire were acting as a school for citizenship", or "holy lecture-halls" as Augustine himself puts it.[17] In order to carry out this moral task, Augustine was endowed with a tremendous tool: the privilege and responsibility to preach. He

---

12. John Cavadini, "Simplifying Augustine", in John van Engen, ed., *Educating the People: Exploring the History of Jewish and Christian Communities* (Grand Rapids: Eerdmans, 2004), p. 65, n. 8.

13. Cavadini, "Simplifying Augustine", p. 70, n. 33.

14. Cavadini, "Simplifying Augustine", p. 71.

15. Cavadini, "Simplifying Augustine", p. 81.

16. Brown, *Augustine*, pp. 246-247.

17. Epp. 91.2 and 138.2.9, cited in Brown, *Augustine*, p. 338.

preached to nurture his community, especially keen to build and strengthen its moral foundation, in order to realise an earthly shadow of the heavenly city of God as much as possible within the limitations of a fallen world.

At the crux of Augustine's socially-conscious sermons lay Christ's command to love one's neighbour. Scholars have argued how Augustine actually understood the love of neighbour — especially in relation to the love of self — over the years of his career, beginning from his earliest philosophical treatises to his mature works. Christian love tells us two things about the neighbour. Firstly, the neighbour has an ontological status equal to the self as an object of love. Secondly, the neighbour is to be loved as much as the self in loving God, a prerequisite for one to attain the *beata vita*. For Augustine, love is simply the source of all ethics; neighbour-love is the engine which gives a moral, social, and political thrust in his sermons.

Although neighbour-love played a central role in Augustine's ethics, I will not examine this to any further extent and refer the reader to more in-depth accounts.[18] Rather, I turn to another important, though often neglected concept of peace *(pax)*. In Augustine's maturing moral and political theology, *pax* gradually emerges as a "flagship" concept, as seen in his sermons and other writings. Augustine drew upon two principal sources. One was the secular, legal, and political notion of peace in the late antiquity, as best exemplified by *pax Romana,* and the other was scripture. A question, however, remains to be answered: why and how did he decide to use *pax* to conceptualise his moral and political thinking? Especially noteworthy is the context of the first decade of the fifth century, when Augustine was entangled in the prolonged battle against the Donatists. It was an embryonic period for his moral and political theology. With deepening insight into the biblical notion of peace through his exegesis and sermons, he eventually formulated an ecclesiological theory of peace, anticipating a fuller, more socio-political expression in Book 19 of *De Civitate Dei*.

4. *Pax est ordinata:* Augustine on Peace

Book 19 of *De Civitate Dei* is a political treatise based primarily on Augustine's exegesis of key biblical texts. At its centre, Augustine places *pax,* cul-

---

18. See, for example, John Burnaby, *Amor Dei: A Study of the Religion of St. Augustine* (London: Hodder & Stoughton, 1938); O'Donovan, *The Problem of Self-Love;* and most recently Eric Gregory, *Politics and the Order of Love: An Augustinian Ethic of Democratic Citizenship* (Chicago: University of Chicago Press, 2008).

minating in the famous "table of peace" (19.13.1). Listing different levels of peace, ranging from material substance to rational nature, from personal to social life, he succinctly defines peace as a kind of ordering: "peace is something ordered" *(pax est ordinata)*. The definition marks a culmination of his prolonged preoccupation with, and at the same time the decisive transformation of, another crucial concept in his ethics, *ordo* (order). How were the twin concepts of *pax* and *ordo* related in the development of Augustine's moral theology?

In one of his earliest philosophical treatises, *De Ordine,* Augustine understood *ordo* within a markedly Neoplatonist framework as being nearly synonymous with truth. One's happiness *(beata vita)* lay in acquiring truth, the perfect knowledge of the cosmic order of things *(ordo rerum),* which was thought to be attainable by the chosen few (II.18.47–19.51). Soon, within a matter of a few years, Augustine came to realise the flaws of his argument, especially in light of his deepening understanding of the scriptures. Roughly by the turn of the fifth century Augustine discarded the earlier, simplistic view of happiness. With his more realistic awareness of the fallen condition of human beings, Augustine redefined happiness as the prime gift of God's salvation. The concept of order too needed to be reconsidered, especially in relation to an eschatologically deepened insight into the work of divine providence. God was now understood to govern this world through two channels (dual order): one was the order of nature *(ordo naturae)* created by God, and the other was what can be characterized as "the providential order", God's ordering of human will and institutions in the imperfect, interim world between the fall and the eschaton.[19]

In relation to Augustine's doctrine of order, *pax* originally appeared as a minor derivative notion, signifying the tranquillity of the creation order and a perfect state of the ontological relationship between God, creation, and man. Then, for most of the 390s, peace was developed separately from order. Eschatologically redefined, *ordo* alone, however, proved inadequate to explain the "historical" nature of human sociality and the fragile reality of human morality. Meanwhile, *pax* gained importance in Augustine's theology as a result of his intensive reading of the scriptures. A decisive breakthrough came in the first decade of the fifth century, when peace became Augustine's key concept in his ecclesiology developed in reaction to the Donatists. It marked a fundamental shift in his social thinking: the central concept changed from *ordo* to

---

19. Cf. Robert A. Markus, *Saeculum: History and Society in the Theology of St. Augustine,* second edition (Cambridge: Cambridge University Press, 1988), pp. 86-93.

pax. Finally, in *De Civitate Dei* (413-427), *pax* reincorporated *ordo* as the theoretical basis and providence as the historiographical framework of Augustine's political theology.[20]

Political peace *(pax civitatis),* for the mature Augustine, was ontologically grounded to the extent that it was something ordered, yet it belonged not to the natural order but to the providential order, as an unnatural but necessary good used commonly by the city of God and the earthly city for different ends. Political peace was established in an earthly political community *(res publica)* united by civic consensus on the common objects of love. It was maintained by political authority endowed with judicial power to enforce the law and to punish and correct wrong-doers. In its final form, Augustine's theory of peace understood politics as a provisional and residual function: provisional, because it was necessary only within the bounds of human history, and residual because the more it was based on love, the less it became domination. Politics, in the end, was an inherently ethical matter, fundamentally concerned with the moral quality of a community.[21]

5. *Pax Ecclesiae:* Augustine and the Donatist Controversy[22]

Crucial to Augustine's development of the concept of *pax* was his ecclesiastical campaign against the Donatists that began soon after his ordination as priest in 391. By that time, both sides had become enmeshed in a complex web of slander, intrigue, and violence. Augustine found himself thrown into an antagonistic stalemate akin to "a Cold War", as Peter Brown describes it, and tried to protect his flock from interference by the Donatists by promising not to meddle with them in return.[23] His campaign stretched over three decades, which can be divided roughly into five periods:[24]

Period 1: from 391 to 395, when Augustine was occasionally engaged in epistolary dialogue and open debate with local Donatists, while producing a pamphlet *(Psalmus Contra Partem Donati,* 393) and his first

20. Cf. Kayama, "From *Ordo* to *Pax,*" pp. 189-251.

21. Cf. Kayama, "From *Ordo* to *Pax,*" pp. 252-253.

22. Cf. Kayama, "From *Ordo* to *Pax,*" pp. 138-169.

23. Brown, *Augustine,* pp. 225-226; cf. en. ps. 21(2).31.

24. For a generally accepted periodisation, cf. Geoffrey Grimshaw Willis, *Saint Augustine and the Donatist Controversy* (London: S.P.C.K., 1950), pp. 36-92, which slightly differs from mine in details concerning the dates of the work and the actual periodisation of events.

controversial treatise (*Contra Epistulam Donati Haeretici*, 393/4) which is now lost;

Period 2: from 395 to 400, when Augustine became more involved in the controversy now sweeping northern Africa, attending the third Council of Carthage (397) and stepping up his campaign by frequent pastoral correspondence with Donatist bishops (epp. 33, 43, 44, 49, 51, 52), repeated proposals for open debate, and writing another non-extant work, *Contra Partem Donati* (397);

Period 3: from 400 to 405, the most prolific period during which he realigns the different strands of his thought — ontology, Christology, anthropology, eschatology, and historiography — into a systematic ecclesiology elaborated in three major anti-Donatist treatises, *Contra Epistolam Parmeniani* (c. 400), *De Baptismo Contra Donatistas* (400), and *Contra Litteras Petiliani* (401-405), and also actively participating in the successive Councils at Carthage that resulted in the imperial Edict of Unity in 405;

Period 4: from 405 to 411, between the Edict of Unity and the decisive Conference of Carthage *(collatio)* in 411, a period in which Augustine finally came to endorse political intervention, not merely for the sake of civic protection but more controversially to "coerce" the heretics into Catholic unity, as argued extensively in his correspondence (epp. 88, 93, 105, 128);

Period 5: 411 and after, having played a significant role in shaping the deliberations of the *collatio* in 411, Augustine became preoccupried with the return of schismatics to the Catholic church. His literary work consisted of two versions, a full record and a convenient digest, of the *collatio* and repeated pleas to the authorities for merciful punishment (epp. 133, 134), as well as an apologia for the policy of religious coercion (ep. 185).

Augustine's deepening involvement in the controversy simultaneously spurred intense theological reflection on the nature and function of the church, bringing his ecclesiastical theory of peace into its fullest expression. In the first two periods, the term *pax* was constantly used, but still isolated from its role in his biblical exegesis and the ethics of dual order. Not until the third period did Augustine systematically reorganise his ideas into an ecclesiology with a new "flagship"-concept, *pax*, spurred by a dire need to solicit the allegiance of his people in order to build and solidify his community. By the time he won the decisive victory at *collatio* in 411, Augustine had been prepared to justify the authority of the Catholic church, Christian participation in socio-political activities, and even his notorious endorsement of religious coercion, all in the name of the "peace of the church" *(pax ecclesiae)*.[25]

In this protracted controversy, both the Donatist and the Catholic churches had a long history of appealing constantly to peace in defence of the authority of each camp. The most notable example was Optatus of Milevis, whose deployment of *pax* in his anti-Donatist treatise *De Schismate Donatistarum* (c. 384) may be regarded as a precursor of Augustinian peace.[26] But it was Augustine who conceived a comprehensive theory of "ecclesiastical peace", providing a theological justification of the Catholic church and a moral and social principle of peacemaking in the spirit of love. He grounded it within the framework of a renovated doctrine of dual order, which enabled him to understand peace as a multi-layered phenomenon, simultaneously cosmic, Christological, and historical.

At the very bottom lay ontological eudaemonism, in which the whole creation order was protected by God the giver of peace to all; each soul was naturally driven toward peace to attain happiness.[27] Yet, Augustine no longer claimed that true happiness and peace could be reached by human efforts for two reasons. First, true peace was ultimately a salvific gift of Christ: Christ alone could mediate this divine gift to sinful human beings, as testified by Luke 2:14 ("on earth peace to men of good will").[28] The other reason was Augustine's deepening understanding of eschatology. Salvific peace was only bestowed at the eschaton, on the Day of Judgement, upon the righteous and the faithful. Any form of peace obtained by human beings was only an interim, historical phenomenon, which remained imperfect, a shadowy image of true peace at best, within the boundaries of human history.[29]

This ontology, transformed by Christology and eschatology, opened a new way for Augustine's re-evaluation of human morality. For Christians especially, the interim world was now a designated field of their moral life. The earthly life was no longer a battle between good and evil, Christians and pagans. Rather, he repeatedly referred to Christ's parable of the wheat and the chaff (Matt. 13:24-30; Lk. 3:17), to describe the essential character of the earthly life.

---

25. Augustine's reference to *pax ecclesiae* can be found as early as DVR. 6.11 (in 388). For *pax ecclesiastica*, cf. inch. exp. Rom. 5.13 and Q83. 75 (c. 394/395).

26. Cf. Kayama, "From *Ordo* to *Pax*," pp. 154-159.

27. See, for instance, serm. 25.4 & 7 and 53A.12 for peace as the right order and tranquillity of soul and body; serm. 53.16 for spiritual purification.

28. E.g., serm. 70.3. For *pax Christi*, see also inch. exp. Rom. 18.12, 23.12.

29. See serm. 168.2; cf. also epp. 55.6.10, 69.1, 118.3.13.

It was the "commingling" *(permixtum, commixtio)* of the good and the bad, of the saved and the damned, although the identification of who belonged to which group was a divine secret only to be disclosed at the eschaton.[30] Without knowing their final destination, therefore, Christians were to live like "pilgrims" in the world, were not allowed to escape from it, but were still expected to lead a morally good life based on Christ's commandments. Taking Luke 2:14, for instance, Christians were to pursue peace on earth which Christ gave to men of good will.[31] In other words, it was a "pilgrims' peace", which they were urged to use well, while always taking its imperfectibility and relativity into account.

In the pilgrimage of peacemaking, the church came to the fore as a school to instruct and mobilise its people, with Augustine as headmaster, to defend the "peace of the church". The church was a shadowy but true representation of the heavenly home for the earthly pilgrims. It was a providential institution by which the faithful were guided through the snares and conflicts of earthly life to the life of everlasting peace. It was the guardian of salvific peace with a special mission to disseminate the "gospel of peace" (Eph. 6:15) throughout the world, as the prophet had foretold in his blessing on the "herald of peace" (Is. 52:7).[32] For Augustine, therefore, it was all too obvious that the "peace of the church" belonged to the Catholic church now extending all over the world; its universality gave it legitimacy, compared to the partiality of the Donatist church confined to North Africa.[33]

Apart from his written works against the Donatists, Augustine also preached on the peace of the Catholic church with intense fervour. Like Optatus a few decades earlier, Augustine repeatedly preaches from Psalm 33:15 [34:14]: to "seek peace, and pursue it".[34] Another favourite passage was Christ's seventh beatitude in Matthew 5:9. Peacemaking *(pacare, pacificare)* was a moral mission blessed by Christ, which aimed to make peacemakers out of sinners. For instance, in a sermon (53A) preached at a later stage of the Donatist controversy, Augustine describes the act of peacemaking as starting from within — "pacify yourself" — and then promoting "the business of reconciliation" between troubled neighbours (ibid. 12). The Christian ethic of peacemaking aimed to teach believers to "love peace" *(amor pacis)*

---

30. Cf., e.g., ep. 43.21-22 on Matt. 13:24-30, and 23.6 on Lk. 3:17.

31. Cf. serm. 101.5, 11. Cf. also serm. 89.4 on Eph. 2:14.

32. For Eph. 6:15, cf. en. ps. 59.11; for Is. 52:7, serm. 113A.9. Cf. also Petil. 2.69.154; serm. 101.5, 11.

33. Cf., e.g., serm. 71:28; also Parm. 1.1.1, bapt. 1.1.2, epp. 93.9.29, 105.4.14-15.

34. Cf. serm. 16.1, 4, 5, serm. 25.7; also. en. ps. 34.18, 84.12, 98.7, 84.12, 143.9, 147.16.

was the recurrent theme of Augustine's ecclesiastical campaign against the Donatists.[35]

6. Preaching Peace

How did Augustine actually preach peace? In answering this question, three sermons (357, 358, 359) deserve special attention, all of which were delivered just before and after the *collatio,* the Conference of Carthage (the 1st, 3rd, and 8th of June 411), where the Catholics won a decisive victory over the Donatists.[36]

In the first two sermons, Augustine speaks openly on the "peace of the church". Sermon 357 was preached on the 17th of May, two weeks prior to the *collatio,* during the Pentecost Ember days. It is rather uncharacteristic of Augustine that he does not expound on biblical texts, but gives an overt exhortation of peace in order to set the tone of the whole homiletic series: Christ commands us to love peace, that is, to share it even with the haters of peace. Beginning with a praise of peace as "our beloved and our mistress" (1), Augustine emphasises that peace is not a material but a spiritual good which can be shared without fear of loss or causing jealousy; the more it is shared, the more it increases, like the Lord's bread which fed five thousand people (1-2). The congregation are hence encouraged to become peacemakers themselves: "[b]e at peace therefore, brothers and sisters, with each other", but "if you want to draw others [the Donatists] to peace, you must have it yourself" (3).

Reiterated here is the need to "cure" them.[37] The rhetoric is undoubtedly paternalistic, but Augustine tries carefully to avoid a high-handed call for assimilation, insisting that "those who love peace take pains to increase the possession by adding other possessors." The preacher encourages his congregation to accept their adversaries as brothers, when the controversy is settled once and for all (ibid.). The sermon culminates in an urgent call for tolerance, "to show them a Christian and Catholic meekness". The Donatists are to be received "very, very gently", just like abusive patients treated by "mild doctors" who would not "return abuse for abuse" (4). Citing Matthew 5:45 ('he makes the sun rise upon the good and the bad'), Augustine urges: "[p]ut up with it, I beg you, my brothers and sisters", especially "at this critical moment." In the

---

35. Cf. Bapt. 1.9.12, 3.1.1, 4.5.7-8, 7.10, 14.23, 22.39; also Petil. 2.78.174, epp. 43.23, 61.2, 76.2, 87.10, 88.5, 185.10.43.

36. For other sermons on peace during this period, cf. serm. 23, 25, 47, 81, 168.

37. Kolbet illustrates this point in terms of moral education (psychagogy) (*Augustine and the Cure of Souls,* p. 10).

repentant spirit of the Pentecost Ember season, Catholics must "give this kind of peaceable answer to one who doesn't love peace" with "persistent meekness" (ibid.). The exhortation of peace concludes with a prayer to Christ, "the Lord our God, our physician", for "our brothers [the Donatists], whose cure and restoration to health is our present concern" (5).

In just two days,[38] Augustine gave another sermon on "peace and charity" (serm. 358): referring to Psalm 120:7 ('though they hate peace, we are at peace'), he instructs his people not to cause any trouble that might be advantageous to the Donatists at this critical moment. Such a call for peace may be quite tactical, but the underlying message is plain: "peace and charity" are what the Lord commands and loves (1). Augustine insists that the adversary should be reconciled in Christ's peace, by sharing and possessing it together (2). Crucial to the success of such peace is "charity from a pure heart" (1 Tm. 1:5), which was apparently a favourite passage cited frequently by Augustine, since the whole congregation shouted out along with him (4). Christ's love creates a broad space in the heart: in this breadth of love, on the one hand, the Donatists are invited "to share in the possession of peace" (4), and on the other, the Catholics are urged to receive them "out of a love of peace" and "in a fraternal and peaceful manner" (5). In any case, disorder must be avoided, first and foremost because Christ is "the author of peace, the sower of peace, the lover of peace", commanding us to be the peacemakers whom He blessed in Matthew 5:9 (6).

Sermon 359 was delivered a few months after the *collatio.* While the tone of voice is a good deal more confident, Augustine now faces a new problem: how to receive the Donatists into his congregation. Preaching on Sirach 25:1 ('concord between brothers, and the love of neighbours, and a husband and wife in agreement with each other'), Augustine praises how admirable such a concord is, but also admits how rare and difficult it is to achieve (1). Still, the scriptures encourage us to seek the brotherly concord, because its reward is God Himself, the eternal inheritance which the Catholic church has always hoped to acquire with the Donatists (4). The *collatio* presented a great showcase for such Christian concord. All we wish, Augustine insists, is "to correct" them, taking each error *"not [as] a matter of litigating, but of loving,"* and "it is possible only in one church for the sake of peace, for brothers to be in concord with each other" (5, italics added). The Donatists deserve to be called "brothers", because, even if one may be a bad brother, still he is a brother (6). While

38. Or somewhat later between the 26th and 31st of May. See *The Works of Saint Augustine,* vol. 10, p. 194, n. 1.

there are many former Donatists already received in the church (7), those who still resist ferociously present "a test of charity" to the Catholics and "they too must be loved" (8). In the final section (9), Augustine turns back to Sirach 25:1, referring especially to the love of neighbours, and urges his congregation to treat even a vicious adversary as a neighbour, saying "you should love him, too, in order to gain him, too" (9).

In these sermons on peace, Augustine searched earnestly for a way to reconcile the two bitterly divided parties. Nevertheless, the preacher put himself in a precarious position when he legitimised the policy of "religious coercion" against the Donatists. Over the years of his involvement in the controversy, his remarks on the issue often appeared contradictory and ambiguous. Although his own admission of the "change of heart" was candid and casual, his support of the coercive policy was firm and thorough. To generations of scholars, Augustine's final justification of coercion has proved profoundly problematic, resulting in diverse interpretations.[39] Despite the ambiguities, a subtle coherence underlying his ostensible change of view on coercion can be discerned. It may not be a "doctrine", as Brown rightly points out, but it is more consistent and comprehensive than an "attitude" as he prefers to describe it.[40]

For Augustine, religious coercion was, in essence, not so much a political matter as an ecclesiastical issue. It was a matter of Christian leadership, a bishop asking his fellow Christians for due assistance as Christian magistrates endowed with legislative power acting as "secular shepherds". Two authorities were expected to complement each other as an integral part of overall pastoral care for stray sheep. In line with his exhortative sermons on peace, Augustine explained the role of Christian leadership in a twin sermon on Ezekiel 34 preached around 414 (serm. 46 and 47).[41]

In the first, extremely lengthy interpretation of Ezekiel 34:1-16 (serm. 46) Augustine expounds the theme of "the shepherds", stating that Christ is the one true shepherd who sets the standard of pastoral care, or "stewardship" *(dispensation)* as he calls it (2, 5). He urges his congregation to feed the sheep properly, not as bad shepherds who feed themselves instead (2, 7, 8); to strengthen a feeble sheep rather than killing it (10, 12); to put up with what is

39. Cf. particularly Brown, "St. Augustine's Attitude to Religious Coercion", *Journal of Religious Studies* 54 (1964): 107-116; idem, *Augustine*, pp. 207-239; and Markus, *Saeculum*, pp. 133-153.

40. Cf. Brown, "St. Augustine's Attitude to Religious Coercion", pp. 107-108.

41. The importance of these sermons is suggested in O'Donovan, *The Desire of the Nations: Rediscovering the Roots of Political Theology* (Cambridge: Cambridge University Press, 1996), p. 202.

bad (13); and to call back the stray sheep persistently (14). Most important, it is the spirit of "love" *(charitas)* that yields unity, whereas pride *(superbia)* leads to division (18, 30); therefore, Christ the true shepherd never deserts the scattered sheep even in the harshest weather (23). This is the role model of Christian ministry, although bad shepherds exist even among the Catholics, but far more apparently among the Donatists.[42] Towards the end of the sermon, Augustine accelerates his criticism, and finishes somewhat abruptly, saying "the Catholic emperors are quite right in forcing you into unity" (41).

In the second part (serm. 47), preached shortly afterwards,[43] Augustine covers the rest of Ezekiel 34 (17-31), while he changes the theme from "the shepherds" to "the sheep", blaming the Donatist ministers for neglecting their people. All through the sermon, his argument revolves around the topic of judgement, which is the key function of Christian leadership, ecclesiastical or secular. Augustine first declares that bishops too are sheep along with the congregation fed by the true shepherd: bishops are under Christ's judgement alongside their flock. He then points out that the true shepherd is waiting to judge (3), now "warning us and not yet judging" (5). Characteristically, Augustine depicts this world as the interim time of God's patience, where weeds are inevitably mixed with good seeds, tolerated until separation (6). The Lord is now speaking by way of admonition, so that weeds may be corrected (8, 12). This is how the true shepherd feeds, judging with patience and mercy, which human shepherds — apparently ecclesiastical but also secular by inference — are expected to imitate (6, 12). From his incessant call for patience, to restrain from rash judgement on their sheep, we sense the general dislike of the death penalty widely shared by the church in those days.[44] The twin sermon on the ideal Christian ministry culminates in his familiar invitation to the "peace" of the Catholic church, which Ezekiel prophesies in terms of the "testament of peace" (34:25 in serm. 47.22; also 47.13, 17) and of "the planting of peace" (34:29 in serm. 47.28).

Preaching peace in this way, Augustine sought to rebuild his community by enquiring after the moral quality of its members and urging them to accept former adversaries in the spirit of forgiveness, tolerance, and love. Of course, the same logic could easily justify the coercive assimilation of the Donatists. Nevertheless, as Brown points out in the epilogue of the 2000 edition of *Au-*

---

42. A hint of Catholic self-criticism pointed out in *The Works of Saint Augustine,* vol. 10, p. 293, n. 1.

43. For the dating, cf. *The Works of Saint Augustine,* vol. 10, p. 323, n. 1.

44. Pointed out by O'Donovan, *The Desire of the Nations,* p. 202. On Augustine's view of the death penalty, see also Brown, *Augustine,* p. 238.

gustine of Hippo, Augustine was more optimistic about the human condition in his sermons than in his writings.[45] At least in his bitter battle with the Donatists, Augustine tried hard to live up to his expectation and responsibility as a bishop (shepherd) taking care of the souls (sheep) that had been bitterly wounded in the prolonged controversy. For all his realistic understanding of the imperfectability of human morality, he still endeavoured to improve the moral foundation of his congregation as much as possible within earthly limitations.

7. Preaching as a Moral Pedagogy for Earthly Pilgrims

For Augustine, preaching was an inherently moral act. Delivering sermons to explicate and disseminate the Word of God for the salvation of the souls of his people, he sought simultaneously to communicate with his congregation about the objective of their earthly life as a moral life of pilgrimage in pursuit of happiness and peace in the spirit of Christian love within the limits of this world. Preaching peace, in short, Augustine engaged in what may be termed as "a moral pedagogy of peacemaking for earthly pilgrims".[46] It was a social *doctrina christiana,* an educational programme *(disciplina)* containing punishment *(correctio)* as a tool for restoring the broken *pax ecclesiae* in the spirit of Christian love. Crucial to the curriculum was the last instruction on love, since "love of peace" equipped with three moral principles *(reconciliation, forgiveness of sins,* and *tolerance)* was fundamental to the pilgrims' communal life in the interim world. Augustine's leadership and his acceptance of religious coercion were essentially ecclesiastical, rather than political, in nature. Still, his sermons during this period, together with his letters and other writings, certainly prepared the path to the mature political theology that was fully demonstrated in *De Civitate Dei.* Augustine's ecclesiastical theory of peace could be regarded justifiably as an embryonic "political theory".[47]

Ontological eudaemonism was the foundation of Augustine's preaching, particularly in respect to its moral orientation. Just as eternal happiness was reflected in temporal happiness no matter how perverted it might be, any human action or institution contained a degree of goodness that earthly pil-

---

45. Brown, *Augustine,* pp. 510-513.
46. Cf. Kayama, "From *Ordo* to *Pax,*" pp. 169-188.
47. Cf. Markus, *Saeculum,* p. 143.

grims were expected to seek in their pursuit of happiness and peace. The outcome was Augustine's persistent inquiry into the morality of earthly pilgrims, although he was all too aware of its downside to build a constructive ethic on what he discovered. If moral betterment meant to make this world as humane as possible, he was too pessimistic to believe in the possibility of humanising its fallen condition; yet he was too much a moralist to discard any possibility of minimizing its dehumanising factors.

The ontological nature of Augustine's moral theology was, in the end, a mixed blessing for him. On the one hand, it contributed to his sustained interest in the relative goodness of the earthly life amidst his eschatological insight into its fallen condition. On the other hand, it had a serious side-effect, as demonstrated in his endorsement of religious coercion. For the ontological ethic implied a rather simplistic analogy between two authorities, ecclesiastical and secular, as two hierarchically distinguished entities, the former with a higher and the latter with a lower moral value, overriding a more quintessentially biblical view that they just represented two distinct worlds or aeons.

In fact, when he asked the assistance of political authorities out of a sincere ministerial concern, Augustine could justify that it was just an ecclesiastical shepherd requesting secular shepherds to contribute to the *pax ecclesiae*. He could also intervene in some unfavourable political decisions (especially concerning death penalties), with little doubt about the legitimacy of his intercession as a bishop to curb any miscarriage of secular justice.[48] In the Donatist controversy, at least, Augustine failed to honour what he believed in otherwise, i.e., the biblical distinction between the two spheres of judgement — *civitas Dei* and *civitas terrena* — which was to be retrieved fully in his *opus magnum*.

According to Augustine, preaching communicates what theology finds, and the preacher should toil to cultivate the moral soil of his community through such communication. Preaching itself is not a political act in the modern sense of the word, but it can certainly nurture the moral sensibility of each member, showing a set of criteria for judgement concerning what is relatively good in this world and what action should be taken to prevent the worst from occurring. Preaching can be moral without falling prey to indoctrination, if we are to learn carefully from Augustine's failure in his endorsement of religious coercion.

---

48. Cf. Brown, *Augustine*, p. 238.

From Justification to Justice:
The Cranmerian Prayer Book Legacy

Joan O'Donovan

Political and moral theology at their best are faithful intellectual undertakings involving the widest and richest possible engagement of the inquiring mind with the scriptural text and with the exegetical and theological inheritance. They have the twofold purpose of glorifying God by drawing out in an orderly fashion the implications of His actions for our common and individual human actions, and also, thereby, of serving the political and moral reflection and deliberation of all His faithful people. The greater part of Oliver O'Donovan's theological contribution thus far should be appreciated against this sort of wide-ranging normative expectation.

There is, however, a type of theological undertaking which falls short of the best, but which is still vital to the ongoing witness of particular churches with historical traditions of thought and practice. This is the exercise of interpreting one's own church tradition to those within it and to those outside it. It is an apologetic and a critical exercise, frank about the theological weaknesses, as well the strengths, of one's tradition; attuned to its ecumenical as well as its distinctive aspects. This exercise is indispensable to a church's theological energy and discipline, both in its internal conversations, ministries, and practices, and in the engagements of its missionary outreach.

As a Church of England clergyman, Oliver O'Donovan has been deeply committed to this latter theological undertaking, producing many occasional and less well known pieces, such as his recently republished exposition of historic Anglican doctrine, *On the 39 Articles: A Conversation with Tudor Christianity.*[1]

---

1. London: SCM Press, 2011 [originally published Exeter: Paternoster Press, 1986].

My paper is also of this ecclesiastical genre, belonging to a larger project of interpreting the Reformation tradition of English church establishment to a generation in Britain and elsewhere which is largely out of touch and out of sympathy with it. Among the various elements of Tudor church establishment, the most determinative for the English church, after the printed Bibles, have been the Tudor editions of the prayer book. As many readers will be aware, the 1552 edition, with some key insertions from the earlier 1549 edition, comprised the bulk of the 1662 *Book of Common Prayer (BCP),* which has remained the only legally prescribed order of worship (prescribed by Parliamentary act) for the English national church on ordinary, festive, and state occasions. Thus, we may confidently assert that the 1662 *BCP* has contributed much of the spiritual foundation and guiding framework of an English ecclesial, moral, and political tradition.[2]

It is hardly surprising, then, that the steady attenuation of English church establishment marking recent decades has had an important liturgical component, alongside its other theological, social, and political components. The last fifty years of large-scale liturgical revision have resulted in, on the one hand, an ongoing proliferation of liturgies, and on the other, a trend toward simpler ecumenical forms that underplay certain controlling principles and emphases of the historic prayer books. The demise in parish churches of the traditional Sunday services of Matins and Evensong, together with a more Catholic handling of the weekly 'parish Eucharist', have, broadly speaking, entailed the liturgical abandonment of lengthy and coherent scripture readings and of preaching which attends seriously to the task of scriptural exposition. They have entailed a distancing from core Reformation themes, and as well, the sacrifice of liturgical solemnity and beauty for popular accessibility. Within the more self-consciously evangelical constituency, which sustains a focus on scripture reading and exposition, worship has consistently veered in a populist, youth-oriented, informal, and non-liturgical direction.

Running parallel with these liturgical trends in the Church of England has been a progressive weakening and dismantling of other aspects of historic church establishment: of the national scope and public prominence of the church's parochial and non-parochial ministries and of the interconnections of ecclesial and civil government. While English church-state relations are currently in some constitutional flux, it would appear that an increasingly pluralistic religious establishment is taking shape, involving Christian and

2. Exported through British colonial and missionary enterprises, the 1662 *BCP* has also supplied the historical foundations of liturgical development in most Anglican churches in the world today.

non-Christian communities, which the civil authorities are tending to manage more aggressively than previously, through multilateral co-operative arrangements or 'partnerships'.[3]

It is noteworthy that some significant members and representatives of the religious constituencies concerned have not been persuaded that their spiritual and practical interests will be best served by trading the constitutional umbrella and distinctive public presence of traditional church establishment for a government-orchestrated pluralism of individual and communal religious rights. Their preference has been for a continuing church establishment that gives public representation to minority religious voices, while increasingly sharing public space with them, so tempering claims of civil equality with those of historical identity and tradition.[4]

Such 'conservatives' have good reason to mistrust the ethos of the emerging establishment as being excessively managerial, legalistic, and juridical. They may justifiably fear the prospect of religious groups and their members conducting themselves as centres of competitive demand for public resources (symbolic and material), enmeshed in externally regulated relationships with one another, in which each is continually guarding its own and inspecting another's claims and another's compliance with the rules, always vigilant that government adjudication of religious rights is sufficiently uniform and egalitarian.[5]

This legalistic, juridical, and managerial ethos is one of which we have all had experience, as it continues to invade every social and institutional sphere across our advanced liberal-democratic societies, despite widespread popular complaint, the fulminations of media gurus, and the legislative tinkering of politicians. An oppressive surveillance of rights provision and protection,

3. Alongside the continuing bilateral relations between the government and the Church of England, in which the latter effectively acts as a gateway for other Christian denominations to utilise public resources in developing and maintaining public ministries, the Home Office in 2003 launched an ambitious programme of multilateral cooperative relations between government and 'faith communities' in which the Church of England is merely one among equals. See *Working Together: Cooperation between Government and Faith Communities* (London: Home Office Communities Unit, 2004).

4. For views along these lines from the Jewish, Muslim, Hindu, and Sikh communities, see, e.g., the essays of Bhikhu Parekh, Rabbi Sylvia Rothchild, Ramindar Singh, Daoud Rosser-Owen, and Tariq Modood's introductory essay, in Tariq Modood, ed., *Church, State and Religious Minorities* (London: Policy Studies Institute, 1997).

5. This competitive scenario is subjected to telling criticism in Luke Bretherton, 'A New Establishment? Theological Politics and the Emerging Shape of Church-State Relations,' *Political Theology* 7, no. 3 (2006): 371-392.

combined with the pervasive threat of litigation, continues to inflate the public and private regulation of social institutions, organisations, and agencies, depriving many labourers in diverse fields of work, care, and professional endeavour of their proper freedom of judgement, and the exercise of their skills and wisdom as experienced practitioners.

From a Reformation theological perspective, our struggle with this sustained assault on human freedom will be futile unless we understand it as the contemporary form of sinful human striving after justification by works of the law, and, concomitantly, as both cause and symptom of our diminished participation in the real spiritual and material goods of human community. It is important, therefore, for the Church of England's ministry and engagement, that she retrieve from the Tudor prayer book legacy an understanding of human moral agency, action, and community as primarily evangelical, conformed to the church's practice of worship, and only peripherally as juridical, conformed to the practice of secular jurisdiction. This is my present task.

The Dialectic of Proclamation and Jurisdiction

Broadly speaking, the Tudor prayer books communicate a theological vision of moral community common to the mainstream of English and continental magisterial reformers. The vision, therefore, comprises the shaping context of the prayer books, as well as their tradition-shaping substance. It presents the moral life of persons-in-society as controlled by two universal authorities and practices: on the one hand, the authority of God's saving word of judgement given in Jesus Christ which is directly constitutive of the church's practice of proclamation; on the other, the authority of the human community's binding public judgement operating under God's word of judgement and mercy. These two authorities and practices determine human moral agency and action in its twofold eschatological and historical reality: as restored through Christ's conquest of sin and death on the Cross and awaiting fulfilment; and as struggling under the wages of sin and subject to the law's condemnation. While the vision projects a theoretical and institutional separation of these different, even antithetical, communal practices, it also projects their interdependence in this eschatological age in which the old Adam is being overtaken by the new.

For the English reformers, as for their continental mentors, it is in the church's practice of proclamation that human moral agency and action is renewed and human goods decisively appropriated, where God's judgements are heard and received by the community. The reformers conceive renewed moral agency and action as human judgement about good and evil conforming to God's revealed judgements, and coming to fruition in human action. The first and determinative human judgement, which forms the ground and possibility of all others, is the individual and communal judgement of faith, in which sinful human beings accept the Father's judgement of condemnation and reconciliation directed towards themselves in the death and resurrection of His Son. The Father's judgement of condemnation and reconciliation is, at one and the same time, His condemnation of the history of sinful human judgement and action, put to death with Christ on the Cross; His vindication of faithful human judgement and action, raised from the dead and exalted with the resurrected and ascended Christ; and His promise of the fulfilment of all that He has vindicated, in the consummation of Christ's kingdom. The individual and communal act of faith is, then, a complex act of repentance for past sin, trust in Christ's accomplished work of reconciliation, and hope for a wholly renewed common life in Christ.

The Tudor reformers emphatically present the act of faith as originating not within sinful human subjectivity, but within the divine subjectivity of the Holy Spirit, who, as the spirit of the risen and ascended Christ, incorporates believers into His resurrection life and makes available to them the spiritual benefits of their redemption. As the Spirit communicates Christ's benefits in a pre-eminent way in the practice of worship, of word and sacrament, so it is within this regular communal practice that faith is generated, nourished, strengthened, and purified. In regarding worship as the central communicative act of their faith, the Tudor reformers also regard it as the first practical obedience of faith, paradigmatic for all obedience.[6]

Their conviction that the renewal of human moral freedom springs from the church's practices of Gospel proclamation rather than from juridical practices is, then, the moral correlate of their soteriological conviction that sinful human beings are justified solely by God's grace in Christ and not by their works. As judgement over the faithful belongs exclusively to God in Christ who is both judge and judged, so the primary response of the faithful to God's judgement in Christ is one of evangelical proclamation — of joyful, thankful, humble, and adoring worship — rather than one of public judgement, whether in the civil or ecclesiastical realms. In one theological move, the reformers

6. My choice of terms here expresses my debt to Bernd Wannenwetsch's rich exploration of the church's common worship as the grammar of the Christian life and the first instance of her corporate obedience to God's rule, in *Gottesdienst als Lebensform — Ethik für Christenbürger* (Stuttgart: Verlag W. Kohlhammer, 1997); ET *Political Worship: Ethics for Christian Citizens*, trans. Margaret Kohl (Oxford: Oxford University Press, 2004).

repudiated the medieval Roman conception of the church as a priestly hierarchy of proclamation wedded to jurisdiction, and the mediaeval discipline of sacramental penance in which priests, besides 'retaining or remitting' the guilt of sins, judged confessing sinners as to their degrees of sin and guilt, and assigned earthly punishments (penances).[7]

Correspondingly, the mainstream of English Reformers, following Luther, reinterpreted the apostolic authority of the ordained ministry as essentially proclamatory and non-jurisdictional: as authority to preach and teach God's word, to intercede on behalf of the gathered church, to give pastoral counsel, exhortation, and consolation to those within their care; and they reinforced this interpretation by assigning jurisdiction over external church polity to the lay magistrate and his ecclesiastical representatives. The predominant Anglican view was that episcopal jurisdiction in the church's external polity derived from the royal 'plenitude', lacking an independent Christological basis; so that when the bishops issued binding public judgements in whatever ecclesiastical sphere, they did so as the monarch's ministers.[8]

*   *   *

Let us now explore how the Cranmerian prayer books display the paradigmatic role of public worship in determining moral agency and action as evangelical proclamation, beginning with a brief word on their content and on Thomas Cranmer's contribution to their production.[9]

7. The medieval bishop's exercise of the church's 'power of the keys' retained the intimate relationship between judgement in 'the sphere of conscience' and in the church's external polity, despite such opposing tendencies toward their separation as the growth of private penance and of papal jurisdictional supremacy. Medieval penitential theology, and especially the theory of papal indulgences, continued to place human juridical acts at the core of the church's mediation of salvation in Christ.

8. This reforming view was subscribed to by such Henrician, Edwardine, and Elizabethan luminaries as William Tyndale, Christopher St. German, Thomas Cromwell, Richard Sampson, Edward Fox, Thomas Starkey, William Marshall, John Rogers, Hugh Latimer, Nicholas Ridley, John Ponet, John Jewel, and John Whitgift. Within reforming circles, it was only seriously challenged by the rise of Calvinist ecclesiology in the 1570s. Thomas Cranmer's attempt in 1540 to reconcile this position with the New Testament record of the apostolic church accepts the Eusebian view that God's plans for the governance of His church reached fruition only with the advent of Christian empire (John Edmund Cox, ed., *Miscellaneous Writings and Letters of Thomas Cranmer,* Parker Society [Cambridge: Cambridge University Press, 1846], pp. 116-117).

9. Thomas Cranmer (1489-1556) served as Archbishop of Canterbury for twenty years, under King Henry VIII and King Edward VI in his minority. Although he completed much of the groundwork of liturgical reform during Henry's reign, the king's theological and ecclesial

The original and revised books of 1549 and 1552 contain all the orders of English services, including the daily offices of morning and evening prayer, the Litany, the ministration of Holy Communion, public and private baptism, confirmation, the solemnization of matrimony, visitation and communion of the sick, and burial of the dead — the ordination and consecration of deacons, priests and bishops occupying a separate book until the 1552 revision. These new orders were variously related to their mediaeval English predecessors, some more closely, some more remotely. Minimally, their production involved translation, shortening, and simplification of the old Latin liturgies, to increase clerical and lay understanding and enable greater lay participation. Frequently it involved more radical overhauling of their structure and content, as in the reduction of the daily monastic and clerical offices or hours from eight to two (morning and evening). Always, it involved theological reorientation to central Reformation themes. Theological reorientation, along with structural modifications, were more pronounced in the 1552 edition[10] which was adopted by the Elizabethan church with a few significant revisions.

While the production of both prayer books, naturally, involved the collaboration and scrutiny of episcopal committees, their chief architect, translator, adaptor, editor, and composer was Archbishop Cranmer. His contribution extended beyond the liturgical texts *per se* to the design of calendars for Bible readings, psalms, and collects (appointed prayers). Scholarship has shown that his inspiration and sources were far-ranging, temporally and geographically, from patristic writings to a host of more contemporary Catholic, Lutheran, and Reformed liturgies, manuals, books of private devotions, and catechisms.[11]

---

traditionalism prevented Cranmer's labours from bearing much public fruit, apart from the related project (pursued jointly with Thomas Cromwell) of providing an official vernacular Bible. The accession of the reform-minded minor, Edward VI, in 1547 enabled Cranmer to make his lasting liturgical and theological contributions to the English church, in the production of two *Books of Common Prayer* (1549 and 1552), and the publication of the Forty-Two Articles (1553).

10. E.g. the Communion saw radical structural revision, with the dismantling of the traditional sequence of prayers comprising the 'Canon' of the Mass, retained in 1549. The removal and dispersion of prayers was primarily intended to eliminate any lingering suggestion of: (1) the Eucharistic celebration as a repetition of Christ's offering, and a meritorious work performed by the priest for the church; and (2) the doctrines of transubstantiation of the host, or even of Christ's corporeal presence in the received elements.

11. For contemporary discussions of, and researches into, the 1549 and 1552 *Books of Common Prayer*, see John E. Booty, *The Book of Common Prayer 1559: The Elizabethan Prayer Book*, The Folger Shakespeare Library (Charlottesville: University Press of Virginia, 1976);

Common Worship as Paradigmatic for Moral Agency and Action

Let us now look more closely at how the English liturgies disclose renewed moral agency and action as a structured response to, and communication of, God's word of judgement in Jesus Christ, which is His word in its trinitarian fullness. This is a fourfold disclosure: of its divine-human basis and form, its common and communicative character, its outer rule and its inner rule.

(1) The Christological Basis and Form

All the regular services of the Tudor church point to Christ's accomplished work of righteousness on the Cross as the divine-human basis of God's salvation of sinners and the primary object of faith, from which flow 'good works'. However, the service of Holy Communion focuses on Christ's passion and death as the sole ground of the world's redemption, the pivotal representative act of God's incarnate Son that accomplishes the reconciliation to the Father of humankind and the world. In the theologically lavish language of the Eucharistic prayer of institution (consecration): Jesus Christ 'made there (by his one oblation of himself once offered) a full, perfect, and sufficient sacrifice, oblation, and satisfaction, for the sins of the whole world'.[12] The divine-human sufficiency of Christ's sacrifice, here affirmed, comprehends the death of humanity to sinful corruption, and its resurrection to restored and perfected life. The intrinsic perfection of the Son of Man's oblation and the Father's merciful acceptance of it are two inseparable moments of one act: God's judgement against the disordering forces of fallen humanity and His judgement for the luminous integrity of faithful human being. Even Christ's ascension into glory and empowerment of His resurrection community with the Spirit of truth and holiness are the further unfolding of His climactic representative triumph on the Cross.

The whole sequence of pre- and post-communion prayers points to Christ's unrepeatable suffering and death as the sole merit on which the Father's forgiveness of sinners is grounded, and to faith in the merit of Christ's passion as the sole form in which sinners lay hold of the Father's forgiveness.

Geoffrey Cuming, *The Godly Order: Text and Studies Relating to the Book of Common Prayer* (London: Alcuin Club, 1983), and *A History of Anglican Liturgy,* 2nd ed. (London: Macmillan, 1982).

12. Booty, ed., *The Book of Common Prayer 1559,* p. 263. Unless otherwise indicated, all prayer book quotations are from this edition.

Both the pre-communion penitential prayers and exhortations and the post-communion prayers of congregational thanksgiving and oblation preclude any contribution of sinful human beings to their justification: they preclude any moment or process in which sinful human beings are made acceptable to God through a dialectic of divine grace (infused or acquired) and human moral effort, of the sinner obtaining merit (condign or congruent) and of God rewarding it. It is entirely the Father's abundant mercy and Christ's righteousness, received by faith, which bring sinners into God's presence, and remove from them the imputation of sin.

Significantly, the penitent faithful offer up to the Father 'our praise and thanksgiving', along with 'ourselves, our souls and bodies', to be 'a reasonable, holy, and lively sacrifice'[13] only after we have been spiritually united with Christ by spiritually partaking of His flesh and blood.[14] Likewise, it is only after we have received sacramental assurance of the Father's 'favour and goodness toward us', and of our being 'members incorporate' of Christ's 'mystical body' and 'heirs through hope' of His 'everlasting kingdom',[15] that we beseech the Father so to 'assist us with thy grace' to 'do all such good works as thou has prepared for us to walk in'.[16] We are bold to offer up ourselves to God and to ask for His grace to act well because the faith freely imparted to us, uniting us to our crucified, risen, and ascended Saviour, is lively and fruitful, issuing in works of love. The same triune God who inspires our trust in Christ's justifying work on the Cross discloses to us His will for our lives, and inclines our desire to active obedience. The post-communion prayers express the sure expectation that the faithful will, and do even now, participate in the community of renewed moral agency and action that is the spiritual body of their risen and ascended Saviour.

The Eucharistic liturgy displays the church, then, as a twofold fellowship: a fellowship of faith in *our* justification by Christ's sinless oblation on the Cross that overcomes the law's death-dealing condemnation by fulfiling its life-giving justice; and a fellowship, by our common faith, in a host of spiritual and practical blessings inhering in Christ's victory over the anti-human tyranny of sin and death. The corporate Communion of the faithful in the sacrament of Christ's body and blood invokes the Holy Spirit's corporate communication of the sanctifying fruits of faith, which are the forms of our earthly participa-

13. *BCP*, p. 264.
14. *BCP*, p. 264.
15. *BCP*, p. 265.
16. *BCP*, p. 265.

tion in Christ's spiritual promises. These are the inclinations and practices of reverent fear and adoring love of God, and humble gratitude and obedience towards Him, of self-forgetful and self-denying love of our neighbours, and of resistance to the temptations of the corrupt 'flesh'.

(2) The Common Moral Agency of the Worshipping Church

All the liturgies of the 1552/59 prayer books convey the pivotal ethical insight that the Holy Spirit's gift of renewed moral agency is not to the individual but to the community of persons. From 1552 onwards, the voice of the worshippers is decisively the collective 'we' rather than the singular 'I', conveying the expectation that perfected moral agency in the Kingdom of God will be wholly common, communicative, and consensual: that it will be mutual participation in the Spirit's judgements, mutual sharing in the knowledge, love, and freedom of Christ. It is this full manifestation of reconciled community that the church's practice of worship proclaims in word and deed, in preaching and sacraments. But the liturgies do not identify the gathered faithful in this age of waiting with any institutional church, or with the entirety of earthly institutional churches; nor do they affirm that institutional practices of worship are, in and of themselves, the pure moral action of reconciled community. Rather, they affirm that human moral renewal is divinely given where the word of God is purely preached and the sacraments administered according to Christ's commandments.

The English liturgies display the subject of every obedient act of worship as the whole company of Christ's faithful people, to which every worshipping individual and congregation is joined in a spiritual communion of faith, hope, and love. Despite their explicit tendency to identify the church universal with 'the church militant' on earth, out of reticence about communion of the living with the dead in Christ,[17] they nevertheless offer indications that the worshipping subject extends across time as well as space. These reside primarily in the historical catholicity of the liturgical material: in the inclusion of ancient confessions of faith, and of forms and prayers drawn from a wide spectrum of ancient and contemporary sources, Eastern and Western.[18]

17. Notably, the prayer for 'the whole state of Christ's church' in the 1549 Communion service becomes the prayer for 'the whole state of Christ's church militant here in earth' in the 1552 service, and no longer incorporates thanksgiving for the lives of the saints and petitions for the faithful departed (*The First and Second Prayer Books of Edward VI*, Everyman's Library, intro. Douglas Harrison [London: Dent, 1910], pp. 221-222, 382).

18. Cranmer was not only ecumenical in his contemporary liturgical borrowings but

The priority of the communal moral subject is also expressed in the public rite of infant baptism, which begins by presenting the incorporation of the candidate into the community of Christ's resurrection promises as God's response to the obedient prayers and confessions of the whole gathered church present in the local congregation and in the god-parents;[19] and proceeds to present the pledges of openness to Christ's promises made for the candidate by the godparents as the candidate's *own* pledges, which he/she must come to acknowledge as such with maturity of will and understanding.[20] The doubly representative action of the godparents, in which both the assembled church and the infant candidate participate, is not merely legal, political, or social, but spiritual: a communicating action of Christ's Spirit.

(3) The Conformity of Common Worship to the Outer Rule of Scripture

The obedient proclamation of worship, displayed by the English liturgies, conforms to the outer rule of Scripture as the authoritative revelation of God's word of salvation in Jesus Christ, comprehending all God's judgements and actions towards His creatures. As the foremost act of the faithful subject, obedient worship re-presents the apostolic *recollection* of the saving history of Jesus Christ, which is the original and foundational human *hearing* and *speaking* of God's saving word, upon which all subsequent hearing and speaking depend. This is the hearing and speaking of those privileged disciples of Christ who heard and saw their master in the flesh, and were uniquely commissioned and empowered (in-spirited) to testify of Him. As the writings in the New Testament canon have transmitted their authentic and authoritative testimony to later generations of the church, the liturgical reading of these writings occupies the primary place in worship.

At the same time, the faithful are united with the whole history of God's

---

frequently retained more of the tradition than even Lutheran colleagues. For example, he preserved more of the traditional canticles (regularly chanted Scriptural texts), versicles, and responses in Morning and Evening Prayer, and over seventy of the church's ancient and medieval collects (set prayers), in translated and adapted forms, for which he was largely responsible.

19. The minister's opening bidding addressed to the whole congregation, and his subsequent address to the god-parents before they make promises for the candidate (*BCP,* pp. 270, 272-273).

20. The minister's concluding exhortation to the godparents: 'Forasmuch as these children have promised by you to forsake the devil and all his works etc.' (*BCP,* p. 276).

incarnate Word of judgement and promise to sinful humanity only as the apostolic recollection reveals this Word to be the fulfilment of the transcending hope embodied in the history of Israel: hope for a wholly efficacious priestly sacrifice and intercession for the sins of God's elect; hope for an irreversible, messianic deliverance of God's people from the alien tyranny of impiety, injustice, and deception thwarting their common pursuit of holiness; hope for a prophetic promulgation of the Mosaic law that will elicit perfect obedience by its sanctifying power. Moreover, in revealing the universal and cosmic dimensions of Christ's saving work, the apostolic recollection also fully reveals the representative status of Israel's communal history, as encompassing the history not only of the whole human community, but of the ordered totality of created beings.

The Tudor liturgies recognise the rule of Scripture as a canonical totality by taking much of their speech directly from its different parts (in translation), and by giving a central place to sequential reading of the books in their canonical order. The services of Morning and Evening Prayer, intended by Cranmer to be daily offices for laity as well as clergy, rehearse the words of Scripture in said or sung psalms, canticles, the Lord's Prayer, and other prayers, and at the same time, include lengthy, sequential readings from both Testaments. To ensure that the bulk of the Bible would be read, Cranmer rearranged the lectionary according to the civil calendar rather than the liturgical year, so that the Old Testament would be largely covered in the course of one year, the New Testament (excepting the Apocalypse) every four months, and the Psalter every month.[21]

In addition, Cranmer and his Anglican successors asserted unequivocally the priority of Scripture-reading to preaching in public worship, defending it against increasingly virulent Presbyterian and Separatist objections. They insisted that human proclamation had to wait on the promise of God's self-revelation through His chosen voices: the act of congregational listening had to precede that of clerical interpretation.[22]

---

21. In his *Preface* to the 1549 prayer book (reprinted in 1552 and 1559), Cranmer laid down the purpose of the church's 'Common Prayers' or 'Divine Service' to be the ordered (sequential) reading of Holy Scripture, without interruption, repetition, or unnecessary embellishment (*BCP*, pp. 14-15). Accordingly, he removed from the services of Morning and Evening Prayer, as from the first part of the Communion service, many of the non-Biblical elements interleaved with the Biblical ones in the earlier liturgies.

22. Later Elizabethan divines such as John Whitgift and Richard Hooker were forcefully articulating the Cranmerian view when they construed the disciplined reading of the whole Scripture in the church's worship as the first part of her chief corporate duty of preaching: e.g. Hooker, *Of the Laws of Ecclesiastical Polity,* Bk. 5, ch. 19.1.

For Cranmer, the canonical order of Scripture rendered it a progressive revelation not only of God's saving purposes, but also of the ontological grounding, the character and the elements of human good works. In Morning Prayer, he gave liturgical recognition to the inception of Scriptural revelation with the divinely-created totality of finite beings and goods in their ordered relationships. Its Canticles pay striking attention to God's revelation of His majesty and glory, goodness and mercy in bringing forth and sustaining the ordered totality of creatures (e.g., *Te Deum laudamus, Benedicite omnia opera Domini Domino* [Song of the Three Young Men, vv. 35-68], *Jubilate Deo* [Ps. 100]). Correspondingly, the congregational praise and thanksgiving address all aspects of God's self-revelation in creating, redeeming, and sanctifying humankind and the world, conforming to the full scope of God's being and work revealed in the sequence of biblical psalms and lessons (readings).

Nevertheless, Cranmer followed his continental mentors in giving liturgical priority to God's explicit commandments as disclosing the moral implications of all His recorded judgements and actions. Moreover, the regular prayers of the church display Christ's commandments as the hermeneutical key to the totality of divine commandments, and so, to the Bible as the external rule of Christian morality. For Cranmer and his liturgical circle, Christ's commandments, interpreted within the whole of His ministry, are the authoritative disclosure of God's law given with the creation, the sure revelation of perfect human conformity, inward and outward, to His eternal will. They do not supersede, but fulfil and interpret, God's previous revelations to Israel of the order of created beings and ends, the shared goods and structures of human community, the right relations of human beings to God, to one another, and to the non-human creation.[23]

Cranmer's evangelical commandment ethic is reflected in the structure of the 1552 Eucharistic liturgy, which opens with the Lord's Prayer and a rehearsal of the Decalogue. The company of the faithful is gathered by the public proclamation of its common rule and by a petition for its true, spiritual keeping. But such keeping of God's law is only open to those who penitently confess their past failings, ask God's forgiveness, and deliverance from their 'manifold sins and wickedness', and partake of the memorial of Christ's death, as He commanded. Thus, the communion service begins and ends on the same note: the eschato-

23. This view controls Cranmer's 'Homily Of Good Works Annexed Unto Faith' published in the official 1547 collection of Edward VI for regular use in church pulpits. Here his summary of the law of Christ displays a traditional dependence on Christ's critical exchanges with the Pharisees and on his exhortations to perfection in the Sermons on the Mount and on the Plain. Cox, ed., *Miscellaneous Writings and Letters*, pp. 148-149.

logical existence of justified sinners, directed, sanctified, and governed by the triune God 'in the ways of thy laws, and in the works of thy commandments'.[24]

(4) The Conformity of Common Worship to the Inner Rule of the Holy Spirit

The regular services of 1552/59 display in their structure and their prayers the correspondence between the external determination of renewed moral agency and action by the rule of the Father in Jesus Christ, revealed in the Scriptures and the inner determination by the promised rule of the divine Spirit, through whose acts the faithful participate in the freedom and lordship of their risen and ascended Saviour. This is freedom not only from the law's condemnation of past sins, but from the oppressiveness of the law's present demands, encountered as external and alien constraints on the subject's willing and acting. The promised rule of the Holy Spirit (also referred to as God's 'heavenly' and 'special' grace) communicates to the faithful the lordship over the law of Christ's perfect obedience to His Father's will, in which true human knowledge is wedded to proportionate and appropriate desires and affections.

As the ordinary and seasonal collects (set prayers) eloquently express, the Holy Spirit will make Christ's lordship present to the faithful, moment by moment, by particular operations, illumining their judgements, strengthening their resolution, generating appropriate desires and affections, bringing about effectual action in that unique succession of moral situations comprising their individual and communal histories. So the collect for Easter Day beseeches: 'Almighty God, which through thy only begotten Son Jesus Christ hast overcome death, and opened unto us the gate of everlasting life, we humbly beseech thee, that as by thy special grace preventing us, thou dost put in our minds good desires, so by thy continual help, we may bring the same to good effect; through Jesus Christ our Lord, who liveth and reigneth with thee and the Holy Ghost, ever one God, world without end.'[25]

---

24. *BCP*, p. 266. While recognising the generic meaning of 'the law' as 'the ministration of death', Cranmer's Christocentric commandment ethic, like that of William Tyndale, recognises the indispensable role of the law within the gospel's 'ministration of life'. For both theologians, the law is 'the pathway' of the faithful to Christ's eternal kingdom, intrinsic to the inward and outward, individual and communal, obedience issuing from faith in the crucified, risen, and ascended Christ. Their conception has obvious affinities to, while remaining distinct from, Melanchthon's and Calvin's explications of the law's pedagogical use.

25. *BCP*, pp. 152-153: Cranmer's translation and adaptation of the Latin collect from the

In the promised renewal of the moral subject, there is no disjunction between knowing and willing, reason and desire, the will and the affections, the different virtues; neither is there conflict between the moral judgements of individuals, or between individual and communal judgements; for the Spirit's gift of the freedom and love of Christ is the unifying thread of the individual as of the common moral life, 'the very bond of peace and all virtues'.[26]

The Christocentric and pneumatological ethic of the English liturgies takes seriously the petition of our Saviour's prayer: 'Thy kingdom come. Thy will be done in earth as it is in heaven.' For it sets forth as a present hope a communion of persons whose equality resides in their liberty and their liberty in their single obedience to God's will. The double rule of the Christian moral life requires recognition of the equal standing of believers as recipients of Christ's promises: it is as fellow sharers, even now, in the external rule of God's revealed word and in the internal rule of Christ's Spirit of freedom and love that the faithful are, individually, empowered and obliged to proclaim God's judgements to one another through preaching, teaching, interceding, exhorting, consoling, and counselling, exercising moral judgement on their neighbour's behalf as well as for themselves. In all these acts the faithful stand alongside one another as equal beneficiaries of God's merciful and saving judgements; they do not stand above their fellows, exercising condemnatory judgement on them.[27] They also stand alongside those who have not yet heard or received God's saving judgement in Christ, whom they are commissioned, as servants of the Spirit's work, to gather into the community of proclamation.

Public Worship and Public Judgement

In displaying the eschatological determination of human moral agency and action by God's word of judgement given in Jesus Christ, Tudor public worship is not silent about the secular determination of moral community by the practices of public judgement. On the contrary, it both defines and empowers the

---

Sarum Processionale. M. R. Dudley, ed., *The Collect in Anglican Liturgy: Texts and Sources 1549-1989* (Collegeville, MN: The Liturgical Press, 1994), p. 73.

26. From Cranmer's own composition for Quinquagesima, 1549, echoing Eph. 4:3 and Col. 3:14 (*BCP,* p. 106; Dudley, p. 65).

27. The firm foothold of the English liturgical ethic in Christ's resurrection promises is an antidote to all attempts to interpret God's prior revelations of moral community in rationalistic, self-contained systems (whether of principles, ends, virtues, or practices) cut off from their eschatological *telos.*

secular practices of governing and being governed. The church's central liturgical act of such defining and empowering is the ordered reading of the Scriptures, which provide the ultimate measure, not only of true proclamation, but of just public judgement in church and commonwealth, no human judgement having validity that is repugnant to God's revealed judgements.

For Cranmer, as for the mainstream of English reforming divines, the authority, purposes, and limitations of public judgement, as well as the principles of communal right, justice, and obligation, have been definitively revealed to God's chosen people: to the 'Old Israel' by God's appointed giver and interpreters of His law, and to the 'New Israel' by the example, commands, and judgements of Christ and His apostles.[28] But while they looked to the Israelite polity of the Old Testament, especially the united monarchy, for the authoritative model of the supreme governor's unitary jurisdiction over both the clerical and lay estates of the commonweal, they did not accept the unity of proclamation and judgement that it represented.

Rather they construed the ruler's practice of public judgement, whether in ecclesiastical or civil polity, as operating at the boundary of proclamatory community, at the site where moral judgement and action have broken down, or are breaking down and giving way to disordered judgements, passions, and affections. Thus, the prayer for the 'church militant' in the communion service characteristically beseeches God that all the king's ministers and all 'put in authority under him . . . may truly and indifferently minister justice, to the punishment of wickedness and vice, and the maintenance of God's true religion and virtue.'[29] Similarly, Cranmer's official sermon of 1549 against rebellion portrays the 'godly order' of the commonweal as requiring that 'kings and governors' be the 'common revengers, correctors and reformers of all common and private things that be amiss', executing 'the right judgment of God's wrath against sin.'[30]

Cranmer's sermon displays a typical understanding of coercive public judgement as an incomplete or deficient representation of God's judgement,

28. Late scholastic and renaissance theories of natural law (right, justice) which gave epistemological priority to unassisted reason over Biblical revelation, were not much in evidence among Cranmer's clerical reforming colleagues, despite their penetration of humanist and legal circles.

29. *BCP*, p. 382.

30. 'A Sermon Concerning the Time of Rebellion', in Cox, ed., *Miscellaneous Writings and Letters*, p. 193. Delivered at St. Paul's Cathedral in the wake of the western and eastern rebellions of 1549, and intended for general publication, Cranmer's sermon was a collaborative effort with the Italian émigré Peter Martyr (Pietro Martire Vermigli).

deficient in that it represents only God's condemnation of sin and merciful preservation of sinful human community against its ravages, but not His saving judgement toward His creatures. It cannot re-present the judgement of Christ's suffering and triumphant love that justifies and regenerates the contrite sinner. Although it may furnish the context and even the external form of 'correction', it does not accomplish the inward reconciliation and communion of formerly antagonistic wills, promised to those who participate through faith in Christ's resurrection life.[31]

Nevertheless, despite the manifold deficiencies of public judgements, which the English reformers discuss at some length,[32] the English liturgies show them as *serving* the church's proclamation of God's judgements in their Trinitarian fullness. In the sphere of church polity (including liturgical practice), they are seen chiefly to curb the more subtle spiritual vices of moral and intellectual pride, which cause believers, without sufficient Biblical warrant, to pit their own judgements against common judgement, disrupting the seemly order of common practice and breaking the bond of communal peace.[33] While the requirement of conformity or uniform practice is impotent, of itself, to bring about conversion of the subject's heart and growth in virtue, it may, by compelling individual conceit to defer to outward unity and concord, be an extraneous instrument of the Spirit's proper action. So subjects pray for the blessing of being 'godly and quietly governed' (again, the prayer for the church militant). Only however, by the Spirit's guidance may they come to obey gladly a common policy with which they do not agree, for the sake of sustaining communal peace and good order.

---

31. Running through Cranmer's 1549 sermon against rebellion is an implicit contrast between the prophetic judgement on sin spoken by the preacher and the political judgement on crime enacted by the ruler, as diverging representations of divine wrath. Whereas the former proclamation never separates God's wrath against sin from His saving purposes in Christ, and so is a direct instrument of the Spirit's work of repentance, faith, and regeneration, the latter necessarily does, being at most, a remote instrument of the Spirit's saving work. Cranmer's sermon itself is a sustained prophetic condemnation of the vice on both sides of the conflict and call to repentance, and at the same time, an unambiguous statement of the remit of political authority (*Miscellaneous Writings and Letters*, pp. 190-202).

32. A seminal text for this discussion was Thomas Starkey's *Exhortation to Unity and Obedience* (London, c. 1540), which is modestly indebted to Thomas Aquinas's discussion of human law in *ST* 1a2ae.95.2.

33. Cranmer's essay 'Of Ceremonies, Why Some Be Abolished and Others Retained', incorporated in the Tudor prayer books, *BCP*, p. 18.

Conclusion

To recapitulate, my intention has been to show the Cranmerian *Books of Common Prayer* to be the core theological articulation of an English reformation ethical and political legacy that continues to deserve our attention. In the midst of the legalistic and juridical ethos of contemporary liberal society, interpenetrated as it is with the technological project of mastering human and non-human nature, we stand in fresh need of the English reformers' insight into the diverse ways in which the constitutive practices of church and civil government, those of evangelical proclamation and coercive judgement, determine human moral agency and action. Especially we need to be reminded that only the eschatological renewal of human moral agency and action through the church's practice of proclamation, centred in her common worship, can overcome the tyranny of the law in all its social and psychological manifestations; because this renewal is our incorporation, even now, into the community of Christ's obedience, which is His lordship over and fulfilment of God's law. The church's practice of common worship holds out to the faithful the possibility of proclaiming in their moral judgements the history of the Father's own creative and saving judgements in His Son.

In showing us how the obedient act of worship is paradigmatic for renewed moral agency and action, the Cranmerian liturgies also show us how the freedom of Christ's resurrection community orders and sustains the freedom of fallen humanity to participate in the created order of human goods (albeit in a distorted and fragmentary way), and to protect and sustain that participation through coercive public judgement. In so doing, they define and empower the determination of moral community by public judgement. But this role of common worship depends on its publicity, an aspect of which, historically, has been its recognition in public law as the action of the one, holy, catholic, and apostolic church. The dialectical relationship between proclamation and public judgement continues to warrant careful probing today; and our response to the various forms of civil-church establishments, both longstanding and emerging in our contemporary world, should not be one of dogmatic rejection, on the legalistic and juridical grounds of egalitarian religious rights, as is all too common in advanced liberal polities, but one of critical receptivity to the longer Christian tradition.

Governing Diversity:
"Public Judgment" and Religious Plurality

Jonathan Chaplin

Introduction

This chapter explores how a contemporary government administering what Oliver O'Donovan terms "public judgment" might respond to the existence of a plurality of religions, worldviews, or (as I shall now call them) comprehensive doctrines represented among its citizenry.[1] The prevailing secular liberal answer to this question is that governments must adopt a stance of neutrality towards such doctrines — an expectation which has been thought to imply that coercive laws can only be justified by appeal to "public reasons," that is, reasons accessible in principle to all citizens irrespective of their comprehensive doctrines. Adherence to the procedure of public reason then implies a stance of equal treatment in the face of the plurality of competing comprehensive doctrines represented in the citizenry. This position is often designated as "pluralism," and this is how O'Donovan names it.

O'Donovan rightly rejects the secular liberal account of pluralism and the account of public reasoning on which it depends, on the grounds that it severs many citizens' deepest religious or moral commitments from their political deliberations and actions. But he also questions Christian accounts of plural-

1. I use this Rawlsian term for shorthand not as implying agreement with all Rawls means by it.

I am grateful to Joshua Hordern for valuable research assistance in the preparation of this paper and to the editors for their comments. The argument, however, is my own.

ism. He specifically takes distance from one of the best-articulated such accounts, that advocated by neo-Calvinists working in the line of Abraham Kuyper. Indeed he did so in his Kuyper Prize Lecture delivered at Princeton Theological Seminary in 2008, entitled "Reflections on Pluralism."[2] This lecture is his most sustained treatment of the question to date and serves as the focus of my exposition of his position. I suggest that he may have attributed to Christian pluralism problematic notions which it does not share, and that his own notion of "public judgment" may allow a political stance closer to "Christian pluralism" than he seems to admit.

My focus is on the Kuyperian or neo-Calvinist articulation of "pluralism."[3] This is my own position, though the paper is not intended (merely) as a tribal riposte. Something like the neo-Calvinist position is embraced by a wide variety of political theologians today, and not only in North America where many Christians have embraced it warmly. Versions of it were endorsed by most European Christian Democrats in the course of the twentieth century, where it gave rise to what has been named as "consociational democracy." It is an issue underlying many debates about the appropriate goal of Christian political witness in contemporary societies, which means, as O'Donovan rightly perceives, that it is at bottom a question of mission, and therefore also one of the "authority of the gospel."

A Plurality of Pluralisms

What O'Donovan means by "pluralism" can be clarified with the aid of a typology of pluralisms proposed by two contemporary neo-Calvinist authors, Richard Mouw and Sander Griffioen, in *Pluralisms and Horizons*.[4] Mouw and Grif-

2. Oliver O'Donovan, "Reflections on Pluralism," in *The Kuyper Center Review*, Vol. 1: *Politics, Religion, and Sphere Sovereignty*, ed. Gordon Graham (Grand Rapids: Eerdmans, 2010), pp. 1-13 [henceforth cited as *Lecture*].

3. Statements of Christian pluralism influenced by neo-Calvinism include Richard Mouw and Sander Griffioen, *Pluralisms and Horizons: An Essay in Christian Public Philosophy* (Grand Rapids: Eerdmans, 1994); James W. Skillen, *Recharging the American Experiment: Principled Pluralism for Genuine Civic Community* (Grand Rapids: Baker, 1994); Nicholas Wolterstorff's contribution to Robert Audi and Nicholas Wolterstorff, *Religion in the Public Square: The Place of Religious Convictions in Political Debate* (Lanham, MD: Rowman & Littlefield, 1997); Luis Lugo, ed., *Religion, Pluralism, and Public Life: Abraham Kuyper's Legacy for the Twenty-First Century* (Grand Rapids: Eerdmans, 2000). An Anglican defense of pluralism is Rowan Williams, *Faith in the Public Square* (London: Bloomsbury, 2012).

4. Mouw and Griffioen, *Pluralisms and Horizons*.

fioen identify three categories of social plurality which must be carefully attended to in any discussion of pluralism. The first is *associational plurality* — the plurality of human associations of many kinds naturally emerging in many societies.[5] The second is *directional plurality* — the plurality of "spiritual directions" or comprehensive doctrines present in contemporary societies. The third is *contextual plurality* — the plurality of cultural contexts in which associational and directional plurality appear. Each of the three types may be thought of either in a descriptive or in a normative sense, thus generating six types:

1. descriptive associational pluralism
2. normative associational pluralism
3. descriptive directional pluralism
4. normative directional pluralism
5. descriptive contextual pluralism
6. normative contextual pluralism

The variety in which O'Donovan is chiefly interested in his *Lecture* falls within the category of "directional plurality," or a plurality of comprehensive doctrines. More specifically his focus is on the implications of such doctrines for what he calls "practical principles," i.e. principles of practical moral reasoning; I return to this focus in the next section.

To be sure, O'Donovan also recognizes the phenomenon of "associational plurality," rightly identifying it as an instance of the wider ontological plurality of created entities, which are not only individuals but also forms of human association.[6] Indeed he accepts associational plurality in both the descriptive and the normative senses, since human associations disclosing aspects of created goodness are evidently not only to be taken note of but also approved of.[7] He also acknowledges the general phenomenon that Mouw and Griffioen term "contextual plurality," such as is manifested in the plurality of human languages. But these two types of plurality are peripheral to his interest in directional plurality.

---

5. The term "associational plurality" captures what Kuyper speaks of as societal "sphere-sovereignty." See Abraham Kuyper, "Sphere Sovereignty," in James Bratt, ed., *Abraham Kuyper: A Centennial Reader* (Grand Rapids: Eerdmans, 1998), pp. 461-490.

6. O'Donovan, *Lecture*, p. 8. Subsequent page references in the text are to this article.

7. See, e.g., Oliver O'Donovan, *Resurrection and Moral Order: An Outline for Evangelical Ethics*, 2nd ed. (Leicester: Apollos; Grand Rapids: Eerdmans, 1994), pp. 32, 189, 218-219, 230; Oliver O'Donovan, *The Desire of the Nations: Rediscovering the Roots of Political Theology* (Cambridge: Cambridge University Press, 1996), pp. 262-263, 266.

O'Donovan is quick to point out in his *Lecture* that the use of the suffix "-ism" in the term "pluralism" is apt to mislead since it suggests a kind of philosophical belief rather than a state of affairs. Yet he sees this ambiguity as revelatory, since he goes on to argue that pluralism does indeed function as a particular and controversial philosophical position even though it purports to rise above such positions. It is, he says, a "reflexive doctrine of doctrines, which insinuates a view of itself and its own status into its account of the status of other doctrines" (p. 9). He is also correct to note that even descriptive usages of the term do not refer to uninterpreted facts, for to denote a society as "plural" is, as he puts it, "to let the spotlight fall on social difference rather than conformity" (p. 1), which discloses a particular concern (one I allude to later). Yet it seems to me quite legitimate to depict those interpreted states of affairs as descriptive examples of "plurality" without implying any moral or theological approval of the states of affairs so depicted. One can characterize "plurality" without being committed to "pluralism." Mouw and Griffioen thus distinguish "descriptive associational pluralism," the "*highlighting* [of] the fact of a plurality of associational patterns," from "normative associational pluralism" which involves "*advocating* associational plurality as a good state of affairs."[8]

The substance of my discussion of O'Donovan's view of pluralism is organized around three questions he poses to it in his *Lecture:* first, in what sense, if any, does pluralism actually exist? second, how does pluralism relate to plural traditions of practical moral reasoning and plural comprehensive doctrines? and third, how should government deliver "public judgment" in the face of a plurality of practical principles and comprehensive doctrines?

1. Does "Pluralism" Exist?

This is an arresting question, since most observers today would simply take it as obvious that we live in "pluralist" societies. But O'Donovan presses us to think harder about what we mean by the claim. An important observation by Mouw and Griffioen can help us get going. They note that all three types of plurality — associational, directional, and contextual — are simultaneously visible in any particular social situation. For example, all human associations reveal the impact of their cultural context (an African rural family looks different from a Japanese urban professional one); and each betrays the influence, however indirect or unconscious, of one or more spiritual directions (a tradi-

---

8. Mouw and Griffioen, *Pluralisms and Horizons,* pp. 17-18.

tional Catholic family looks different from a radical libertarian one). "Spiritual directions," then, are not abstract, disembodied entities possessed of independent existence and agency, but are the spiritual energies of concrete human beings led by diverse spiritual loyalties, often acting in association, and always in specific cultural contexts.

O'Donovan notes this important point, but in responding to it he ventures a further judgment which seems puzzling and unpersuasive. He is certainly right to observe that things like comprehensive doctrines are different from concrete entities like persons and associations (p. 7). One might say that such doctrines animate concrete entities but are not concrete entities themselves. But his observation occurs while making the wider, and I think problematic, point that things like comprehensive doctrines are not entities that could be plural at all: "Entities can be plural if they can be numbered alongside one another. And entities can be numbered alongside one another if their mode of being is as individual members of a kind." Moreover, only entities that can be plural can enter into any kind of association with each other and so be seen as partaking in the same society — the sort of society which pluralists want to call "a plural society." Comprehensive doctrines, or "isms," however, are only "hypothetical intellectual entities:" "[D]o such entities as isms, possessing the ontological structure implied in treating them as members of a kind in association with one another, actually exist? Do we confront here, as with a plurality of animal kinds, a basic datum of the created universe, or, as with plural languages, do we confront a fruit of providence in response to Babel? Or do we confront only an imagination?" (p. 9).

But these are not the only alternatives. Granted, a comprehensive doctrine is not "a basic datum of the created universe" nor a "fruit of providence." But it is surely not only "an imagination." Comprehensive doctrines may not exist as entities but entities are not the only really existing things in the universe, or at least not the only things that work real effects. "Marxism" may be the product of Marx's "imagination" (and that of his followers) and it may also be false in many respects, but there is no doubting its "reality." I suggest that comprehensive doctrines be understood as "imaginary" in the different sense that Benedict Anderson intends when he speaks of nations as "imagined communities"[9] — not as entities given in nature like kinship groups, nor as constructed institutions like states, but as profoundly formative shared interpretations of the world that exercise enormous cultural power and com-

9. Benedict Anderson, *Imagined Communities: Reflections on the Origin and Spread of Nationalism*, rev. ed. (London: Verso, 1991).

mand the intense loyalties of their adherents. Comprehensive doctrines are history-shaping.[10]

But if comprehensive doctrines are "real" in the sense proposed, what is the relation between such "imagined" doctrines and the ontological structure of creation? The relation is surely this: if the search for ultimate meaning and truth, which Christians interpret as the search for God, is itself programmed into human creatureliness — if "our hearts are restless until they find their rest in Thee" — then the larger meaning-systems humans devise as they engage in this quest, wittingly or not, testify to this creaturely striving toward God. It is part of the ontological structure of human persons that they engage in such striving. What Rawls calls comprehensive doctrines or what Mouw and Griffioen call spiritual directions are, then, so many attempts to articulate this universal human striving after meaning and truth — after God. Plural comprehensive doctrines may not arise out the original good creation but they are only possible on the basis of this creaturely impulse. If so, then it is hard to see why they may not be classified as individual members of a "kind" (albeit a very special kind of kind).[11] They are instances of the kind, "human (mis)formulations of ultimate truth." If so, I see no reason why they could not be "numbered," although only counting them would not be a very profitable exercise.

Christians will also go on to say that all humanly constructed comprehensive doctrines amply disclose the results of the fall, of the restlessly inventive imaginings of humans suffering from chronic spiritual blindness — to which God's response is, as Judge, to "scatter the proud in the imaginations of their hearts" (Luke 1:51), and as Redeemer, to offer "to the people who walked in darkness . . . a great light" (Isaiah 9:2b).[12] This point, too, is acknowledged among many Christian pluralists, especially adherents to neo-Calvinism, who, as O'Donovan notes, "[b]y taking the epistemic dimensions of original sin seriously . . . [invite] us to expect deep social division at the level of 'worldview' that may have to be coped with politically" (p. 11). So to assert that comprehensive doctrines are real and that they have an anchor in the ontology of creatureliness is not to suggest that they are true perceptions of created reality. There is one order of creation, and human formulations of it in comprehensive

10. See the account by neo-Calvinist philosopher Herman Dooyeweerd of dynamic "ground motives" at work in western culture, in *Roots of Western Culture: Pagan, Secular, and Christian Options* (Toronto: Wedge, 1979).

11. They are not instances of what O'Donovan in *Resurrection and Moral Order* terms either "generic kinds" or "teleological ends" (p. 32) since these are grounded in created order as originally given.

12. See O'Donovan, *Resurrection and Moral Order*, p. 19.

doctrines are true insofar as they capture that order reliably; all formulations are fallible and some are woefully misguided.[13]

Evidently, however, some such formulations contain valid insights into dimensions of created order. The neo-Calvinist philosopher Herman Dooyeweerd acknowledges the point by pointing to the genuine "states of affairs" uncovered even by thinkers wearing the distorting philosophical lenses of one or other "ism."[14] O'Donovan acknowledges something similar in cautioning that "the Christian moral thinker . . . has no need to proceed in a totalitarian way, denying the importance and relevance of all that he finds valued as moral conviction in the various cultures and traditions of the world."[15]

Yet O'Donovan seems to read the neo-Calvinist position as assuming that the spiritual fragmentation of fallen society is in some sense to be accorded theological legitimacy, that "the ruptures of original sin . . . will normatively take an ideological form within society" (p. 11). But this was never their position. While they worked to reach a fair public accommodation of different comprehensive doctrines contending in the public realm of the late nineteenth-century Netherlands, they never saw such spiritual splintering as normative in itself. Nor do Mouw and Griffioen; for them "normative directional plural-ism" is incompatible with Christian faith.[16] Neo-Calvinists, then, can agree with O'Donovan that directional plurality is, as he puts it, an "accident," i.e. a contingent state of affairs consequent upon the fall.[17]

At one point O'Donovan himself comes close to recognizing the need for the kind of public accommodation of directional plurality favored by neo-Calvinists, where he acknowledges that Christian eschatology mandates "sec-ularity" in the sense of an acceptance of the incompleteness of the reign of

13. Mouw and Griffioen, *Pluralisms and Horizons*, p. 18. Thus the kind of "pluralism" which O'Donovan thinks some modern Christians have succumbed to through a desire to sidle up to prevailing cultural attitudes (*Desire of the Nations*, p. 226), is not what neo-Calvinists support.

14. Jonathan Chaplin, *Herman Dooyeweerd: Christian Philosopher of State and Civil Society* (Notre Dame, IN: University of Notre Dame Press, 2011), p. 46.

15. O'Donovan, *Resurrection and Moral Order*, p. 89.

16. Thus the following critique of "pluralism" would also be endorsed by neo-Calvinists: "A polytheistic society negotiates multiple claims with no cohesion but what it can impose on them, so that, in effect, it enforces its own sovereignty. Late-liberalism, one may say, in taking up the banner of 'pluralism,' has made itself self-consciously polytheistic." Oliver O'Donovan, *The Ways of Judgment* (Grand Rapids: Eerdmans, 2005), p. 76. Henceforth cited as *WOJ*, followed by page number. Nor would most neo-Calvinists support the "moral pluralism" O'Donovan rightly criticizes in *A Conversation Waiting to Begin: The Churches and the Gay Controversy* (London: SCM, 2009), pp. 49-53.

17. See O'Donovan, *Resurrection and Moral Order*, pp. 91-97.

truth in this age. In a statement that could be readily echoed by Christian pluralists he writes: "Secularity is a stance of patience in the face of plurality, made sense of by eschatological hope."[18]

There is, then, a fundamental difference between interpreting directional plurality as itself normative and supporting a normative political principle to govern its fair public accommodation. The nature of that principle will be the third question I shall address. The next one concerns the nature of moral reasoning and its relationship to comprehensive doctrines. This is important because O'Donovan thinks that pluralism is premised on a serious misunderstanding of the nature of such reasoning — indeed that once the nature of such reasoning is understood it is no longer possible to regard comprehensive doctrines as "plural" at all.

2. Pluralism, Practical Reasoning, and Comprehensive Doctrines

The focus of O'Donovan's *Lecture* is the challenge a society is thought to face when its members adhere to diverse principles of practical moral reasoning, or as he abbreviates them, "practical principles."[19] This challenge, he says, is a source of significant "anxiety," and it is this anxiety which is the motivating concern behind the interpretive choice to describe a society as "pluralist." Here is his formulation of how pluralists see the problem:

> Pluralism singles out for attention something inherently worrying, which is a difference of practical principle. When sectional cultures in society act on contrary assumptions and pursue divergent courses in their relations with each other, when there are incompatible modes and expectations of public conduct, then we are anxious. . . . If each one of us, or each community, thinks about our activity in such idiosyncratic ways that our neighbors lack all practical understanding of us, it is necessary, so it is alleged, to deploy a different kind of thinking to govern our interactions. (p. 2)

The pluralist solution to this troubling existence of a plurality of practical principles of conduct is to propose a new type of public discourse which over-

18. Oliver O'Donovan, *Common Objects of Love: Moral Reflection and the Shaping of Community* (Grand Rapids: Eerdmans, 2002), p. 69. See also *WOJ*, p. 22.

19. For a fuller account of practical reasoning, see O'Donovan, *Common Objects of Love*, pp. 13-19; and O'Donovan, *Self, World, and Time*, Vol. 1 of *Ethics as Theology* (Grand Rapids: Eerdmans, 2013).

arches such incompatible principles, namely "public reason." But the imperatives of what purports to be "public" reason have the effect of severing public
principles from the nurturing moral traditions by which alone they can be
sustained or appear persuasive to their adherents, so that they are experienced
by many citizens as alien, arbitrary impositions. Public reason then becomes
"a regime of practical thinking detached from all fundamental principles of
action" (p. 2). The conclusion is that "[t]he concept of an absolute public reason
is . . . incompatible with the terms of any open practical inquiry, and especially
with a Christian one" (p. 7). I will not rehearse this critique of Rawlsian-style
public reason further here because it has been effectively stated elsewhere by
many Christian critics.[20]

Let me offer four qualifying remarks on O'Donovan's way of framing the
problem of pluralism. First, he is right to note that the challenge of the presence of diverse practical principles in a single society is not a novel one, as
liberal defenders of pluralism seem to imply. Such liberals construe pluralism
in inflated terms as "a new metaphysic of society . . . as though the coming of
a new cultural demographics were a moment of metaphysical disclosure: an
underlying reality we had overlooked became suddenly clear, and we were
disillusioned of our simple idea that society is based on things held in common" (pp. 2-3).[21] But, he reminds us, the cultural and religious plurality of our
societies is not remotely as complex as that prevailing in, for example,
nineteenth-century India. Quite so. I wonder, however, whether the specific
challenge presented to our own societies by a plurality of practical principles
is more vexing than O'Donovan concedes. It is not only that in societies such
as our own several deeply divergent practical principles contend with increasing aggressiveness in the public square and press their demands on government. It is also that there is deep disagreement over what practical reasoning
itself is or even whether it is possible to engage in it any longer (the relativist
position); and, if not, whether we are, after all, left simply with a stand-off
between rival power-bids (the perspectivist position).[22] To acknowledge the
depth of moral plurality is not necessarily to imply any "new social metaphysic" but it is, perhaps, to imply the need for a "new social hermeneutic," a

20. See, e.g., Audi and Wolterstorff, *Religion in the Public Square;* Nigel Biggar and Linda
Hogan, eds., *Religious Voices in Public Places* (Oxford: Oxford University Press, 2009).

21. The idea that societies are *constituted by agreement* on core moral commitments, and
the charge that modern liberalism and pluralism deny the fact, are recurring themes in O'Donovan's work. See, e.g., *Desire of the Nations,* p. 222; *Common Objects of Love.*

22. On the distinction between "relativism" and "perspectivism," see Alasdair MacIntyre,
Whose Justice? Which Rationality? (London: Duckworth, 1988), p. 52.

reading of the *zeitgeist* in which a genealogy of the peculiarly modern and postmodern sources of deep moral plurality occupies a prominent place.[23]

Second, O'Donovan's formulation of the pluralist problem already implies a pejorative judgment on the state of affairs in question which would not necessarily be accepted by Christian (or other) pluralists. O'Donovan speaks of "sectional" cultures thinking in "idiosyncratic" ways, implying that they are somehow deviating from — or at least standing out from — some existing, widely-shared moral consensus which is non-sectional. But many Christian pluralists question whether such a consensus any longer exists, holding instead that contemporary western societies are marked by the presence of multiple moral minorities, alongside, perhaps, a still-dominant overarching secular modernist framework of moral reasoning now itself rapidly decomposing under the acids of postmodernity into several eclectic and unstable variants.[24] *That* dominant framework is, of course, not one which Christians would want to concede as the non-sectional, non-idiosyncratic position — as O'Donovan has compellingly argued elsewhere.[25] There is, no doubt, legitimate disagreement over this diagnosis of our contemporary situation. Not all Christians would accept the rather bleak picture just offered, some insisting that a residual Christianity remains alive in our public cultures and others doubting whether secular modernism is any longer dominant. These differences cannot be resolved here, but the disagreement between O'Donovan and Christian pluralists is likely to turn in part on such competing diagnoses.

Third, O'Donovan claims, in the passage quoted above, that pluralists regard the scope of moral disagreement as so extensive as to rule out *all* mutual moral understanding across communities. But few liberal, or Christian, pluralists would describe our societies so bleakly. The latter, at least, would hold that, while some moral disagreements may be deep and intractable, and some modes of conduct "incompatible," these divergences are not ubiquitous and so do not rule out the possibility of significant remaining consensus on practical principles, on the basis of which some other disagreements may be successfully negotiated.

23. Alasdair MacIntyre offers one such hermeneutic in *Whose Justice?* Charles Taylor offers another in *A Secular Age* (Cambridge, MA: Harvard University Press, 2007).

24. I press a similar point against what I call O'Donovan's "organic" notion of representation in "Representing a People: Oliver O'Donovan on Democracy and Tradition," *Political Theology* 9, no. 3 (2008): 295-307 (Special Issue: The Political Theology of Oliver O'Donovan). O'Donovan is not persuaded: Oliver O'Donovan, "Judgment, Tradition and Reason: A Response," *Political Theology* 9, no. 3 (2008): 404-407.

25. E.g., O'Donovan, *Desire of the Nations*, pp. 271-284.

Fourth, the "public reason" solution O'Donovan refers to in the passage quoted above is the specifically *secular liberal* response to the problem of plurality. It is, however, not the one embraced by most of those who call themselves Christian pluralists, certainly not the neo-Calvinists, many of whom are as critical of this liberal solution as O'Donovan is.[26] So O'Donovan's spirited assault on liberal public reason is not in itself an assault on Christian pluralism.

Those four qualifications entered, let me return to the main question of how diverse practical principles relate to comprehensive doctrines. I begin by noting five claims O'Donovan makes in the *Lecture* about the activity of practical reasoning.

First, practical principles are not produced by isolated individuals but by shared traditions of reasoning, "community beliefs that generate a universe of reasons" (p. 5).[27] Second, practical reasoning is "discursive" rather than "deductive." It is made up of complex "connected chains of reasoning" moving back and forth between basic beliefs and practical consequence, chains which display, or at least seek, an overall coherence, yet without being rigidly syllogistic. (O'Donovan's claim that pluralists erroneously hold to a "foundationalist" construal of practical reasoning in which conclusions are thought to flow deductively from comprehensive doctrines, is not one I recognize.) Third, practical reasoning aspires to "universality," it seeks to give an account of the general human good, not merely to express its own idiosyncratic conception of that good. Fourth, practical reasoning aims at what O'Donovan calls "rational communication," the intended audience for which is not only members of one's own moral community but those of others who are willing to engage in and learn from conversation. "Since agreement in the truth is what human beings are made for, they will search for it wherever the possibility arises and we will encounter new and intriguing coalitions of thought. To free ourselves for the search, we need only to liberate ourselves from determinist theories of society that think they can tell us in advance just which agreements are, and which are not, possible" (p. 7). Indeed it is precisely because moral reasoning is discursive rather than deductive that a disagreement of practical principle is never simply a stand-off between two "incommensurable" positions. Indeed in order to *discover the existence* of a disagreement it is necessary to enter into the chain of reasoning of one's opponent: "I enter into a kind of counterpoint

26. See, e.g., Mouw and Griffioen, *Pluralisms and Horizons,* and Wolterstorff's contribution to Audi and Wolterstorff, *Religion in the Pubic Square.*

27. In *Common Objects of Love* he writes: "moral reflection . . . has effect in organized communities" (p. 21).

to the train of reasoning the other is engaged in, I begin to accompany him as I challenge him and question him. I enter into the sequence of his reasoned propositions, governed by a logic of moral thought from which neither he or I can be exempt" (p. 13). Fifth, any reconciliations of contending moral positions that may be achieved "in this age" can be construed as the fruit of the Spirit's work, and as an outcome of mission, a conviction that makes room for Christian hope (pp. 12-13). To this fifth point I would only add that some reconciliation is already possible on account of the experience of a common order of creation shared by all human beings irrespective of their comprehensive doctrines or practical principles (or of their response to revelation and redemption).

This is a highly instructive and appealing account of moral reasoning. But while liberal pluralists might well resist one or more aspects of it, many Christian pluralists, and probably most neo-Calvinists, would find it congenial at every significant point. If there is irreconcilable disagreement about pluralism between O'Donovan and the neo-Calvinists, it is not here.

In the *Lecture*, O'Donovan does not say very much about how the diverse "community traditions" of practical reasoning that he acknowledges do exist relate to comprehensive doctrines. I suggest that comprehensive doctrines can best be understood as the larger intellectual frameworks adhered to by particular traditioned communities, supplying a deep layer of conviction guiding a community's practice of moral reasoning. This, at least, is how they are understood by most contemporary neo-Calvinist pluralists. And such a position, again, seems quite compatible with the account of practical reasoning developed by O'Donovan.

3. Governing Diversity

The third question posed by O'Donovan to pluralism is the specifically political one of how governments should respond to the fact of a plurality of practical principles and comprehensive doctrines among their citizenry. Here again we find potential for convergence with Christian pluralism that O'Donovan seems to have underestimated. He frames the question in what first appears to be rather an oblique way: "how do isms stand before the equalizing regime of democracy?" (p. 10). This framing emerges as follows. Adherents of pluralism take pluralism to be part of a defense of democracy, to which the principle of equality is foundational. But before it is a principle of election, equality is a principle of legality — that of equality before the law — and that principle is administered by courts. So the question of how government should respond to the diversity of comprehensive doctrines or practical principles presented to it by its citizens resolves centrally into that of how *courts* should respond to such diversity (a judgment reflecting his view that "the fundamental organ of government is the court" [p. 10]). But every application of the principle of equality presupposes the ontological question of "what entities make a recognizable demand for equal treatment" in a particular situation, and, in the context of a court, that appears in the first instance as the question of what counts as a "legal person" capable of being a party to a case.

Here O'Donovan makes the important observation that while courts are obliged to treat legal *persons* equally (i.e. impartially) they are not obliged to treat legal *reasons* equally. On the contrary, they are to treat them *unequally* by ruling some as valid and others as invalid. "Reasons enter court in competition . . . which is the court's business to terminate by giving effect to their inequality. Reasons enter court in order to eliminate one another" (p. 10).[28]

Legal persons, moreover, can be either individuals or communities. Thus, "when a community defined by its doctrine and practices appears before the courts, that community will have equal standing with any other legal person" (p. 11). It is indeed very important to recognize that communities of belief — churches or other religious associations, or bodies like the British Humanist Association (BHA) — can claim legal standing in court and present legal reasons for consideration deriving from their beliefs. The effective freedom to "manifest" one's religion in public (to use the language of the important Article 9 of the European Convention on Human Rights) is a matter not only of individuals but also of communities. Thus, for example, if the BHA turns to the courts to secure the addition of secular humanism to the religious education curriculum in state schools it can expect to be accorded the same status of legal personality as that granted to a church defending its entitlement to hire only officers who share its theological or ethical convictions.

So the issue can now be formulated more precisely as that of what a court is to do when corporate persons present comprehensive doctrines (or practical principles derived from them) as candidates for legal reasons. And O'Donovan here draws the inescapable conclusion that such legal reasons will be treated in exactly the same way as any putative legal reason, namely assessed for their intrinsic jurisprudential validity. He makes the point in reference to the Archbishop of Canterbury's controversial proposal in 2008 that English law might

---

28. As he puts it elsewhere: "Practical reason equalizes those who dare to engage in it" (*WOJ*, p. 50).

in some way accommodate aspects of sharia law. This argument, he rightly notes, "is not an argument for doctrinal equality. It is an argument for the legal standing of communities that do in practice resolve some of their problems in the light of their doctrine. Neither in this case nor in any other can doctrine be accorded the status of legal persons, so that the apparatus of government adopts a position of indifference in respect of them" (p. 11). This very important distinction is not always adhered to in the language — and perhaps not always the thinking — of Christian pluralists. No court — indeed no other organ of government — can be impartial as between reasons grounded in comprehensive doctrines; such grounding gives them no immunity from the rigorous testing facing any putative reason.

However, on the strength of this entirely valid conclusion O'Donovan goes on to venture a larger judgment about pluralism which is questionable: "the fact that courts cannot give [doctrines] this status explains why it is in the courts that the unfulfillable promises of pluralism for the equal treatment of all belief have been most spectacularly disappointed" (p. 11). I take it that this remark applies chiefly to the courts of western liberal democracies, since there are many jurisdictions elsewhere (e.g. Indonesia, Israel, Lebanon, or northern Nigeria) which do contain systems of "legal pluralism" in which tribunals of religious communities are accorded considerable devolved legal competence to administer aspects of religious personal law.[29]

Two observations on O'Donovan's assessment of the legal and political aspects of pluralism are in order. First, while it is indeed the case that some pluralists, even some Christian pluralists, wish to get more out of western courts than they have done so far, I do not think that their chief demand has been that courts "treat all doctrines equally." One of the main legal principles by which "pluralist" demands are adjudicated in some western courts is that of "reasonable accommodation," whereby exemptions from generally applicable statutory obligations are granted to individuals or associations, in cases where the goal of substantive equality of treatment is thought to require it. This amounts to the recognition that a uniform, exceptionless application of such obligations can bring about injustice, if an insistence on conformity to a statutory obligation would impose a disproportionate burden on the (religious) conscience of an individual or an association.[30]

29. Strictly, however, even systems of legal pluralism do not imply courts' granting "doctrinal equality" to different beliefs *within the same sphere of law;* they delegate legal power to a new sphere of law, within which a new set of valid legal reasons applies.

30. The legal principle of accommodation is itself a legal reason already recognized in such jurisdictions, so in granting accommodations, courts are not showing deference to ex-

The practice of legal accommodation is a very important way in which courts do in fact seek to recognize the legal significance of plural doctrines for persons and associations adhering to them. O'Donovan does not mention it in his Kuyper Lecture but does allude to it elsewhere when commenting on the question of how western governments might respond to requests for the accommodation of sharia law: "We have, indeed, a good deal of interreligious pluralism to cope with in the West which we have not coped with *here* before. But we have coped with it elsewhere, largely by resort to an older doctrine of secular provisionality in which government is seen as necessarily flexible and responsive to conditions. In just such a spirit the Archbishop of Canterbury recently proposed certain very modest accommodations between British law and *sharia*-based community jurisdiction. . . ."[31] What O'Donovan calls "secular provisionality," Christian pluralists would call "just accommodation" (the difference of language arising from contrasting, though not incompatible, construals of the phenomenon of religious diversity: for O'Donovan, primarily from the standpoint of Augustinian eschatology; for Christian pluralists, primarily from the standpoint of the normative role of the state).

The second observation is that the concerns of pluralists, including Christian pluralists, have always been much wider than legal ones. Whether or not it is the case that "the fundamental organ of government is the court," it is the case that other organs of government have been expected by pluralists to play, and have played, a significant role in responding to the aspirations and demands of plural religious and cultural communities. I would suggest that the legal accommodation of such plurality is but one instance of a wider political process of accommodation, whereby — to use O'Donovan's words — "deep social division at the level of 'worldview' . . . [is] coped with politically" (p. 11). The ways in which this has been done in western liberal democracies are too numerous to list, but here I briefly describe one which has been central to the model of pluralism advocated by European Christian Democracy (to which neo-Calvinism has been one contributor). Political scientists refer to its institutional expression as "consociational democracy," and it embraces two major

---

ternal non-legal doctrines (sharia law, for instance) but rather acting in accord with their own legal principles.

31. O'Donovan, "Judgment, Tradition and Reason," p. 411. See Jonathan Chaplin, "Legal Monism and Religious Pluralism: Rowan Williams on Religion, Loyalty and Law," *International Journal of Public Theology* 2, no. 4 (2008): 418-441. At one point O'Donovan endorses "a true Christian instinct to defend small and imperiled cultural and linguistic communities liable to be overwhelmed by the homogenising pressures of Western technological culture" (*Desire of the Nations*, p. 267).

components, one situated at the point of inputs into the policy-making process, the other at the point of outputs from it.

At the point of inputs, Christian Democrats have striven to ensure that the institutions of representative democracy do not pre-emptively disadvantage religious or other minority voices against gaining an adequate hearing in representative processes. One example of this is in electoral systems, where an "adequate" hearing has been understood to mean a "proportional" hearing, leading to an advocacy of some variant of proportional representation, a system removing a major barrier to minority groups' ability to win representation in parliaments.[32] Parallel to this are various arrangements whereby representatives of diverse religious or other communities are appointed on an equitable basis to consultative bodies in various policy areas.

At the point of outputs, a key aspiration of Christian Democrats has been to secure equitable treatment for religious or other minority organizations in various public services, such as education, health, social welfare, and broadcasting. Here "equitable treatment" has been thought to mean first, the legal freedom to establish provider organizations and to maintain them according to the sponsoring organizations' ethos without being subjected to intrusive legal constraint, and, second, access to adequate (perhaps proportionate) public funding where such services substitute for one which the state is already committed to funding. The principal example of this in the UK is the state funding of church (and more recently Muslim) schools, though the arrangement has been more widely established in countries such as Germany, the Netherlands, and Belgium.[33]

These arrangements are designed, *inter alia,* to allow such communities to maintain their distinctive religious or moral identities — their traditions of practical reasoning — without being forced to retreat into private enclaves divorced from participation in wider society and beyond the reach of public scrutiny. They are ways in which citizens can sustain what O'Donovan (citing Bernd Wannenwetsch) calls "homologous identities" (p. 4) in which private and public identities can be kept coherent. In my view these legal and political arrangements are eminently justifiable, not only as a way for communities to defend their identities but also as a proper extension of the principle of personal and associational religious freedom. Any such arrangement must, of

32. O'Donovan himself is not enthusiastic about proportional representation (see *WOJ*, p. 177).

33. For a comparative survey of such arrangements, see Stephen V. Monsma and J. Christopher Soper, *The Challenge of Pluralism: Church and State in Five Democracies* (Lanham, MD: Rowman & Littlefield, 1997).

course, remain within the existing law of the land, and precisely what the law will allow will be a matter for continuing negotiation.

Before turning to O'Donovan's notion of "public judgment" let us pause briefly to ask whether his view of "establishment" is compatible with this model of equitable Christian pluralism.[34] O'Donovan holds that a "confessionally Christian government" — such as is sustained by the establishment of the Church of England — may in certain situations be theologically legitimate (though he nowhere claims it is ever theologically mandatory).[35] That would seem to stand in tension with the foregoing argument in favor of equitable public treatment of plural claims of persons or associations bearing diverse comprehensive doctrines. One could argue that, strictly speaking, it does, though I concede that the tension need not in practice generate serious political division and may even be welcomed by a majority of citizens in a plural society. Some European consociational democracies have managed to maintain (weak forms of) establishment without generating widespread unease. It is certainly the case that, as O'Donovan himself notes, contemporary forms of establishment in western societies are entirely compatible with the legal recognition of full religious freedom for persons and communities.[36] Establishment does not inhibit legal accommodation and may, contingently, lend plausibility to it, such as, for example, where an established church seeks to champion the public standing of other denominations or religions.[37]

4. Pluralism and "Public Judgment"

To conclude my discussion of what "governing diversity" might mean, I now want to explore the thought that the consociational arrangements outlined

34. For O'Donovan's theological account of establishment, see *Desire of the Nations*, pp. 217-224.

35. O'Donovan, *Desire of the Nations*, p. 195. See David McIlroy, "The Right Reason for Caesar to Confess Christ as Lord: Oliver O'Donovan and Arguments for the Christian State," *Studies in Christian Ethics* 23 (2010): 300-315.

36. O'Donovan, *Desire of the Nations*, p. 224.

37. On O'Donovan's claim that the passing of the First Amendment of the U.S. Constitution implied "a concept of the state's role from which Christology was excluded, that of a state freed from all responsibility to recognise God's self-disclosure in history" (*Desire of the Nations*, p. 245), see my "Political Eschatology and Responsible Government: Oliver O'Donovan's 'Christian Liberalism,'" in Craig Bartholomew et al., eds., *A Royal Priesthood? The Use of the Bible Ethically and Politically: A Dialogue with Oliver O'Donovan* (Grand Rapids: Zondervan; Carlisle: Paternoster, 2002), pp. 265-308.

above might actually be seen as a direct implication of the role of government construed in O'Donovan's terms as the administering of "public judgment."

For O'Donovan, "[t]he authority of secular government resides in the practice of judgment" (*WOJ*, p. 3). Government action is fundamentally about the concrete *rendering* of justice in active deeds of governance by a political community. Judgment is "an act of moral discrimination that pronounces upon a preceding act or existing state of affairs to establish a new public context" (*WOJ*, p. 7). The following four aspects of O'Donovan's notion of public judgment are relevant to the matter at hand.[38] First, *judgment is characteristically public* (*WOJ*, p. 10). "Political judgment prevents the fragmentation of the public space into myriad private spaces. . . . The alternative to public judgment is not *no* judgment but *private* judgments, multitudinous and conflicting, frustrating each other and denying everyone the space of freedom" (*WOJ*, p. 23). Thus, any species of "pluralism" which denied to government the task of delivering singular (i.e. universally binding) public judgments and left society to resolve its own conflicts through a clash of many rival "judgments" would collapse into anarchy. Christian pluralists would wholly agree. What they would also argue is that government's "singular" judgments should include the possibility of — and might in some circumstances mandate — an accommodation of claims made by persons and associations pursuant to their comprehensive doctrines. The same conclusion emerges from O'Donovan's notion that public space is also a realm of "public freedom" (*WOJ*, pp. 55-57). While the goal of judgment is not merely to protect our private freedoms, in securing public freedoms government will also preserve those private freedoms, including religious freedoms.

Second, *the normative criterion of right public judgment is God's own judgment*. We judge truthfully "when, within the limits of human understanding, we judge of a thing as God has judged of it" (*WOJ*, p. 16). We are enabled to do so because of the light provided by "the generic judgments of God known to us through divine law, natural and revealed, and through salvation history," judgments which "disclose the categorical structure of all events, and so teach us how to appraise particular events" (*WOJ*, p. 17). We are thereby enabled to engage in "descriptive truth," which is a matter of "appropriate predication." Appraising particular events in conformity to the way God appraises them involves, among other things, the reliable discernment of the complexity and variety of created kinds, and so of the "events" whose identity is determined

---

38. The following discussion draws on my "Oliver O'Donovan's *The Ways of Judgment*," *Scottish Journal of Theology* 61, no. 4 (2008): 477-493.

in relation to them. Although O'Donovan does not say so, it seems a legitimate extension of his point that "appraisal" could also include taking a view on what is to count as a legitimate comprehensive doctrine for purposes of legal accommodation. The likely future "event" of an Islamic association seeking permission from a court to use sharia law in private tribunals would seem to require just such an appraisal. It is hard to see how such acts of discrimination could be excluded from the task of public judgment. They do not amount to judging the truth of a doctrine, only whether it falls under the relevant law.

The claim that public judgment is done rightly insofar as it conforms to God's judgment does not imply for O'Donovan that public judgment should be done by *the church,* only that it is the task of the church, and of individual Christian citizens, to call government to right judgment by utilizing the possibilities of (what he elsewhere terms) "public speech" made available to all citizens in contemporary representative systems.[39] O'Donovan is quite aware that particular governments might actually come up with a wide variety of "appraisals" of a situation which might misdescribe circumstances, subtly or egregiously. Churches and Christian citizens, then, must work to commend to government what they take to be right "appraisals" and oppose wrong ones as best they can, and in so doing they will find themselves alongside many other communities of belief, with whom they will variously find themselves in agreement or disagreement.

Third, *public judgment mandates particular kinds of equal treatment.* On the one hand, O'Donovan denies that justice can be reduced to equal treatment, for justice is essentially "attributive," requiring judgments which correctly discern the particularity of every situation or claim: "Attributive justice elaborates difference . . . since differentiation is the law of every social organism" (*WOJ,* p. 42). On the other hand, there are specific circumstances when equal treatment is indeed mandated, namely where attributive justice discerns an undifferentiated, universal claim. One is where humans stand "on the threshold of death," for example, in the allocation of acute health care; another is where they stand "on the threshold of social exclusion," that is, where they "lack essential resources to participate in social communications as such" (*WOJ,* p. 45). These two circumstances do not relate directly to judgments about *religious plurality,* but a third circumstance that he notices does: the human entitlement to "equality before judgment" itself, i.e. equality before the law (*WOJ,* p. 49). We have already seen that this requires, *inter alia,* that government accords equal treat-

---

39. O'Donovan, *Desire of the Nations,* pp. 268-271. Where public freedom of religious expression is well protected, they will be enabled to do so.

ment to conscientious claims made by persons and associations pursuant to their diverse comprehensive doctrines. Doing so, we might add, also serves to pre-empt another possible source of "social exclusion."

Fourth, *the scope of the judging role of government meets its boundary in the roles presumptively reserved to individuals and non-governmental associations* (*WOJ*, p. 136). Thus, governments engaging in public judgment will, as far as possible, seek to respect and protect the legal autonomy of associations founded to pursue some comprehensive doctrine.

Fifth, *human judgments informed by God's judgments will be appropriately complex* (*WOJ*, p. 18). Public events are complex not only because they disclose the variegated design of created order, but also because that enduring order is disclosed through the succession of ever-changing temporal circumstances that constitute human history and which accord to each particular society its own idiosyncratic character. Judgment has to be framed as a suitable response to this historical idiosyncrasy as well as to the differentiated universal order underlying it. Thus it is not only that law must truthfully express the moral claims of that universal order, but that "[t]he truth of a law must also be a truth about the society in which it will function" (*WOJ*, p. 19). So, for example, the Mosaic law of divorce was not a falling away from the truth about marriage; rather it "told the truth about the Israelites' hardness of heart" (*WOJ*, p. 20). "Every change in the law aims to squeeze out, as it were, the maximum yield of public truthfulness available within the practical constraints of the times. Sometimes it does this by attempting more, sometimes by attempting less" (*WOJ*, p. 193). The implication, again, would seem to be that public judgment will remain open to allowing flexible accommodations of moral and religious plurality.

These five implications of public judgment, I suggest, converge to offer significant support for the political aspirations of Christian pluralism. The point is not that a society could ever be "governed by diversity" but rather that just governance will include a reasonable accommodation of particular claims advanced, by persons or associations, on the basis of a diversity of comprehensive doctrines.

Conclusion

I have suggested that O'Donovan's account of "pluralism" is both instructive for, and at certain points corrective of, accounts developed by neo-Calvinist and other Christian pluralists, but also that most of the problematic commitments he rightly identifies in secular liberal pluralism are not in fact held by most Christian pluralists. I have argued that O'Donovan's account of the nature of practical reasoning does not, as he seems to suppose, undermine the political claims of Christian pluralists but could be readily embraced by them. Finally, I have argued that, contrary to his apparent perception, O'Donovan's notion of public judgment can after all justify some of the central aspirations of Christian pluralists. A government administering what O'Donovan calls "public judgment" may find it legitimate — even mandatory — to grant a variety of specific legal and political accommodations to adherents of plural comprehensive doctrines such as are represented in contemporary western societies. On closer inspection, the distance between the two accounts turns out not to be as great as he has supposed. In any event, this chapter is an invitation to explore that possibility further.

Communication

Brent Waters

I think it fair to characterize much of Oliver O'Donovan's work as an astute, and at times quarrelsome, encounter with late modernity. He captures its twin liberal and authoritarian tendencies in an incisive manner, exposing their contradictory, yet nonetheless formative influence. Late moderns are somehow simultaneously devoted to autonomy and dependency. The ubiquity of information and telecommunication technologies is a fitting image of our present circumstances: individuals are happily creating "unique" lifestyles by utilizing homogenizing technologies upon which they are growing utterly dependent. O'Donovan, however, has no desire to ease this tension. Consequently, he rejects the secular options of liberal individualism or Hegelian collectivism, and he has little use for such theological proposals as accommodating Christian ethics to late modern practice, refusing late modernity in favor of antiquity, or forming a counter social and political reality. Rather, O'Donovan portrays the late modern world for what it is, namely, another moment in the historical and providential unfolding of God's vindicated creation, and it cannot be overemphasized that this unfolding is ongoing; that creation is being drawn toward its unrealized destiny of the *parousia.* In making this argument he turns to the Christian history of expectation and how human life should be ordered in light of what is expected, drawing especially upon St. Paul, St. Augustine, and Hugo Grotius. As a result critics, friendly or otherwise, often miss his teleological and eschatological emphases, accusing him, for instance, of being a quixotic defender of early liberalism, or worse, the champion of a resuscitated Christendom. Yet O'Donovan is not seeking the restoration of Eden or Geneva, but is focused, in this time between the times, upon a new heaven and earth; he is not so much interested in condemning or replacing late modernity as he is in urging late moderns to quit being fixated exclusively on the present age, and begin aligning their lives along a trajectory of restless expectation.

An entire essay, or even book, could be written examining the broad contours of O'Donovan's assessment of late modernity, and explicating the moral and political implications. But I have chosen to focus on one piece within this larger scheme: communication.[1] My reason for doing so is that it offers a useful concept which, with further development, might help to militate against the libertarian and authoritarian tendencies of late modernity. It may, perhaps, be understood as advice to citizens of the heavenly city on how to order their lives as faithful and restless pilgrims during their sojourn in the earthly city.

According to O'Donovan, communication is the basic form of the social life, derived from its root in *koinōnia,* which can be variously translated as "community," "communion," or "communicate."[2] In O'Donovan's words: "To 'communicate' is to hold some thing as common, to treat it as 'ours,' rather than 'yours' or 'mine.' The partners to a communication form a community, a 'we' in relation to the object in which they participate."[3] Although communication entails reciprocity, it is neither a bestowal nor an exchange. Something can become "ours" without the parties surrendering their respective claims. Rather, the principal purpose of communicating the goods of creation is to ground human equality in a given social reality, for in relation to God as creator no single individual can be the basis of a communication. Such things as gifts, meals, and property can be communicated, and there are spheres of communication such as the church, family, and workplace. Civil society in turn is composed of differentiated spheres of communication that share "enkaptic relations." An enkaptic relation requires each sphere to have an internal order that is relevant to the goods its members communicate with each other, and they overlap with other interdependent spheres. But this interaction must be limited if the respective spheres are to remain differentiated. A family, for example, orders itself in line with the goods it communicates, and is dependent upon other spheres, such as medicine and the workplace, to sustain itself. This relation, however, does not suggest that a family should organize itself as if it were a hospital or business firm, or that hospitals and businesses should be

---

1. See Oliver O'Donovan, *The Ways of Judgment* (Grand Rapids: Eerdmans, 2005), chapters 13-16, and *Common Objects of Love: Moral Reflection and the Shaping of Community* (Grand Rapids: Eerdmans, 2002).

2. See O'Donovan, *The Ways of Judgment,* pp. 242-243.

3. Ibid., p. 242.

organized as if they were families. It is precisely the differences among the differentiated spheres that enable communication or *koinōnia* as the form of the social life.

O'Donovan employs two crucial concepts in his account of a differentiated civil community. The first is that of a *people*. Civil community is not merely a collection of autonomous individuals, but the outgrowth of institutions and practices of a particular people. A people share an imaginative perception of a common good they are, or should be pursuing. This imaginative construct is not arbitrary, for it stems from a commonly held and binding tradition and culture, which in turn is instantiated in a series of "overlapping and interlocking" spheres of communication,[4] to a large extent echoing St. Augustine's insistence that a people are bound together by their common objects of love.[5] A people tacitly agree on what the goods of creation are and why they should be loved, and on what social spheres are needed and how they should be ordered in communicating these goods. To begin with a people as the centerpiece of political ordering provides a needed check to the liberal and authoritarian tendencies of late modernity. On the one hand, communicating the goods of creation requires a form of governance beyond a minimalist protection of civil rights, for such a structure cannot promote the common identity and good of a people. On the other hand, the priority of social communication resists unwarranted governmental encroachment that smothers the common identity of a people under the weight of bureaucratic regulation and control. In short, political ordering does not create civil community, but "discovers and defends the social order" of the people it governs.[6] Government represents a people, and a people see themselves in what represents them, thereby resisting the "state-totalitarianism"[7] endemic to late modernity in both its liberal and authoritarian manifestations.

The second concept is that of *place* or *locality.* Territory and borders are definitive features of a people. Goods can only be communicated within a particular place or locale, and boundaries are needed to differentiate the "you" and the "I" that can become a "we." Practically, the spheres of communication require a physical place and space in which their respective goods are communicated. A family needs a place to reside; work is performed in some locale. More broadly, a place incorporates the totality of diverse communications in

4. See ibid., p. 150.

5. See Augustine, *City of God,* 19.24; see also O'Donovan, *Common Objects of Love,* chapter 1.

6. See O'Donovan, *The Ways of Judgment,* p. 157.

7. See ibid., pp. 155-156.

which the particular spheres cohere in a singular locale. According to O'Donovan, it is a "high achievement to define society in terms of place, rather than blood-relationship," for such a "universal" conception embraces "all the forms of society that arise within a formally defined" place or bordered territory. This emphasis upon place helps resist both the "platonic temptation" to abolish or escape the constraints of locality which is amplified by the late modern drive to become dwellers of a worldless world, and the liberal project of transforming any and all places into property that can be owned and traded.[8] Identifying a society with a particular place resists the "totalitarian pretensions" in both liberal and authoritarian guises. Such identification acknowledges a plurality of societies which co-exist, each producing differing forms of governing their respective communications. Society is not a generic phenomenon, but entails a particular people in a particular locale that produces a particular state, and not idealistic models of political ordering that attempt to replace concrete locality with a vague and inclusive universality — a dangerous tactic of replacing bordered place with borderless space.

What might Christian moral and political theology gain from O'Donovan's account of communication? A comprehensive answer cannot be offered in this essay, but some venues of further inquiry suggest themselves by looking briefly at O'Donovan's assessment of one of the most ubiquitous features of the late modern world: the market. A market is a venue designed to facilitate exchange, and is often associated with but not limited to commercial exchanges. No human act can be entirely or exclusively commercial. A commercial act is predicated upon acts of production and consumption that in turn are embedded within various spheres of communication and broader social contexts. Individuals do not exchange merely for the sake of trading, but exchange in order to procure goods and services that are necessary to sustain the spheres in which the respective parties communicate. I exchange my money with the grocer, for instance, to put food on the family table. Exchange is thereby necessary to sustain a market, but is "not fundamental to community."[9] Rather, it is an instrumental device enabling a pursuit of the common good, in turn tacitly acknowledging that communication, as opposed to consumption, is what fulfills human community. Given the socially embedded character of all human action, work is not merely an instrumental act enabling production and consumption but is also an act of culture, endowing goods

8. See ibid., pp. 256-257; cf. Barry Cooper, *Action into Nature: An Essay on the Meaning of Technology* (Notre Dame, IN, and London: University of Notre Dame Press, 1991), part 11.
9. See O'Donovan, *The Ways of Judgment*, pp. 246-247.

and services with a deeper meaning that promotes communication.[10] A carpenter and playwright, for example, do not only produce, respectively, a dining room table and a play to be consumed, but also enable the communication of a family and community. Although the production and consumption of goods and services are not the defining features of civil community, they are nonetheless indispensable thereby necessitating the market and its rule of exchange. It is the market that sustains the differentiated spheres of communication, but it does so not through exchange itself but in providing a "common space" into which people enter and meet. The market is a "sign of a local society," for a physical locale is needed where products are actually released and taken.[11]

O'Donovan's account of communication offers a conceptual scheme with which to resist some of the more corrosive features of late modernity. This potential may be illustrated by noting briefly two instances. First, the emphasis upon a people serves as a reminder to avoid the old trap of confusing ends and means. The production and consumption of goods and services are important instrumental activities, but they are not ends in themselves. GDP informs us about the rates of productivity and consumption, but tells us little about whether or not they are aiding the communication of the goods of creation. That determination is a normative judgment based upon the tradition and culture of a people, and the ensuing political question is the extent to which government should regulate the market in ensuring that the communicative spheres comprising a people is best served, sustained, and protected.

Second, the emphasis upon locality explodes the late modern myth that place is now largely irrelevant. With the development of technologies providing speedy transportation and instantaneous exchange of information, the ideal late modern lifestyle is nomadic in which the constraints of locale have presumably been overcome. Late modern nomads can allegedly do their work and communicating anywhere and nowhere in particular. It is, however, a deception. Locality has not been overcome, but rendered less visible and immediate, creating the semblance of unencumbered mobility. Yet even the most itinerant nomad must eventually find a place to sleep, eat, access the web, and recharge the gadgets and devices. But these are merely pauses in a world of either physical or imaginative perpetual motion in which nomads presume that their liberation from locality is extended to the invisible individuals pro-

---

10. In this respect work should be regarded as "the essence of social communication," and "unemployment is the paradigm of social breakdown" (ibid., p. 251); cf. Hannah Arendt's distinction between labor and work in *The Human Condition* (Chicago and London: University of Chicago Press, 1998), parts III-IV.

11. See O'Donovan, *The Ways of Judgment*, p. 255.

ducing the goods and services they voraciously consume. In O'Donovan's trenchant words: "For me, as for slave-owners of the early modern colonies, it is all too easy to overlook those on whom the gratifying of my desire depends, and to succumb to the illusion that the tips of my fingers on keyboard and mouse have freed *them* from the constraints of place too!"[12]

I am largely sympathetic with O'Donovan's account of communication, because it offers a potentially useful concept for resisting the corrosive liberal and authoritarian tendencies of late modernity. To preserve the closely related notions of a people and locality is to also withstand efforts to diminish human identity to monochromatic options of consumer or citizen. Human identity is multifaceted, formed in and emerging out from overlapping layers of private and public associations rather than behavior dictated by either the market or the state. It is in and through these "bonds of imperfection,"[13] as the "gift of God" for being human,[14] that the goods of creation are properly communicated, and in turn aligning creation and its creatures toward the end for which they were created.

There is within O'Donovan's account of communication, however, an understated but nevertheless intriguing tension, in respect to the market, and economic exchange more broadly. He asserts, rather baldly, that "market-exchange is a purely instrumental device."[15] Yet he also contends that "market-transactions . . . are also communications."[16] Can he have it both ways? If the market is only instrumental, then the paramount moral consideration is its function rather than structure. So long as a market enables a people to communicate its goods then it presumably makes no difference if its exchanges are relatively free or controlled. But if market transactions are also communications then apparently its structure cannot help but serve certain ideological priorities regarding the preservation of a people and its locality. And herein lies the tension: if a people and its locale are being eroded, a condition which is seemingly endemic to late liberal societies, then blame cannot be assigned to an instrumental market that reflects rather than causes this decline. Yet if the market is the source of such erosion then it must be regulated and controlled by asserting political power, often within varying authoritarian guises. Neither option is a happy one in respect to O'Donovan's account of communication: an instru-

12. Ibid., p. 260.

13. See Oliver O'Donovan and Joan Lockwood O'Donovan, *Bonds of Imperfection: Christian Politics, Past and Present* (Grand Rapids: Eerdmans, 2004).

14. See O'Donovan, *The Ways of Judgment*, pp. 249-250.

15. Ibid., p. 255.

16. See ibid., pp. 246-247.

mental market provides the production and consumption of wanted goods and services, but in turn erodes the values and virtues that hold a community together over time and in place. Conversely, a controlled market results in a scarcity of needed goods and services that makes communication more difficult to achieve. We seemingly must choose between a market that is adept at promoting either vacuous consumerism or endemic impoverishment, in neither case sustaining the communications of a people. The market is apparently a necessity that proves to be either cancerous or parasitic.

In contending that markets are instrumental but their exchanges are nonetheless communications, O'Donovan is not posing a stark contradiction. Rather, has he not captured the curious circumstances of the late modern global market? Both liberal and authoritarian regimes depend upon market exchange to acquire necessary goods and services, yet neither free nor protectionist policies can sustain communication because neither can preserve a people and locality. In most respects, there is nothing new or novel about late modern market exchange. Technology has simply increased the speed and efficiency of production, trade, and consumption, and as noted above the so-called irrelevancy of place is an illusion. Yet there are features of this market which are unprecedented, entailing fluidity and a range of derivative pursuits, particularly in regard to finance, in which it is not clear what if, anything, is being exchanged. It is not so much a situation of trying to put new wine into old wineskins or old into new, but more like adding a few novel ingredients into the vat that has produced some unexpected changes in fermentation and undetermined taste.

O'Donovan's account of communication offers a conceptual framework for ascribing the normative social and political ordering of a vindicated creation awaiting, in this time between the times, its fulfillment in Christ. Much of his corpus describes what this ordering entails, especially in terms of the challenges posed by late modernity.[17] These challenges are particularly prescient in his discussion of communication, for late moderns are seemingly indifferent, if not hostile, to the very notions of a people and locality. Yet the subtle tension involving market exchange exemplifies the ambiguity of our present circumstances, for it is not clear where exactly to assign blame, and therefore to propose a remedy, for this indifference and hostility. The market is neither the cause nor the solution for sustaining the communication of the goods of creation.

---

17. See esp. Oliver O'Donovan, *Resurrection and Moral Order: An Outline for Evangelical Ethics* (Grand Rapids: Eerdmans, 1986).

Is there a way to gain some more clarity on this ambiguity, not at this juncture to resolve it, but to simply acknowledge and begin exploring it? One potential venue is to visit briefly O'Donovan's principal inspiration: Johannes Althusius. O'Donovan's account of communication draws upon the Althusian principle of symbiotic association. In brief, the civil community is not composed of individual citizens but private and public associations such as families, guilds, collegiums, and estates. Consequently, government represents a people rather than creating them, suggesting a kind of proto-federalism.[18] Althusius wrote agonizingly lengthy and detailed tomes, and what O'Donovan takes from him is admittedly sparse. This is not a criticism, however, for if I learned nothing else from my teacher I learned the rule of nominal plundering: seize only what you need from an author, and no more. As a result, you will be relieved to know that you need not endure a summary of Althusius's work in order to find some useful treasure that O'Donovan left behind. Nor am I hinting that O'Donovan is or should become an Althusian. Some writers contend that if one begins with Althusius one inevitably ends with the European Union — though, as someone residing on the other side of the pond, I have no idea if this is a good or desirable end. Rather, I want to focus on the context that prompted Althusius's work.

Much of what Althusius wrote was provoked by a reaction against Jean Bodin. To oversimplify, Bodin proposed a top-down model of political and social ordering. The state creates civil society by assigning and granting certain duties, rights, and privileges to individual citizens. What holds a civil community together is the state's monopoly on coercive power rather than any particular tradition, culture, or locale as exemplified in an empire. In contrast, Althusius propounded a bottom-up model in which the state represents a differentiated society of private and public associations held together by a common tradition, culture, and locale that the state is obligated to honor and protect. Bodin carried the day, and his general principle of the centrality of the state was refined by subsequent generations of political theorists.

Why did Bodin's argument carry the day? There are a number of answers to this question, but one I submit is that they presupposed two differing universal backgrounds against which they developed their particular and respective foregrounds of political and social ordering. The particular has no meaning in the absence of the universal; the specific is known in contrast to the general. Again, to oversimplify, Althusius presupposed a background of a

---

18. See, e.g., Thomas O. Hueglin, *Early Modern Concepts for a Late Modern World: Althusius on Community and Federalism* (Waterloo, ON: Wilfrid Laurier University Press, 1999).

universal Christian culture. There were admittedly severe disagreements over what this culture entailed, but it was an argument over a shared reality. Various civil communities were pluriform expressions of this universal culture, albeit in conflicting ways. Hence Althusius's insistence that the power of the commonwealth should be dispersed among the symbiotic associations, both private and public, comprising the civil community in order to protect their autonomy and preserve their respective communications. The borders of the commonwealth were roughly contiguous with that of the locality populated by a people that it represented. Althusius developed a splendid codification and philosophical justification for late medieval society, at the very time that its formative Christian culture was already in tatters and could not sustain what he was championing. What he offered was a description of Minerva's owl that was already well along in its flight.

Bodin presupposed the universality of the state, and in doing so turned the Althusian model on its head. Power should be centralized in the state, and reallocated by granting selective duties, rights, and privileges. In this scheme private associations could be ignored or tolerated so long as they did not unduly disturb the peace or directly threaten the authority of the state. Moreover, the state did not represent a particular people nor was it obligated to protect its locale. Rather, the state consisted of individual citizens or subjects, and its borders were determined by the territory it could either defend or seize. The state, then, with its monopoly of coercive power, could govern widely divergent cultures. Although subsequent generations of political philosophers argued over what form the state should take, and the extent it should or should not encroach upon the private affairs of the individuals it governed, its necessity and universality was never seriously challenged.

I have recounted this context not to reenter the debate between Althusius and Bodin, but to suggest that we might be facing a similar situation in which the universality of the state is being supplanted by the universality of the market. This prospect is reflected in Philip Bobbitt's contention that we have entered a period of transition from the nation-state to the market-state.[19] According to Bobbitt, the nineteenth century was the era of the nation-state in which citizens were expected to serve the interests of the state, which was achieved primarily through imperial expansion. This led to inevitable conflict, and a long war was fought in the twentieth century to establish the predomi-

19. See Philip Bobbitt, *The Shield of Achilles: War, Peace, and the Course of History* (New York: Knopf, 2002), and *Terror and Consent: The Wars for the Twenty-First Century* (New York: Knopf, 2008).

nance of the nation-state in which state exists to serve the interests of its citizens. The victory was short-lived, however, for with the rapid expansion of global markets and trade liberalization the transition to the market-state was initiated.

Unlike more exuberant enthusiasts that proclaimed the end of history with the collapse of the Berlin wall,[20] Bobbitt readily admits that the disappearance of the nation-state is far from imminent. He acknowledges that virtually everyone continues to live in nation-states and will continue to do so in the foreseeable future, but they do so in a world that is increasingly better suited for the market-state. This odd circumstance is seen in the dual and conflicting identities of citizen and consumer. Citizens, for instance, want secure borders to protect their jobs and assets, but consumers want few, if any, restrictions, upon free flowing trade, capital, and labor. These conflicting interests produce a political dilemma: the state attempts to exert greater territorial control over a population aspiring to become, both physically and imaginatively, increasingly nomadic (willingly, unwillingly, or unwittingly). If we are entering a contextual shift from the universality of the state to the market, or in Bobbitt's terms from nation-state to market-state, then it may help to account for O'Donovan's tension regarding the market and why the concept of communication is a useful tool for theologians to assess this shift in both a critical and a constructive manner. To initiate this exploration I will pose two questions, and I have no intention of answering either of them as I am staking out some areas for future inquiry.

First question: what is a market? Or, perhaps more accurately, what is the market becoming? To speak of the market in our present circumstances requires that we speak about a global market, or to invoke the popular but inelegant word, "globalization." In order to speak intelligibly, however, two myths must be dispelled: (1) that what is referred to as globalization is a unique phenomenon. This is, of course, nonsense. For as long as human beings have exchanged goods and services with others who are not their own at some distance, a global market (of sorts) has existed, and over time its extent and number of participants has ebbed and flowed.[21] Contrary to Thomas Friedman, the world was already flat when many of its inhabitants believed it really was flat. What is now unprecedented is the scale of the global market made possible,

20. See, e.g., Francis Fukuyama, *The End of History and the Last Man* (New York: Avon Books, 1992).

21. See William J. Bernstein, *A Splendid Exchange: How Trade Shaped the World* (New York: Atlantic Monthly Press, 2008).

in part, by technological developments enabling ease of transport and information exchange, and the creation of unparalleled levels of production, consumption, trade, employment, wealth, and capital. (2) Globalization signifies the triumph of democratic capitalism. This again is nonsense. Adam Smith did not invent the market. Markets have been a central feature of human life for as long as history has been recorded, and it is a remarkably flexible device that is able to accommodate either gradual or rapid social change, as well as a widely varying range of participants holding disparate ideologies and interests. In this respect, it is important to note that the biggest players in the current global market, especially in energy and capital investment, are not private or publicly traded corporations but state-owned and -operated firms.[22]

The global market is still predominantly a space, but one that can be configured physically or virtually. I can either purchase an item by entering a local store, or I can "virtually enter" a web site and have it delivered to my home. O'Donovan is right to insist that cheerfully clicking my way through a web site creates the illusion that locality is irrelevant. Let us imagine, for example, that I need a new computer so I can continue to write books and articles that are read by very few people. While on a trip in a hotel room late at night I order the computer online, and request delivery on the day I will return home. In the few minutes that it took me to complete this task, I initiated a series of global transactions. Although the lead office of the company from which I purchased the computer is located in Texas, the server hosting the web site is in Vancouver. An office worker in Dublin reviews and processes my order. The hardware and software were manufactured in such places as Bucharest, Tokyo, Seoul, and Taipei. My computer is assembled in Shanghai, and air-freighted and delivered to my door by a corporation headquartered in Memphis. Unfortunately, I can't get the bloody thing to work, so late that night I ring the twenty-four-hour customer service hotline and speak to a patient representative in Bangalore who helps me correct the problem. I may now sleep in peace knowing that my new computer is working like a charm, while the service rep takes her lunch break, no doubt muttering something about stupid Americans.

What this scenario illustrates is that although locality may be invisible to me as I happily click away, it is certainly not rendered irrelevant. Yet the extent to which market space is contiguous with physical proximity is made prob-

---

22. See, e.g., Ian Bremmer, *The End of the Free Market: Who Wins the War Between States and Corporations* (New York: Portfolio, 2010); cf. Stefan Halper, *The Beijing Consensus: How China's Authoritarian Model Will Dominate the Twenty-first Century* (New York: Basic Books, 2010).

lematic, or at least ambiguous. Distance is not a deterrent to exchange, but promotes and enlarges it. The market creates "virtual spaces" wherever and whenever exchange is needed. It would appear that the global market inevitably erodes communication since its virtual spaces enable anonymous exchange among late modern nomads. Locality has not been eliminated, but has been effectively separated from territory. To a large extent, I think this is probably true, but the characterization is too sweeping. Territorial protectionism, for example, does not necessarily promote communication. To return to my computer, if it were required that all manufacturing and distribution had to be confined to a hundred-mile radius of where I reside, most of the individuals involved in their production and consumption would still remain anonymous. Moreover, it is quite possible that I could not afford such a computer given insufficient supply and lack of competition. In addition, although the individuals and their locales spread around the world remain invisible to me, my purchasing helps provide employment that enables their participation in communicative associations. The global market is a space, but not one determined by fixed boundaries, but is fluid with an ebb and flow, embracing its participants somewhat like an undulating tide. It is this fluidity that prompts further inquiry into the relationship between communication and the market: can a fluid market be a potential instrument for assisting communication among a greater number of people? To what extent does communication depend upon a locale of physical proximity, or can it be conducted at a distance among mobile people? Can communicative spaces be created that are intended to be impermanent, non-territorial, transportable, but *not* nomadic?

Second question: what is association? Or, what is association coming to be? A prerequisite for communicating the goods of creation is a people sharing a common place. Traditionally such place was delimited by territorial constraints. A community resulted predominantly, though not entirely, from the accident of proximity, and a distinct lack of physical and social mobility over time. This is not the case for late moderns who are adept at forming associations of shared interests for relatively brief or extended periods of time through the creation of temporary physical and virtual spaces accomplished through a combination of information and transportation technologies. This, of course, begs the question of whether or not communication can occur periodically and at a distance. There are, I believe, two popular but failed strategies that are often employed in answering this question. The first strategy may be characterized as the Amish option in which a territorial enclave is carved out for the purpose of isolating its members as much as possible from the contagion of the outside world. There is admittedly some appeal to this option, but it is unclear if selective isolation — such as refusing to connect to the electrical grid or internet — actually preserves or enhances communication. Moreover, the livelihood of such territorially sequestered communities remain dependent upon trading with outsiders, so even Amish agricultural products and crafts eventually find their way into the global market. The second strategy — resistance is futile — succumbs to present circumstances by privileging virtual space over territorial place. It is far from clear, however, if a so-called virtual community is anything more than a contradiction in terms. Perhaps I am just too old to make the transition to social networking, but I don't believe that Facebook is an adequate substitute for communicating face-to-face.

Both of these strategies fail because it is assumed that territorial place and virtual space, the former implying permanence while the latter is transient, are mutually exclusive; either one or the other. Yet the issue at stake may not be either/or but both/and. Is the late modern world emerging, or could it emerge, as a network composed of symbiotic and enkaptically related communities that are sustained by overlapping social spaces that are simultaneously territorial and virtual? Spaces or localities in which communication occurs through both physical proximity and at a distance, and on both an ongoing and periodic basis? An example which comes to mind is that I am a member of a theological faculty. The seminary has a territorial location, and the community is composed of an accidental collection of students, teachers, staff, and administrators. Within this common place we go about our respective tasks, presumably to the benefit of our common good. I also participate in a community of scholars sharing common interests, who are spread across the world. We meet or converse periodically in temporary physical and virtual spaces. These two associations overlap and to a large extent are mutually enriching. I see no compelling reason why I must choose one to the exclusion of the other. Yet admittedly there are also tensions. The concerns and conversations I share with my faculty colleagues are not the same as those with members of my guild. Moreover, the same market forces exerting institutional pressures in respect to student recruitment, mode of instruction, financial management, and campus maintenance are the same ones enabling the guild to thrive by reducing the costs and enhancing the ease of exchanging information, conversing, and traveling.

This simple illustration is emblematic of broader tensions endemic to late modernity, such as the one between the twin identities of citizen and consumer in the emerging market-state. Despite the growing desire of late moderns to be unfettered nomadic wanderers, they remain very much tied to localities that are fixed and territorial. Any extensive wandering requires passports and visas, and governments determine that they reside someplace long enough to pay taxes. Yet the ability to create temporary, periodic, and virtual spaces cannot be ignored or easily dismissed. Consequently, for the sake of future inquiry, locality as a prerequisite for communication needs to be acknowledged, but the ensuing theological task is not to steadfastly resist any notions of locality that might erode a presumed territorial foundation. Rather, is not the challenge to conceive locality in terms of a series of overlapping, enkaptic, and global social spheres or spaces which on the one hand are territorial, relatively permanent, and ongoing, while on the other hand are also temporary, periodic, and virtual? And is it not also the task to conceive an ordering of these spheres or spaces that ultimately promotes communicating the goods of creation instead of lesser goods, such as exchange? And in particular, how might the global market be used as an instrument in achieving this ordering?

There are, of course, many other questions that could be posed for future investigation. Some examples that come readily to mind is what is work coming to mean, and how it is related to labor and employment? What is property? What are private spaces and what are public spaces? How should these spaces be related and to what extent do they overlap? Why is communication a useful conceptual tool that should be employed by theologians in pondering and assessing our late modern circumstances? In lieu of offering an answer, I simply note two agenda items for future investigation.

First, communication helps resist false claims of universality. F. D. Maurice offered the salient observation that the longing for universal association or fellowship is a good desire.[23] This good desire is embodied supremely in the church's affirmation of its catholicity. Moreover, the church's universality does not destroy or negate particularity; the church is one but pluriform. Consequently, the church upholds and assists the various social spheres in which the goods of creation are communicated in pluriform ways. This good desire, however, can be easily corrupted, the most striking example being that of a quest for universal empire. The centralization of imperial power destroys the particularity of conquered nations; their respective customs and traditions are displaced by generic edicts and inconsiderate policies. The eventual goal is to homogenize vanquished peoples into a singular artifact of imperial will and power. Maurice, for instance, contends (incorrectly, I think) that Rome imposed Latin as the only valid idiom for public and commercial discourse. He then makes the eccentric, but nonetheless intriguing, observation

---

23. See F. D. Maurice, *Social Morality* (London: Macmillan and Co., 1869).

that the Holy Spirit has given the gift of tongues to resist such imperial pretensions.[24]

Although the late modern nation-state has purportedly renounced any overt interest in establishing empires (they are, after all, expensive to maintain), the universal and homogenous state, as George Grant was fond of reminding his readers,[25] is nonetheless a ubiquitous and lamentable reality, and its unconstrained expansion should be resisted. The encroachment of the state, in both its more liberal and authoritarian forms, has a withering effect upon symbiotic and communicative associations, distorting civil community into an artifact of the state's will. Displacing the universal and homogenous state with the universal and homogenous market, however, is not a good exchange. Although the global market may be an excellent tool for resisting the encroachment of the state, it too can have a corrosive effect upon communicative associations when consumption and exchange become ends in themselves. It may seem odd to indict the market of attempting to demolish particularity since it is presumably designed to satisfy diverse needs and wants. But when production, consumption, and exchange are pursued on a mass scale, homogenization is likely if not inevitable. The goods and services afforded by the global market are growing increasingly similar if not identical due to the scale of demand. What is somewhat unique is the occasional local spin on how these goods or services are used; for example, the growing popularity of KFC for Christmas Eve dinners in Tokyo. In short, the danger is reducing civil community to individual consumers in which all interaction is perceived as exchanges resulting in voracious and insatiable consumption.

This does not mean that the state and the market are inherently evil. To the contrary both are necessary prerequisites for communicating the goods of creation; the former is required for protection and the latter for provision. The problem is when either of these partial goods is elevated to *the* universal or ultimate good. Both must remain limited if they are to fulfill their respective instrumental purposes. Life in its fullness cannot be obtained by being either a citizen or a consumer. Communication offers, at least in principle, criteria for properly limiting and orienting the state and market. Establishing such criteria, however provisionally, will require a normative account of what communicating the goods of creation entails, particularly in respect to this uncer-

24. See ibid., p. 291.

25. See George Grant, *Technology and Empire: Perspectives on North America* (Toronto: House of Anansi, 1969), esp. pp. 79-109.

tain transition from nation-state to market-state. But what is the source or sources that should be plundered in devising this account?

This question leads to the second agenda item for future inquiry: can the church be a model of a non-territorial people, but for whom locality remains central in communicating the goods of creation? The church is composed of the people of God with their particular customs and traditions that endure over time. Yet Christians are not a people that are tied to a particular territory. They are not required to reside or even visit such notable places as Jerusalem, Rome, or Canterbury. But as a people they do require a place in which to gather, and that space is created wherever and whenever two or three gather in Christ's name. Some of these spaces are relatively fixed, such as a cathedral, but others are often temporary and almost always periodic. I have my doubts whether these spaces can be virtual, but I leave it as an open question.

Whenever and wherever Christians gather in their Lord's name, they create a space in which they commune; they are bound together as a people in the church, the *koinonia* of Jesus Christ. Yet is important to emphasize that in these spaces it is not the gathered, but, as O'Donovan insists, the gathering church that demarcates the locale.[26] This is not a fine semantic distinction, but a reminder of the church's and creation's eschatological destiny in Christ. In this time between the times, the work of the church, as well as the governing of creation, is pursued in expectation of the *parousia*. To borrow imagery from St. Augustine, Christians are therefore a restless people, never quite at home anywhere in a world they are nonetheless called to love and serve. Consequently, in contrast to the identities of native citizen or nomadic consumer, a third option of *expectant pilgrim* is offered. Unlike natives, pilgrims know that their destiny is not determined by blood and soil, but by water and the Spirit. They are free to go wherever in the world they are called to be. And unlike nomads, pilgrims do not wander aimlessly or where they will. They know where they are headed, but often tarry along the way in particular places for extended periods of time. Consequently, theological precepts of social and political ordering are offered with a provisional certitude, subject to reformation and amendment in light of the changing circumstances of the providential unfolding of God's vindicated creation being drawn toward its appointed destiny.

To what extent this kind of sojourning ecclesiology might inform the secular ordering of civil community is a task for future inquiry and delibera-

---

26. See Oliver O'Donovan, *The Desire of the Nations: Rediscovering the Roots of Political Theology* (Cambridge: Cambridge University Press, 1996), pp. 175-178.

158

tion. The precept of communication, perhaps with some selective plundering of the principle of subsidiarity and doctrine of the orders of creation, might help to forge discourse to delimit and reorient the earthly city, particularly the state and market, toward its proper destiny. This is an important and daunting task to take on in this time of transition from nation-state to market-state, and we should be grateful to Oliver for urging, at times provoking, his fellow theologians to get on with it.

What Is "the Public"?
Theological Variations on Babel and Pentecost

Brian Brock

Where does the public sphere lie and what sort of conceptual description will best bring its essential contours into view? The main task of this paper is to show how several classic Christian proposals define the scope, content, and conceptual level of the idea of the "public sphere." Such an investigation seems especially useful if we are prepared to consider many of today's most heated popular and scholarly disputes about political questions to be inflamed by a much longer, deeper, and largely unconscious struggle to agree about what the public sphere actually is. The multi-layered complexity of the ongoing negotiation of the shape and architecture of the European Union provides one example of the conceptual and practical issues involved in such definitional clarifications. Each party holds divergent assumptions about what the public sphere, government, oligarchic interests, definitions of secularity, and so on are, each entailing an account of how these terms interrelate. As a result, political negotiation is both difficult and productive because divergent and contested definitional constellations yield different and contested sets of practical recommendations for the shape of the public square, and so what activities are understood to be legitimate or indispensable within it.

In this paper I will survey two broadly related theological approaches to the question of the source and soul of the public sphere. I will first examine Augustine's claim that a society is an artefact of the agglomeration of a population's loves, and how Oliver O'Donovan has deployed this framing of the question in his political theology. I will then briefly outline Dietrich Bonhoef-

With thanks to Scott Prather for his editorial comments on this paper.

fer's elaboration of a different Augustinian theme, that a true public springs from the divine activity of forgiveness and reconciliation, moving on to show how this account of the public orients the political theology of Bernd Wannenwetsch. I will not follow the familiar convention of defining the public as the inverse of the private, preferring instead to explore the idea of the public on its own theological terms.

Augustine was the first western theologian to produce a robust Christian account of the public and its theoretical relation to the church and state. His preferred term for what we think of today as the public is a "society," defined as a community of shared loves, is the foundational definition upon which his accounts of the church and state and their interrelations rests. On some readings the ballast of his position is carried by an analysis of the immanent dynamics of human affective attachment and its production of political alliances. On such a reading Augustine's account of the public sphere attunes contemporary political theology to the processes of congregation automatically at work in fallen human society. But he also made a claim that places some tension on this first concept, that a society based on false love, that is, on a love other than God, is not a true society.

In his political theology, Bonhoeffer develops this latter strand of Augustine's thought, being centrally concerned with the role of repentance and reconciliation in his framing of a definition of the (or a) public. Though Bonhoeffer's emphasis on the constitutive role of reconciliation and forgiveness in sustaining the public sphere highlights the trust social contractarian political thought eclipses (as has been recognized in some recent philosophical accounts),[1] I will further suggest that a Christian account of these terms is not reducible without remainder to a philosophical account due to its insistence that true forgiveness and reconciliation are precipitated and facilitated by Christ's forgiveness. The trajectory of Bonhoeffer's account demands that theological accounts of the public sphere take seriously the radical nature of human conflict, and the magnitude of the task of overcoming it, presuming that any public that does not do so cannot remain a public in any meaningful sense.

My proposal is that O'Donovan's interests follow Augustine (and Hobbes)[2]

1. Michael Hardt and Antonio Negri, *Commonwealth* (Cambridge, MA: Belknap Press, 2009), pp. 179-188; Sheldin Wolin, *Politics and Vision: Continuity and Innovation in Western Political Thought*, expanded ed. (Princeton: Princeton University Press, 2004), pp. 581-606.

2. While clearly critical of Hobbes's political thought in a range of ways, O'Donovan does take him to be the beginning of modern political thought (cf. Oliver O'Donovan, *Desire of the Nations: Rediscovering the Roots of Political Theology* [Cambridge: Cambridge University Press,

in unpacking the import for political ethics of the post-lapsarian location of human social interaction. As a result, politics is primarily concerned with guilt and wrong in the public sphere. In contrast, Wannenwetsch follows an alternative Augustinianism developed by Bonhoeffer (and in the tradition of Rousseau), that is primarily concerned with the conceptual and practical implications of the need for repentance, reconciliation, and the overcoming of estrangement if any public is to endure. I am not suggesting that either account offers the definitive theological definition of the public. I aim rather to thematize the noticeable difference of emphasis between these two accounts in a manner that might aid those wishing to incorporate the substantial theological insights evident in both approaches.

In both approaches a public is generally understood as first and primarily a community of people who can converse with one another and make political decisions together. This agreement on the formal features of political life allows different but complementary descriptions of the content of this conversation, so drawing attention to the fundamental component of trust which grounds all social bonding. In both strands a "public" is understood as at root a form of faith, an embodied and communicative goodwill and hope for life together. We are reminded in a shocking way of the indispensability of this fundamental trust and desire for reconciliation in those moments when antagonistic political parties find themselves in paralyzed deadlock over crucial tasks of governance, such as forging a budget. Within a broad agreement on this emphasis, however, what distinguishes the two strands of political theology I wish to investigate here is their different weighing of two of Augustine's most well known beliefs about political life; on the one hand that societies are born from the confluences of immanent human loves, and on the other that a society not sharing a love of God is no real society.

I will suggest that a core task of a Christian political theology is to develop readers' sensitivities to the ways that any public is built up and maintained, so that healthy trends in a public can be identified and something constructive offered about how to keep it from breaking down. The gain in looking at the origin and internal dynamics of the public, understood as a fragile entity based on collective trust, believing, hoping, and loving, is to go beyond the modern narrowing of political philosophy to questions of the development of procedural rules or accounts of the limits of what can or cannot be allowed in the public sphere (a narrowing championed in the hugely influential *A Theory of*

1996], p. xi), a judgement which warrants my interest here in isolating the larger points of convergence between their framings of political philosophy.

Justice of John Rawls). On my reading O'Donovan approaches this critical task via the question, "How does a public come into being?" a question he presses in order to expose the essential ligatures that must link up in the formation of any public. Wannenwetsch asks a slightly different question: "How is a public sustained?" This line of questioning assumes that the sustainability of the public sphere depends on more than a suite of tricks and techniques that can be deployed to maintain political consensus, and demands a more substantive account than is offered by purely reactive and negative accounts that focus almost exclusively on responding to its metastases.

Without a deep account of what generates and sustains a healthy public, purely procedural discussion of the behaviours appropriate to the public sphere are doomed to repeat platitudes. There are well-known historical reasons why modern political thought tries to do without this deeper explanation, reasons I believe are susceptible to theological narration. I will set out my version of that theological narrative before moving to my main theme, the public as defined by O'Donovan and Wannenwetsch.

Prehistories of the Public

Paralleling almost every form of political thought, Christian theology has an *Urgeschichte* of political disunity, the divine punishment of humanity's hubristic self-exaltation at the tower of Babel. Modern western political philosophy achieved its current form only by overturning the previous hegemony of the Genesis account of the beginnings of society, language, authority, and so government. We no longer recall that Locke's hugely influential *Two Treatises on Government* devotes one of its two books to explaining why the divine command to Adam to exercise dominion is an inappropriate foundation for a theory of government. Hobbes's political philosophy begins from a primal prehistory that is darkly post-lapsarian. In *The Origin of Inequality* Rousseau's approach is more subtle, taking up all the themes of the creation account he wishes to displace with his secularized Eden protology by suggesting that the primeval biblical history is proto-democratic in depicting the essence of the social order as a primal grant of reciprocated trust.

I return to the primal stories which underlie the conceptual superstructure of modern political philosophy in hopes of providing a fresh view of what is at stake in discussion of the nature and proper content of the public sphere. Primal stories draw attention to what are considered to be the most important features of a subject. For our purposes protologies serve to answer at least two questions. Out of what phenomenon does a public arise? What is the essence of a public as a living and dynamic entity that coalesces and can dissipate? These questions are particularly important for those of us who have been freshly reminded in both ecclesial and national contexts that it is perilous to take the continuing solidity of any given public for granted.

Given this exorcism of scripture from modern political thought, it is worthwhile for political theologians to revisit the basic conceptions of human political life to which they are committed by scripture. It is clear that the depiction of edenic interpersonal relations is strongly bracketed by the terminus of these innocent relations in the Babel episode (Gen. 11:1-9). In the Babel narrative the biblical authors express their understanding of what every subsequent society ought to expect to be the main problems of political life. Here the loss of shared language is linked with the breakdown of the space of public communication and so the fragmentation of society. But in distinction from the main strands of social contract theory, in which a primal contract resolves this political agonism, the New Testament depicts the recovery of community as found only in a divine transcending of political disunity which at the same time preserves differences of language, culture, and human agency (Acts 2:1-4).

At Pentecost, the immediacy of the Holy Spirit causes words of praise and proclamation to spring to human lips. Like the light which God created and which gives the world time to be with him, language is the condition for human communication and so communion. Given the central role played in the Old Testament by the concept of the Word and its role in the formation of inter-human and human-divine covenants, this structural and structuring function of language is revealed as one of the most important of the divine gifts. For this reason, the Old Testament prohibitions against lying, false oaths, and the false use of God's name are prominently placed and regularly elaborated.[3] The function of the Babel narrative is to unpack the tragic knock-on effect of the Fall in terms of the loss of the communal fabric sustained by language. In it human self-exaltation inexorably calls down the divine punishment which is simultaneously a protective measure, the confusion of language that immediately leads to political fragmentation.

In short, the sin of Babel is not building a tower but doing so in a quest for self-emancipation on which God can only smile in pity. In the doomed

---

3. The protection of language is prominent in both tables of the Decalogue (Ex. 20:7, 16), the violators of language are regularly excoriated in the Psalms (cf. Ps. 120, 10:7), and in the prophetic literature, the eschatological people are pictured as having no lies in their mouths (Is. 53:9, Zeph. 3:13). The latter metaphor carries straight into the New Testament (Rev. 14:5).

attempt to make a name for themselves rather than be named by God humans are depicted as contracting centripetally, hoarding rather than moving out centrifugally in the life of free sharing of the goods of creation for which they were meant. The power of language, instead of serving communal life, is teamed with human technological knowledge not to continue life with God, but to overcome him to possess and control his gifts.

Though it may come as a surprise given the evident political power of the possession of unified language, in the New Testament the Holy Spirit speaks into the heart of the punishment of Babel (Babylon) not, as we might expect, to restore the original unity of language, but to create a new unity within and beyond linguistic diversity. John's apocalypse also pictures a final reconciliation of the peoples that does not elide differences (Rev. 7:9-12), a vision that is surely also a reflection on the early church's powerful experience of this political unification after Pentecost. In the song of praise of Christ evoked by the unifying Spirit, those speaking different languages find their way opened toward one another and a unity of hearts. Without this unity, diversity of languages engenders diversity in aims, and it is a work of divine grace not to allow social unities which naturally coalesce around self-exaltation to become the rule.

In the relation of the Babel and Pentecost moments of salvation history Christian theology is offered a rich conceptuality for rethinking contemporary definitions of the public sphere.

Augustine

In a famous remark Augustine grounds his theory of society in the shared love of earthly goods. He does so in a manner that allows him to make subtle distinctions between the value of the goods to which a public is attached and so to evaluate the unity itself.

> A people, we may say, is a gathered multitude of rational beings united by agreeing to share the things they love. There can be as many different kinds of people as there are different things for them to love. Whatever those things may be, there is no absurdity in calling it a people if it is a gathered multitude, not of beasts but of rational creatures, united by agreeing to share what they love. The better the things, the better the people, the worse the things, the worse their agreement to share them.[4]

4. Augustine, *City of God*, XIX.24. Translated by O'Donovan in *From Irenaeus to Grotius:*

Augustine's analysis asks us to become sensitive to the meaning of collective expressions of love and its opposite, hatred. This provides an alternative to the habit of modern political philosophy to begin with discussion of the structures of government, a clarification of the concepts of the private and the public, or attempts to negotiate the relation of secular and religious language within public discourse. Oliver O'Donovan makes much of this strand of Augustine's political theology.

Oliver O'Donovan

While O'Donovan has written voluminously in political theology, here I will only sketch the main political themes he draws from Augustine in his little book *Common Objects of Love*. In it O'Donovan encapsulates this Augustinian starting point with a question, "What unifies agents into a community of action?"[5] He opens his answer by outlining Augustine's decisively premodern epistemology. We know anything only because we are affectively attached to things that engage our attention; before study, deliberation, and decision we are beings who love. "All knowledge, then, has an affective aspect, just as all love has a cognitive aspect."[6]

The "disinterested" knowledge of the natural sciences can therefore only be a practical stance we cultivate in the interest of investigation. We can more or less successfully bracket out our feelings in the course of an inquiry, but those feelings remain, and as has been so often shown in revisionist accounts of modern science, are often the actual motor and tiller of our supposedly disinterested behaviour. O'Donovan's point is to question the modern mania for epistemology which assumes that the most critical questions are resolved by asking how we know what we know. He stresses, conversely, that humans cannot avoid evaluative and affective judgements and that this must be taken into account at the most basic strata of our political theories.

He stands here in direct opposition to theories like Rawls's neo-Kantian veil of ignorance which renders justice precisely by attempting to extract our knowledge of whether we care for or love others from our political deliberations. But it is also worth noting that he stands in continuity with such theories

---

A Sourcebook in Christian Political Thought, ed. Oliver O'Donovan and Joan Lockwood O'Donovan (Grand Rapids: Eerdmans, 1999), p. 162.

5. Oliver O'Donovan, *Common Objects of Love: Moral Reflection and the Shaping of Community* (Grand Rapids: Eerdmans, 2002), p. 1.

6. O'Donovan, *Common Objects*, p. 11.

by setting up his argument on the basis of human individual and collective love of objects that is more fundamental than love of persons (including God).

> Loving is the corporate function that determines and defines the structure of the political society; it is the key to its coherence and its organization. Loving *things,* not loving *one another.* Augustine also affirmed that members of a community loved one another; but that is a second step. The love that founds the community is not reciprocal, but turned outward upon an object.[7]

This premise sets up the later accounts offered of tradition and history which are framed as in the most basic sense projects of human identity formation.[8]

Tracing two of his further distinctions allows us to begin to see the implications of O'Donovan's chosen starting point. First, we must distinguish between willing and loving. Willing is the flagship concept in modern political thought, but occludes the reality that our acts are often responses to persons, ideas, or other realities outside of us. Love names the positive attitudinal disposition of response, and is not reducible to the acts which it motivates. "The object of love is not an act of our own, but simply — to use an Augustinian phrase again — the 'enjoyment' of its object; and 'enjoyment' is not the name of something we do, but of a relation in which we stand."[9] This distinction allows a second: public moral deliberation can never be simply about acting. Because we also are beings with affective attachments, even when we engage in public discussions about proposed collective or governmental actions, making no explicit reference to our ontological presuppositions, our positions nevertheless derive their intelligibility from the thick descriptions of what we take to be the true and the good in an ultimate sense.[10]

The concept of secularity plays an important role at this juncture. The Christian concept of secularity is an eschatological notion, suggests O'Donovan, composed of a refusal to give up claims to knowledge of God and a simultaneous acceptance in patient hope of the incompleteness of all human knowledge.[11] The western political doctrine of secularity codifies this hope by formalizing the church's rather late realization that voices who dispute its theological claims might nevertheless speak truth about many other questions, including the proper course of action a political body ought to pursue. At this

---

7. O'Donovan, *Common Objects,* p. 26, italics in original.
8. O'Donovan, *Common Objects,* p. 34.
9. O'Donovan, *Common Objects,* p. 16.
10. O'Donovan, *Common Objects,* p. 17.
11. O'Donovan, *Common Objects,* p. 42.

point the blessing in the punishment of Babel becomes more apparent. As part of what is decidedly a curse, the fragmentation of political unity, a legitimate reticence to claim to possess the whole truth and nothing but the truth becomes possible, and this is a blessing for public discourse.

O'Donovan sees the Good Samaritan as a paradigmatic exemplar of the proper virtue of secularity in his setting aside of nationalist and religious prejudices, those false social representations which keep him from noticing and responding to proximate need.[12] Notice, however, that his interest is in the moment of the Samaritan's relinquishing his prejudices before acting, not in the moment of the actual giving of care to the fallen victim. This emphasis grows from a definition of secularity primarily concerned to foster a healthy resistance to premature unification of political plurality of belief, and O'Donovan's heavy reliance on the imagery of the final judgment makes it clear that his is the secularity of the "unfulfilled promise,"[13] not a secularity generated by any present experience of reconciliation.

An emphasis on the overcoming of estranging political differences in order to respond to proximate human need is further eclipsed in his more programmatic account which conceives political reconciliation primarily in terms of its final eschatological consummation rather than its inbreaking into contemporary human affairs.[14] When O'Donovan does discuss the dispersal of Babel[15] it is not reconciliation that is understood to bring humans back into political society with one another, but place: "It is a high achievement to define society in terms of place, rather than blood-relationship, language, economic practice, or whatever, and so conceive it as a concrete universal, embracing all the forms of society that arise within a formally defined area of spatial contiguity."[16] It relevant to note that the discovery of place by a people is here depicted as a *society's* achievement.

Because society is a public conversation in which a community discovers and expresses its shared loves in the mode of designating the objects and ideas with which it wishes to represent its essence and self-assessment, it creates icons which

. . . form the communal self-understanding which structures all other shared meanings. They include representative objects, representative per-

12. O'Donovan, *Common Objects*, p. 44.
13. O'Donovan, *Common Objects*, p. 42.
14. O'Donovan, *Common Objects*, p. 40.
15. O'Donovan, *Ways of Judgment* (Grand Rapids: Eerdmans, 2005), pp. 254-256.
16. O'Donovan, *Ways of Judgment*, p. 256.

sons, representative histories and representative ideas [including forms of governmental organization]. They express what the society is, and they express what it is good for; they are forms of that knowledge of itself which is at the same time love of itself. They constitute the central core of the society's common way of seeing the world and living in it. And because the existence of a society is not atemporal, they constitute the core of its continuing identity in time, providing intelligible connections between past and present. In this function we refer to them as the "tradition" of the society.[17]

To have such designated representations is simultaneously to recognize threats to them[18] and to be provided with the tools to explain events which seem to have evoked strong collective passions. Tensions are sure to arise when a community's chosen representations are challenged. The resurgence of anti-flag burning amendments in the US as a backlash against supposed anti-patriotism provides one example of this dynamic. Even more explosive is the clash between the western tradition of free speech and habitual irreverence toward sacred cows with the Muslim prohibition of pictures of Mohammed. O'Donovan's treatment suggests that in such cases a bifurcation of a society is well underway as indicated by the divergence of the objects of its affection. The suppression of such bifurcations is a legitimate aim of legal judgement,[19] which properly admits its utter inability truly to heal such divisions by legislative or judicial acts alone.[20]

The gain of O'Donovan's account is to make more visible the ways public discourse is the tradition of a society's self-definition, and how such conversation can be threatened from both inside (by factionalism) and outside (by terrorism). He is less interested in explaining what to do about the wounds and scars done in publics which break them down, and more on exploring what is to him a genuine wonder, that society functions at all if it forgets that it is secular, that is, a convergence of this-worldly self-interest. His Augustinian answer to this mystery is that humans have practical needs and love earthly goods, and so suboptimal associations are continually generated in the interactions of the thinking, desiring, social animal. But Augustine is also quite explicit on a quite different point that finds richer development in another strand of western the-

17. O'Donovan, *Common Objects*, p. 32.
18. O'Donovan, *Common Objects*, p. 37.
19. O'Donovan, *Ways of Judgment*, pp. 57-58.
20. "The human judge may know the Holy Spirit's help in judging, but cannot shed the Holy Spirit abroad in those who are judged. Human judgment cannot assure mankind regeneration and new life." *Ways of Judgment*, p. 87.

ology: "the just live by faith which works by love. . . . But where there is not this justice, there is certainly no association of men united by a common agreement as to what is right . . . and so there is no commonwealth."[21]

Dietrich Bonhoeffer

The theological account of the public presented by Dietrich Bonhoeffer in his *Ethics* is organized by a more positive initial assumption, that political community of any type can only be maintained as it digests political insults. This beginning is clearly if not explicitly a comment on the blind spots of early modern contractarian political philosophies and draws on the Pentecost narrative.[22] This overcoming of political antagonisms can happen in one of two ways, Bonhoeffer believes. There may be a "scarring over" in which political wounds and guilt "are not justified, not removed and not forgiven" but the pain they cause slowly subsides. Government can serve this scarring by limiting vendettas and summary justice on the grounds that "Not all wounds that were made can be healed; but it is critical that no further wounds be inflicted." Government serves to put out the fires of wounded pride and violent revenge, and in this task, "What matters is only whether the past guilt is in fact scarred over. If so, then at this point, within the historical conflicts of the nations, both domestic and foreign, something like forgiveness takes place, though it is only a weak shadow of the forgiveness that Jesus Christ gives to believers."[23]

21. Augustine, *City of God* XIX.23, ed. and trans. R. W. Dyson (Cambridge: Cambridge University Press, 1998), pp. 959-960. Though far less frequently noticed, Augustine also makes this point standing firmly within what I have called the Pentecost moment: "[W]hat is the point of speaking, what is the point of singing, if one does not sing Zion's songs? The song of Jerusalem is our own language. The song that tells of love for this world is a foreign tongue, a barbaric language we have picked up in our captivity. Anyone who has forgotten Jerusalem will therefore be dumb before God." Augustine, "Exposition of Psalm 136," in *Expositions of the Psalms: 121-150,* ed. Boniface Ramsey, trans. Maria Boulding (New York: New City Press, 2004), p. 236.

22. "Leibniz grappled all his life with the idea of a universal script consisting, not of words, but of self-evident signs representing every possible idea. It was an expression of his wish to heal the world, which was then so torn to pieces, a philosophical reflection on the Pentecost story." Dietrich Bonhoeffer, *Letters and Papers from Prison* enlarged edition, ed. Eberhard Bethge (London: S.C.M. Press, 1971), p. 53.

23. Dietrich Bonhoeffer, *Ethics,* in *Dietrich Bonhoeffer Works,* Vol. 6, ed. Ilse Tödt, Heinz Eduard Tödt, Ernst Feil, and Clifford Green, trans. Reinhard Krauss, Charles West, and Douglas Scott (Minneapolis: Fortress Press, 2005), pp. 143-144.

Bernd Wannenwetsch

This second possibility of restoration through forgiveness is the core insight orienting Bernd Wannenwetsch's account of the public. Wannenwetsch's work did not grow genetically from reflections on Bonhoeffer's thought, but Bonhoeffer's account of political theology does encapsulate the main lines of Wannenwetsch's theological instincts. If societies cannot continue without some form of forgiveness of wrongs, begins Wannenwetsch, and if the forgiveness of Christ is taken as its paradigm, what role does the church play in identifying and maintaining the true substance of the public? Wannenwetsch takes the church to be a community in which reconciliation is being accomplished, and what is being learned in this process is being fed back into the plural secular public, so sustaining it. The very existence of the modern secular public sphere, even though it explicates its union as nothing more than the convergence of rational self-interest, is intrinsically dependent on "dark publics" where the skills of trust and non-egoistic relationship must be learned which sustain the secular public realm.[24]

"[T]he worshipping community is the true public"[25] is the bold claim with which Wannenwetsch begins as he unfolds the political import of the church's own distinct rationality and order. This is a community exploring its own special form of political life by discovering and learning to overcome the concrete divisions that are tearing any given public apart. Wannenwetsch draws a contrast between the political rationalities of church and parliamentary democracy in order to illustrate how the political life of the church may sustain the essential core of democratic public converse. In a parliament, for instance, rules of order permit the curtailing of debate, allowing majorities to rule and minorities to be silenced. But the church, governed by the law of the Spirit, can wait for consensus. This waiting is not for the final divine reconciliation, but its advent here and now. In the face of its internal conflicts, the church is a community defined by its desire to regulate this conflict neither by giving conflict free rein nor by making everything a matter of constitutional debate and formal rulemaking.

---

24. Bernd Wannenwetsch, *Political Worship: Ethics for Christian Citizens,* trans. Margaret Kohl (Oxford: Oxford University Press, 2004), p. 306. I cannot go into the discussion here, but the shift from the nomenclature of "society" to that of "public" is as important as it is complex. Cf. O'Donovan, *Ways of Judgement,* pp. 10-12, 55-59. One of Wannenwetsch's fundamental commitments, to the Lutheran account of good works, takes good works to be intrinsically public and private in specific ways at all times. Wannenwetsch, *Political Worship,* p. 201, cf. pp. 171-175.

25. Wannenwetsch, *Political Worship,* chapter 8.

> The church . . . is called to solve afresh any conflicts which arise, instead of trying to exclude them through some formal *a priori* — perhaps through the constitutional exclusion of persons or groups which have proved to be the source of special conflict. But its special political character means that the form of life in which it exists in salvation history — that is, reconciliation — is also the *medium* through which it solves conflicts.[26]

The church is by definition that community which has been formed by the divine assault on political alienation. Humans drawn into this divine work willingly seek the breaking down of political divisions and the forgiving of wounds. Only a church exploring this work of peace given and discovered can have something to offer the variegated societies with whom its members live the rest of their dispersed lives. Wannenwetsch does not think of this society as a model to which secular society can or should be made to conform, nor as a purveyor of ideal concepts of society, but supremely as a forum for finding political agreement — its core designator being that this is a group learning to live together as reconciled beings. Its very essence is thus to be a generator of practical *ad hoc* political solutions. In it the formerly estranged learn in practical ways what it takes to resolve their enmity. Thus the proper way to approach the role of the church in secular society is to understand it as a community characterized by its commitment to redescribing the antimonies of its political life, learning to see its situation in fresh ways that can only enrich secular discourses by offering alternatives to dominant concepts that have forced all parties into narrow, sterile, and unnecessary oppositions.[27] The essence of the public that is the church is therefore the will and desire to find agreement *beyond* the opposition grounded in individual and party interest.

I can only briefly sketch the mechanics of Wannenwetsch's account of this ecclesial process of breaking down political deadlocks and sterile conceptual polarization. He summarizes the process thus: "Christians make their specifically political contribution, moulded as it is by the experience of worship, when they speak and act publicly as people who have learned to trust the power of the Word instead of relying on the effect of slogans — as people who are practicing eirenic listening and speaking."[28] If O'Donovan exposes the

26. Wannenwetsch, *Political Worship*, p. 155.

27. Bernd Wannenwetsch, "'Members of One Another': *Charis*, Ministry and Representation; A Politico-Ecclesial reading of Romans 12," in Craig Bartholomew, Jonathan Chaplin, Robert Song, and Al Wolters, eds., *A Royal Priesthood? The Use of the Bible Ethically and Politically; A Dialogue with Oliver O'Donovan* (Carlisle: Paternoster, 2002), p. 197.

28. Wannenwetsch, *Political Worship*, p. 279.

reliance of political philosophy on willing to the exclusion of an awareness of the fragmentation or consolidating forces of collective affect, one of Wannenwetsch's foremost critiques of modern political philosophy is its lack of resources to stem the displacement of hearing by seeing in politics, the politics of profile and visibility. Politics loses its footing when it ceases to be built on an engaged listening, coming instead to take its orientation from the desire to manage appearances that renders political actors deaf because listening and attending have been displaced by an obsession only to be seen to be saying the right things.[29]

In contrast, continues Wannenwetsch, the story of the descent of the Spirit at Pentecost shows how the concord produced by the Spirit is based on the overcoming of profound divisions which nevertheless does not erase distinctiveness. People are united beyond their cultural and political identities to form a surprisingly novel public by the experience of their shared listening. In being captured by the power of the divine Word which always arrives through human mouths the nations are simultaneously empowered for the " 'peaceful hearing' which may be considered the most political of all the virtues."[30]

This virtue of listening to the Word of peace and reconciliation offered in other people's words is learned in the church created by the Spirit of Christ, in which reverent attention to the spoken word as the source of divinely given new life is practiced. Listening with respect and humility to human words, as learned in the worship service, lays a challenge on the congregation to listen to one another, a listening which learns what it means, in practice, to hear the words of others as conduits of divine speech. In such a training ground the toxic politics of suspicion can be unlearned in which moral rules are only technical instruments for preserving power, words are used tactically, and everyone is assumed to be either corrupt or corruptible. The suspicion of suspicion cannot put suspicion to rest, but must be displaced by learning what it means to take people's proffered words seriously, rather than looking behind and through them to a supposedly more "true" meaning. For Wannenwetsch, the import of re-learning to trust words cannot be overstated in a modern political context.

> What must be appreciated here is first, and quite simply, the phenomenologically unequivocal fact that trust in this Word is inherent in the practice

---

29. Wannenwetsch, *Political Worship*, p. 283.
30. Wannenwetsch, *Political Worship*, p. 285.

of worship as such. Worship gathers people together around a Word which they trust. . . . Denied the search for hidden meaning behind, above and beneath the Word uttered (and here Luther's theology agrees with Wittgenstein's philosophical ideas), the hermeneutics of suspicion is shown the door. It is replaced by an elemental trust which starts from the assumption 'that the Words of God are more understandable and more sure than all the words . . . of men'. . . . Accordingly, it is only if an elemental trust in the Word is developed, and only in that framework, that the paradigm change in political hermeneutics can begin: as resistance to the disembodying of human communication in the attitude of suspicion.[31]

Because the community is learning to trust the divine Word and the unifying work of the Spirit, it can expect that its process of finding political agreement need not be prematurely ended nor that it will run on indefinitely without any decision: like new life or healing or the earth's fertility, political consensus can only be born, not manufactured nor controlled by humans. People must work, engaging their passions and wills, to discover the agreement of mutual assent. Though this process is both pleasurable and frustrating, the consensus that is found there can only arise in its unpredictable time.[32] Secular politics, structurally and definitionally, forgoes any trust in this divine Word, yet it remains essential, concludes Wannenwetsch, that within society people exist who know and seek that consensus in which every voice has been heard and a decision agreeable to all emerges. Democracy and public space exist only because some possess this "clue" about the importance of consensus, of which the church is a standing reminder. "The fact that the [secular] political arena is not itself the ideal place for learning to trust the words of other people must not blind us to the fact that this arena is, for all that, dependent on this trust in words. Consequently, it is essential for political culture to find places where trust in the word can be learnt, where words can be found to count and not to deceive."[33] None of the foregoing is meant to suggest that the church cannot become a "mere" institution where antimonies are not overcome but may even uncontrollably fester. Wannenwetsch is exploring what the church is when it expresses its essence to guide the church toward this generative center and to help us also spot the antagonisms that render the gathering of the church a mockery, a Judas-like handing over of the prince of peace (a fate about which the very words of institution warn

31. Wannenwetsch, *Political Worship*, pp. 296-297.
32. Wannenwetsch, *Political Worship*, p. 304.
33. Wannenwetsch, *Political Worship*, p. 306.

Christians in 1 Cor. 11:23). In the final analysis Wannenwetsch is offering a hermeneutic that makes visible the *type* of actions which are the essence of the church but are not confined to it.

Conclusion

What, then, to return to our initial question, is a public? I have suggested that Augustine and O'Donovan draw the basic co-ordinates of their definition firmly, though not exclusively, from an account of the Fall. Created good, properly human powers have gone astray and attached themselves to creaturely objects. Because they have, humans find themselves in groupings generated by the various modalities of love of self rather than love of God. In O'Donovan's reading of Augustine the earthly city is the locus of politics because the political (in distinction from the social) is linked to governmental restraint and redirection of false loves rather than to an analysis of how God generates and sustains human social forms.[34] Such an account parallels modern contractarian assumptions about the public being formed by self-interest grounded in a rational and willed compact, while insisting that the union which underlies publics is more unpredictable and unstable than the contractarians assume in being a less rational and volitional affair than a matter of projected desire. Societies are entities unpredictably formed from loves fallen away from their true end, but a public emerges not because of this creaturely-social phenomenon of having common loves, but in the governmental restraint or redirection of wayward loves.[35]

I have suggested further that Bonhoeffer and Wannenwetsch place more weight on the other side of Augustine's thought, that a society based on false

34. I take this to be indicated by the analysis of *Common Objects* outlined above. But this is also entailed in the centrality of the concept of judgement and its negative definition. "In political judgement wrong has epistemological priority over right — which is to say that there are no formal "principles" of justice before we render actual judgement on some concrete wrong, which, in its turn, is measured, not in relation to some prior principle of justice, but in relation to created order as such. The wrong is not a mere negative of some right, but guilt and injury. Guilt and injury, however, cannot be elucidated *a priori*, only condemned *a posteriori*. The determination of wrong, then, is constantly repeated in an ongoing practice of judgement, which elaborates general categories of guilt and injury out of concrete condemnations." *Ways of Judgment*, p. 58.

35. "St Paul's new assertion is that the performance of judgment alone justifies government; and this reflects his new Christian understanding of the political situation." O'Donovan, *Desire of the Nations*, p. 148.

love is no genuine public. Only that community formed as people opened up to the other's claims, listening to one another and being changed by one another and recognizing this essence in its institutional structures can be called a true public. Aside from the redeeming work of Jesus Christ through the Spirit, a true public is therefore impossible. Bonhoeffer and Wannenwetsch clearly locate the core of their account in an understanding of the reconciling work of the Trinitarian God. On this view "public" indexes the quality of people's commitments to one another beyond self-interest and the reflection of this quality in institutional configurations. The closer we come to this type of interpersonal relation the closer we come to a true public, and the more others are simply "managed" by institutional and procedural means the further we fall from it, inside or outside the church. The interest of Wannenwetsch in assessing the relative moral value of various political techniques parallels the efforts of contemporary political philosophy along similar lines, but his account of the purpose of any such techniques (such as arbitration, structures for parliamentary debate, etc.) reorients this interest by refusing contemporary political philosophy's stated aim to avoid allowing material claims about justice and truth to enter the fundamental strata of public discourse.

These reflections have the potential to shed fresh light on such disputes as those over the banning of headscarves in France. In Wannenwetsch's terms, the vehement protest their banning provoked reveals a failure of listening and the impulse to seek consensus by those in political power. In such conflicts we can see how a rigidly secularist public sphere can be as apolitical and totalizing as any fundamentalist religion in ruling certain forms of speech and behaviour out of bounds. What O'Donovan has helped to make visible is that there is no neutral or procedural mechanism which can adjudicate between legitimate and illegitimate limits for the content of the public sphere. The attentiveness he advocates, however, is not one grounded in a hope that all parties will find an arrangement to which they can consent, but by the danger of assuming this shared view too quickly and so contributing to the construction of the "false universals" that French secularism is so imperiously enforcing with the headscarf ban.

Given his central interest in preventing this coalescence of denuding public agreement, O'Donovan does not follow Wannenwetsch to ask, "What can we *materially* hope for in *this* public from the ruling of the one God who promises to bring peace to the nations?" Because he does not we are often left with the frustrating sense that social antagonisms represent clashes of irreconcilable idolatrous powers to be adjudicated by the courts when they break into open conflict.[36] Recently Wannenwetsch has gone as far as suggesting that such conclusions inevitably follow from Augustinian accounts of politics that foreground the Babel moment.

> I am increasingly convinced that there is a fundamental theological problem in the way in which Augustine set up the framework for Christian political existence by making human forms of desire constitutive for it. Even if we grant that for the champion of a theology of grace, every human act of loving God is but a response to the love that God has shown before, and hence grant the latter a constitutive role in the gestation of the heavenly city, the imagery of such a responsive love as generative of the *civitas caelestis* would still sit uneasily with the Biblical tradition that expects the heavenly Jerusalem, as Rev 21:2 has it, to be "coming down out of heaven from God," instead of "emanating" from an appropriately ordered economy of human desire.[37] And when it comes to the earthly city, Augustine's framework makes it next to impossible to see God's loving providence at work in the gestation of this polity.[38]

Wannenwetsch presses again the crucial question of how Christian eschatology shapes Christian political theology. Is the "real" political reconciliation for which the church hopes and prays something which lies over the temporal horizon or something on which the church depends in its present? He is firmly convinced that the image of a "city coming down" directs our attention to the reality of the eternal city of God now, and its emanation from outside the immanent capacities of creatures. Eschatology is understood here in kairotic or messianic rather than teleological terms.

Put precisely, in what sense is eschatological hope *politically* fertile? The hope depicted in O'Donovan's account of the public suggests a Christian political ethic characterized by the "alertness, patience and worship"[39] of those

36. "The alternative to public judgment is not *no* judgment, but *private* judgments, multitudinous and conflicting, frustrating each other and denying everyone the space of freedom." *Ways of Judgment*, p. 23.

37. [Original quotation cites here: Bernd Wannenwetsch, "Representing the Absent in the City: Prolegomena to a Negative Political Theology according to Revelation 21," in L. G. Jones, R. Hütter, and C. R. Velloseo Ewell, eds., *God, Truth, and Witness: Engaging Stanley Hauerwas* (Grand Rapids: Brazos Press 2005), pp. 167-192.]

38. From Wannenwetsch, " 'For in Its Welfare You Will Find Your Welfare': Political Realism and the Limits of the Augustinian Framework (Response to Luke Bretherton)," unpublished manuscript.

39. O'Donovan, *Common Objects*, p. 70.

whose primary aim is to resist the seductions of their age as they await their appointment with the final judge.[40] But Christian political theology that hopes for real political reconciliation in this age can ask for an eschatology that awaits real divine peace-making in the present without losing the political lessons of Babel. A Pentecostal hope of this variety offers comfort to a contemporary church struggling with depoliticization in offering a way out of the debilitating political pessimism about the Babelite state of political life that post-temporal political eschatologies make all too tempting.

40. O'Donovan, *Common Objects,* p. 71.

The Ways of Discernment

Hans Ulrich

I

It is a great honor to have the opportunity to present here some thoughts which have been — as the editors have put it — "inspired" by Oliver O'Donovan's book, *The Ways of Judgment*. In my own context of reflection *The Ways of Judgment* has been so thought-provoking that it has been very difficult to select a single theme which could illuminate our common work in theological ethics in a short space. I hope that this essay may serve as a partial answer to Oliver's stimulating reply to some of my own thoughts on theological ethics, a debt which I am still to repay.[1] His reply was about the "object of theological ethics" (as he translates *Gegenstand*) and the question for ethics as a "science" *(Wissenschaft)*. The present essay is an indirect response to that, but hopefully to the point.

The line of thought I pursue here follows from O'Donovan's claim that there is an act of judgment which theology has to describe in order to serve as a reminder, in a kind of reverse apologetic, of what the 'ways of judgment' are and should be. If that is so, may it not also be the case that there are further basic 'acts' which should be described and which would also serve, paralleling the ways of judgment, as a reminder in an apologetic reinterpretation of other phenomena or institutions which are also fundamental for our human life? Would it not also be appropriate to reflect through a similar method 'the ways

1. See Oliver O'Donovan, 'The Object of Theological Ethics', *Studies in Christian Ethics* 20 (2007): 203-214.

179

of understanding' which would serve as a reminder of what 'science' or 'knowledge' is about? Oliver O'Donovan notes at the beginning of *The Ways of Judgment* that there is

> a crisis that is more pressing on unbelievers than on believers. . . . In our days it is not religious believers that suffer a crisis of confidence. Believers *did* suffer a serious one two or three generations ago, and the results of that crisis in small church attendance and the de-Christianizing of institutions are still working themselves out around us. But that crisis was precipitated by the presence of a rival confidence, a massive cultural certainty that united natural science, democratic politics, technology, and colonialism. Today this civilizational ice-shelf has broken up, and though some of the icebergs floating around are huge — natural science and technology, especially, drift on as though nothing has happened — they are not joined together anymore, nor joined to the land.[2]

Here a new apologetic task opens up, that of recalling to their proper orientation the fundamental acts that constitute human existence, in order to ensure that they preserve the context of human life. Does this apologetic approach work also in the case of the icebergs of "science" and "technology"? This has been a particular concern for me: my own cooperation with people from the fields of technology and the natural sciences over many years has repeatedly raised the question whether there is a way of reminding them of their "orientating" task.

II

The Ways of Judgment

It is significant that O'Donovan's book is not merely about "ways" of judgment but about "*the* ways" of judgment. There are certain discernible and assignable "ways" along which judgment proceeds, "ways" which direct us in our judgment as long as we do not deviate, "ways" which open up the landscape of justice in its specific ordering. "Ways," in my reading, does not mean "manners" (even if this meaning is not totally excluded), but ways for walking along within a specific area — the area of justice, the sphere or the "context" which is the only one where we, human beings, can live according to our human condition.

2. *WJ*, p. xii.

We can find this distinguished meaning of "way" and "ways" within the biblical language in a highly differentiated semantic field.[3] There are "the ways of God (YHWH)" which we, human beings, cannot understand, but which are the ways God is leading us, and there are the ways of the just which God alone knows (cf Psalm 1). There are "the ways" whereby God led Israel from Egypt, in which it was Israel's challenge to follow these ways and not to deviate from them. The ways by which God leads his people are at the same time the ways of the Torah. We should not readily suppose a metaphorical transition from the way through the desert and the way of living as presented in the Torah. The way of living is at the same time the way of life and the way we are to live, as we can learn from some exegetical work on the semantics of "way" in the biblical traditions. The Hebrew phrase *derech chaiim* or *orech chaiim* has at least a threefold meaning, all running together in the Torah which teaches the way of life, the way of living, and the way we are to live.

Israel has learned the Torah by following God's leading out of Egypt and by learning the Torah anew in other situations. In a further step of reflecting the reality of living, the Torah appears as the second creation, as we read in Psalm 19:

> The law [*Torah*] of the Lord is perfect,
>   reviving the soul;
> the decrees [*edut*] of the Lord are sure,
>   making wise the simple.

To follow the Torah implies wise understanding. There is no Hebrew word for obedience other than the word "listen" (and then "preserving" — not "observing"). This means that the way of life has to be taught and this teaching then needs understanding. In Psalm 119:34 we read:

> Give me understanding, that I may keep your law
> and observe it with my whole heart.

Those who follow the Torah become wise. To be wise means to be experienced in the Torah. Martin Buber translates what the English version calls "decrees" *(edut)* as *Vergegenwärtigungen* ('visualisations') (Ps. 19:8; Dtn. 6:17;

---

3. For overviews, see Kathrin Liess, *Der Weg des Lebens: Psalm 16 und das Lebens- und Todesverständnis der Individualpsalmen,* Forschungen zum Alten Testament. Reihe 2, 5 (Tübingen: Mohr Siebeck, 2004); and Markus Philipp Zehnder, *Wegmetaphorik im Alten Testament: Eine semantische Untersuchung der alttestamentlichen und altorientalischen Weg-Lexeme mit besonderer Berücksichtigung ihrer metaphorischen Verwendung,* Beihefte zur Zeitschrift für die alttestamentliche Wissenschaft, vol. 268 (Berlin: de Gruyter, 1999).

Jer. 44:23).[4] The Torah provides *the* context of living as it is constituted by God's presence. This context has to be understood, otherwise the people of God would get lost.

The Act of Discernment (Understanding)

Like 'judging', 'understanding' is a key word in the biblical writings.[5] Importantly, it is closely connected with judging, as we see in Psalm 82: the unjust rulers do not "understand." Expanding on O'Donovan's description of judgment as act, we can now see that there are further basic acts that we should be aware of. The act of understanding is one of these. Understanding is not something that happens to a person, but that something that has to be *done*. Understanding is an act — as is clear from Psalm 82, where we are told that God accuses the unjust rulers because they fail to understand. The NRSV translation is that they "have neither knowledge nor understanding" (v. 5). The Hebrew text, however, uses the language of acts: the act of getting knowledge and the act of understanding. The unjust do not understand: that is, they do not act in a way that displays understanding.

However "understanding" is a rather vague translation of the Hebrew word which we encounter here. The Hebrew word is very often translated in English Bible versions as "discern." This translation is quite close to the Hebrew word which may even be translated as "distinguish" or "differentiate." The act of "discernment" is about distinguishing issues, phenomena, things contrary to indifference and confusion. The act of discernment is the basic act of the wise man who signifies reality in its given differentiation. The Hebrew word finds its Greek equivalent in *krinein*. Significantly, this Greek word covers both the act of judgment and the act of discernment. It would be a story of its own to describe the semantic field of *krinein*.[6] I will deal here first with the Hebrew language, in which the Greek is rooted.

---

4. Martin Buber and Franz Rosenzweig, *Die Schrift und ihre Verdeutschung* (Heidelberg: Schneider, 1954).

5. The Hebrew Bible shows c. 170 references.

6. Cf. Ingeborg Bertau, *Unterscheidung der Geister: Studien zur theologischen Semantik der gotischen Paulusbriefe* (Erlangen: Palm & Enke, 1987). See for its meaning especially in O'Donovan's work: Gerard C. den Hertog, 'Urteilen als Kernaufgabe des bürgerlichen Regiments: Ein Vergleich von Johannes Calvin und Oliver O'Donovan', in Matthias Freudenberg and Georg Plasger, eds., *Kirche, Theologie und Politik im reformierten Protestantismus: Vorträge der 8. Emder Tagung zur Geschichte des reformierten Protestantismus* (Neukirchen: Neukirchener Theologie, 2011), pp. 37-50.

The act of discernment is tightly connected with the act of judgment. So we find Solomon asking God for a "heart" able to "listen" (1 Kings 3:9). And God then presents Solomon according to his prayer a heart that is discerning and wise and enables him to judge (1 Kings 3:12). The act of discernment is the central act of wisdom. Wisdom is a practice of discernment.

As far as the various Hebrew words in this semantic field are concerned, we have to bear in mind (as Gerhard von Rad has shown in his work on wisdom in Israel)[7] that there are no sharp distinctions between some of the Hebrew words used here. This reflects the phenomenon of wisdom in its manifold richness. One of these words denotes pointedly the act of "discernment." This act characterizes or should characterize those who have to judge. It is not enough to know the rules of law; there is also needed a hermeneutics of the lived context. The core act here is that of discernment: that is, of 'understanding', observing the way in which the underlying distinctions determine the context of living.

Understanding the Context and Its Limits

O'Donovan has shown the connection between judging and understanding, for example when in his chapter on imperfectibility he describes the need for "contextual truth," that is, the understanding of circumstances and situations. This understanding is, as he notes, "in principle unlimited."[8] There does, however, have to be set a limit, otherwise there would be no effective judgment possible. As he writes:

> Neither the court nor the legislative chamber is the place to explore some aspects of the situation that more extensive and humane reflection, not to mention divine insight, would uncover. They have to cut things short, and act.[9]

The limitation is also marked by this "divine insight": it is, one might say, positively and beneficially limited by God's insight and God's final judgment,[10] which are in that way present to us.

The "context of living" we are talking about, then, includes both this ben-

---

7. Gerhard von Rad, *Wisdom in Israel*, trans. James D. Martin (London: S.C.M., 1972).
8. *WJ*, p. 22.
9. *WJ*, p. 22.
10. See the story of Cain and Abel (discussed in *WJ*, p. 28).

eficially limited context of human understanding and judgment and the context covered by God's very own "understanding" and His very own act of judgment. Only because of this distinction are human discernment and judgment possible in a clearly determined form. (We will come back to the topic of "limits" in its theological meaning later.)

Discernment and Judgment — Related to God's Acts

The act of discernment as it is connected with judging is not about differentiation in general but about the distinctions as they are set by God in His active presence. The act of discernment is about the way of life within the reality where we as human beings find ourselves. The distinctions of the act of discernment turn upon our remaining within God's presence and guidance. So we read in Psalm 16:11:

> You show me the path of life.
> In your presence there is fullness of joy;
> in your right hand are pleasures forevermore.

Discernment is discernment of this 'path' (orech). This is true for the individual as it is for God's people. They are wandering through the desert. The desert is without any already given way. The way in its coherence and continuity has to be marked by an ongoing discernment as it is taught through God's guidance and judgment. This is contrary to the idea, argued by Markus Philipp Zehnder, that the way will be realized by the prolonging of rites and customs.[11] Continuity is given only by an explicit act of handing over (just as the Greek word for 'tradition' is a cognate of paradidonai, which means the ongoing practice of handing over).

Asking for the coherence of discernment and judgment we could here follow Hannah Arendt's posthumously edited work on judging, Das Urteilen.[12] Like thinking and willing, judging is according to Arendt one of the three basic acts of the human mind. Partly following Immanuel Kant, she sets the act of judging in the context of a common world which is the context also for all political action and interaction.[13] The constitution of the common world de-

11. Zehnder, Wegmetaphorik im Alten Testament.
12. Hannah Arendt, Das Urteilen: Texte zu Kants Politischer Philosophie (Munich: Piper Verlag, 1985).
13. See further her essay, 'Verstehen und Politik', in Zwischen Vergangenheit und Zukunft

pends on this human practice of understanding. The question which follows from this is if, and arising out of what practice, we can find a common world without reflecting the geography of it as given with the limits beneficially granted by God's acts. We will later find the same issue with regard to the ways of teaching and learning. This would imply understanding this common world within the context of creation, renewal, and redemption, and would mean distinguishing a common world and the context of living as these are grounded in God's acts. In addition it might be noted that for Arendt understanding is unlimited activity in which we seek to find a common world in order to "reconcile" ourselves with that world — one in which terrible events such as the Holocaust and Nazi totalitarianism have occurred. The endeavor of "understanding" is one of reconciliation (which is, incidentally, a traditional concept of hermeneutics).[14]

The Biblical Tradition on Discernment

Reflection on this within the biblical traditions also relates to a common world, but it is important to recognize that the common reality is one which is determined by God's acts. In particular, as Bonhoeffer emphatically reminded us, it is is determined by the fact that God has reconciled 'the world': our world is constituted by an act of God. All this assumes that understanding is possible only because of a renewal of our minds (Rom. 12:2) which renewal gives rise to a new awareness of the reality granted by God.

There is no reality where God's people can live separated from God and His acts. This is very much the notion of reality as we find it in biblical traditions and its theological reflections. To be outside this reality means to be separated from God's acts — those acts which exclusively are God's acts and which are constitutive for our human world. These acts are addressed to His people. These are acts without which we His creatures cannot live, and cannot live together. So we read for example in Psalm 130: "If you, O Lord, should mark iniquities, Lord, who could stand? But there is forgiveness with you, so that you may be revered." Who could stand without receiving forgiveness from

(Munich: Piper Verlag 1994), pp. 110-127; translated as 'Understanding and Politics (The Difficulties of Understanding)', in *Essays in Understanding: Formation, Exile, and Totalitarianism*, ed. Jerome Kohn (New York: Schocken Books, 1994), pp. 307-327. Arendt is also very instructive on the relation between judgment and opinion, the role of opinion (as opposed to scientific knowledge) in politics, and the relation of judgment and the *vita contemplativa*.

14. Arendt, 'Verstehen und Politik'.

God? It is wisdom to raise this question. Wisdom is about the relation and distinction between God's acts and human affairs, and — most important — the distinctions which arise from this and which mark out the contours of the way of living.

Thus wisdom discerns what (for example) needs forgiveness, forgiveness which, as we hear in Psalm 130, God alone is able to grant. Only because of God's forgiveness are we human beings enabled and authorized to forgive, as we pray in the Lord's Prayer. Forgiveness is one of the constitutional acts of God, which mark beneficially the limits of human acts. Compare this with the following words of Jürgen Habermas:

> Secular languages which only eliminate the substance once intended leave irritations. When sin was converted to culpability, and the breaking of divine commands to an offense against human laws, something was lost. The wish for forgiveness is still bound up with the unsentimental wish to undo the harm inflicted on others. What is even more disconcerting is the irreversibility of past sufferings — in injustice inflicted on innocent people who were abused, debased, and murdered, reaching far beyond any extent of reparation within human power. The lost hope for resurrection is keenly felt as a void. . . .
>
> . . . the unbelieving sons and daughters of modernity seem to believe that they owe more to one another, and need more for themselves, than what is accessible to them, in translation, of religious tradition — as if the semantic potential of the latter was still not exhausted.[15]

Habermas's view is based on a taken-for-granted distinction between religious and non-religious traditions. The distinction between believers and non-believers turns upon the search for something more, something wished for. In biblical traditions this distinction is marked as that between the wise man and the fool. There it is not a question of feeling a void but of losing the way of wisdom — precisely because there is no wise discernment outside God's acts, that is, outside an active confidence in God's acts, God's forgiveness, God's judgment, God's *edut*, God's reconciliation. In particular, reality will be disclosed exclusively by those acts of God which are focused on the sacrifice of His Son. As Paul says, wisdom appears as the wisdom of the cross. It is the wisdom of a *theologia crucis*, which alone 'declares what reality is' *(dicit quod*

---

15. Habermas, 'Faith and Knowledge', in *The Future of Human Nature,* trans. William Rehg, Max Pensky, and Hella Beister (Cambridge: Polity Press, 2003), pp. 101-115 (here pp. 110-111).

res est), as Martin Luther puts it. The distinction of wisdom and foolishness depends on that confidence, on trust in God's present acts.

Von Rad's description of the biblical reflection on the "limits of wisdom" is in its logic basically equivalent to O'Donovan's description of the limits of judgment.[16] Referring to Proverbs 19:21 ("Many plans are in a man's mind, but Yahweh's decree [*azat*] endures"), von Rad notes:

> Here, too, it is a question of limits of which a man must remain aware in his attempt to master life. There is no thought, however, of the well-known and much lamented limitation of man's range of vision. That would be something still comparatively harmless. It is a question not of something which a man does not know, but ought to know and perhaps even could know, but of something which he can never know. Once again this simply establishes the fact as such. What it means for a man is left open. One can almost suppose that in the case of this limitation, where it becomes clear that even in every human plan God still has the last word, the wise men saw, rather, something beneficial. God could protect man even from his own plans.
>
> The ancients became aware of this limitation in that utterly incalculable and therefore mysterious factor which seemed to intrude between the preparation of a project and its realization. Here, so the teachers thought, one can experience the hand of God. Of course, such sentences do not purport to be sound doctrines about the theological distinction between human and divine activity (man in planning, God in action). They are simply examples from life by means of which one can demonstrate clearly the intervention of the divine mystery.[17]

Wisdom is constituted by the openness to that always present mystery. Von Rad continues:

> This, however, also provides an answer to our question as to the specific theological position of what was said about the limits of wisdom. The purpose of what was said in this respect was not to conceal an intellectual difficulty. Rather, it filled the gap which opened up between two types of empirical statement which were diametrically opposed to each other. Of course it approached man by way of a warning, but certainly not with the intention of making him aware of his lack of freedom.

16. See *Wisdom in Israel,* trans. James D. Martin (London: S.C.M., 1972), esp. his chapter "Limits of Wisdom," pp. 97-110.

17. Von Rad, *Wisdom in Israel,* p. 100.

When did Israel ever complain of this mysterious presence of God in every human activity? This divine presence, on the one hand limiting human planning, on the other carrying men beyond the goal which they had envisaged — to experience human limitations in this way was, in the last resort, a comforting doctrine. By this dialectic of the two points of view the wise men have influenced the religious thinking of the entire Western world.[18]

The way of wise discernment will be marked by conflicting or even contradictory experiences which the wise man will be aware of so long as he does not give way to a kind of certainty which lacks trust in God's acts. That kind of certainty is foolish. In refusing such dialectical tensions, it fails to be open to different experiences and to the renewal of one's mind (Rom. 12:2), an openness which is not simply a kind of open-mindedness but is rooted in the recognition of God's acts, in particular His acts of teaching and transforming our minds.

As the ways of judgment have to be realized in ways of representation, so the ways of wise discernment have to be realized in ways of teaching and learning. Wisdom has to be taught and made explicit. It becomes real in its articulation.

Learning the Practice of Wisdom

The wisdom of discernment has to be learned. This wisdom is given not as a detached knowledge about the differences between God and humankind or even as a gnosis about the mystery. Rather it works as a practice, a discerning practice keeping track of God's ways. It is a characteristic of wisdom that it integrates different and even contradictory experiences, unlike the 'purifying' processes typical of the modernist scientific mentality as discussed by Bruno Latour.[19] So we read again in von Rad's description:

They (sc. the wise men) could not give . . . practicable directions for the road. They were aiming at something much more important: by means of their teachings, derived from experience, they set the pupil in the midst of the constant oscillation between grasp of meaning and loss of meaning, and

18. Von Rad, *Wisdom in Israel,* pp. 105-106.
19. Bruno Latour, *We Have Never Been Modern* (Cambridge, MA: Harvard University Press, 1993).

in this way they induced him to make his own contribution in this exciting arena of knowledge of life. In this way they probably achieved more than if they had trained their pupils to find a better solution for theological problems. Reduced to its bare essentials, these regulations of theirs for a fruitful life seem determined by a remarkable dialectic.

[On the one hand] Do not hesitate to summon up all your powers in order to familiarize yourself with all the rules which might somehow be effective in life. Ignorance in any form will be detrimental to you; only the "fool" thinks he can shut his eyes to this.

Experience, on the other hand, teaches that you can never be certain. You must always remain open for a completely new experience. You will never become really wise, for, in the last resort, this life of yours is determined not by rules but by God.[20]

Summary: God's Acts and the Wisdom to Discern God's Acts

The only "reality"[21] in which human beings can live as God's creatures is constituted by those acts of God which we not only presuppose (or have to presuppose) in our living but which we all along engage. Otherwise we would follow quite different rules of living.

Listening to the biblical traditions we find articulated the manifold acts of God.

Theological traditions have conceived God's acts as acts of creation, of government and preservation, of salvation and reconciliation, and of redemption. These are acts which are exclusively God's acts. In our awareness there is first of all the act of forgiveness and judgment. These acts are not the anyhow assumed fundamental condition for human living, but the actual reality which we all along engage and experience.

This is what the biblical traditions of wisdom teach us — as we learn it also from Jesus' teaching when we read in Matthew 6:25-30:

> [25]Therefore I tell you, do not worry about your life, what you will eat or what you will drink, or about your body, what you will wear. Is not life more than food, and the body more than clothing? [26]Look at the birds of the air; they neither sow nor reap nor gather into barns, and yet your heavenly Father feeds them. Are you not of more value than they?

20. Von Rad, *Wisdom in Israel*, p. 106.
21. See Gerhard von Rad's critical reflection on "order" (pp. 106-107).

^{27}And can any of you by worrying add a single hour to your span of life? ^{28}And why do you worry about clothing? Consider the lilies of the field, how they grow; they neither toil nor spin, ^{29}yet I tell you, even Solomon in all his glory was not clothed like one of these. ^{30}But if God so clothes the grass of the field, which is alive today and tomorrow is thrown into the oven, will he not much more clothe you — you of little faith?

It is unwise to think of the human condition without realizing what we as human beings receive from God. Any of God's acts open our eyes to the proper context of human living. So, for example, Matthew 9:2-8 teaches us that health is inseparable from the need for forgiveness from God, which only Jesus has authority to grant. The health of God's creatures is not well understood if it is reduced to the awareness of physical strength. Thus from John 9:3 we learn that blindness is not understood if it is reduced to physical blindness: the blind man belongs to God's story with His people. Wisdom does not, as some exegetes have suggested, distinguish between a physical, material sphere and a spiritual sphere. The distinction is rather between God's acts as they define our human condition and much more restricted perceptions of the issue, focused on false questions such as the question about the relation between guilt and illness. The real question is how forgiveness — or the renewal of our minds (Rom. 12:2) — is constitutive for our way of life.

What we learn here is that within the context of God's acts we are able to discern the differences which mark out our human way of life. "Is not life more than food?" It is in the context of God's reality that Jesus appeals to wise discernment; outside of such a context the command not to worry about one's life would be simply arbitrary.

Further decisive discernment is possible when we keep in sight that God's reality includes the coming kingdom. So we hear:

^{31}Therefore do not worry, saying, 'What will we eat?' or 'What will we drink?' or 'What will we wear?' ^{32}For it is the Gentiles who strive for all these things; and indeed your heavenly Father knows that you need all these things. ^{33}But strive first for the kingdom of God and his righteousness, and all these things will be given to you as well.

This consoling admonition calls on us to discern between bodily needs that are unquestionably basic on the one hand and the righteousness of the Kingdom of God on the other. But it is declared against the background of God's acts, and this is what prevents it from being arbitrary or even cynical.

Only within this context is it possible to discern between the fundamental worry (as the Greek word indicates) and daily tasks of care and providence. And this act of discernment is not constrained by limits of our human capacities, but is related to the acts of God which positively limit our duties and requirements and so transform them.

As we find significant distinctions in Jesus' teaching, so we find many further distinctions throughout the New Testament, not least in Paul's letters. There is the distinction between *soma* and *sarx,* between freedom and liberty, between different meanings of justification, between different meanings of conscience, between different meanings of many things. All of these numerous distinctions refer to the acts of God: His act of justification, His act of liberation, His act of vocation, His act of judging, His act of reconciliation, His act of forgiveness, His act of communication, and so on. These distinctions denote the way of life. Moral theology has to represent these distinctions: this is the task of its discernment. The ethics of Dietrich Bonhoeffer provide some especially fine examples: consider, for example, his distinction between the natural and unnatural on the one hand and the "contra natural" on the other. The logic of this discernment — as of other discernments in his ethics — is rooted in the awareness of God's acts as they are focused in the story of Jesus Christ as constitutive for our real context of living.

III

Science and Wisdom: Some Examples

There is a whole order of distinctions which can be brought to our attention if we follow the biblical ways of discernment. The Bible's distinctions describe our context of living in a different way from scientific approaches which follow their own logic of discernment and develop their own categories — despite being committed to the perpetual task of revision and self-criticism. The central issue here is to remind the sciences of the wisdom about reality, a reality which is constituted by the limits that are given by God's acts, and then to cooperate with them, so that they become curious about that wisdom,[22] and do not float around like icebergs without orientation or help.

In general we should say that there is a broad field of concurrence between

22. This has been the focus of my interdisciplinary work with the molecular biologist Walter Doerfler over many years.

science and wisdom — and it is wisdom that is responsible for that concurrence. Let me give a few examples. They aim to show how a critical apologetics (of science) works, one which reminds the sciences of the ways of discernment they are required to pursue if they are to look not only for any kind of knowledge but for a knowledge which contributes to our understanding of the *conditio humana*. We know too much, but what we know we do not understand. Science should be about a knowledge seeking understanding.

Within the current discussion about the human genome we find a very specific kind of reflection on the limits of knowledge. On the one hand the question, as it is in every area of science, is about what kind of limits we face in planning further research and further applicable techniques. And science of course aims to overcome these limits. For example, there is the highly complex interplay between the immediate functions of the (so called) genome and a whole array of interconnected processes and elements. This is often discussed as the relation between "genetics" and "epigenetics." An awareness of this complexity guards against a too simplistic or even false idea of a genetic determinism.

But what we have to be aware of is not the distinction between more or less transparent physiological processes of development, but between the description of these processes in all their complexity (which is an endlessly demanding task) and a different approach, which can not only enter into dialogue with this scientific endeavor, but also draws the attention of science to God's creation and the story of God with His creatures. Thus if we wish to try to understand aspects of an individual's life in a way that enables us also to help them understand themselves better, we should — by contrast with a description of developmental processes correlated to genetically indicated characteristics — seek to discern the story in which that individual's life is situated. The story is no less complex or easy to discern than the processes of development.

Wisdom as we find it in the biblical traditions holds those different ways of knowledge and understanding together. So we hear in Psalm 139:

> [13]For it was you who formed my inward parts;
> you knit me together in my mother's womb.
> [14]I praise you, for I am fearfully and wonderfully made.
> Wonderful are your works;
> that I know very well.
> [15]My frame was not hidden from you,
> when I was being made in secret,

intricately woven in the depths of the earth.
[16]Your eyes beheld my unformed substance.
In your book were written
all the days that were formed for me,
when none of them as yet existed.
[17]How weighty to me are your thoughts, O God!
How vast is the sum of them!
[18]I try to count them — they are more than the sand;
I come to the end — I am still with you.

According to Martin Buber, the Hebrew word for "wonderfully made" should be translated as "singled out," i.e. singled out by God within a particular individual's story. The days of one's life are written in God's book. This description is different from any reflection on the genetic determination of one's life by one's genome and its interactions. In other words, there is still another context for thinking about experience, and it is wise to be aware of it — wise, in order to recognize the context of living as something limited beneficially and positively by the story of the acts of God in which human beings are placed. Scientific research has shown that the genome of every person is different, but it is unable to understand what this means; and this not only because the processes are so complex, but also because there may be nothing there *to* understand given the nature of the scientific logic of discovery.

It would be another story to show what happens when the logic of creation is included in a scientific context. Creation is exclusively God's act, distinct from any kind of process of production or making. And it "begins" beyond any beginning. The very beginning remains in God's mystery — as the Hebrew text of Genesis 1 suggests, when it begins with Beth. The Aleph remains in God's wisdom. There is no mandate to grasp the origin of creatures, and it is wise not to try to find one.

Another example of the need of wisdom arises from reflection on the concurrence of God's act of "vocation" (as O'Donovan discusses it in his critical analysis of the debate about homosexuality) and the struggle to discern our own path through life, and in this sense to gain self-knowledge, a task that also involves integrating scientific knowledge. To know oneself, we can learn here, is not possible without listening to God's call. Related to this act we have to discern — according to Psalm 1 — what is given to us to know about ourselves and what we entrust to God's realization of our path — just as Jesus prays in Gethsemane that the Father's will be done. In this sense we pray in the Lord's Prayer: "your will be done" *(genetheto)*. There is no plain Socratic *gnothi seau-*

ton (know yourself), but the recognition of my "soul" brought back into the context of God's *edut* (God's *Vergegenwärtigungen*) as we read in Psalm 19.

Just as O'Donovan has taught us in relation to the field of political theory, so here also in relation to the biosciences it is striking how the practice of discernment works out in our search for understanding the *conditio humana*. There is an apologetic task here of alerting different disciplines and different forms of human activity (one might also mention economics here) to the question of their meaning. Do we understand what biomedical research should and could be about? Do we understand what particular kinds of technology could be about? What are the distinctions we need, what is the wisdom we have to learn? There are of course very enlightening examples of practicing wise discernment: Brian Brock's book *Christian Ethics in a Technological Age* might be mentioned in this regard.[23] And many distinctions have been developed which may be regarded as paradigmatic. Within the field of medicine one might instance the distinction between "therapy" and "enhancement." And, as we have learned from Gerhard von Rad's description, this is exactly the way of establishing wisdom.

IV

The question for wisdom concerns also "the ways of discernment" themselves. Do we understand what understanding and discernment should be about? Do we understand "the ways of discernment"? This question implies an assumption of their coherence — so that we can realize that we are on "the ways" as they are predetermined for us.

From here, then, we have to describe the ways of discernment equivalent to the ways of judgment. As judgment has to be *represented* in appropriate institutions, so discernment has to be *"realized"* by practices (and institutions) of *teaching* and *learning*. Discernment has to be taught — and God himself is the one who teaches us His ways of discernment. Parallel to the description of the institutions of "judgment" we have to discuss the "institutional" forms of teaching and learning wisdom. Gerhard von Rad points also to the institutional forms of wisdom in Israel. This institutional form is intrinsic to the character of wisdom insofar as wisdom is constituted by God. The prayer for God's teaching — as in Psalm 16 or in Psalm 25 — corresponds to this character. From here we have to show in what sense any teaching does have its

23. Brian Brock, *Christian Ethics in a Techological Age* (Grand Rapids: Eerdmans, 2010).

paradigmatic location within the church. The ways of discernment pass through this teaching if the church, the people of God, is still His wandering people.

As the description of the institutional form would be parallel to "the ways of judgment," so it is the eschatological fulfillment which is already there in God's acts, in God's renewal of our understanding — and the gift of "new hearts of wisdom," as we read in Jeremiah 31:

> [33]But this is the covenant that I will make with the house of Israel after those days, says the Lord: I will put my law within them, and I will write it on their hearts; and I will be their God, and they shall be my people. [34]No longer shall they teach one another, or say to each other, "Know the Lord," for they shall all know me, from the least of them to the greatest, says the Lord; for I will forgive their iniquity, and remember their sin no more.

Between Naturalism and Religion? Jürgen Habermas, Robert Spaemann, and the Metaphysics of Creation

Holger Zaborowski

In 2005, a collection of Jürgen Habermas's writings was published under the title *Between Naturalism and Religion.*[1] This title is indicative of Habermas's most recent philosophical interests and, more specifically, of the philosophical program that characterizes his work at the beginning of the twenty-first century — still an attempt to complete the project of modernity. Habermas realizes the contemporary challenges of naturalism, particularly in its deterministic guise — not merely in philosophy, but also in the natural and social sciences, and in the wider culture — and provides an in-depth critique of these challenges. This does not come as a surprise for someone familiar with his philosophy. A thinker whose work has so significantly been influenced by the Kantian and idealist traditions and their anti-naturalistic emphasis on the "fact of freedom," as it were, cannot but interpret the most recent rise of radical kinds of naturalism and scientistic determinism as a key challenge for philosophy. According to Habermas, nature, as construed by scientific reasoning, is not the ultimate framework for an adequate understanding of reality. For him, not only the question of human freedom — one of the most crucial questions of the philosophical tradition — is at stake in this debate. At stake is another question. It is the question of the essence and future of philosophy.

"If we describe an event," Habermas notes in his important 2001 lecture "Faith and Knowledge," "as being a person's action, we know for instance that

---

1. Jürgen Habermas, *Zwischen Naturalismus und Religion: Philosophische Aufsätze* (Frankfurt am Main: Suhrkamp Verlag, 2005); ET: *Between Naturalism and Religion: Philosophical Essays,* trans. Ciaran Cronin (Cambridge: Polity, 2009).

we describe something which can be not *only* explained like a natural process, but also, if need be, justified."[2] There is, therefore, a "difference between the language games of justification and mere description," that is to say that there is also a difference between philosophy and the descriptive sciences (or, to be more precise, the sciences as far as they proceed descriptively).[3] In his view, this difference cannot be overcome. Habermas does not share, therefore, the high hopes of some scientists: their "belief in a science which will one day not only supplement, but *replace* the self-understanding of actors as persons by an objectifying self-description is not science, but bad philosophy."[4] Against this kind of bad philosophy, he defends what he considers good philosophy. It is a philosophy that knows about its limits while at the same time being aware of its possibilities and, indeed, of its responsibilities as far as human self-understanding and its intellectual defence is concerned.

Habermas's recent interest in questions of the philosophy of religion, however, came as a surprise to many interpreters of his philosophy, even though it clearly predates his lecture on "Faith and Knowledge."[5] The topic of religion was largely absent in his earlier writings. They showed at best an Enlightenment non-concern with religion, if not a sceptical, critical, and even dismissive view of religion. Now, Habermas has clearly recognized a certain significance of religion not just for the private, but particularly for the public sphere.[6] He does, however, not limit himself to a mere acknowledgement of a *de facto* return or continuous significance of religion — hardly a controversial state-

2. Jürgen Habermas, "Faith and Knowledge," in Jürgen Habermas, *The Future of Human Nature* (Cambridge: Polity Press, 2003), pp. 101-115, p. 107; the German text was first published in Jürgen Habermas, *Glaube und Wissen* (Frankfurt am Main: Suhrkamp Verlag, 2001).

3. Habermas, "Faith and Knowledge," p. 107.

4. Habermas, "Faith and Knowledge," p. 108.

5. For an English translation of some of the writings that show his increasing concern with religion and theological issues, see Habermas, *Religion and Rationality: Essays on Reason, God, and Modernity,* ed. Eduardo Mendieta (Cambridge, MA: The MIT Press, 2002). Important in this context is also his encounter with then Cardinal Joseph Ratzinger: Jürgen Habermas and Joseph Ratzinger, *The Dialectics of Secularization: On Reason and Religion,* ed. Florian Schuller, trans. Brian McNeil (San Francisco: Ignatius Press, 2006). For theological discussions of his recent view of religion, see particularly Rudolf Langthalter and Helga Nagl-Docekal, eds., *Glauben und Wissen* (Berlin: Akademie-Verlag, 2007); Michael Reder and Josef Schmidt, eds., *"Ein Bewußtsein von dem, was fehlt": Eine Diskussion mit Jürgen Habermas* (Frankfurt am Main: Suhrkamp Verlag, 2008).

6. See, for example, his "Religion in der Öffentlichkeit: Kognitive Voraussetzungen für den 'öffentlichen Vernunftgebrauch' religiöser und säkularer Bürger," in *Zwischen Naturalismus und Religion: Philosophische Aufsätze,* pp. 119-154.

ment for anyone who does not limit his focus on Europe.[7] It seems as if Habermas who, in the wake of Max Weber and others, considers himself "tone-deaf to religious connotations,"[8] finds an ally in religion for his criticism of naturalism in its strong form. He now — that is, in the age that he considers "postsecular" — favours a limited cooperation between religion and philosophy: "Postsecular society continues the work, for religion itself, that religion did for myth. Not in the hybrid intention of a hostile takeover, to be sure, but out of a concern to counteract the insidious entropy of the scarce resource of meaning in its own realm."[9] How is this to be understood? What is religion's contribution to this cooperation?

In the lecture "Faith and Knowledge," Habermas explains to what extent religion, particularly Judaism and Christianity, can help to formulate arguments against naturalism and the naturalistic reductionism that appears to be so influential in bioethical debates. He writes that "[i]n the controversy, for instance, about the way to deal with human embryos, many voices still evoke the first book of Moses, Genesis 1:27: 'So God created man in his own image, in the image of God created he him.' [. . .] This *creatural nature* of the image expresses an intuition which in the present context may even speak to those who are tone-deaf to religious connotations."[10] What Habermas considers necessary in this situation is what he calls a "nondestructive secularization" by means of a "translation." "Those moral feelings," he argues, "which only religious language has as yet been able to give a sufficiently differentiated expression may find universal resonance once a salvaging formulation turns up for something almost forgotten, but implicitly missed."[11]

It is, first of all, evident that Habermas has not radically changed his view of religion. He still views history as a history of progress and emancipation from religion, but admits a failure of philosophy. It has not yet sufficiently advanced as to be able to leave religion behind by providing a "salvaging formulation." If this has been achieved, so he implies, there may no longer be need for religion from a philosophical perspective or, at least, there may no longer be need for the kind of cooperation between religion and philosophy that Habermas now envisages. The problem of this position is not as much its

---

7. For an instructive sociological discussion of the public role of religion in the contemporary world, see José Casanova, *Public Religion in the Modern World* (Chicago: University of Chicago Press, 1994).

8. Habermas, "Faith and Knowledge," p. 114.

9. Habermas, "Faith and Knowledge," p. 114.

10. Habermas, "Faith and Knowledge," p. 114.

11. Habermas, "Faith and Knowledge," p. 114.

inherent functionalist view of religion. A religious believer can accept that a non-believing philosopher tries to make use of some tenets of his religion while still holding that there is a substantial dimension of one's belief that resists any attempt to functionalize it or to subject it to the kind of philosophical "work" that Habermas suggests. There is, it seems, a more significant problem of such an enterprise, not just from the viewpoint of a believer. For Habermas seems to suggest that religious knowledge "expresses" merely an "intuition" that philosophers such as himself need to render the object of their thinking such that it is no longer merely an expression of an intuition or a "feeling," but a well established rational insight. Habermas here remains very faithful to his Kantian and Hegelian legacy. His position is merely more modest or, as he would perhaps claim, more realistic with respect to the temporal framework of the project of a philosophical overcoming of religion. While only religious language seems to have given a "sufficiently differentiated expression" to this intuition as of now, the future seems to be more promising to Habermas insofar as he thinks that a rational and, therefore, universal account of the "moral feelings" at stake can at least in principle be developed and sufficiently be justified on the basis of his understanding of philosophy.

Yet, if we remind ourselves of a simple and well known fact, Habermas's optimism may prove very questionable. Both the translation of Christian theology into philosophy and secularization, as conceived of by Habermas, are by no means new projects. Despite its impressive history, however, the modern Western tradition of a secularization of religion by means of translation seems to have failed so far with respect to an idea that stands at the centre of the Enlightenment project altogether, that is, the idea of the human person and his dignity. This is not the thesis of an anti-modernistic thinker, but the very implication of his argument.

Habermas, to be sure, would be able to solve the tension: modernity, he famously argued, is an "unfinished project" and therefore in need of continuation and completion rather than a post-modern or anti-modern dismissal. What is needed, then, is not so much fundamental criticism of modernity as more patience with it. However, even if this is the case (and the question remains if Habermas does not also need to translate the Christian eschatological understanding of history "non-destructively" in order to justify his view of history as progress), another more important question remains. It is the question if it is at all possible and, if so, how it is possible to achieve what Habermas suggests. Can we so easily translate one very complex idea, embedded in an equally complex life-world, into another context without losing important elements and dimensions of this idea? There is no doubt that Habermas does not sufficiently consider this question. In spite of its sophistication, his understanding of translation remains very simplistic and, given the existing problems of translation of simple words even from one language into another similar language, rather naïve. If translation were as easy as Habermas seems to suggest, the question as to why it has not yet happened in a "sufficiently differentiated" manner, or why he has not done it himself, becomes even more urgent.

The key problem of Habermas's proposal thus concerns the relation between Christian doctrine and both secular and post-secular philosophy. This is most obvious in the concluding paragraph of "Faith and Knowledge." Habermas begins this paragraph almost as if he is a theologian: "Because he is both in one, God the Creator and God the Redeemer, this creator does not need, in his actions, to abide by the laws of nature like a technician, or by the rules of a code like a biologist or a computer scientist. From the very beginning, the voice of God calling into life communicates within a morally sensitive universe. Therefore God may 'determine' man in the sense of enabling and, at the same time, obliging him to be free."[12] As far as this understanding of God and God's relation to man as a free creature is concerned, most Christian theologians, it seems, would happily agree with Habermas. They would, however, not agree with the statement that immediately follows the sentences that have just been quoted: "Now," as Habermas points out, "one need not believe in theological premises in order to understand what follows from this, namely, that an entirely different kind of dependence, perceived as a causal one, becomes involved if the difference assumed as inherent in the concept of creation were to disappear, and the place of God be taken by a peer — if, that is, a human being would intervene, according to his own preferences and without being justified in assuming, at least counterfactually, a consent of the concerned other, in the random combination of the parents' sets of chromosomes."[13] Already earlier, Habermas made the intriguing statement that "in order to understand what *Gottesebenbildlichkeit* — 'in the likeness of God' — means one need not believe that the God who is love creates, with Adam and Eve, free creatures who are like him."[14] The question is whether the "difference assumed as inherent in the concept of creation" can be maintained without any kind of premise concerning the existence of God. Habermas seems to suggest that this is possible insofar as all that is needed is a translation

12. Habermas, "Faith and Knowledge," p. 115.
13. Habermas, "Faith and Knowledge," p. 115.
14. Habermas, "Faith and Knowledge," p. 114.

of a theological idea into the context of secular, that is, non-theistic, thought. In other words, all that is necessary is a position *between* naturalism and religion that, in addition to standing between two antithetical sets of principles, as it were, is able to bridge the gap between these two sets, not in the sense of a dialectical synthesis, strictly speaking, but in the sense of choosing certain elements from either set as far as they prove useful. But while Habermas is certainly right in arguing that "one need not believe in theological premises in order to understand what follows" from these premises for anyone who believes in them, the question is simply whether this still follows — that is, whether or not the conclusion based on these premises, is true — for those who do not consider the premises true. Maybe it is exactly the "difference" that Habermas wants to preserve that gets lost in the kind of translation that he suggests.

Habermas's idea of philosophy as a rational justification seems to face an insurmountable problem at this point. As long as he does not consider the premises true, the argument based on these premises may well be valid, but it cannot be true. Whatever follows from the religious understanding of creation for the believer, does not follow for the non-religious philosopher however much he is capable of understanding the reasoning of the believer. For if there is no creator and no understanding of what creation is in the argument, there is simply no proper argument left. It seems as if, particularly given the level of contemporary sciences, the "place" at stake can only be taken either by God or by a peer (who has taken the place of the will of nature or, to be more precise, who is the rational expression of a previously "blind" nature — for nature remains the ultimate framework of reference). The "place" at stake, as it seems, cannot remain empty. Naturalism, then, is the only possible option for someone who abandons the idea of God. There is no way to go beyond this alternative (which Habermas implicitly acknowledges when he defends a "soft naturalism" somewhere else).[15]

Does this mean that philosophy cannot but fail to find a position between naturalism and religion altogether? Can the answer to the naturalistic challenge *only* be a decidedly theological answer? It may be a tempting answer, not uncommon in our time, to argue that only theology can provide the remedy to the challenges of naturalism (and many other reductionist ideologies). This answer, however, is also problematic for it fails, among many other things, to

15. For his defence of a "soft naturalism," see "Von den Weltbildern zur Lebenswelt," in *Jürgen Habermas, Nachmetaphysisches Denken II: Aufsätze und Repliken* (Berlin: Suhrkamp, 2012), pp. 19-53.

recognize the potential of a philosophical answer that examines the order of creation by means of reason without presupposing the very often merely formal and abstract concept of reason that is so common in modern philosophy. It is also problematic because theology has been from the very beginning the enterprise of translating concepts and ideas not only into different languages, but also into different cultural, social, and philosophical contexts. So Habermas's idea of the need of a translation is perhaps not totally misleading. It seems, however, that one would have to translate the biblical concept of creation and its implications *differently* into the discourse of philosophy. Is there, then, a philosophical translation, different from the one provided by Habermas?

There seems to be such a different translation. It is a translation that does not attempt to translate the doctrine of creation into a very different idea, the mere idea of "recognition of the self in the other," for instance, but that aims to appropriate this doctrine philosophically such that it will lead to a philosophy of creation. There is no doubt that such a philosophy is controversial, particularly if the concept of creation is modelled on the radical Christian understanding of a creation out of nothing.

Aristotle famously remarked that all but one philosopher maintained that there was no creation of time and that time and, therefore, motion, are eternal.[16] Here, Aristotle refers to Plato's *Timaeus* and the idea of creation expressed in this text.[17] The *Timaeus* has undoubtedly provided many challenges for interpreters. Suffice it to say that, even if the reference to creation in this text is to be read literally and if Plato thus held a doctrine of creation, what he meant by creation is substantially different from the doctrine of creation as developed by the Christian tradition and as presupposed by Habermas. This doctrine has been the object of explicit philosophical criticism particularly in modernity. Heidegger's remarks on the doctrine of creation and the radical difference between philosophy and any conception of creation come to mind.[18] And for Nietzsche, it only makes sense to speak of humans as creators: "Only as creators can we destroy!"[19] God himself, as Nietzsche suggests in *Daybreak,* does

16. Aristotle, *Physics* VIII, I (250 b10 ff.).

17. Plato, *Timaeus,* 27 d 5ff.

18. See, for example, Martin Heidegger, *Einführung in die Metaphysik* (Tübingen: Niemeyer, 1958), p. 4; ET: *Introduction to Metaphysics,* trans. Gregory Fried and Richard Polt (New Haven: Yale University Press, 2000), pp. 5-6.

19. Friedrich Nietzsche, *The Gay Science: With a Prelude in German Rhymes and an Appendix of Songs,* ed. Bernard Williams, trans. Josefine Nauckhoff, poems trans. Ardian del Caro (Cambridge: Cambridge University Press, 2005), Book II, Aphorism no. 58, p. 70.

not claim to be a creator (his death notwithstanding): "*On the seventh day.* — 'You praise that as my *creation?* I have only put from me what was a burden to me! My soul is above the vanity of creators.'"[20] It therefore seems to fall to the theologian to talk about creation and God as the creator if the concept is not to be totally dismissed. A philosophy of creation seems to be impossible. It is a *scandalon,* not only to non-believers, but also to many believers. Could one not argue that it is only possible to talk about creation because of one's faith in God's revelation? Should, therefore, the concept of creation not be left to theologians?

There are, however, important counter-voices to this view. F. W. J. Schelling's later philosophy, most commonly known as a philosophy of revelation, is essentially a philosophy of creation.[21] In the context of his time, Schelling attempted to provide an answer to two important challenges. The first one was the "logicisation," as it were, of reality in the wake of Hegel's all-comprehensive system of philosophy. The second one was the challenge of both the increasingly successful natural sciences and of naturalist philosophies that were closely related to the sciences. While Hegel appeared to be trapped in a philosophy of mere consciousness, thus never capable of reaching reality as it really is (at least so Schelling's criticism goes), the sciences may talk about reality, but fail to understand reality non-reductively and thus to do justice to the "fact of freedom," that the later Schelling could only account for with respect to God's freedom. It is with respect to these shortcomings (and also to the shortcomings of his own earlier philosophy) that Schelling becomes aware of the need of what he calls a positive philosophy, a philosophy that, as one can argue, is not afraid of taking the limits of mere thought and thus God's revelation, first and foremost in creation, philosophically seriously.

Schelling's later philosophy, to be sure, has its own intrinsic limits and ambiguities, both from a theological and a philosophical perspective. It still participates in the legacy of German idealism, whether it completes it or not, in such a way that it is today mainly, but not exclusively, of historical interest.

---

20. Friedrich Nietzsche, *Daybreak: Thoughts on the Prejudices of Morality,* ed. Maudemarie Clark and Brian Leiter, trans. R. J. Hollingdale (Cambridge: Cambridge University Press, 2007), Book V, Aphorism no. 463, p. 193.

21. Several works of the later Schelling are now available in English translation. See, for example, his *The Grounding of Positive Philosophy: The Berlin Lectures,* trans. Bruce Matthews (New York: State University of New York Press, 2007). For a short discussion of Schelling's philosophy (with further references), see my "Why There Is Something Rather Than Nothing: F. W. J. Schelling and the Metaphysics of Freedom," in John Wippel, ed., *The Ultimate Why Question* (Washington, DC: Catholic University of America Press, 2010).

Schelling's philosophy can thus be considered a transitional philosophy, leading the way toward the recognition of historicity, existence, and the givenness of reality that characterized much of twentieth-century thought. But in its very transitional character, it raises the question whether or not the doctrine of creation can philosophically be appropriated in the contemporary context. Is there a way to continue Schelling's philosophy of creation without its ambiguous undertones?

One can argue, as we will see, that Robert Spaemann's philosophy of the human person does not only provide, but essentially is such a philosophy of creation. In his *Persons: The Difference between 'Someone' and 'Something'*, magisterially translated into English by Oliver O'Donovan, Spaemann provides the outline of such a philosophy.[22] Persons, Spaemann shows in this book, "are" not their nature (as animals "are" their nature). Persons "have" their nature, that is, persons have a free relation to their nature. A person cannot leave his or her nature totally behind (this would imply suicide). Nor can a person make his or her nature the absolute framework of his or her self-understanding (this would imply an impossible denial of one's freedom). In the person, nature and freedom are thus related in an unsurpassable way.

According to this view of who a person is, "nature as such" is not normatively significant. Ethics, therefore, cannot be based on the sciences or on a naturalistic view of reality. "In nature," Spaemann argues, "there is not the slightest trace of a reason" for taking on a moral principle.[23] If nature were the ultimate framework for our understanding of reality, a Nietzschean *amor fati* would be all that is left. For whatever happens, happens naturally, and because of the blindness of nature, no decision can be made whether what happens naturally (and all that human beings do happens then by definition naturally) is good or bad. For a strictly naturalistic position, there are, according to Spaemann's persuasive argument, simply no principles that allow the differentiation between good and bad.

How, then, can we understand not simply moral principles, but our decision for (or against) moral principles, that is, our being a person who freely relates to his or her nature? If we follow Spaemann's argument, one answer to this question is given by religion. Religion, as he shows, confirms our self-

22. Robert Spaemann, *Persons: The Difference between 'Someone' and 'Something'*, trans. Oliver O'Donovan (Oxford: Oxford University Press, 2006). For a discussion of Spaemann's philosophy, see my *Robert Spaemann's Philosophy of the Human Person: Nature, Freedom, and the Critique of Modernity* (Oxford: Oxford University Press, 2010); for the following, see particularly chapter 5.

23. Spaemann, *Persons*, p. 96.

understanding as a person. For according to religion "nature is not the last horizon, but something we 'have'. Taken as a whole, nature is 'creation', and its teleological structures allow us to discern the creator's will for humankind. Nothing less than a personal will can be the source of normative 'natural right' for persons."[24] There is therefore a strong link between ethics and religion. It is in fact so strong that Spaemann does not even indicate which other answers to the question at stake there are. It seems as if only religion, as outlined by Spaemann, could justify the self-understanding of persons as "having" and not simply "being" their nature.

Is this still a philosophical argument? Does his reference to "'creation'" and the "creator" not betray Spaemann's religious interests and thus invalidate the philosophical significance of his argument? Spaemann, to be sure, develops his argument against the background of his own religious belief. He openly admits that he refers to Christianity as a model for his understanding of religion.[25] His reasoning, however, does not presuppose Christianity and its truth as a foundation. It is not built on religious premises, understood as the premises of one particular religion such as Christianity. One could rather argue that he, following Kant's practical philosophy,[26] postulates a religious view of reality. Such a view needs to be postulated in order to make sense of the experience of being a person that Spaemann examines with almost phenomenological precision. For a "religious understanding of subjectivity can treat it as a person, i.e. an existent that was 'meant to be' subjective and could not be otherwise."[27] If there were no divine creator, Spaemann points out, the self-understanding of the person would inevitably prove illusory. He explains what this means in what can be read as a translation of the Christian concept of creation into a philosophical discourse, that is, a discourse that is modelled, but in its truth claim not founded, on the truth of a specific historical religion. There is, as he maintains, an unstable, dialectical "balance between transcendence and reflection" in human consciousness.[28] In the act of thinking, the human mind goes beyond itself and thus transcends itself. The thinker hopes that what he

24. Spaemann, *Persons*, p. 96.
25. Spaemann, *Persons*, p. 94.
26. For Habermas's critical account of Kant's philosophy of religion, see his "Die Grenze zwischen Glauben und Wissen: Zur Wirkungsgeschichte und aktuellen Bedeutung von Kants Religionsphilosophie," in *Zwischen Naturalismus und Religion*, pp. 216-257 ("The Boundary between Faith and Knowledge: On the Reception and Contemporary Importance of Kant's Philosophy of Religion," in *Between Naturalism and Religion*, pp. 209-247).
27. Spaemann, *Persons*, p. 95.
28. Spaemann, *Persons*, p. 93.

thinks about is real and that the object of his thinking is not merely a product of his thinking. The thinker's reaching out for reality, however, can become again the object of his reflection. Reality could be a mere thought. Every attempt of the thinker to go beyond himself may just be another way of remaining within himself or, as Spaemann put it, "every thought about what lies beyond thought is itself a thought."[29] Can human thinking ever achieve Being in such a way that it is not just another thought?

Spaemann leaves open whether or not "the gap between thinking of Being and Being itself" can ever be bridged by means of human thinking alone. Hegel, he argues, undertook the enterprise to bridge this gap. Spaemann, however, seems to imply that Hegel ultimately failed. He follows Schelling's later philosophy (and its criticism of Hegel's thought) and argues that "Being is always 'unanticipated' (unvordenklich),"[30] that is, Being cannot be thought of prior to its actual being given such that there are intrinsic limits of mere logical thought. It is, however, given to us: in the conception of God. "In conceiving of God and of his own creation," Spaemann holds, "reflection comes to a standstill, confronted with itself as Being."[31] For this reason, religion is "undialectic."[32] As the "form" in which the Absolute is "already present, and already known to be present,"[33] it is not subject to an endless dialectic of transcendence and reflection, but allows a reconciliation of the two. Spaemann points out that an example of such an understanding of God and of the human person can be found in Descartes' philosophy: "And Descartes, the first to base his whole philosophy on subjective reflection, could only assure himself that subjectivity was real by way of the conception of God he found there, i.e. in religion."[34] One does not, it seems, need to go beyond Cartesian modernity to be able to follow Spaemann's argument. One can even argue that, particularly if one takes modernity's discovery of subjectivity seriously, one will have to follow his argument.

Spaemann's (and, if we follow his interpretation, Descartes') view of subjectivity — not a religious view in the strict sense of the word, but a view that, modelled on what can be found in a concrete religion, postulates a philosophical concept of the Absolute as present in a way that cannot be anticipated — is opposed to what he calls "naturalist monism." According to such a naturalist view, our self-understanding as persons — the concept of subjectivity alto-

29. Spaemann, *Persons,* p. 93.
30. Spaemann, *Persons,* p. 94.
31. Spaemann, *Persons,* p. 94.
32. Spaemann, *Persons,* p. 95.
33. Spaemann, *Persons,* p. 94.
34. Spaemann, *Persons,* p. 94.

gether — is ultimately a misunderstanding. For this kind of naturalism reduces the dialectic of transcendence and reflection to a merely natural phenomenon: "From this point of view transcendence with its posit of Being is but an impotent reduplication, constantly overtaken by reflection on its conditions, while reflection itself is merely a natural phenomenon."[35] Naturalism, then, is based on "transcendence without reflection."[36] There is nothing but nature. There is also a position that is characterized by "reflection without transcendence." Spaemann calls this position "spiritualism." Such a "spiritualism" disregards the natural and, because freedom or human reason is taken to be an absolute, understands reality as an object or product of mere reflection. While the naturalist subjects everything to the workings of nature, thus losing any possibility of ever understanding himself as a free and rational being, the "spiritualist" tries to understand himself as a free and rational agent at the cost of losing any possibility of ever understanding himself as a (natural) being. It goes without saying that neither naturalism nor spiritualism can understand the truth of the human person, that is, the person's free "having" his or her nature. In either case, the balance between nature and freedom, between transcendence and reflection that is constitutive of the person, cannot be adequately expressed. It can only be understood reductively: one is not only subject to the other, but one of the two is ultimately an illusion.

According to Spaemann's interpretation of modernity, naturalism and "spiritualism" stand in a dialectic relation to one another; they are antithetical positions that can dialectically collapse into one anther without ever leading back to the lost middle ground.[37] Vis-à-vis the challenges of naturalism, "spiritualism," and their dialectic, Spaemann's philosophy of the human person establishes a position not between these two sets of ideas, but beyond these positions and their dialectic. What is required to go beyond this dialectic, is, as we have already seen, a view of reality that takes seriously that the Absolute is always already present — in a way that cannot be anticipated, but always already bridges the gap between thinking and Being such that the unstable balance between reflection and transcendence can come to rest without annihilating one or the other. This is to say that what is required is to postulate a philosophy of creation that takes a religious view of reality philosophically seriously.

35. Spaemann, *Persons,* p. 95.
36. Spaemann, *Persons,* p. 95.
37. For his interpretation of the dialectic of modernity, see my *Robert Spaemann's Philosophy of the Human Person,* chapter 3.

On the basis of this kind of thinking, it is still possible to speak of, and to justify, the dignity of the person: "Dignity," Spaemann argues,

> signals something sacred. The concept is a fundamentally religious-metaphysical one. Horkheimer and Adorno saw this clearly when they wrote that the only argument against murder is a religious one. This was not, of course, employed as an argument for murder, but rather for taking a religious view of reality. It is a mistake that persists into our time to think you can drop our religious view of reality without losing something else, something you would not so readily choose to do without.[38]

The reference to Adorno and Horkheimer — two philosophers who were extremely important for Habermas and his philosophical development[39] — clearly shows that Spaemann, himself a Catholic, has not a Catholic or Christian philosophy in mind when he reminds his readers of the need of a "religious view" in the context of philosophy. What he has in mind is a philosophical understanding of religion, that, while possibly being modelled on a concrete historical religion such as Christianity, implies a philosophical theology, that is, a philosophical way of talking about God or the Absolute. Spaemann, therefore, also has in mind a metaphysical understanding of philosophy. Unlike Habermas who calls his thinking (as well as our age) not only "post-secular," but also "post-metaphysical,"[40] Spaemann does not abandon metaphysics in the sense of trying to understand what reality really is, that is, in the sense of discovering the truth of Being and, therefore, the truth of the Absolute and its presence.

While Habermas is certainly right when he points out that there is need for a translation of many religious concepts into the universal language of

---

38. Spaemann, "Human Dignity and Human Nature", in Robert Spaemann, *Love and the Dignity of Human Life: On Nature and Natural Law* (Grand Rapids: Eerdmans, 2012), pp. 27-44, pp. 41-42.

39. See in this context particularly Habermas, "To Seek to Salvage an Unconditional Meaning without God Is a Futile Undertaking: Reflections on a Remark of Max Horkheimer," in *Religion and Rationality*, pp. 95-109; "'Ich selber bin ja ein Stück Natur' — Adorno über die Naturverflochtenheit der Vernunft: Überlegungen zum Verhältnis von Freiheit und Unverfügbarkeit," in *Zwischen Naturalismus und Religion*, pp. 187-215 ("'I Myself Am Part of Nature' — Adorno on the Intrication of Reason in Nature: Reflections on the Relation between Freedom and Unavailability", in *Between Naturalism and Religion*, pp. 181-208).

40. For this understanding of our age, see particularly Habermas, *Nachmetaphysische Denken I* (Frankfurt am Main: Suhrkamp Verlag, 1988); ET: *Postmetaphysical Thinking: Philosophical Essays*, trans. William Mark Hohengarten (Cambridge: Polity, 1995); *Nachmetaphysisches Denken II*.

philosophy, he may not be right in his view of what needs to be translated, or how the translation ought to proceed, when it comes to the concept of the human person and the person's dignity as created in the image of God. It may not be possible to "recover," as Habermas's post-metaphysical thought suggests, "the meaning of the unconditional without recourse to God or an Absolute."[41] It may not be possible then to transcend the limits of nature. It may be necessary to take the position of a metaphysics of creation as a translation of the theological concept of creation into a philosophical language. Spaemann's philosophy of the person provides an example for such a translation. While his understanding of religion is modelled on Christianity, it seems that one would not have to be a Christian to understand his metaphysics of creation as a postulate, not as a foundation or presupposition of his argument. One would have to take seriously one's own self-understanding as a person that puts into question any kind of deterministic naturalism. This is by no means an irrational argument. It is, however, an argument that requires the recognition of oneself, and of the other human being, as a person. It thus requires the *morality* of a person.

41. Habermas, "To Seek to Salvage," p. 108.

The Nature of Family, the Family of Nature: Prescient Insights from the Scottish Enlightenment

John Witte, Jr.

In a series of writings spanning four decades, Oliver O'Donovan has brought his formidable mind and elegant pen to bear on fundamental questions of sex, marriage, and family life. His first point of departure, as a Christian ethicist, is the Bible. Genesis 1 and 2 are axiomatic for him: that marriage was created as a "one flesh union" between a man and a woman designed for them to "be fruitful and multiply." So is Matthew 19: that a marriage should not be "rent asunder" too easily nor a subsequent remarriage entered too quickly. So is 1 Corinthians 7 that stipulates both the natural ability that some people have to pursue the single life and the "conjugal rights" that married people have to share their bodies and sexual needs with their spouse. So are the Mosaic family laws and the Pauline household codes that culminate in the masterful depiction of marriage in Ephesians 5 as a mutually sacrificial, loving, and intimate "mystery," modeled on the union of Christ and the church.[1]

O'Donovan's second point of departure, as an historian of ideas, is the Western Christian tradition. He has expounded the Bible's teachings on sex, marriage, and family life in learned conversation with the great sages of the

---

1. Oliver O'Donovan, *Resurrection and Moral Order: An Outline for Evangelical Ethics* (Grand Rapids: Eerdmans, 1986), pp. 20-21, 69-72, 210; idem, "Marriage and the Family," in *Obeying Christ in a Changing World*, Vol. 3, ed. Bruce Kaye (Glasgow: Fountain Press, 1977); idem, *Marriage and Permanence* (Bramcote: Grove Books, 1978); idem, *The Ways of Judgment* (Grand Rapids: Eerdmans, 2005), pp. 261-292; idem, "The Honor of Marriage," in idem, *The Word in Small Boats* (Grand Rapids: Eerdmans, 2010), pp. 150-155; contributor, *Marriage: A Teaching Document from the House of Bishops of the Church of England*, 4th impr. (Nottingham: Church House Publishing, 2000).

Christian tradition — Augustine, Aquinas, Luther, Calvin, Kierkegaard, and scores of others, whose work he knows cold and, of course, in their original languages.[2] From these conversations with the tradition, O'Donovan has lifted up the fundamental "ontology" of human beings who are created as "male and female" and called to be united as "two in one flesh." He has also lifted up the fundamental "teleology" of human marriage as a dyadic union created for the inherent goods of mutual love and companionship of husband and wife, mutual procreation and nurture of children, and mutual stability and security of the household and its members.

In *Resurrection and Moral Order,* he writes profoundly about the nature of human sexuality, marriage, and family life that is reflected in these biblical and traditional teachings:

> In the ordinance of marriage there was given an end for human relationships, a teleological structure which was a fact of creation and therefore not negotiable. The dimorphic organization of human sexuality, the particular attention of two adults of the opposite sex and of different parents, the setting up of a home distinct from a parental home and the uniting of their lives in a shared life (from which Jesus concluded the unnaturalness of divorce): these form a pattern of human fulfillment which serves the wider end of enabling procreation to occur in a context of affection and loyalty. Whatever happens in history, Christians have wished to say, this is what marriage really is. Particular cultures may have distorted it; individuals may fall short of it. It is to their cost in either case; for it reasserts itself as God's creative intention for human relationships on earth; and it will be with us, in one form or another, as our natural good until (but not after) the kingdom of God shall appear.[3]

O'Donovan has calculated — and lamented — the ample moral, social, and personal "costs" of departing from these "natural goods" of marriage and the family. In particular, he has weighed in on some of the red-hot issues that are deeply dividing churches, states, and societies today — promiscuity, pornography, contraception, abortion, artificial reproduction, no-fault divorce, extramarital sex, non-marital birth, same-sex unions, trans-sexuality, and more.[4] On each of these topics, he has guided his readers to a higher herme-

2. See esp. the erudition on display in his leading work in political theology, *The Desire of the Nations: Rediscovering the Roots of Political Theology* (Cambridge: Cambridge University Press, 1996).

3. O'Donovan, *Resurrection and Moral Order,* p. 69.

4. See esp. Oliver O'Donovan, *Church in Crisis: The Gay Controversy and the Anglican*

neutical plane, inviting them to see the bigger theological and moral stakes at work in the bitter battles that now beset us about these intimate matters. He has also led his readers to a deeper theoretical foundation, encouraging them to look carefully at the pervasive (and, for him, deeply disturbing) secular liberal theologies that support the modern sexual revolution — especially the seemingly endless expansion of human rights ideals that privilege individuality and freedom of choice, identity, expression, association, and self-determination.[5]

O'Donovan does not end up with a wistful call for the West to return to the purported glories of Christendom. As an historian, he knows better than to think that the West once had a golden age of domestic life and law that can be readily transplanted into our day. Nor does he call modern pluralistic Western societies — most of them constitutionally committed to religious freedom for all and religious establishment to none — to incorporate biblical and traditional teachings into their legal systems simply because those teachings are true and right. As a moralist, he knows the advantage of keeping the big normative systems of religion and law, church and state in creative dialectical tension. He agrees with a recent statement of the Anglican Bishops: "If *per impossible* the Christian minority today had power to impose on the nation a

---

Communion (Eugene, OR: Cascade Books, 2008); idem, *The Christian and the Unborn Child* (Nottingham: Grove Books, 1972); *Marriage and Permanence* (Nottingham: Grove Books, 1978); *Transsexualism: Issues and Argument* (Cambridge: Grove Books 2007); idem, "Transsexualism and Christian Marriage," *Journal of Religious Ethics* 9 (1983): 135-162; idem, "Discussing Homosexuality with St. Paul: A Theological and Pastoral Approach," in *A Crisis of Understanding: Homosexuality and the Canadian Church,* ed. Denyse O'Leary (Burlington, ON: Welch, 1988), pp. 51-61; idem, "Homosexuality in the Church: Can There Be a Fruitful Theological Debate?" in *The Way Forward? Christian Voices on Homosexuality and the Church,* ed. Timothy Bradshaw (London: Hodder & Stoughton, 1997, 2003), pp. 20-36; idem, "Again: Who Is a Person?" in *Abortion and the Sanctity of Human Life,* ed. J. H. Channer (Exeter: Paternoster, 1985), pp. 125-137, reprinted in *On Moral Medicine,* ed. Stephen E. Lammers and Allen Verhey, 2nd ed. (Grand Rapids: Eerdmans, 1998), pp. 380-386; idem, "The Conjoined Twins," *Medicine, Science and the Law* 52, no. 4 (2002): 280-284; contributor, *Personal Origins: Report of a Working Party on Human Fertilisation and Embryology of the Board for Social Responsibility* (London: Church Information Office, 1985); contributor, *Marriage in Church after Divorce: A Discussion Document from a Working Party Commissioned by the House of Bishops of the Church of England* (London: Church House Publishing, 2000); contributor, *Die Familie im neuen Europa: Ethische Herausforderungen und interdisziplinäre Perspektiven,* ed. Gerhard Höver, Gerrit G. de Kruijf, Oliver O'Donovan, and Bernd Wannenwetsch (Berlin: LitVerlag, 2008); O'Donovan, *Begotten or Made?* (Oxford: Oxford University Press, 1984; repr. 2002).

5. See esp. O'Donovan, *The Desire of the Nations,* pp. 243-284.

matrimonial law satisfactory to itself, to use the power would surely be unjust as well as socially disruptive."[6]

But the Christian church, he insists, must continue to mine Scripture and tradition, reason and conscience for new insights to meet the new challenges of sex, marriage, and family that modernity has posed. And the church must continue to give prophetic witness to the state and society, particularly when its norms and practices depart so radically from what is natural, just, and most conducive to the common good. Part of this prophetic exercise requires the church to get its own moral house in order on issues of sexuality, marriage, and family life — not easy, O'Donovan knows first hand, given the rancorous debates in his own Anglican communion.[7] Part of this prophetic exercise requires Christians to develop a political theology and moral grammar that reaches across confessional divides and works out productive agreements about the "natural goods" of marriage and the family that need social and legal support.

I come to this subject as a legal historian, interested in the interaction of law, religion, and the family in the West. I am particularly drawn to O'Donovan's insights into the unique "nature" of human marriages and families — a nature he sees described in the creation narratives of Genesis 1–2 and also inscribed on our human nature and cultural experience. In this, he is echoing a classic teaching of the Western tradition. Scholars from the earliest Greek philosophers to the latest evolutionary scientists have argued that the human species has found exclusive, monogamous, and enduring marriage as the best vehicle for the mutual protection, support, and companionship of men and women and for the mutual procreation, nurture, and education of children.[8]

The basic argument, as it has evolved in the West, is that exclusive and enduring monogamous marriages are the best way to ensure paternal certainty and joint parental investment in children who are born vulnerable and utterly dependent on their parents' mutual care. Exclusive and enduring monogamous marriages, furthermore, are the best way to ensure that men and women are treated with equal dignity and respect, and that husbands and wives, parents and children provide each other with mutual support, protection, and edification throughout their lifetimes. The positive law of the state must not only

---

6. *Putting Asunder* (1966), p. 14, quoted by O'Donovan, *Resurrection and Moral Order*, pp. 20-21.

7. See esp. O'Donovan, *Church in Crisis*.

8. I develop this argument at length with the late Don S. Browning in *From Private Contract to Public Covenant: What Can Christianity Offer to Modern Marriage Law?* (Cambridge University Press, forthcoming), chaps. 5-10.

support such marriages, the argument continues; it must also outlaw polygamy, fornication, adultery, and "light divorce" that violate the other spouse's natural rights as well as desertion, abuse, neglect, and disinheritance that violate their children's natural rights to support, protection, and education.

This traditional Western argument about the nature of sex, marriage, and the family drew on complex and emerging ideas concerning human infant dependency, parental bonding, paternal certainty and investment, and the natural rights and duties of husband and wives, parents and children. But this argument started with three brute realities that every family law system must address: that human children need help for a very long time, that human adults crave sex a good deal of the time, and that human beings, unlike all other animals, are capable of self-destructive behavior ("sin" is what theologians call it) that society needs somehow to deter.

In this chapter — dedicated to O'Donovan in admiration and appreciation — I offer one little sample of this broader Western argument about the nature of sex, marriage, and family, drawn from the eighteenth-century Scottish Enlightenment. I choose this example, in part, because many of the leading figures of the Scottish Enlightenment have followed O'Donovan's career path — training and teaching at Oxford or Cambridge, and then settling into professorships at various Scottish universities, not least the University of Edinburgh. I choose this example as well because the Scottish Enlightenment teachings on this topic are rather little known in the literature, though they strongly shaped the common law of domestic relations until the twentieth century. And I choose this example because it will surprise some readers, as it surprised me. These Scottish scions of modern liberalism, so famous for their defense of liberty, democracy, market capitalism, and more, were anything but sexual libertines. They defended almost all the traditional Western ideals of sex, marriage, and family life. But, rather than defend them on biblical and theological grounds as earlier Christians had done, they argued from natural law, common sense, practical reason, and social utility.

The Nature of Marriage and Family Life:
Home, Hutcheson, and Hume

The writings of Henry Home, known as Lord Kames of Scotland (1696-1782), were particularly perceptive. A leading man of letters and a leading justice of the Scottish highest court, Home was a friend of Francis Hutcheson, David Hume, Thomas Reid, Adam Smith, and other such Scottish luminaries. He wrote extensively on law and politics, religion and morality, history and economy, art and industry. He was best known for his brilliant defense of natural law, principally on empirical and rational grounds. Home sought to prove the realities of virtue, duty, justice, liberty, freedom, and other natural moral principles, and the necessity for rational humans to create various offices, laws, and institutions to support and protect them. While his rationalist methodology and naturalist theology rankled the orthodox Christian theologians of his day, Home wanted to give his natural law argument a more universal and enduring cogency. A devout and life-long Protestant, he believed in the truth of Scripture and the will of God. But he wanted to win over even skeptics and atheists to his legal and moral arguments and to give enduring "authority to the promises and covenants" that helped create society and its institutions.[9]

Among many other institutions and "covenants," Home defended monogamous marriage as a "necessity of nature," and he denounced polygamy as "a vice against human nature." Home recognized, of course, that polygamy was commonplace among some animals, drawing sundry examples from the work of the French Jesuit naturalist, Buffon.[10] He also recognized that polygamy had been practiced in early Western history and was still known in some Islamic and Asiatic cultures in his day. But, he insisted, polygamy exists only "where women are treated as inferior beings," and where "men of wealth transgress every rule of temperance" by buying their wives like slaves and by adopting the "savage manners" of animals. Among horses, cattle, and other grazing animals, Home argued, polygamy is natural. One superior male breeds with all females, and the mothers take care of their own young who grow quickly independent. For these animals, monogamous "pairing would be of no use: the female feeds herself and her young at the same instant; and nothing is left for the male to do." But other animals, such as nesting birds, "whose young require the nursing care of both parents, are directed by nature to pair" and to remain paired till their young "are sufficiently vigorous to provide for themselves."[11]

---

9. See Henry Home, *Essays on the Principles of Morality and Natural Religion* [1779], 3rd ed., ed. Mary Catherine Moran (Indianapolis: Liberty Fund, 2005), esp. Part I, Essay 2, chapters 6 and 9; and the study by Ian Simpson Ross, *Lord Kames and the Scotland of His Day* (Oxford: Oxford University Press, 1972); William C. Lehmann, *Henry Home, Lord Kames, and the Scottish Enlightenment: A Study in National Character and in the History of Ideas* (The Hague: Martinus Nijhoff, 1971).

10. See Henry Home, *Sketches of the History of Man, Considerably Enlarged by the Latest Additions and Corrections of the Author,* ed. James A. Harris (Indianapolis: Liberty Fund, 2007), 3 vols., Book I, Sketch VI, Appendix: "Concerning Propagation of Animals and Care of Progeny."

11. Ibid., Sketch V, 204, Sketch VI, 261, 263, 271, 278.

Humans are the latter sort of creature, said Home, and are thus predisposed by nature to adopt enduring monogamous pairing. Home expanded on the natural law configuration of marriage and the importance of human childhood dependency developed by Aquinas and his followers, Grotius, Pufendorf, and Locke, adding new insights as well from the science of cultural development (anthropology as we now call it):

> Man is an animal of long life, and is proportionally slow in growing to maturity: he is a helpless being before the age of fifteen or sixteen; and there may be in a family ten or twelve children of different births, before the eldest can shift for itself. Now in the original state of hunting and fishing, which are laborious occupations, and not always successful, a woman, suckling her infant, is not able to provide food even for herself, far less for ten or twelve voracious children. . . . [P]airing is so necessary to the human race, that it must be natural and instinctive. . . . Brute animals, which do not pair, have grass and other food in plenty, enabling the female to feed her young without needing any assistance from the male. But where the young require the nursing care of both parents, pairing is a law of nature.[12]

Not only is the pairing of male and female a law of nature, Home continued. "Matrimony is instituted by nature" to overcome humans' greatest natural handicap to effective procreation and preservation as a species — their perpetual desire for sex, especially among the young, at exactly the time when they are most fertile. Unlike most animals, whose sexual appetites are confined to short rutting seasons, Home wrote, humans have a constant sexual appetite which, by nature, "demands gratification, after short intervals." If men and women just had random sex with anyone — "like the hart in rutting time" — the human race would devolve into a "savage state of nature" and soon die out. Men would make perennial and "promiscuous use of women" and not commit themselves to the care of these women or their children. "Women would in effect be common prostitutes." Few women would have the ability on their own "to provide food for a family of children," and most would avoid having children or would abandon them if they did. Marriage is nature's safeguard against such proclivities, said Home, and "frequent enjoyment" of marital sex and intimacy "endears a pair to each other," making them want only each other all the more. "Sweet is the society of a pair fitted for each other, in whom are collected the affections of husband, wife, lover, friend, the tenderest affections of human nature."

12. Ibid., Sketch VI, 263-264.

The God of nature has [thus] enforced conjugal society, not only by making it agreeable, but by the principle of chastity inherent in our nature. To animals that have no instinct for pairing, chastity is utterly unknown; and to them it would be useless. The mare, the cow, the ewe, the she-goat, receive the male without ceremony, and admit the first that comes in the way without distinction. Neither have tame fowl any notion of chastity: they pair not; and the female gets no food from the male, even during incubation. But chastity and mutual fidelity [are] essential to the human race; enforced by the principle of chastity, a branch of the moral sense. Chastity is essential even to the continuation of the human race. As the carnal appetite is always alive, the sexes would wallow in pleasure, and be soon rendered unfit for procreation, were it not for the restraint of chastity.[13]

Polygamy violates this natural design and strategy for successful procreation through enduring marital cohabitation, Home argued. First, monogamy is better suited to the roughly equal numbers of men and women in the world. "All men are by nature equal in rank; no man is privileged above another to have a wife; and therefore polygamy is contradictory" to the natural order and to the natural right of each fit adult to marry. Monogamous pairing is most "clearly the voice of nature." It is echoed in "sacred Scripture" in its injunction that "two" — not three or four — shall become "one flesh" in marriage. If God and nature had intended to condone polygamy, there would be many more females than males.[14]

Second, monogamy "is much better calculated for continuing the race, than the union of one man with many women." One man cannot possibly provide food, care, and nurture to the many children born of his many wives. Their wives are not able to provide easily for their young when they are weakened from child labor and birth, needed for nursing, or distracted by the many needs of multiple children. Some of their children will be neglected, some will grow up impoverished, malnourished, or undereducated, some will inevitably die. "How much better chance for life have infants who are distributed more equally in different families."[15]

Third, monogamy is better suited for women. Men and women are by

---

13. Ibid., Sketch VI, 264, 267, 269-270. Later, Home condemned mandatory celibacy and abstinence within marriage as "ridiculous self-denial," an "impudent disregard of moral principles," and the "grossest of all deviations, not only from sound morality, but from pure religion" and natural law. Ibid., Book III, Sketch III, 888-890.

14. Ibid., Book I, Sketch VI, 265-266.

15. Ibid., Sketch VI, 266; Sketch VIII, 484.

nature equal, Home argued at length, building on the egalitarian themes of
Locke among others. Monogamous marriage is naturally designed to respect
this natural gender equality, even while recognizing the different roles that a
husband and wife play in the procreation and nurture of their children. Thus
marriage works best when a husband and wife have "reciprocal and equal affection" as true "companions" in life, who enjoy each other and their children
with "endearment" and "constancy." Polygamy, by contrast, is simply a patri-
archal fraud. Each wife is reduced to a servant, "a mere instrument of pleasure
and propagation" for her husband. Each wife is reduced to competing for the
attention and affection of her husband, particularly if she has small children
and needs help in their care. One wife and her children will inevitably be
singled out for special favor, denigrating the others further and exacerbating
the tensions within the household which cause the children to suffer, too.
Packs of wolves might thrive this way, but rational humans cannot. Combining
natural instinct with rational reflection, humans have discovered that monogamy is the "foundation for a true matrimonial covenant" between two equal
adults.[16]

Fourth, monogamy is better designed to promote the fidelity and chastity
humans need to procreate effectively as a species. It induces husband and wives
to remain faithful to each other and to their children, come what may. Polygamy, by contrast, is simply a forum and a catalyst for adultery and lust. If a
husband is allowed to satisfy his lust for a second woman whom he can add
as a wife, his "one act of incontinence will lead to others without end." Soon
enough, he will lust after yet another wife and still another — even the wife of
another man, as the biblical story of King David's lust for Bathsheba tragically
illustrates. The husband's bed-hopping, in turn, will "alienate the affections"
of his first wife, who will embark on her own bed-hopping. Such "unlawful
love" will only trigger more and more rivalries among husbands, wives, and
lovers in which all will suffer. Moreover, by sharing another man's bed, the wife
might well require her husband "to maintain and educate children who are
not his own." This most men will not do unless they are uncommonly smitten
or unusually charitable. Polygamy simply "does not work," Home wrote. "Matrimony between a single pair, for mutual comfort, and for procreating children
implies the strictest mutual fidelity."[17]

Even children understand that monogamous marriage is "an appointment
of nature," Home concluded. As infants they bond with both their mothers

16. Ibid., Sketch VI, 261, 267-268, 287-311.
17. Ibid., Sketch V, 204; Sketch VI, 270, 287-289.

and fathers and when they grow older they work to keep the couple together. "If undisguised nature shows itself anywhere, it is in children," Home wrote. "They often hear, it is true, people talking of matrimony; but they also hear of logical, metaphysical, and commercial matters, without understanding a syllable. Whence then their notion of marriage but from nature? Marriage is a compound idea, which no instruction could bring within the comprehension of a child, did not nature cooperate." From the "mouths of babes" come profound truths about our most basic institution.[18] We hear in these words of Home the seeds of a children's right point of view — their right to be born in a society whose customs and laws protect their inclination, need, and right to be raised by their parents of conception unless illness, accident, or death of a parent intervenes.

Home's argument for monogamy and against polygamy was typical of the arguments from nature, reason, and experience that the Scottish Enlightenment mustered in favor of traditional forms and norms of marriage. Some of these writers supplemented these with arguments from Scripture and Christian tradition, but most, like Home, sought to prove their case on rational and empirical grounds so much as possible. For example, the great Scottish philosopher of common sense Francis Hutcheson (1694-1746) grounded his argument for the natural law of monogamy, fidelity, and exclusivity again on the natural needs of mothers and children:

> Now as the mothers are quite insufficient alone for this necessary and laborious task, which nature also has plainly enjoined on both the parents by implanting in both that strong parental affection; both parents are bound to concur in it, with joint labor, and united cares for a great share of their lives: and this can never be tolerable to them unless they are previously united in love and stable friendship: as new children also must be coming into life, prolonging this joint charge. To engage mankind more cheerfully in this laborious service nature has implanted vehement affections between the sexes; excited not so much by views of brutal pleasure as by some appearances of virtues, displayed in their behavior, and even by their very form and countenances. These strong impulses plainly show it to be the intention of nature that human offspring should be propagated only by parents first united in stable friendship, and in a firm covenant about perpetual cohabitation and joint care of their common children. For all true friendship aims at perpetuity: there's no friendship in a bond only for a fixed

18. Ibid., Sketch VI, 265.

term of years, or in one depending upon certain events which the utmost fidelity of the parties cannot ensure.[19]

"Nature has thus strongly recommended" that for humans all sex and procreation occur within a "proper covenant about a friendly society for life," Hutcheson continued, using the typical covenantal language for marriage favored by Scottish Presbyterians. "The chief articles in this covenant" are mutual fidelity of husband and wife to each other. A wandering wife causes the "greatest injury" to her husband by bringing adulterine children into the home who dilute his property and distract him from "that tender affection which is naturally due to his own [children]." A wandering husband causes great injury to his wife and children by allowing his affections and fortunes to be squandered on prostitutes, mistresses, and lovers. (Hutcheson's commentators, including Princeton President John Witherspoon who regularly lectured on his writings, added the dangers of tracking in syphilis and other sexual diseases, too.)[20] Other articles of the "natural marital covenant," Hutcheson wrote, include "a perpetual union of interests and pursuits" between husband and wife, a mutual commitment to "the right education of their common children," and a mutual agreement to forgo separation and divorce. It is against reason and human nature, Hutcheson wrote, "to divorce or separate from a faithful and affectionate consort for any causes which include no moral turpitude; such as barrenness, or infirmity of body; or any mournful accident which no mortal could prevent." Such "libertinism" is "not only unjust, but also unnatural." Divorce should be allowed only in cases of adultery, "obstinate desertion, capital enmity, or hatred and such gross outrages as take away all hopes of any friendly society for the future or a safe and agreeable life together."[21]

Similarly, the famous Scottish philosopher David Hume (1711-1776), for all his skepticism about traditional morality, thought traditional norms of sex, marriage, and family life to be both natural and useful. He summarized the natural law configuration of marriage crisply: "The long and helpless infancy

19. Francis Hutcheson, *Philosophiae Moralis Institutio Compendiaria, With a Short Introduction to Moral Philosophy,* ed. Luigi Turco (Indianapolis: Liberty Fund, 2007), p. 218.

20. See John Witherspoon, *Lectures on Moral Philosophy,* ed. Varnum Lansing Collins (Princeton: Princeton University Press, 1912), Lecture XI. Witherspoon's lectures are heavily drawn from his teacher Francis Hutcheson; among the students in those lectures was American founder James Madison.

21. Hutcheson, *Philosophiae Moralis,* pp. 220-222. See also Francis Hutcheson, *Logic, Metaphysics, and the Natural Sociability of Mankind,* ed. James Moore and Michael Silverthorne (Indianapolis: Liberty Fund, 2006), pp. 206-207.

requires the combination of parents for the subsistence of their young; and that combination requires the virtue of chastity and fidelity to the marriage bed."[22] Hume used many of the same arguments that Home had mustered against polygamy. This "odious institution" denied the natural equality of the sexes. It fostered "the bad education of children." It led to "jealousy and competition among wives," and more. Moreover, said Hume, polygamy forced a man, distracted by his other wives and children, to confine his other wives to the home — by physically threatening, binding, or even laming them, by isolating them from society, or by keeping them so poor and weak they could not leave. All this is a form of "barbarism," with "frightful effects" that defy all nature and reason.[23]

Hume offered similar natural and utilitarian arguments against "voluntary divorce." Many in Hume's day argued for divorce as a natural expression of the freedom of contract and a natural compensation for having no recourse to polygamy despite a man's natural drive to multiple partners. "The heart of man delights in liberty," their argument went; "the very image of constraint is grievous to it." Hume would have none of this. To be sure, he recognized that divorce was sometimes the better of two evils — especially where one party was guilty of adultery, severe cruelty, or malicious desertion, and especially when no children were involved. But, outside of such narrow circumstances, he said, "nature has made divorce" without real cause the "doom of all mortals." First, with voluntary divorce, the children suffer and become "miserable." Shuffled from home to home, consigned to the care of strangers and step-parents "instead of the fond attention and concern of a parent," the inconveniences and encumbrances of their lives just multiply as the divorces of their parents and stepparents multiply. Second, when voluntary divorce is foreclosed, couples by nature become disinclined to wander, and instead form "a calm and sedate affection, conducted by reason and cemented by habit; springing from long acquaintance and mutual obligations, without jealousies or fears." "We need not, therefore, be afraid of drawing the marriage-knot, which chiefly subsists by friendship, the closest possible." Third, "nothing is more dangerous than to unite two persons so closely in all their interests and concerns, as man and wife, without rendering the union entire and total. The least possibility of a separate interest must be the

22. David Hume, *Enquiries Concerning the Human Understanding and Concerning the Principles of Morals* [1777], 2nd ed., ed. L. A. Selby-Bigge (Oxford: Clarendon Press, 1902, 2nd impr., 1963), pp. 206-207.

23. David Hume, *Essays Moral, Political, and Literary,* rev. ed., ed. Eugene F. Miller (Indianapolis: Liberty Fund, 1987), Essay XIX "On Polygamy and Divorces," pp. 182-187.

source of endless quarrels and suspicions." Nature, justice, and prudence alike require their "continued consortium."[24]

William Paley and the Utilitarians

The natural law writings of William Paley (1743-1805), a Cambridge philosopher and later an Anglican cleric with a strong following among Scottish philosophers, provide a good illustration of how these natural law arguments could be pressed into a more utilitarian and natural rights direction. Paley was known in his day as a "theological utilitarian." He sought to define those natural principles and practices of social life that most conduce to human happiness — in this life, and sometimes in the next. Those principles and practices, he said, could be variously sought in Scripture and tradition, divine law and natural law, morality and casuistry — all of which, for Paley, contributed and came to "the same thing; namely, that science which teaches men their duty and the reasons of it."[25]

Marriage is among the natural duties and rights of men and women, Paley wrote, for it provides a variety of public and private goods. His list of marital goods was a nice distillation of traditional arguments:

1. The private comfort of individuals, especially of the female sex. . . .
2. The production of the greatest number of healthy children, their better education, and the making of due provision for their settlement in life.
3. The peace of human society, in cutting off a principal source of contention, by assigning one or more women to one man, and protecting his exclusive right by sanctions of morality and law.
4. The better government of society, by distributing the community into separate families, and appointing over each the authority of a master of a family, which has more actual influence than all civil authority put together.
5. The same end, in the additional security which the state receives for the good behaviour of its citizens, from the solicitude they feel for the welfare of their children, and from their being confined to permanent habitations.
6. The encouragement of industry . . . and morality.[26]

24. Ibid., pp. 187-190.
25. William Paley, *Principles of Moral and Political Philosophy* [1785], ed. D. L. LeMahieu (Indianapolis: Liberty Fund, 2002), pp. 1-25. See further D. L. LeMahieu, *William Paley: A Philosopher and His Age* (Lincoln: University of Nebraska Press, 1976).
26. Paley, *Principles,* pp. 167-168.

Paley worked systematically through the respective "natural rights and duties" of husband and wife, parent and child. In marriage, a husband promises "to love, comfort, honor, and keep his wife" and a wife promises "to obey, serve, love, honor, and keep her husband" "in every variety of health, fortune, and condition." Both parties further stipulate "to forsake all others, and to keep only unto one another, so long as they both shall live." In a word, said Paley, each spouse promises to do all that is necessary to "consult and promote the other's happiness." These are not only Scriptural and traditional duties of marriage. They are natural duties, as can be seen in the marital contracts of all manner of cultures, which Paley adduced in ample number. These natural duties, in turn, give the other spouse "a natural right" to enforce them in cases of adultery, "desertion, neglect, prodigality, drunkenness, peevishness, penuriousness, jealousy, or any levity of conduct which administers occasion of jealousy." What St. Paul called the "mutual conjugal rights" of husband and wife is simply one expression of the natural rights that husband and wives enjoy the world over.[27]

If the couple is blessed with children, the parents have a "natural right and duty" to provide for the child's "maintenance, education, and a reasonable provision for the child's happiness in respect of outward condition." A parent's rights to care for their children "result from their duties" to their children, said Paley.

> If it be the duty of a parent to educate his children, to form them for a life of usefulness and virtue, to provide for them situations needful for their subsistence and suited to their circumstances, and to prepare them for those situations; he has a right to such authority, and in support of that authority to exercise such discipline as may be necessary for these purposes. The law of nature acknowledges no other foundation of a parent's right over his children, besides his duty towards them. (I speak now of such rights as may be enforced by coercion.) This relation confers no property in their persons, or natural dominion over them, as is commonly supposed.

But a parent "has, in no case, a right to destroy his child's happiness," Paley went on, and those that do will suffer punishment, if not lose custody of their child. Moreover, while parents have a right to encourage and train their children to a given vocation and to give their consent to their children's marriages, "parents have no right to urge their children upon marriages to which they are averse." Children, in turn, have "a natural right to receive the support, education, and care" of their parents. They also have a "natural duty" to "love,

27. Ibid., pp. 194-196.

honor, and obey" their parents even when they become adults, and to care for their parents when they become old, frail, and dependent.[28]

Paley worked systematically through the various sexual sins that deviated from these private and public goods of marriage, and the natural rights and duties of the household — now marshalling natural, rational, and utilitarian arguments against them. His arguments against incest, polygamy, and polygyny differed little from those of the other natural law theorists whom we have already sampled. More original were his combinations of natural law and utilitarian arguments against fornication, prostitution, adultery, and easy divorce.

Paley opposed fornication — "sex or cohabitation without marriage" — mostly because it "discourages marriage" and "diminishes the private and public goods" it offers "by abating the chief temptation to it. The male part of the species will not undertake the encumbrance, expense, and restraint of married life, if they can gratify their passions at a cheaper price; and they will undertake anything rather than not gratify them." Paley recognized that he was appealing to general utility, but he thought an absolute ban on fornication was the only way to avoid the slippery slope to utter sexual libertinism. "The libertine may not be conscious that these irregularities hinder his own marriage . . . much less does he perceive how *his* indulgences can hinder other men from marrying; but what will he say would be the consequence, if the same licentiousness were universal? or what should hinder its becoming universal, if it be innocent or allowable in him?"[29]

Fornication furthermore leads to prostitution, Paley went on, with its accompanying degradation of women, erosion of morals, transmission of disease, production of unwanted and uncared for children, and further irregularities and pathos. Fornication also leads naturally to a tradition of concubinage — "the kept mistress," who can be dismissed at the man's pleasure, or retained "in a state of humiliation and dependence inconsistent with the rights which marriage would confer upon her" and her children. No small wonder that the Bible condemned fornication, prostitution, concubinage, and other such "cohabitation without marriage" in no uncertain terms, said Paley, with ample demonstration. But, again, in these injunctions the Bible is simply reflecting the natural order and moral sense of mankind:

> Laying aside the injunctions of Scripture, the plain account of the question seems to be this: It is immoral, because it is pernicious, that men and women

28. Ibid., p. 210.
29. Ibid., pp. 168-169.

should cohabit, without undertaking certain irrevocable obligations, and mutually conferring certain civil rights; if, therefore, the law has annexed these rights and obligations to certain forms, so that they cannot be secured or undertaken by any other means, which is the case here (for, whatever the parties may promise to each other, nothing but the marriage-ceremony can make their promise irrevocable), it becomes in the same degree immoral, that men and women should cohabit without the interposition of these forms.[30]

Adultery is even worse than fornication, said Paley, because it not only insults the goods of marriage in the abstract. It injures an actual good marriage, leaving the innocent spouse as well as their children as victims. For the betrayed spouse, adultery is "a wound in his [or her] sensibility and affections, the most painful and incurable that human nature knows." For the children it brings shame and unhappiness as the vice is inevitably detected and discussed. For the adulterer or adulteress, it is a form of "perjury" that violates their marital vow and covenant. For all parties in the household, adultery will often provoke retaliation and imitation — another slippery slope to erosion of marriage and the unleashing of sexual libertinism and seduction. Both nature and Scripture thus rain down anathemas against it.[31]

Paley opposed "frivolous" or "voluntary" divorce as well, using arguments from "natural law" and "general utility." Like many other Protestants, he thought that divorce and remarriage of the innocent spouse was both natural and necessary in cases of adultery, malicious desertion, habitual intemperance, cruelty, and crime — although he recognized that the "Scriptures have drawn the obligation tighter than the law of nature left it," and that separation from bed and board might be considered an option for some Christians. But Paley was against voluntary divorces or separations for "lighter causes" or by "mutual consent," grounding his opposition in arguments from nature and utility. Such "lighter" divorces were "obviously" against natural law if the couple had dependent children, Paley thought. "It is manifestly inconsistent with the [natural] duty which the parents owe to their children; which duty can never be so well fulfilled as by their cohabitation and united care. It is also incompatible with the right which the mother possesses, as well as the father, to the gratitude of her children and the comfort of their society; of both which she is almost necessarily deprived, by her dismiss[al] from her husband's family."[32]

30. Ibid., pp. 169-173.
31. Ibid., pp. 176-180.
32. Ibid., pp. 186, 190.

"Causeless," "voluntary," and "lighter divorces," unilaterally sought, are not so obviously against natural law for childless couples, Paley argued, but they are still "inexpedient" enough to prohibit. The worry is, again, the mixed signaling of such a regime, Paley argued, and the "gradual slide" down the slippery slope toward "libertinism." If such easy divorces are available, especially on a unilateral basis, each spouse will be tempted to begin pursuing their own separate interests rather than a common marital interest once the heat of their new love has begun to cool. Each will begin hoarding their own money, developing their own friendships, living more and more independently from the other. "This would beget peculation on one side, mistrust on the other, evils which at present very little disturb the confidence of married life" but eventually will destroy it from within. The availability of easy divorce will discourage spouses to reconcile their conflicts or "take pains to give up what offends, and practice what may gratify the other." They will have less incentive to work hard "to make the best of their bargain" or "promote the pleasure of the other."[33]

Limiting divorce to cases of serious fault will stop this inevitable downward spiral in a marriage, Paley believed. Forcing couples to stay together for better or worse, "though at first extorted by necessity, become in time easy and mutual; and, though less endearing than assiduities which take their rise from affection, generally procure to the married couple a repose and satisfaction sufficient for their happiness." The availability of easy divorce, by contrast, will heighten the natural temptation of each spouse, especially the husband, to succumb to "new objects of desire." However much in love they were with their wives on their wedding day, and however hard they try, men are "naturally inclined" to wander after "the invitations of novelty" unless they are "permanently constrained" to remain faithful to their wives even as their wives lose their "youthful vigor and figure." Thus "constituted as mankind are, and injured as the repudiated wife generally must be, it is necessary to add a stability to the condition of married women, more secure than the continuance of their husbands' affection; and to supply to both sides, by a sense of duty and of obligation, what satiety has impaired of passion and of personal attachment. Upon the whole, the power of divorce is evidently and greatly to the disadvantage of the woman: and the only question appears to be, whether the real and permanent happiness of one half of the species should be surrendered to the caprice and voluptuousness of the other?"[34]

33. Ibid., pp. 187-189.
34. Ibid.

Paley's natural law and theological utilitarian arguments in favor of traditional understandings of sex, marriage, and family life would find enduring provenance among many utilitarians into the nineteenth century. The most famous of these utilitarians, Jeremy Bentham (1748-1832), endorsed most of these same propositions that Paley had set forth, even though Bentham famously eschewed the natural law and natural rights language that had so inspired Paley's theory of marriage. Bentham thought most traditional sex, marriage, and family norms could be rationalized on utilitarian principles alone.[35]

Summary and Conclusions

Home, Hutcheson, Hume, and Paley were just a few of scores of other Enlightenment writers from the seventeenth to the nineteenth centuries who defended traditional Western norms of sex, marriage, and family using this surfeit of arguments from nature, reason, custom, fairness, prudence, utility, pragmatism, and common sense. Some of these natural law theorists were inspired, no doubt, by their personal Christian faith, others by a conservative desire to maintain the status quo. But most of these writers pressed their principal arguments on non-biblical grounds. And they were sometimes sharply critical of the Bible — denouncing St. Paul's preferences for celibacy, the Mosaic provisions on unilateral male divorce, and the many tales of polygamy, concubinage, and prostitution among the ancient biblical patriarchs and kings. Moreover, most of these writers jettisoned many other features of the Western tradition that, in their judgment, defied reason, fairness, and utility — including, notably, the establishment of Christianity by law and the political privileging of the church over other associations. Their natural law theory of the family was not just a rationalist apologia for traditional Christian family values or a naturalist smokescreen for personal religious beliefs. They defended traditional family norms not out of confessional faith but out of rational proof, not just because they believed in them but because they worked.

It was precisely this rational, utilitarian, and even pragmatic defense of the natural law configuration of marriage that made it so appealing to modern English and American jurists as they sought to create a common law of marriage that no longer depended on ecclesiastical law or church courts. Great English and American common lawyers, like Blackstone, Viner, Dane, Mans-

---

35. *The Works of Jeremy Bentham*, ed. John Bowring, 11 vols. (Edinburgh: William Tait, 1843), 1:119-121, 348-357; 2:499, 531-532; 3:73, 202-203; 6:63, 522; 7:579-581.

field, Kent, Story, Strong, Field, and others used these arguments regularly. They echoed in English, Scottish, and American cases until the early twentieth century in defense of monogamous marriage, and in support of criminal sanctions against sexual activities outside of marriage.

Even the most robust natural law theorists of early modern and modern times, however, understood that the natural law of sex, marriage, and family could not do it all, because it was not self-executing. The natural law might strongly incline many humans to behave in certain ways in their sex, marriage, and family lives, and many humans in fact follow these natural inclinations without prompting. But the reality is that a good number of folks stray on occasion from the naturally licit path, and some do this all the time. Natural law needs the positive laws of the state to teach these basic norms of sex, marriage, and family life to the community, to encourage and facilitate citizens to live in accordance with them, to deter and punish citizens when they deviate, and to rehabilitate and redirect them to healthier relationships consistent with the norms of natural and civil liberty. The nineteenth-century common law notion of marriage as a good and desirable civil status captures this insight that natural law and positive law must work together to ensure fair and stable sex, marriage, and family lives for citizens. It sends the right signals to the community, and confirms the natural inclinations of many of its citizens. The positive law systems of many democracies today are not doing this, unleashing precisely the kind of social, psychological, and economic pathos on private lives and on public goods that the Scottish Enlightenment philosophers predicted.

Natural law not only needs the positive laws of the state to teach and enforce its norms; it also needs broader communities and narratives to stabilize, deepen, and improve these natural norms and the natural inclinations they induce. The natural law norms of sex, marriage, and family life ultimately depend on deeper covenantal and sacramental models and exemplars of love and faithfulness, trust and sacrifice, commitment and community to give them content and coherence. They depend upon other stable institutions besides the state (churches, neighborhoods, schools, health organizations, and more) to teach, encourage, and implement these natural law norms. Marriage is "a multidimensional institution," and it depends upon multiple value systems and multiple institutions to be fully stable and functional. The prophetic church has a critical role to play here, and O'Donovan's vision of that role is indispensable.

Body Integrity Identity Disorder
and the Ethics of Mutilation

Robert Song

Introduction

Christian theology teaches the goodness of the material world, a goodness that was declared in creation, vindicated in the resurrection, and will be fulfilled in the world's redemption. The material world includes the human body, and acceptance of the body as the gift of a good Creator, as something neither to be worshipped nor to be escaped, lies at the heart of Christian thinking about the practice of medicine. It has also grounded a critique of those technological modes of thought characteristic of the modern world that explicitly or implicitly suggest the desirability of disembodiment and celebrate the freedom of the self to live unencumbered by the fatedness of gross matter.

The critique of the technological mind-set is extremely attractive, and has rightly received much attention.[1] Nevertheless in its outworking in relation to modern medicine, it runs certain dangers, particularly when it treats of certain experiences, standardly treated as psychiatric disorders, in which people find themselves in some sense alienated from and in conflict with their bodies. The

1. For an eloquent recent example, see Brian Brock, *Christian Ethics in a Technological Age* (Grand Rapids: Eerdmans, 2010).

The final, definitive version of this paper has been published in *Studies in Christian Ethics*, vol. 26 no. 4, November 2013, pp. 487-503, by SAGE Publications Ltd. (http://online.sagepub.com). doi: 10.1177/0953946813492921. All rights reserved. © Robert Song. I am grateful to Chris Cook, Gerard Loughlin, Susan Parsons, Jean Porter, Helen Savage, Brent Waters, and Vanessa Williams for their comments on the themes of this article.

most obvious example of this is the experience of transsexualism, where a person finds himself or herself feeling at odds with his or her anatomical sex. The affirmation of the goodness of the body might suggest that the clinical response must be psychotherapeutic in nature, and must eschew sexual reassignment surgery.[2] Yet the case may not be so straightforward. I will explore this, not through a study of transsexualism, which involves broader questions of sexuality and gender, but through the much more unusual situation in which individuals desire the amputation of a healthy body part. By considering the appropriateness of a surgical remedy for psychological distress in this situation, we may be able to shed some light on the proper role of medicine in a world which, though fallen, remains good.

The Making of a New Diagnostic Category

Some years ago Robert Smith, a consultant surgeon at the Falkirk and District Royal Infirmary in Scotland, defied received medical wisdom by performing an above-knee amputation of the perfectly healthy leg of a man who was evidently in great psychological distress and who was convinced that he would continue in this state until his leg was removed. A couple of years later Smith carried out a similar operation on a second person, but in response to hostile newspaper reports was subsequently prevented by his NHS hospital's ethics committee from performing a third.[3] He reported that the patients on whom he had operated apparently felt 'incomplete' with four limbs, but believed that they would feel 'complete' if a limb was surgically removed. The results of the operations appear to have been remarkable: in both cases minimal postoperative analgesia was required, and the patients, whose lives and careers had previously been blighted by frequent depressive episodes, found themselves transformed and without any subsequent need for psychiatric treatment.[4]

The numbers of people who are gripped by the desire for the kind of radical surgery undertaken by Smith are exceptionally small, unsurprisingly,

2. See, for example, Oliver O'Donovan, *Transsexualism: Issues and Argument* (Cambridge: Grove Books, 1982).

3. Clare Dyer, 'Surgeon Amputated Healthy Legs', *British Medical Journal* 320 (2000), p. 332. The patients had received psychiatric assessment, and the procedure had been discussed in advance with the ethics committee of the General Medical Council.

4. Robert C. Smith, 'Body Integrity Identity Disorder: The Surgeon's Perspective', in Aglaja Stirn, Aylin Thiel, and Silvia Oddo (eds.), *Body Integrity Identity Disorder: Psychological, Neurobiological, Ethical and Legal Aspects* (Lengerich: Pabst Science, 2009), pp. 41-48.

and until the advent of the internet were largely invisible to each other, to the medical world, and perhaps, in a sense, to themselves. Nevertheless there is now enough evidence to suggest a number of commonalities amongst them.[5] The most commonly desired impairment is amputation, of one or more arms, legs, fingers, or toes, though some wish to be blind, others to be paraplegic, others to wear plaster casts or orthopaedic braces. Many have lived with these desires since childhood, and for some the experience is related to an early memory of seeing an amputee or a person using crutches or the like. Those in this situation will often go to exceptional lengths to fulfil their desires, not only by pretending to be disabled through the use of wheelchairs or opaque contact lenses or plaster casts, but in some cases endangering their own lives in a bid to be free of unwanted limbs. To take one example, the manager of an ice works was found by the police early one morning with his legs crushed by an Archimedean screw, but holding a walking stick which he 'happened' to have with him and with which he had switched off the machinery. Both his legs were amputated, and he returned to work a mere three weeks later, using a wheelchair and apparently a happy man. Others are reported as having resorted to immersing their legs in dry ice, using chain saws on themselves, laying their legs on railway lines, shooting themselves in the leg, refusing treatment to reattach limbs, and so on.[6] Just as intense as the psychological suffering can be from the unresolved tension of feeling incomplete ('Can one's head explode from BIID pain?'),[7] so can the relief and lack of regret after having had an amputation similarly be profoundly felt. There are several reports of complete resolution by surgery;[8] and there is some evidence that this is not regretted

5. The largest surveys to date are reported in Michael B. First, 'Desire for Amputation of a Limb: Paraphilia, Psychosis, or a New Type of Identity Disorder', *Psychological Medicine* 35 (2005), pp. 919-28 (52 participants); and Rianne M. Blom, Raoul C. Hennekam, and Damiaan Denys, 'Body Integrity Identity Disorder', *PLoS ONE* 7.4 (2012), e34702. doi:10.1371/journal. pone.0034702 (54 participants). Valuable web resources can be found at transabled.org and biid-info.org.

6. Gregg M. Furth and Robert Smith, *Amputee Identity Disorder: Information, Questions, Answers, and Recommendations about Self-Demand Amputation* (Bloomington, IN: 1stBooks, 2002), pp. 41-47; Robert Smith, 'Less Is More: Body Integrity Identity Disorder', in Stephen W. Smith and Ronan Deazley (eds.), *The Legal, Medical and Cultural Regulation of the Body: Transformation and Transgression* (Farnham: Ashgate, 2009), pp. 147-157, at 148-150.

7. http://twitter.com/wylz/statuses/8442830218 (accessed 13 March 2013).

8. For a case history, see Arjan W. Braam and Nicole de Boer-Kreeft, 'Case Report — The Ultimate Relief; Resolution of the Apotemnophilia Syndrome', in Stirn et al. (eds.), *Body Integrity Identity Disorder*, pp. 70-76; and for a first-hand account, see Andrew Becker, 'Body Integrity Identity Disorder (BIID) and Me', in ibid., pp. 103-106.

into old age — witness the statement of one 76-year-old woman who had had a leg amputated at the age of 23: 'living with an amputation is nothing compared with a lifetime of mental torment'.[9]

This phenomenon was first brought to the attention of modern medicine by the psychologist John Money in 1977,[10] although evidence of someone wanting to have his leg amputated has been unearthed from the late eighteenth century.[11] On the basis of two case histories Money, who was primarily a sexologist, deduced a connection between a desire to have one's leg amputated and an erotic attraction towards amputees. The former he named 'apotemnophilia' (literally, 'love of amputation'), intending with this designation to categorise it as a paraphilia, an erotic obsession with becoming an amputee. As it happens, while Money was right to note the connections between amputation and sexual arousal for many of those affected, later work surveying larger numbers has suggested that the erotic aspect is not universal, and that even for those for whom it is present, in only a minority of cases is it the predominant motivation for seeking amputation.[12]

Other psychologists, noting that it is typically first experienced in childhood and that some sufferers report the coldness and asexuality of their upbringing, have suggested that it might be a form of attention-seeking, deriving from a desire to receive the sympathy in their identity as disabled that was lacking to them in their early years. But these explanations have not been found widely persuasive, partly because the desire to be impaired appears in many cases to be extremely stable and largely recalcitrant to any kind of psychotherapeutic intervention, but also because people typically keep these desires secret and will frequently spend many years at home pretending in the desired body shape long before venturing out into the open. Others still have tried to understand it as a body dysmorphic disorder, a preoccupation with a particular bodily feature such as the nose, hair, or skin which the person perceives as being ugly or unattractive and which causes distress or loss of self-

9. Smith, 'Less Is More', p. 155.

10. John Money, Russell Jobaris, and Gregg Furth, 'Apotemnophilia: Two Cases of Self-Demand Amputation as a Paraphilia', *Journal of Sex Research* 13 (1977), pp. 115-125.

11. See Carl Elliott, *Better than Well: American Medicine Meets the American Dream* (New York: Norton, 2003), p. 214, citing Jean-Joseph Sue, *Anecdotes Historiques, Littérraires et Critiques, sur la Médicine, la Chirurgerie, et la Pharmacie* (Paris: Chez La Bocher, 1785).

12. First, 'Desire for Amputation of a Limb'. The case for understanding it as a paraphilia continues to be argued by Anne A. Lawrence, 'Parallels between Gender Identity Disorder and Body Integrity Identity Disorder: A Review and Update', in Stirn et al. (eds.), *Body Integrity Identity Disorder*, pp. 154-72.

esteem of a magnitude sufficient to demand clinical attention. But again the disparallels are substantial, amongst them that those desiring amputations rarely see the body part as ugly, and are motivated not by the desire to be more socially acceptable or attractive but by the felt need to be more personally complete or authentic.[13]

The seeming failure of psychological explanations and the typical absence of other psychiatric symptoms (apart from depression, which is very likely better understood as a consequence of these experiences than a cause of them) has prompted a drift towards a neurological account. On this view the disjunction between the body and the experienced body image is the result of physical damage to the part of the cerebral cortex which correlates to the conscious representation in one's mind of the shape of one's body. This part of the brain is situated in the right hemisphere, which would make some sense of the observation that there is a disproportionate desire for amputations on the left side of the body. The desire for amputation would be the inverse of the phenomenon of the phantom limb, where a person experiences a missing or severed limb as somehow still present. On this account it is taken to be the result of a developmental neurological anomaly, which creates an internal mismatch and a consequent acute sense of inner tension that requires resolution, one that is felt to be most easily addressed through removal of the affected limb.[14]

There may well of course be multiple aetiologies of broadly the same set of symptoms, and it may be that an approach which integrates neurological and psychological perspectives will eventually prove to be more plausible. However, none of these approaches captures another feature of the phenomenon, namely its effect on the individual's sense of self. For most people the loss of a limb is experienced as a catastrophe, whereas for those who yearn for amputation the same event is the object of intense longing. Because they have never known a time when they experienced the limb as their own, they do not regard the losing of a limb as adventitious or disastrous, but as an integral constituent in their sense of themselves. For this reason, the psychiatrist Michael First has proposed that it be regarded as an identity disorder; noting several parallels with gender identity disorder, including discomfort with the anatomical identity, the frequency of role-playing in the desired identity, and

13. See further Smith, 'Less Is More', pp. 150-152.

14. Paul D. McGeoch, David J. Brang, and V. S. Ramachandran, 'A New Right Parietal Lobe Syndrome?' in Stirn et al. (eds.), *Body Integrity Identity Disorder*, pp. 225-237. Ramachandran sets this in a broader account of brain-body relations in *The Tell-Tale Brain: A Neuroscientist's Quest for What Makes Us Human* (New York: Norton, 2011), pp. 255-258.

the success of surgery as a treatment in many cases, he suggests that it be designated body integrity identity disorder.[15]

The name has many attractions. In contrast with apotemnophilia, it suggests that it is not universally or primarily experienced as related to sexual desire. In contrast with amputee identity disorder, it indicates that amputation is not the only kind of desired impairment.[16] As an 'identity disorder', it at least clarifies that it is not a psychosis and is not ordinarily accompanied by other psychiatric signs or symptoms. Yet it also carries its own problems. By being discussed and categorised within the disciplines of psychology, neurology, and psychiatry, it also locates the problem within the body and mind of the deviant individual, and fails to ask what the relation is between the individual body and the social body. That is, it fails to question how the cultural context in which and by which individuals are significantly constituted itself has effects on the experienced reality of this kind of estrangement from one's body. And by adopting the language of 'identity disorder', it suggests that there is a secure psychiatric understanding of identity, of what a well-ordered identity might be, and therefore what might constitute a disordered identity.

The Bioethical Discussion: Respect for Autonomy

For the majority of philosophical bioethicists who have addressed the questions surrounding the moral legitimacy of a surgical response to BIID, unquestionably the central point of concern has been that of respect for autonomy.[17] Of course other arguments have been canvassed. Sabine Müller, for

15. First, 'Desire for Amputation of a Limb', pp. 926-927. First considers here the possibility that BIID be included in future editions of the *Diagnostic and Statistical Manual of Mental Disorders (DSM)*, an eventuality that is likely to be precluded more by its statistical rarity than the imprecision of the diagnostic category. In the event, BIID has not been included in the recently published *DSM-5* (Washington, DC: American Psychiatric Association, 2013), though it is referred to incidentally as differentiable from body dysmorphic disorder (pp. 247-248) and gender dysphoria (p. 458).

16. The same criticism could be made of the recently proposed 'xenomelia' (i.e. having an 'alien limb'), the repugnant sound of which is scarcely calculated to ease the sense of shame and social isolation BIID sufferers already feel.

17. In addition to the articles by Müller and Savulescu discussed below, see, for example, Annemarie Bridy, 'Confounding Extremities: Surgery at the Medico-Ethical Limits of Self-Modification', *Journal of Law, Medicine and Ethics* 32 (2004), pp. 148-158; Tim Bayne and Neil Levy, 'Amputees by Choice: Body Integrity Identity Disorder and the Ethics of Amputation', *Journal of Applied Philosophy* 22 (2005), pp. 75-86; the articles collected in *American Journal*

example, employs the principlism of Tom Beauchamp and James Childress to argue a case against surgery for BIID.[18] On her interpretation of their principles, the principle of nonmaleficence allows an amputation to be carried out only if it is medically indicated, which is prima facie unlikely since amputation is permanent and is in response to no unambiguous medical need; the principle of beneficence requires that the benefit of the treatment outweighs the harm, but here she finds the alleged examples of patients who have benefited to be too few in number to form a reliable basis for surgical intervention (though she grants that this might be justified under the principle of beneficence in order to prevent potentially lethal attempts at self-mutilation); and the principle of justice would prevent public funding of elective amputations on the grounds of the costs of treatment, of lost income and tax, and the consequent financial implications for health and welfare provision.

These are all relevant considerations which would have to be taken into account in an overall assessment of the ethics of elective surgery for a person with BIID. However, it is the question of whether BIID patients have autonomy which has excited most attention. Müller herself argues that they do not on the grounds that they lack substantial autonomy. Just as we would not accede to the demand for removal of the leg of a schizophrenic patient who was under the delusion that he was acting on the instruction of visiting aliens, so '[i]n all cases of BIID that have been investigated by psychiatrists, the diagnosis states that the amputation is obsessive or results from a monothematic delusion, comparable to anorexia, Capgras syndrome, or anankastic counting'.[19] However, her argument is not wholly persuasive. Of course each case must be considered individually, as in all assessments of capacity, and in every case the possibility of delusional or other psychiatric grounds for lack of capacity must be acknowledged. But the lack of correlation of BIID with other psychiatric disorders also needs to be noted.[20] It is not clear that the desire to have a limb

---

of Bioethics 9.1 (2009); D. Patrone, 'Disfigured Anatomies and Imperfect Analogies: Body Integrity Identity Disorder and the Supposed Right to Self-Demanded Amputation of Healthy Body Parts', *Journal of Medical Ethics* 35 (2009), pp. 541-545; and Christopher James Ryan, Tarra Shaw and Anthony W. F. Harris, 'Body Integrity Identity Disorder: Response to Patrone', *Journal of Medical Ethics* 36 (2010), pp. 189-190.

18. Sabine Müller, 'Body Integrity Identity Disorder (BIID) — Is the Amputation of Healthy Limbs Ethically Justified?' *American Journal of Bioethics* 9 (2009), pp. 36-43. Cf. Tom L. Beauchamp and James F. Childress, *Principles of Biomedical Ethics*, 7th ed. (New York: Oxford University Press, 2013).

19. Müller, 'Body Integrity Identity Disorder', p. 40.

20. Michael B. First, 'Origin and Evolution of the Concept of Body Integrity Identity Disorder', in Stirn et al. (eds.), *Body Integrity Identity Disorder*, pp. 49-57, commenting on his

amputated is delusional: unlike those who suffer from somatoparaphrenia, who do not recognise one of their limbs as their own and maintain that it belongs to someone else, people with BIID fully accept that the limb is theirs.[21] Nor is the desire necessarily clinically obsessive: at all events, obsessive desires that are of psychiatric significance need to be distinguished from mere persistent wishes, which need not as such indicate a lack of autonomy.

Even if those with BIID are otherwise psychiatrically healthy and do have substantial autonomy in at least some cases, does their autonomous desire to have an amputation create an obligation on medical professionals to supply what they demand? The case for respecting patient autonomy, even in controversial choices such as the elective amputation of healthy limbs, is made by Julian Savulescu.[22] Appealing to both Kant and Mill, he argues that we should respect people's autonomous decisions rather than refuse them on paternalistic grounds, even when these encompass such contentious behaviours as sadomasochism, requests for futile treatment, or extreme body modification. This does not permit anybody to choose anything they like: people have an obligation to make rational choices, but those who disagree with them should seek to argue with them and encourage them to make more rational choices, rather than impose decisions on them. Thus, 'whether an individual's decision is ultimately respected (by doctors, family and friends) turns on whether that individual is competent or incompetent, not on whether the decision is rational or irrational'.[23] There are constraints on whether an individual's wishes should be finally decisive, but these centre on distributive justice, harm to others, and in some circumstances the public interest, not on whether others regard their choices as rational or desirable.

The Moral Theological Discussion: The Goodness of the Body

Savulescu's argument represents a liberal autonomism of a particularly pure variety, and is one that is found widely attractive in contemporary bioethics. While others may calibrate the balancing considerations slightly differently

own interview study: 'apart from the desire for amputation this was a psychiatrically healthy sample' (p. 53).

21. Bayne and Levy, 'Amputees by Choice', p. 81.

22. Julian Savulescu, 'Autonomy, the Good Life, and Controversial Choices', in Rosamond Rhodes, Leslie P. Francis, and Anita Silvers (eds.), *The Blackwell Guide to Medical Ethics* (New York: Wiley-Blackwell, 2006), pp. 17-37.

23. Savulescu, 'Autonomy', p. 27.

from him (interpreting harm to others or the requirements of justice in more exacting ways, for example), the principle of respect for autonomy is pivotal — and indeed is becoming increasingly pre-eminent in many interpretations of bioethical principlism.

Yet the appeal to autonomy as the central axis of an ethic of body modification faces a fundamental problem. In relation to body integrity identity disorder, ironically it is unable to make intelligible any conception of the integrity of the body. Whether the idea of autonomy is interpreted by reference to the clinically-determined possession of capacity or in terms of one or another philosophical account of rational self-direction, it does not possess of itself the resources to enable an exploration of the question whether the body has any intrinsic intelligibility, and if so, what the moral implications of that might be. As a consequence, because of the final refusal of any constraints outside of the choosing will, constraints which this mode of thought can only construe as paternalism, the danger is constantly courted of degeneration towards a narcissistic or consumerist attitude towards the body. The body, instead of being in some sense integral with the self, is prone to becoming externalised, alienated, and mobilised to serve the projects of the self. Such an understanding is incapable of capturing any sense of the goodness of the body beyond that which we contingently decide to award to it.

By contrast, in the Christian tradition the goodness of the body is declared to belong to its participation in the created order, a participation which entails that the body may never be volatilised into mere formless extension. Creation, as Oliver O'Donovan puts it, must be understood 'not merely as the raw material out of which the world as we know it is composed, but as the order and coherence *in* which it is composed'.[24] Creation has form and is *in*-formed: it has an intrinsic intelligibility that is in principle capable of being recognised and is not merely a projection of the active, knowing self. Creation is the gift of a good God to which human beings belong, which they are to love, and in which they are to live: the good is to be found in and through creation and its fulfilment, not in escape from it or denial of it. For O'Donovan this licences a recovery of the notion of the 'natural', which can to some extent be discerned without resort to revelation: according to this, there is point to saying that it is natural for children to be brought up by human beings and not by chimpanzees, and natural for babies to be born by natural birth rather than by Caesar-

---

24. Oliver O'Donovan, *Resurrection and Moral Order: An Outline for Evangelical Ethics* (Leicester: InterVarsity Press, 1986), p. 31.

ean section, and natural for people to prefer pleasure to pain, health to disease, and life to death.[25]

This does not imply any quick or crude naturalistic ethics, nor any blithe or unhermeneutical assumptions about the body's legibility, but rather that human beings are called to recognise that the body is in-formed, and are to seek to bear witness to that in-forming in their actions and dispositions. Thus in relation to medicine, however we finally decide to intervene or operate on our bodies, we may never treat them as so much matter, mere ingredients out of which we may form whatever strange devices might emerge from our fevered imaginations. We may not distance ourselves from them in such a way that we are freed to exercise an unfettered *dominium* over them that pays no attention to their formed nature, but rather we are to nourish and cherish them (Eph. 5:29).

Nor does this care for our bodies or recognition of the good that they express preclude any intervention at all in them. The invocation of the category of the natural may not be taken to be a means of short-circuiting the task of moral discernment. That we may properly talk of natural birth by contrast with Caesarean sections does not imply that Caesareans are never medically appropriate. The pangs of childbirth have been greatly increased because of the first sin (Gen. 3:16), and at times they may increase to the point at which surgical delivery is medically justified. The practice of medicine (and within that, of surgery) is precisely one of the ways in which we exercise responsibility towards our bodies in a world that is still groaning for its redemption. But this gives rise to the question: how are we to discern what kinds of surgical intervention might be a sign of responsive care, and what kinds might be a sign of an untrammelled technological manipulation of the body? Must we interpret the elective amputation of a healthy limb as an implicitly docetic denial of the goodness inherent in the body? Or in a fallen world might it be a medically justified response to the facticity of a mismatched mind and body?

The Ethics of Mutilation

Within the tradition of moral theology these questions have been treated under the heading of the ethics of mutilation. Taking its bearings from Thomas Aquinas's account in the *Summa Theologiae*, the discussion of the

25. Cf. Oliver O'Donovan, *A Conversation Waiting to Begin: The Churches and the Gay Controversy* (London: SCM Press, 2009), p. 90.

moral legitimacy of mutilation has sought to interpret the meaning of the given form of the body in the context of particular circumstances. The question we have to ask of it is whether it can furnish us with appropriate analogies which could help us with the detailed moral discernment that is required in the case of BIID.

Aquinas's investigation of mutilation appears in *ST* II-ii.65.1, and forms part of his exploration of the vices of injustice and, within these, of injuries to the person. He appears to have had in mind at least three different kinds of situation: the use of amputation as a punishment by a public authority, the ascetic practice of those who have made themselves eunuchs for the sake of the kingdom of heaven, and the surgical removal of gangrenous limbs in order to save a patient's life. Each of these is addressed through the application of a basic principle:

> A limb is part of the whole body and it therefore exists for the sake of that whole, as the imperfect for the sake of the perfect. The individual limb must therefore be dealt with in the way the benefit of the whole demands.[26]

According to this principle, which was subsequently termed the 'principle of totality', if a particular part of the body is detrimental to the good of the whole body, then it may be removed for the sake of the body as a whole. And conversely, 'if a limb is healthy and working in accord with its natural function, it cannot be removed without detriment to the whole body'.[27] Applied in the penal context, Aquinas argues that this implies that just as a person may be deprived of their life for major crimes, so they may be deprived of a limb for lesser crimes, since the whole human being is ordained to the whole community of which they are a part. Applied in the case of the ascetic, it implies that self-castration can never be justified, since the sin which self-castration is intended to guard against is grounded in the exercise of the will, and spiritual well-being can be ensured without need to resort to physical means of this kind. Applied in the medical case, it indicates that an individual may legitimately consent to the amputation of a limb that may potentially poison the body as a whole, and do so without reference to anybody else, since the health of each person is the responsibility of that person.

Aquinas did not of course have BIID in mind when he composed this

---

26. 'Dicendum quod cum membrum aliquod sit pars totius humani corporis, est propter totum, sicut imperfectum propter perfectum. Unde disponendum est de membro humani corporis secundum quod expedit toti' (*ST* II.2.65.1).

27. *ST* II.2.65.1 (my translation).

article. When he writes of amputation of a healthy member, he is thinking of those driven by sexual urges to compromise their chastity. By contrast, those who suffer from BIID are not spiritual giants giving up all for the sake of the kingdom of heaven, but ordinary people seeking some modicum of psychological resolution. Therefore, despite his injunction that 'in any other case [than those he explicitly accepts] it is quite wrong to mutilate another',[28] it would be wise not to strain his teaching beyond the natural arc of cases he might have anticipated.

In response to new circumstances since his time, there has inevitably been evolution in the tradition of moral theological reflection on the subject, and we need to investigate this to see whether it might illuminate the problem of surgical intervention in BIID cases. One major period when close attention was paid to the topic was during the middle decades of the twentieth century when novel questions were raised by techniques of organ transplantation. Much of the discussion was given over to establishing the validity of mutilation of a person for the good of a neighbour. Such operations might be needed, not only in minor cases such as would be required in the course of blood transfusion, medical experimentation, and the like, but were also used to argue for organ transplantations, so long as they were not disproportionately burdensome to the donor. These could not be justified by appeal to the principle of totality, it was persuasively argued in an influential article by Gerald Kelly, SJ, since this was a principle of subordination of part to the whole which could only be justified in relation to the physical body: it could not be applied to the body politic — evidently departing at this point from Thomas, who had justified the death penalty on this basis, as we have just seen — nor to the Mystical Body of Christ. Instead organ transplantation should be allowed as an exceptional case under the law of charity for the benefit of the neighbour.[29]

Mutilation of the body for the sake of the neighbour is not the salient issue in relation to BIID, but in the course of his discussion Kelly comments on a

28. ST II.2.65.1.

29. Gerald Kelly, SJ, 'The Morality of Mutilation: Towards a Revision of the Treatise', *Theological Studies* 17 (1956), pp. 322-344. Cf. Albert R. Jonsen, 'From Mutilation to Donation: The Evolution of Catholic Moral Theology Regarding Organ Transplantation', Catholic Social Concerns Lecture Series (University of San Francisco: Lane Center for Catholic Studies and Social Thought, 2005). The reference to the Mystical Body of Christ refers to an effort from the 1940s to develop a version of ecclesial ethics which would justify organ transplantation between members of the Church, and therefore between all human beings on the grounds that all members of the human race have been redeemed (Jonsen, 'From Mutilation to Donation', pp. 4-5).

number of principles and cases which had been discussed by the manualists and which are of greater relevance to our concerns.[30] I will comment on a number of these under five points.

First, the general principle of totality is that mutilation of the body for one's own good is permitted 'when it is proportionately necessary or useful for the good of the whole (i.e. the person)'.[31] Kelly's gloss on 'the whole' as 'the person' might be taken here to affirm that mutilations can be performed for the sake of the whole individual, body and soul, which would of course be central to a discussion of surgery for BIID. That is, if amputation of a limb were being undertaken for the good of the whole person, rather than just as a physical response to a clearly physical malady, it might then be justified under this principle. However, given the context of Kelly's general polemic against justifying organ transplantation by reference to the principle of totality, it may be safer to infer that 'person' here is being contrasted with 'social whole' rather than with 'physical body'.

Second, following on some teaching of Pius XII that mutilations are permissible in order to avoid serious and lasting damage, Kelly infers that purely prophylactic surgical removals might be permissible, even of healthy limbs or organs: this might include the incidental removal of a uterus, for example, in the course of the resection of cancerous ovaries, if this were medically justified to prevent possible later complications. However, although we now have an explicit example of amputation of a healthy body part, it is clear that he envisages unambiguously medical indications as justifying it: the self-report of the BIID sufferer, even when taken with their evident distress, would not obviously provide the same quality of evidential warrant.

Third, a particular case, which involves amputating a healthy limb but does not assume a medical context or the exercise of clinical judgement, is the probably fictive example discussed by the manualists of the tyrant who offers to an unfortunate individual the choice either to cut off his own hand or to be put to death.[32] Kelly affirms the broad consensus of the tradition that amputation in this context would be justified, suggesting also that this shows that it is at least

---

30. It should be noted that my use of Kelly in the present context is intended as a way of accessing some of the moral discriminations discussed in the tradition that might illuminate the case of BIID through providing relevant analogies. In doing so, I do wish to affirm the continuing significance of casuistry for moral theology, but do not thereby mean to endorse in detail Kelly's method or conclusions, nor to take sides in the controversies of mid-twentieth-century Roman Catholic moral theology.

31. Kelly, 'The Morality of Mutilation', p. 331.

32. Kelly, 'The Morality of Mutilation', p. 336.

'solidly probable, if not certain' that there need be no intrinsic connection be-tween the mutilation and the saving of one's life; that is, the necessity which connects electing to lose a limb with saving one's life need not be the medical need of the physical body, but could be external (in this case, the will of the tyrant). While this may bring us a little closer to BIID, however, the difference still remains that in the one case we have the implacable will of the tyrant, a necessity external to the person whose limb will be severed; in the other we have an individual's psychological condition which is unlikely to generate the same degree of necessity as a gangrenous or necrotising leg on the one hand or a pitiless despot on the other.

Fourth, more relevant still, might be the case of castration for abnormal sexual urges.[33] While this is similar to the situation discussed by Aquinas, the presentation in Kelly is secularised and medicalised, and refers not to self-sacrificial mutilation in the pursuit of spiritual goods, but to psychiatrically-assessed sexual disorder. Clearly his response here would be of great interest for our concerns; but unfortunately he does not stoop to pronounce explicitly on the principle, no doubt because of its connection with sterilisation, and resorts instead to the observation that doctors are unconvinced of the effec-tiveness of the resort to anatomical castration.

Fifth, of all the cases Kelly considers, that which parallels the situation raised by BIID most closely is lobotomy, a surgical intervention for severe psychiatric conditions that became popular in the mid-twentieth century in preference to even more extreme procedures, and remained widely used, if of course controversial, until the arrival of modern antipsychotic drugs. Kelly quotes with approval an instruction to Catholic hospitals:

> Lobotomy and similar operations are morally justifiable when medically indicated as the proper treatment of serious mental illness or intractable pain. In each case the welfare of the patient himself, considered as a person, must be the determining factor. These operations are not justifiable when less extreme remedies are reasonably available or in cases where the prob-ability of harm to the patient outweighs the hope of benefit to him.[34]

Here we do finally have a situation in which casuistry addresses and approves a surgical remedy for psychological distress. Shrewdly Kelly recognised that medical progress might soon make lobotomies more or less obsolete, and that

---

33. Kelly, 'The Morality of Mutilation', pp. 337-338.

34. No. 44 of the revised edition of *Ethical and Religious Directives for Catholic Hospitals*, quoted by Kelly, 'The Morality of Mutilation', p. 340.

the technique was anyway questionable, but the affirmation in principle is apparent.

Surgical Interventions for Psychiatric Disorders

Is this the analogy with BIID which we are after? The parallels are evident. There is a clear surgical intervention intended as a treatment for a psychiatric problem, which does not take the form of an amputation, to be sure, but does equally have major, irreversible consequences for the patient. In both cases surgery may only be performed after a full psychiatric assessment. In both cases surgery should be undertaken only as a last resort, if there are no lesser therapies available, and if the probability of harm should not be greater than the hope of success. If there is a difference it is that some of the conditions for which lobotomies were performed are more serious than BIID: schizophrenias and other psychotic and delusional disorders are typically considerably more debilitating and detrimental to everyday functioning. Yet even here the differences should not be exaggerated: on the one hand BIID is also very frequently accompanied by depression serious enough to give rise to suicidal thoughts, and in many cases leads people to undertake actions with an extremely high risk of incidental death; and on the other, lobotomies were frequently performed (and frequently had relatively better outcomes) in cases of affective disorders, obsessive-compulsive disorders, anxiety disorders, and a variety of other conditions of arguably broadly similar severity to BIID.

On the face of it, therefore, if the objection to surgery in the case of BIID is that it uses a surgical solution to address a psychiatric need, then the same objection ought to obtain in the case of the lobotomies that were endorsed for use in Catholic hospitals. And conversely: if lobotomies were at least on some occasions morally and medically justified, then so too should surgery for BIID be.[35]

This conclusion may seem counterintuitive, or at the very least unexpected. Our instinctive, pre-reflective responses to each case may well differ quite considerably. On the one hand the instruction to the Catholic hospitals

35. A defence of surgery for BIID by reference to the practice of lobotomy might not appear the most appealing of argumentative routes, given the reputation it gained (it was banned in the Soviet Union in 1950 on the grounds that it was inhumane). But this is not really relevant to the point of principle which we are concerned with, namely the moral legitimacy of surgery for mental disorders.

seems reasonable: at any rate if we regard lobotomy techniques as problematic, we are likely to do so because of the variable levels of their success, or their side-effects, or the enforcement of medical power over patients which they represented, but not on grounds of the principle that they are a surgical response to a psychiatric problem. By contrast, many people's initial response to surgery for BIID is questioning, if not downright hostile.

There are, I suggest, two different reasons why the two situations intuitively may feel very different. The first is that they occupy places in two different cultural narratives. Lobotomies, on the one hand, for all the ways they now seem repellent and violent, still represented an effort to find some form of alleviation of suffering for patients whose symptoms had resisted all previous efforts — it was intended as a more tolerable alternative to leaving those patients either wholly untreated and forgotten in asylums, or treated with only partial effectiveness with a variety of shock therapies and the like. Their therapeutic motivation seems evident. By contrast BIID lends itself to being represented as occupying a place in a cultural narrative about the growth of autonomy within bioethics, in which therapy is being gradually supplanted — or at least complemented — by consumerist attitudes towards medicine. As an example of this, one might consider Carl Elliott's inclusion of BIID in *Better than Well,* a book on the intersection of medicine and American aspirations for self-improvement, amidst chapters on cosmetic surgery, Prozac, performance-enhancing drugs, and other enhancement technologies. The demand for surgery for BIID could be presented as another site where the anxious pursuit of authenticity amongst modern Westerners takes the form of bodily enhancement and the subjugation of the body to the socially-mediated quest for competitive self-fulfilment.[36]

A second reason why lobotomy procedures and surgery for BIID might be thought different is that while lobotomies are surgery on the brain for psychiatric disorders, amputation of a limb is surgery on another part of the body. Of course both are surgical interventions to deal with problems which

---

36. Elliott, *Better than Well,* pp. 208-236. Elliott concedes that his attitudes to a surgical response to BIID have shifted since meeting people wanting elective amputation. Contrast Wesley J. Smith's less sympathetic views, commenting on Bayne and Levy's 2005 article: 'If you want to see why Western culture is going badly off the rails, just read the drivel that passes for learned discourse in many of our professional journals. . . . That this kind of article is published in a respectable philosophical journal tells us how very radical and pathologically non judgmental the bioethics movement is becoming.' 'Should Doctors Amputate Healthy Limbs?' http://www.cbc-network.org/2006/11/should-doctors-amputate-healthy-limbs (accessed 12 March 2013).

present psychiatrically, and both are radical and perhaps irreversible, but there is still some difference between neural surgery and the destruction of the function of a limb. Neurosurgery is at least surgery on the diseased organ, one might say, whereas there is no obviously diseased body part in the case of BIID. The problem, on this view, could be argued not to be psychiatry through surgery as such, but psychiatry through *this* surgery.

To take this second claim first, it is surely at least as easy to argue that they are not so far apart in moral significance. Both kinds of surgery have significant adverse consequences, and it is not obvious that one is proportionately worse than the other relative to the seriousness of the conditions they are each addressing. The most one could concede to the point is that if a resolution of the psychological distress of BIID could be found by operating on the brain rather than amputating a limb, this would be medically indicated. But the detailed neurological knowledge needed for this is precisely what is not currently available; the question we are faced with now is how to act in our current, limited state of knowledge.

More importantly, we should observe that if BIID is the result of some specifically neurological malformation or anomaly, that is, some unambiguously physical cause, we cannot interpret surgery for BIID as simply refusing to accept the preferred status of the biological, or as a wilful disregard of the structures of the body in pursuit of cultural or psychological fantasies. Rather it looks more like intervention in a body that is at war with itself, where one organ is in conflict with another, the head saying to the feet, 'I have no need of you' (1 Cor. 12:21). The body does not here point unequivocally to the goodness of creation, but has in its divided nature also become a sign of the fallen creation, a fall which may have originated in the disobedience of the will but which in the increased pains of childbirth is shown also to have bodily consequences. In a case such as this, it is much less clear what the practice of healing, as a sign of both the restoration of the creation and the fulfilment of the kingdom, might look like. Of course it is proper medical practice that all less radical alternatives should be pursued first — psychiatric, pharmaceutical, non-impairing. But in our current, limited state of knowledge, it is not evident that it must necessarily preclude the possibility of amputation in some occasional cases. As in the instruction to Catholic hospitals about lobotomy, the determining factor would be the welfare of the patient himself or herself, considered as a person; the totality which the mutilation would serve would be the whole person, body and soul.

Surgical Interventions for Identity Disorders?

This might provide a limited justification for surgical therapy for BIID. But an anxiety still remains. Even if such surgery were on occasions defensible in principle, might it not yet be doubtful because of the circumstances in which it would be practised? This returns us to the question of the cultural narrative within which BIID is set. One of the concerns behind affirming that psychological suffering could warrant drastic surgery lies in the perception that this would represent a further step in the direction of the instrumentalisation and consumerisation of the body. Once we accept the principle that we may provide surgical solutions to emotional distress, what other practices might we also find ourselves legitimating? How are we to prevent the ever increasing medical colonisation of our cultural imagination, driven (it should be noted) not so much by the calculated expansion of medical power as by the impatient expectations of the patient-consumer? This trend is amplified and given philosophical voice in those conceptions of autonomy, such as those of Savulescu, which not only defend the capacity for informed consent, but also make claims on medicine to supply whatever individuals may demand. On such accounts, surgery for BIID is folded into the category of consumer choice, as a lifestyle preference or a form of self-realisation, even if no doubt an extreme and rare one.

The concern is compounded by the proposed categorisation of the desire for elective impairment as an 'identity disorder'. The notion of one's 'identity' is remarkably fluid, and is perhaps peculiar to the modern West; it is arguably little surprise, and it says little about its usefulness as a cross-cultural psychological or psychiatric classification, that people in modern English-speaking cultures resort to the language of identity and identity disorder, since this is precisely the language that we habitually reach for when handling this kind of issue. The danger with novel categories of psychiatric diagnosis is that under the guise of supposed scientific impartiality they may impose on others patterns of behaviour, of perception and feeling, which are the local products of specific historical and cultural conditions. And because of the reciprocal, reflexive nature of the relation between people's self-interpretations and the diagnostic categories available to them, especially when mediated through support groups, internet blogs, information sites, and the like, such classifications may end up structuring the ways in which people perform their mental torment in ways that preclude alternative interpretations. Indeed in general, as might be surmised from studies of other arguably transient psychiatric phenomena, our understanding of the significance of cultural context for the structure of experience is inchoate in the extreme.[37]

There are also particular reasons for unease here in relation to BIID. Not only are there significant unclarified issues in the choice of classification,[38] but the potential for abuse and for a consumerisation of surgery is also magnified by a significant number of 'wannabes' who are unresolved about precisely which amputation they are seeking, and therefore might end up having several physically successful but psychologically unfulfilling amputations;[39] as well as by the possibility some might choose to downplay or deny a sexual dimension of their feelings in order to secure the desired surgery. Perhaps most importantly, the adoption of an official psychiatric classification might end up essentialising the experience, ossifying in some people a quasi-positivist self-understanding that precluded the possibility of any alternative accounts of their situation. It might leave them grasping onto their identity as sufferers from BIID as the deepest truth about themselves, clinging to the possibility of surgical intervention as their sole hope of salvation, and unable to ask even in principle whether there were any alternatives.

37. See Ian Hacking's discussion of fugue states in nineteenth-century France and multiple personality disorder in late twentieth-century America in *Mad Travellers: Reflections on the Reality of Mental Illnesses* (London: Free Association Books, 1999), and *Rewriting the Soul: Multiple Personality and the Sciences of Memory* (Princeton, NJ: Princeton University Press, 1995). These are discussed in relation to BIID by Elliott, *Better than Well*, pp. 227-234.

38. The previous, fourth edition of the *Diagnostic and Statistical Manual of Mental Disorders*, the standard psychiatric classificatory instrument in use in the United States, defined two different kinds of identity disorder: dissociative identity disorder (formerly multiple personality disorder) and gender identity disorder, but did not define 'identity disorder' as such (*Diagnostic and Statistical Manual of Mental Disorders: DSM-IV* [Washington, DC: American Psychiatric Association, 1994]). The recent, fifth edition has replaced gender identity disorder with gender dysphoria, not because of increased clarity about the notion of an identity disorder, but because of the stigmatizing effects of associating gender nonconformity with mental disorder. It is perhaps even more striking that the WHO's classificatory system, which is more widely used internationally, does not contain the category of identity disorder; see *The ICD-10 Classification of Mental and Behavioural Disorders: Clinical Descriptions and Diagnostic Guidelines* (Geneva: World Health Organisation, 1992). Nor did Michael First offer any views on the matter in proposing the term 'body integrity identity disorder' (First, 'Desire for Amputation of a Limb'). For a defence of the language of identity disorder here, see Avi Craimer, 'The Relevance of Identity in Responding to BIID and the Misuse of Causal Explanation', *American Journal of Bioethics* 9 (2009), pp. 53-55.

39. Erich Kasten, 'Body Integrity Identity Disorder (BIID): Befragung von Betroffenen und Erklärungsansätze', *Fortschritte der Neurologie Psychiatrie* 77 (2009), pp. 16-24, who on the grounds of the roving target of amputation within some individuals finds reason for questioning the neurological account of BIID.

All of these are real reasons for concern, and would have to be taken into account before any settled understanding of the phenomenon or final reckoning of the morality of elective amputation were reached. The historical trajectory to which a technological and autonomist culture seems irrevocably committed is one about which anyone concerned with humane values should entertain suspicion. Nevertheless the spacious panorama which the grand historical narrative opens up should not eclipse the views afforded by the *petits récits*. The lived realities of those people whose autobiographies have been marked by the intense desire to be rid of a healthy body part deserve to be considered in their own terms, rather than being assumed to play a mere bit part in a wider story, and a questionable one at that. They need not be interpreted as lending themselves, whether intentionally or inadvertently, to endless vistas of arbitrary bodily reinvention or florid fantasies about perpetual self-creation.

However, if it is the case that such surgery need not be co-opted into a narrative of technological annihilation of the body, if it is possible to bear witness to the fundamental goodness of the body even as one entertains seriously the possibility of eliminating a healthy body part, then those considering such an action need to recognise certain constraints. Rejection of an expansionist philosophy of autonomy does suggest certain ways of performing desire. Those who live with these desires would need to be open to the possibility of other ways of having their desires resolved than that of surgery. They would need to be willing to interrogate their desires, knowing that desires can be deceptive and that the literal fulfilment of desire might not be identical with the true fulfilment of desire. They would need to refuse the fatalism of assuming that the only solution to the desire to have the limb amputated is to have the limb amputated. They would need to be wary of tying themselves to a particular identity if that identification reified their predicament and made intelligible only one solution. If — hypothetically — the option were available, they would need to be open to the possibility of losing the desire for surgery rather than losing part of their body.

Of course for many the option of losing the desire for surgery, however theoretically attractive it might be, remains consistently alien to their experience. They may have lived with their feelings for as long as they can remember, and may not know what it would be like to experience life without them. They may well know the emotional cost of failed efforts to distance themselves from their feelings and the seeming impossibility of doing so, and thence the attraction of seeking surgery. For them, if they were finally to request surgery, recognition of the integrity of the body would also evoke appropriate attitudes. They would not assume that amputation would be a genuine and final 'cure', rather than just a treatment of their symptoms that will likely bring other problems in train. They would not hope that a diagnosis and surgery would provide a final solution to all their life's concerns, but would merely provide the basis for a liveable way forward, a modicum of peace.

Body Integrity and the Body of Christ

I emphasise the element of choice in performing one's desires in order to avoid the danger of essentialising the experience, a danger which may intensify when the dominant available categorisations use the language of identity. Not all ways of responding to an experience are equal, and some may be genuinely less enclosed, less fatalistic, more self-aware, more liberating than others. Moreover, whether wittingly or not, some may reflect better than others the final truth of human identity as it is displayed in baptism into Christ. For baptism does not confirm us in our identities but is the crisis of all human identities; baptism reveals the reality of a human identity disorder of a depth inaccessible to any diagnostic manual or psychiatric assessment; it directs us to follow one who did not lay claim to his identity as something to be clung to; and it promises us new life as the bearers of his identity and members together of a liberated and complete body.

Would surgery for BIID be justified? No doubt we are not yet in a position to reach a mature conclusion on this. The church would certainly not be free if it were not free to make the judgement, No. But equally, I submit, it would not be free if it were not free to make the judgement, Yes. And this, not as a concession to pastoral 'necessity', nor out of a misplaced emphasis on compassion as the sole ground of discernment. Nor, as I have suggested, need it derive from giving any ground to an autonomy-centred philosophy. Rather it would be based on a serious, principled attention to the welfare of the patient, considered as a whole person, body and soul, which is not the same as a descent into a gnosticising, historicising rejection of the goodness of the body. There is a difference between an argument that we should allow surgery for BIID since we allow consumer demands over the body such as cosmetic surgery, and the recognition that we are here dealing with a genuine problem which may have no obvious organic cause and which is only accessible through people's self-description, but for which surgery under certain circumstances might be a remedy. And the person who made that judgement out of responsibility towards their own health need not do so as someone appealing to their secure and self-dependent status as an autonomous individual, but might also do so as someone called to be an integral part of the body of Christ.

Dolent gaudentque: Sorrow in the Christian Life

John Webster

I

Moral and pastoral theology is a subordinate but not subservient element of theological science. It is subordinate, first, because — like all the various inquiries which make up theology — it must look beyond itself for its principles, ontological and cognitive. Theology is an exercise of sanctified intelligence in relation to an extrinsic object (the high mystery of God in himself and everything in God), an object known as God shares with rational creatures his perfect knowledge of himself and all things. Moral and pastoral theology is subordinate, second, because its access to these extrinsic principles is generally through other elements of theology. Primarily, it is subordinate to exegesis, that is, to the contemplative construal of God's instruction of the redeemed through Holy Scripture; secondarily, it is subordinate to dogmatics as the conceptual reconstruction or expansion of this divine instruction.

The subordination of moral and pastoral theology to exegesis and dogmatics does not, however, exclude a measure of ordered reciprocity between dogmatic and moral-pastoral science. Dogmatics possesses a certain priority because of the directness of its engagement with the being of God and creatures which precedes investigation of creaturely practices. But there is instruction about the order of being which can only be acquired or displayed as we consider those practices which form the matter of moral and pastoral theology. No element of theological science can be pursued in isolation, apart from the company of the other elements. Moral and pastoral theology, applying itself to the study of human action as a movement whose cause, setting, and end are the presence and works of the triune God, is in especially close company with dogmatics, the theological articulation of first principles. Yet dogmatics would risk missing its object if it did not leave itself open to see its object through the eyes of moral and pastoral science; neither is autonomous in respect of the other, but they stand in an ordered and mutually informative and corrective relation of first and second. A double rule obtains, then, for moral and pastoral theology as it investigates creaturely practice. First: *operari sequitur esse* (action follows being); second: *omne . . . quod est per aliud reducitur ad id quod est per se* (whatever is derivative should be traced back to what is of itself).[1] These movements of *following* and *reduction* draw attention to the order of being and causality; coming-to-know is much less tidy. The order of being need not be replicated in the order of knowing; but the order of knowing must not be projected onto the order of being.[2]

A theological description of sorrow among the human emotions will exemplify this ordered reciprocity of dogmatic-metaphysical and moral-pastoral intelligence. The need for the first is both acute and easily overlooked. Sorrow is vividly and destructively present in the lives of very many persons; but understanding and alleviating their distress requires the application (under the tutelage of divine revelation and with the assistance of the Holy Spirit) of speculative or theoretical powers in order to reach understanding of sorrow's nature and causes. For though we customarily expect a formidable array of such powers on the part of psychotherapists, we rarely require them of Christian pastors, and assume that dogmatic-metaphysical reflection provides scant assistance in the cure of souls and threatens to distract us from practice. Not so: gospel-governed dogmatics and metaphysics show us what, in God, the world and creatures are, why their sorrows arise, how they may be eased. Yet moral and pastoral theology is not merely concerned to reduce cases back to their antecedent principles, as if moral ontology constitutes the totality of ethics and the ministry of consolation. Making sense of creaturely sorrow certainly requires intelligent investigation of moral nature as it appears in the light of the church's confession of the gospel: this is the dogmatic-metaphysical element of ethical science. But moral nature is not apart from the enactment of moral history ('nature' is causally but not temporally prior to history, and only to be isolated *rationaliter*); understanding and guiding that enactment,

---

1. Thomas Aquinas, *Summa theologiae* IaIIae 3.6 resp.

2. On the relation of metaphysical and practical concerns in moral theology, see Thomas S. Hibbs, *Aquinas, Ethics and Philosophy of Religion: Metaphysics and Practice* (Bloomington: Indiana University Press, 2007).

and directing it to that which constitutes its healing, is the chief concern of the practical science of moral and pastoral theology.

What follows reflects on sorrow in the lives of human creatures as they are brought into being, sustained, governed, and redeemed by God in his outer works of creation, reconciliation, and perfection. For guidance I have looked backwards:[3] to Augustine's comments on the passions in the ninth and fourteenth books of *City of God,* but most of all to Thomas Aquinas's consideration of sorrow in the course of the remarkably extensive treatment of the passions of the soul in the *Prima Secundae.*[4] The latter treatment is unequalled in the theological literature. There we find an assumption, untroubled by later curricular tensions, that dogmatic and moral theology constitute a single sequence. And we find other things: clear, penetrating understanding of the biblical and theological inheritance; unsentimental observation of human detail; a profoundly evangelical instinct which places both pleasure and pain within the movement by which ruined creatures are returned to fellowship with God.[5]

---

3. Recent philosophical writing on the emotions has found it necessary to undertake a good deal of historical work, retrieving ancient understandings of the passions (examples would include Richard Sorabji's Gifford lectures *Emotion and Peace of Mind: From Stoic Agitation to Christian Temptation* [Oxford: Oxford University Press, 2000], or Simo Knuuttila's *Emotions in Ancient and Medieval Philosophy* [Oxford: Clarendon Press, 2004]), or tracing their eclipse in modern culture (see Thomas Dixon, *From Passions to Emotions: The Creation of a Secular Psychological Category* [Cambridge: Cambridge University Press, 2003]). The philosophical histories lack theological nuance, however, and even in reading classical Christian texts they commonly abstract elements of philosophical psychology from their spiritual-doctrinal setting in talk of the being and action of God.

4. The treatise on the passions comprises twenty-seven questions, divided into one hundred and thirty-two articles. I prescind from Aquinas's earlier treatments of the passions in *Scriptum super libros Sententiarum* III.15 and *De veritate* X.

5. In reading Aquinas, I have been guided by, inter alia, Mark Jordan, 'Aquinas's Construction of a Moral Account of the Passions', *Freiburger Zeitschrift für Philosophie und Theologie* 33 (1986): 71-97; Eileen C. Sweeney, 'Reconstructing Desire: Aquinas, Hobbes, and Descartes on the Passions', in Stephen F. Brown, ed., *Meeting of the Minds: The Relations between Medieval and Classical Modern European Philosophy* (Turnhout: Brepols, 1998), pp. 215-233; Peter King, 'Aquinas on the Passions', in Scott MacDonald and Eleonore Stump, eds., *Aquinas's Moral Theory* (Ithaca, NY: Cornell University Press, 1999), pp. 101-132; Kevin White, 'The Passions of the Soul (IaIIae qq. 22-48)', in Stephen J. Pope, ed., *The Ethics of Aquinas* (Washington: Georgetown University Press, 2002), pp. 103-115; Carlo Leget, 'Martha Nussbaum and Thomas Aquinas on the Emotions', *Theological Studies* 64 (2003): 558-581; Knuuttila, *Emotions in Ancient and Medieval Philosophy,* pp. 239-256; Servais Pinckaers, 'Reappropriating Aquinas's Account of the Passions', in John Berkman and Craig Steven Titus, eds., *The Pinckaers Reader: Renewing Thomistic Moral Theology* (Washington: Catholic University of America Press, 2005), pp. 273-287; Diana Fritz Cates, *Aquinas on the Emotions: A Religious-Ethical Inquiry* (Wash-

II

How may sorrow become an object of spiritual intelligence? How may we penetrate its keenly-felt but only half-understood presence to its deeper reality: its causes and effects, its place in the unfolding history of redemption, the remedies by which it may now be eased, its ultimate banishment by happiness in the holy city which comes down out of heaven from God?

Sorrow is opaque. In the realm of the fall, where emotions are commonly disordered and destructive, sorrow can so perturb us as to inhibit understanding, including understanding of itself. There is a kind of blankness which may accompany sorrow, by which intelligence is stultified. In its intemperate manifestations, sorrow may seem to its sufferers an absolute, irreducible reality, requiring and allowing for no explanation. Like acute bodily pain, sorrow 'can be so intense as to absorb all the soul's energies,'[6] leaving us no desire or willingness or intellectual resources to stand back and think about its nature, causes, effects, and remedies. Such knowledge as we have of it is simply knowledge of the sheer fact of our hurt. The healing of distress requires understanding; but understanding is overcome by distress.

A condition, therefore, of coming to understand sorrow is the awakening of intelligence (as well as of the will and the desires) by the gospel. Deep, disordered emotion is vivid and wakeful; but in the midst of it, reason may slumber and must be roused. The awakening is at the same time an illumination, shedding abroad light in darkness, dispelling shadows, and a healing, restoring our proper creaturely powers of knowledge. This evangelical awakening, illumination, and healing is what is meant by 'revelation'. Revelation is the outer work of divine charity in which, from the Father of lights, there comes down from above to distraught and ignorant creatures every good endowment and every perfect gift, including 'the word of truth' (Jas. 1.17f.). This 'word' is the word of divine instruction, present to us now in the testimonies of the prophets and apostles. If we are to know and govern the passions, Augustine tells us, we need a 'careful and copious exposition of the doctrine of Scripture, the sum of Christian knowledge, regarding these passions. It subjects the mind itself to God, so that he may rule and aid it, and the passions, again, to the mind, to

---

ington: Georgetown University Press, 2009); Robert Miner, *Thomas Aquinas on the Passions: A Study of Summa Theologiae IaIIae 22-48* (Cambridge: Cambridge University Press, 2009); Nicholas E. Lombardo, *The Logic of Desire: Aquinas on Emotion* (Washington: Catholic University of America Press, 2010); Eleonore Stump, 'The Non-Aristotelian Character of Aquinas's Ethics: Aquinas on the Passions', *Faith and Philosophy* 28 (2011): 29-43.

6. Aquinas, *Summa theologiae* IaIIae 37.1 ad 3.

moderate and bridle them, and turn them to righteous uses'.[7] We come to know our sorrow ultimately from divine revelation, proximately from *scriptura divina, qua christiana eruditio continetur;* attending to revelation and Scripture, moreover, is itself a settling of potentially chaotic emotion by subjecting intelligence to the cure of divine rule.[8]

Coming to understand sorrow depends upon coming to understand the entire reordering of creaturely life which the gospel announces: in Jesus Christ, supremely in his resurrection from the dead, God has set an end to sorrow, and in the Holy Spirit is now gathering creatures into happiness in fellowship with himself. There is a confidence proper to the Christian understanding of sorrow which flows from the authority, clarity, and effectiveness of the gospel announcement. Because Jesus Christ is and is present and eloquent, sorrow is not beyond our understanding. Yet the gospel revelation, perfect in itself, has not yet reached its creaturely term. Certainly, 'we have the prophetic word made sure', and the apostle can legitimately exhort believers to 'pay attention to this, as to a shining lamp' (2 Pet. 1.19). But the lamp shines 'in a dark place'; we await the dawning of the day and the rising of the morning star (2 Pet. 1.19). Revelation does not mean the cessation of learning but rather its engagement by a new and wholly adequate object. We 'have' the word; but what we have is not an item of knowledge instantly comprehended and requiring no further appropriation, but something commanding the constant exercise of attention, in prospect of God's eschatological illumination of us. We come to understand sorrow, accordingly, within the incomplete history of God's dealings with creatures, a history which is 'now day and yet night; night in comparison with the future day for which we yearn, day in comparison with the past which we have renounced'.[9] In this age, Augustine continues, 'it is night until there shine forth day in the glorified advent of our Lord Jesus Christ. . . . There is therefore to come day after this night, meanwhile in this night a lantern is not lacking'. But 'even this light by comparison with a sort of ineffable day is called night. For

---

7. Augustine, *City of God* IX.5.

8. In the Christian tradition, reflection on sorrow has, of course, involved conversation with sources other than Holy Scripture; Aristotle and the Stoics, chiefly. That conversation is necessary, Christian faith having only a handful of native concepts, and many borrowings; and it is fruitful, for rational creatures cannot but bring to awareness some aspects of their creatureliness. But theology will be alert to elements which fit only awkwardly with the gospel or which do not fit at all; and even what it finds instructive (Stoic teaching about temperance, perhaps) will be placed in an overarching account of things in which what is annexed by the gospel will be extended, adapted, and given a different role.

9. Augustine, *Enn. in Pss.* LXXVII.4.

the very life of believers by comparison with the life of unbelievers is day. . . .
Night and day — day in comparison with unbelievers, night in comparison
with the angels. For the angels have a day which we do not yet have'.[10]

Understanding of sorrow is given, acquired, and exercised over time. This
time is not random: it is a movement to an end. On the one hand, this counters
the way in which great sorrow can make present pain seem an absolute moment, and so render us inert and unteachable (this is despair). On the other
hand, it means that the knowledge of sorrow which revelation affords is pilgrim knowledge. It possesses its proper certainties: of our calling and the state
into which that calling has introduced us; of the end to which we are being
conducted by God; of the gifts which sustain us, including the gift of revelation
in the knowledge of Jesus Christ and of the enlightening of our hearts to hope
(Eph. 1.17f.). But it remains imperfect knowledge, an element of our movement
towards 'the age which is to come' (Eph. 1.21). Certainty and imperfection are
not dialectically balanced, such that we are poised precariously between stability and chaos. Certainty is our primary and principal state, imperfection
simply the result of the fact that the reconciliation of intelligence to divine
truth is not yet its full redemption. Even so, theological understanding of
sorrow is not to be had in the absence of its exercise; and the gospel does not
eliminate sorrow through understanding so much as instruct its hearers on
when and how to sorrow, how to resist sorrow's aggravations, how to wait for
our end.

III

Sorrow is one of the emotions or passions of the soul.[11] An emotion is not
simply a subjective mood: sorrow, for instance, is more than merely 'feeling

---

10. Augustine, *Enn. in Pss.* LXXVII.4.

11. There is no obviously adequate word in English. 'Passion' has earlier usage behind it,
and may remind the etymologically alert to the element of suffering *(passio)* in emotion; but
in modern usage it tends to connote vehement emotional disturbance. 'Affection', similarly,
underscores our being acted upon, and has especial resonances in the spiritual tradition of
Puritanism, but its usefulness is restricted by the way it is commonly used for one particular
emotion, namely fondness, often with a hint of sentimentality; as a consequence, it lacks the
range required of a generic term. 'Feeling' is too malleable, covering both purely physical states
and subjective moods. 'Emotion' is, therefore, probably as good as it gets, provided that use of
the term does not invoke the nineteenth-century secular psychologies which made heavy use
of the term.

miserable', though it may engender the psychic state of dejection. Emotion has an object. It is a state and activity of a person in relation to circumstances, occurrences and agents other than the self. As such, it is an 'undergoing' or 'suffering': a movement of the inner self in response to being moved from outside, a reaction.

Martha Nussbaum speaks of emotion as an aspect of human vulnerability, that is, of the incompleteness which accompanies the fact that our human well-being involves our orientation to what escapes our control.[12] Call this, rather, an aspect of creatureliness. We do not have our being from ourselves or in ourselves, for we are contingent: absolutely upon God, whose love has given, and sustains us in, being; derivatively upon other creatures from whom we may not detach ourselves without damaging or destroying our well-being. The current term of preference for this element of creatureliness is 'being-in-relation' or some variant of the same: unobjectionable enough, though often descriptively lush, and likely to be used in ways which solve too many problems too quickly and which threaten to confuse uncreated and created being. Aquinas's more spare and powerful term is *coniunctio*.[13] Unlike God who is *a se* and *in se*, human creatures have their being in conjunction, finding themselves by their very nature set alongside and engaged by other things. To this conjunction, human creatures respond by a movement which Aquinas calls *inclinatio consequens apprehensionem* ('inclination arising from cognition').[14] This is the movement of appetite, whether of attraction or repulsion, consequent upon perception of the state of conjunction in which we exist. The picture here — of being intelligently conjoined to objects which draw or repel — reinforces a conception of human nature as 'open': incomplete, not self-contained or fully resolved or at perfect rest. We are mobile, seeking out other realities in order to find out what may help us towards our good, and, in the course of that, recoiling from the evil which inhibits the fruition of our nature. This creaturely dynamic, in which we respond to our 'conjoined' state by cog-

---

12. Nussbaum, *Upheavals of Thought: The Intelligence of Emotions* (Cambridge: Cambridge University Press, 2001).

13. Aquinas, *Summa theologiae* IaIIae 35.1 resp.

14. Aquinas, *Summa theologiae* IaIIae 35.1 resp. In this respect, Aquinas's account is companionable with recent work on the cognitive character of emotions, such as Ronald de Sousa, *The Rationality of Emotion* (Cambridge, MA: MIT Press, 1987); John Deigh, 'Cognitivism in the Theory of Emotions', *Ethics* 104 (1994): 824-854; Robert C. Solomon, *The Passions: Emotions and the Meaning of Life* (Indianapolis: Hackett, 1997); Peter Goldie, *The Emotions: A Philosophical Exploration* (Oxford: Clarendon Press, 2000); Robert C. Roberts, *Emotions: An Essay in Aid of Moral Psychology* (Cambridge: Cambridge University Press, 2003).

nition and appetite, is the motor of emotion, for the emotions are the various movements of attraction to and recoil from other things.

Emotion is intrinsic to human creatureliness, but it acquires a special character in the wake of the depredations of the fall. In our integral state, the 'conjunctions' in which human creatures exist invariably promoted our good, and so always generated pleasurable emotion. Eden's innocence and the happiness enjoyed there were, in part, the absence of evil and of the consequent need to recoil; before the fall, there was no fear that being united to that which is other than ourselves might not lead to our good, and so there was no disinclination. After the fall, the situation and movement of conjunction remains; its absence would spell the end of the creaturely nature in which it is elemental. But intelligent participation in this state and movement makes us aware that our natural vulnerability may cause damage. Evil is present in the world, and so to 'suffer' the world — to enact ourselves as the incomplete, needy creatures that we are — is to risk sorrow.

There are three elements in sorrow: conjunction with evil; awareness of that conjunction; flight. First, the object of sorrow is some present evil; 'it is union with an evil that is the cause, in the sense of the object, of pain or sorrow',[15] the evil being judged evil precisely because 'it denies one some good'.[16] This evil object is properly intrinsic — we sorrow over our own misfortune; but it may have an extrinsic object, as in sorrow over the misfortune of another, though even in such a case there must be an element of intrinsic sorrow if we are to be engaged by the other's situation (in this case, we call the 'intrinsic' element 'sympathy', in which another's sorrow is appropriated). Second, sorrow presupposes perception *(perceptio)*[17] of the present evil, a perception which is not simply bodily (the pain associated with ill-health) but interior (awareness of the loss of well-being). Third, sorrow is flight from the evil which threatens. Aquinas uses the idiom of the movements of approach *(accessus)* and withdrawal *(recessus)* of physical bodies to convey this psychic movement. 'Sorrow is a kind of flight or withdrawal, and pleasure a kind of pursuit or approach.'[18] The generic term for the movement of recoil is pain, of which sorrow — 'internal' pain, the opposite of joy — is a species; 'pain', however, may also be used in a more restricted way to designate an evil which is repugnant to the body, that is, 'exterior' pain, the opposite of physical pleasure.

---

15. Aquinas, *Summa theologiae* IaIIae 36.4 resp.
16. Aquinas, *Summa theologiae* IaIIae 35.1 resp.
17. Aquinas, *Summa theologiae* IaIIae 35.1 resp.
18. Aquinas, *Summa theologiae* IaIIae 36.1 resp.

Emotion is depicted as a movement of aliveness in which creatures seek to fulfil their natures in relation to other realities. Because only certain sorts of unity or conjunction 'contribute to a thing's goodness',[19] withdrawal (sorrow) is as essential to the fulfilment of our nature as approach (pleasure). '[A]pproach is, of itself, directed towards something in harmony with nature; withdrawal is, of itself, directed towards something discordant with nature.'[20] The distinction *(quod est conveniens . . . quod est contrarium)* indicates that sorrow is part of the good order of creaturely life after the fall, a way in which human nature is sustained and protected. Sorrow always has 'some element of good',[21] not, of course, in the sense that sorrow is to be sought out as if it were pleasure, but in the sense that the sheer operation of repugnance for that which harms us indicates the vitality of our nature, indeed, our opposition to death. 'Pain,' Augustine says, 'which some suppose to be in an especial manner an evil, whether it be in mind or in body, cannot exist except in good natures. For the very fact of resistance in any being leading to pain, involves a refusal not to be what it was, because it was something good.'[22]

The principle to which Augustine and Aquinas draw our attention — that sorrow can only exist in good natures — is of immense metaphysical, moral, and psychological importance. It indicates the fundamental asymmetry between good and evil. God is wholly good, and has made a good creation. Pleasure and pain, joy and sorrow, are therefore not commensurable realities. The creature is not poised between them as between two principles; there is no fundamental ambivalence to creaturely being, for the basic movement of the creature is the movement of *life,* that is, animate movement towards the good. Reflecting on the question 'Is sorrow to be shunned more than pleasure is to be sought?' Aquinas announces the principle: *'Bonum est fortius quam malum,* good is stronger than evil', and continues: 'pleasure is desirable because its object is good; and sorrow is shunned because of its evil object. The desire for pleasure is therefore stronger than the aversion for sorrow'.[23] One reason Aquinas advances for this has to do with the supereminence of the good in creaturely being. Aquinas firmly rejects any idea of total evil: 'the cause of pleasure is something agreeable and good; the cause of pain or sorrow is something disagreeable and evil. Now it is possible to find something agreeable and good without anything at all discordant in it; but it is impossible to find any-

19. Aquinas, *Summa theologiae* IaIIae 36.3 ad 1.
20. Aquinas, *Summa theologiae* IaIIae 36.1 resp.
21. Aquinas, *Summa theologiae* IaIIae 39.4 ad 2.
22. Augustine, *De natura boni contra Manichaeos* XX.
23. Aquinas, *Summa theologiae* IaIIae 35.6 sed contra.

thing totally evil and disagreeable, with nothing good in it at all. It is therefore possible for pleasure to be completely perfect; but sorrow is always partial only.'[24] Evil is not a mode of being but declension from being; 'to be' is 'to be good' (though not necessarily in a moral sense); and so sorrow is not on a plane with pleasure as an object of emotion. It is, rather, a negation which accompanies the affirmation of the good which is the dynamic of creaturely life. Such a description, however, functions at the level of theological metaphysics, not psychology. To speak of sorrow as a negation does not mean that it is illusion, or that it has no object, but that it is a real movement whose object is a privation. Privation can exercise great power.

It would be difficult to overestimate the importance of this for understanding sorrow, on a couple of counts. First, it prohibits the conclusion that sorrow is an indication that evil is a natural element of creaturely existence. Quite the opposite: sorrow, not evil, is natural, its operation being the way in which the good creature opposes evil as something supervenient, an intrusion into the good order of creation. Sorrow is thus bracketed on the one side by the state of integrity in which sorrow was not yet, and on the other by eschatological glorification in which sorrow will be no more (Rev. 21.3f.). This, in turn, points to something of moral-pastoral resonance: the prohibition of any tragic understanding of or resignation over sorrow. Both arrest the movement of creaturely life in the realm of reconciliation; both concede too much to present evil; both inhibit the proper operation of sorrow, whose purpose is to direct us to the goodness of God.

IV

In the present passage of human life in which we are being gathered back into fellowship with God, our emotions are caught up by the Spirit's regenerative work, but remain in some measure fragile and unstable. Though they are being educated to serve in the good conduct of our lives, they can still slip the leash, they are not always fitting to circumstances. Noting this feature of the infirmity of human life after the fall, Augustine considers that it signifies, not the natural viciousness of emotion but its imperfection: indeed, 'so long as we wear the infirmity of this life, we are rather worse than better if we have none of these emotions at all'.[25] Augustine does not commend impassibility, which not only deadens

24. Aquinas, *Summa theologiae* IaIIae 35.6 resp.
25. Augustine, *City of God* XIV.9.

emotion but attempts to anticipate in our present life what can only be ours in the next: 'to be quite free of pain while we are in this place of misery is only purchased . . . at the price of blunted sensibilities both of mind and body. And therefore that which the Greeks call ἀπάθεια, and which the Latins would call, if their language allowed them, "impassibilitas," if it be taken to mean an impassibility of spirit and not of body, or, in other words, a freedom from those emotions which are contrary to reason and disturb the mind, then it is obviously a good and most desirable quality, but it is not one which is attainable in this life. . . . When there shall be no sin in a man, then there shall be this ἀπάθεια'.[26] Given that emotions are intrinsic to life in the pilgrim state, what is important is not rooting them out but getting them right, suffering and exercising them as reconciled creatures who are returning to their creator and who are learning how to live well now in anticipation of the future: 'we must live a good life in order to obtain to a blessed life'.[27] Hence the rule: 'a good life has all these affections right, a bad life has them wrong'.[28] To measure ourselves against this rule and deal well with the emotions as we are conducted to God, we need to come to understand two things about ourselves: 'what manner of persons the citizens of the city of God must be in this pilgrimage, who live after the spirit, not after the flesh', and 'what manner of persons they shall be also in that immortality whither they are journeying'.[29] How might this govern our dealing with sorrow?

Sorrow is an especially striking instance of how sin disturbs the emotions which are basic to human nature, and so of the need to make the emotions a matter of rational reflection and governance, in order that right and disordered emotion can be distinguished and the emotions can serve rather than inhibit progress towards God.

Sorrow is not intrinsically morbid,[30] but regenerate persons must sorrow

26. Augustine, *City of God* XIV.9.
27. Augustine, *City of God* XIV.9.
28. Augustine, *City of God* XIV.9.
29. Augustine, *City of God* XIV.9.
30. Augustine criticizes the Stoics for not allowing that sorrow can exist in the mind of the wise person: *City of God* XIV.8. Aquinas, similarly, because he considers the emotions a constituent element of human agency and beatitude (on which see Pinckaers, 'Reappropriating Aquinas's Account of the Passions', pp. 276f.), judges that *tristitia moderata* is a necessary condition for the rational creature's ascent to God. On this, see Miner's treatment of Aquinas on sorrow in *Thomas Aquinas on the Passions,* pp. 188-211. Stephen Loughlin is incorrect to argue that Aquinas simply wants to eliminate sorrow from the life of pilgrims: '*Tristitia et dolor:* Does Aquinas have a Robust Understanding of Depression?' *Nova et Vetera* 3 (2005): 761-783; the opposite view of Eileen Sweeney, 'Reconstructing Desire' — that Aquinas does not commend rational governance of emotion — is surely exaggerated.

in the right way. There was no sorrow in paradise, because there were no objects of sorrow; but *post lapsum* sorrow can be a right affection, *affectio recta*.[31] The proper functioning of sorrow, indeed, indicates that by virtue of divine grace human nature has survived the fall and its powers have not been entirely eradicated. Sorrow is flight from present evil which harms or threatens to harm us, and the flight signifies the enduring good order of human life. It is not flight in the sense of 'rout' (fearful running away as the only escape from what may overcome us), but in the sense of aversion, measured, well-judged turning from what opposes our good. Sorrow arises from a deep sense of and trust in the eminence of the good which is opposed: we are impelled to flight not only by repugnance for evil but by inclination to good.[32] Moreover, the aversion of sorrow is itself an exercise of created power; it is not mere disarray, but action against what is *contra naturam*, and so a movement which affirms that nature by enacting it.

How is sorrow as *affectio recta* to be distinguished from its disordered counterpart? Sorrow is right affection when it is set in motion by and corresponds to rightly ordered love. 'Among ourselves . . . the citizens of the holy city of God, who live according to God in the pilgrimage of this life, both fear and desire, and grieve and rejoice. And because their love is rightly placed, all these affections of theirs are right.'[33] Further, when love is attached to proper objects, reason is able intelligently to moderate sorrow. 'The emotions are not "diseases" [*morbi*] or "disturbances" of the soul [*perturbationes animae*], except precisely when they are not under rational control.'[34] 'Emotion leads one towards sin in so far as it is uncontrolled by reason; but in so far as it is rationally controlled, it is part of the virtuous life.'[35] This *moderatio rationis* ought not to be considered mere suppression of emotion to avoid perturbation and retain equanimity; it is, rather, discrimination of occasions and modes of sorrow, and direction of its exercise.

Sorrow is right affection when it is 'sorrow for evil',[36] propelled into motion by objects which are abhorrent and from which we must take flight. Believers groan inwardly as in present circumstances of bondage they wait for the coming fulfilment of their filial relation to God (Rom. 8.23); they suffer the 'godly grief' which 'produces a repentance that leads to salvation and brings

---

31. Augustine, *City of God* XIV.9.
32. See Aquinas, *Summa theologiae* IaIIae 36.1, 36.2.
33. Augustine, *City of God* XIV.9.
34. Aquinas, *Summa theologiae* IaIIae 24.2 resp.
35. Aquinas, *Summa theologiae* IaIIae 24.2 ad 2.
36. Aquinas, *Summa theologiae* IaIIae 39.1 sed contra.

no regret' (2 Cor. 7.10); they weep with those who weep (Rom. 12.15). These various modes of sorrow — distress at the delay of the fulfilment of our nature in perfect fellowship with God, remorse over wrongdoing, pity for another's misfortune — are indications that created nature is being realised in proper odium towards evil, whether inside us or in some external object.

Sorrow goes wrong when in some way it breaks free from well-ordered love and governance by truthful apprehension of our nature and calling and our regenerate condition. Sorrow gets caught up in the war between the law of the mind and the law of sin; it no longer consents to and delights in the given shape ('law') of the inmost self which faithful reason apprehends, but is captive by 'another law' (Rom. 7.23). As with all the emotions, so with sorrow: evil lies close at hand. What forms does this threat take?

Consider the 'godly grief' of repentance, being 'displeased over sinning' (*displicere quod peccavit*).[37] Penitential sorrow is godly grief when it 'leads to salvation and brings no regret' (2 Cor. 7.10) — we might say it is *productive*, both an aversion from past sin and an intention for amendment of life. 'See what earnestness this godly grief has produced in you, what eagerness to clear yourselves, what indignation, what alarm, what longing, what zeal, what punishment!' (2 Cor. 7.11). To undergo such godly grief is to suffer no loss (2 Cor. 7.9). Worldly grief, by contrast, is no such movement of aversion from evil and towards the promised good; all it produces is 'death' (2 Cor. 7.10). Unlike the godly sorrow whose underlying principle is our being conducted to perfect life, worldly grief inhibits progress. It is a kind of collapse, 'the desertion of better things'.[38]

Worldly grief is a mode of 'aggravated sorrow' (*tristitia aggravans*)[39] or *acedia*;[40] the term has been applied to a range of affective phenomena, but is best understood as referring to *tristitia de spirituali bono* ('sorrow over spiritual good').[41] It is bound up with false judgements: that spiritual goods do not exist, or are not promised, or, for certain persons at least, are impossible to obtain, or even that they are in reality evil. But the root of aggravated sorrow is the unchecked dominion of the flesh, and refusal of or disbelief in the superabundance of regeneration. Sorrow of this order is aversion to God and good, consent to 'the horror, the loathing of the divine good due to the flesh's victory over

37. Aquinas, *Summa theologiae* IIIa.84.8 resp.

38. Augustine, *De natura boni contra Manichaeos* XX.

39. Aquinas, *Summa theologiae* IaIIae 35.1 resp.

40. See Rebecca K. De Young, 'Resistance to the Demands of Love: Aquinas on the Vice of *Acedia*', *The Thomist* 68 (2004): 173-204.

41. Aquinas, *Summa theologiae* IIaIIae 35.2 resp.

the spirit'.[42] Much might be said of the pathology of aggravated sorrow. We are immobilised by it: because it is an aversion to good, it inhibits the flight from evil which is integral to the movement of life.[43] One overcome by *acedia* 'wants to do nothing', is 'dragged away from good work';[44] active concurrence to the propelling energy of divine vocation fails. And this is accompanied by resentment, a sullen frame, listlessness, apathy, shunning of fellowship with God, disgust at spiritual things: all symptoms of 'ceasing to expect a personal share in the divine goodness'.[45] In short: sorrow of this kind 'kills the spiritual life'.[46]

V

Aggravated sorrow is an onslaught on happiness; but Christian faith finds its remedy in the gospel, which quickens the movement of creaturely life. The healing and the proper direction and use of the emotions follow from the gospel's instruction. Emotional restoration requires cognitive advance, that is, coming to truthful apprehension of our nature and state before God. Disordered sorrow is set right by immersion in the gospel's pedagogy, through which we come to know what we must be in this pilgrim state, and what we will be in immortality. We have earlier intimated what kind of knowledge this is: knowledge awakened by divine revelation, acquired over time, imperfect yet of sufficient certainty. What is its content?

The gospel instructs us about sorrow by turning (sometimes dragging) our attention to the alteration of all things which has been effected by the redemptive work of the Son of God and the regenerative work of the Holy Spirit.

'Isaiah says of the man of sorrows that he carried our sorrows' (Isa. 53.3, 5). In willing consent to the Father's determination and appointment, the eternal Son takes upon himself the office and work of the man of sorrows, appropriating the evils which afflict us and with which we afflict ourselves, making them his own and suffering them in the way which is proper to his free majesty. In becoming like us, he acquaints himself with our sorrows and their grief, he bears the pain which they inflict; and all this at the Lord's pleasure, in fulfilment of the divine resolve to bless creatures and cause them to prosper. Be-

---

42. Aquinas, *Summa theologiae* IIaIIae 35.3 resp.
43. Aquinas, *Summa theologiae* IaIIae 35.8 resp.
44. Aquinas, *Summa theologiae* IIaIIae 35.1 resp.
45. Aquinas, *Summa theologiae* IIaIIae 20.3 resp.
46. Aquinas, *Summa theologiae* IIaIIae 35.3 resp.

cause his bearing of sorrow has this end, it is not to be considered merely the removal of an oppressive weight from us onto him, his relieving us of a burden by shouldering it himself. There is more here than an exchange of suffering subject: he appropriates our sorrows in order to eliminate them; he carries them in order to carry them *away*. And because this is so, he will see the fruit of the travail of his soul and be satisfied.

By virtue of the saving mission of the Son of God, the faithful have been set in the domain of consolation, their lives taking place in the new created reality whose ground is the abundance of God's charity in its character as solace and comfort. The principle of this reality is the divine nature. The God and Father of our Lord Jesus Christ is the 'God of all comfort' (2 Cor. 1.3), made known in the cross and resurrection of Christ (2 Cor. 1.10), and presently active as God 'comforts us in all our affliction' (2 Cor. 1.4). His past deliverance of the saints is the ground for hope that 'he will deliver us' (2 Cor. 1.10). Further, the domain of consolation sustains a community of mutual comfort: God comforts us 'so that we may be able to comfort those who are in any affliction, with the comfort with which we ourselves are comforted by God' (2 Cor. 1.4).

The gospel announces the good of our consolation, and instructs us how to repose in that good, there to find pleasure and happiness. Yet we do not delight in that good by instinct; we must come to see that it is, indeed, congenial, *conveniens*.[47] Muddled loves and hatreds, erratic movements of attraction and recoil, must be converted to the good in which our happiness lies. Such conversion, wholly beyond our damaged capacities, is effected by the second saving mission of God, in which the Spirit so moves upon and in us as to bestow the new nature, reintegrate us into the domain of divine consolation, and complete the healing of sorrow. The work of the Spirit is *physical,* the bringing about of a new nature. The Spirit, that is, does not merely propose realities to the minds and wills of creatures as material upon which they are to go to work: that would not be regeneration but merely the provoking of creaturely self-formation. The Spirit reconstitutes the mind and will from within, so that they become capable of embracing and living gospel consolation. Knowledge of and desire for this consolation generate a life-movement in which aggravated sorrow is overcome by a combination of tranquillity and resistance: tranquillity, because such is the divine solace that serene confidence in our situation is proper; resistance, because divine solace enables movement against continuing affliction. In the realm of regeneration as in that of nature, the Spirit works graciously and sovereignly, but benevolently, as the extension

---

47. Aquinas, *Summa theologiae* IaIIae 38.1 resp.

of divine charity, and therefore not simply extrinsically. As Lord he is life-giver, communicating the new nature and quickening it into activity. The Spirit does not simply manifest comfort as an external reality of which we are onlookers in the midst of sorrow; we *are* in the domain of consolation, and that consolation is not only a condition but a form of life.

Animating this form of life is contemplation of the God of all comfort. Living well in the domain of consolation and embracing happiness requires *cogitatio perseverans:* 'the more we think about spiritual goods the more delightful they become to us'.[48] Sorrow is assuaged and rightly ordered by contemplating God and his goodness which embraces us and gives us a share in his benefits. Contemplation of this kind is difficult when we are overtaken by sorrow, for 'contemplation requires complete repose', and sorrow 'can be so intense as to absorb all the soul's energies and make it impossible to learn anything new'.[49] Moreover, in the wake of the fall our capacity for contemplation is impaired, and renewing its exercise requires that the Spirit kindle in us love of wisdom.[50] But the domain of consolation is also the domain of the awakening and illuminating power of the Spirit.

Contemplation of God's goodness enables reason to govern emotion. This governance is not self-governance, but perception of the good of divine governance. Reason governs as it defers to and repeats the divine rule. And so, once again, what matters is taking up our place in the realm of the divine pedagogy. Living in that realm, we are to be eager in seeking out the gospel's teaching which 'subjects the mind itself to God, that he may rule and aid it, and the passions . . . to the mind, to moderate and bridle them, and turn them to righteous uses.'[51]

The creaturely subject of divine consolation, instruction, and governance is the person in the church, whose common life is both the setting for and an instrument of the distribution of God's comfort. *Non unus homo est, sed unum corpus est.*[52] 'Let all . . . who have "tasted" the sweetness of the "Lord," and who own in Christ that for which they have a relish, think that they are not the only ones; but that there are such seeds scattered throughout the "field" of the Lord, this whole earth; that there is a certain Christian unity. . . .'[53] Aggravated sor-

---

48. Aquinas, *Summa theologiae* IaIIae 35.1 ad 3.

49. Aquinas, *Summa theologiae* IaIIae 37.1 resp.

50. Aquinas, *Summa theologiae* IaIIae 38.4 resp.

51. Augustine, *City of God* IX.5. On 'righteous uses' of sorrow, see Paul J. Griffiths, 'Tears and Weeping: An Augustinian View', *Faith and Philosophy* 28 (2011): 19-28.

52. Augustine, *Enn. In Pss.* XLII.1.

53. Augustine, *Enn. In Pss.* XLII.1.

row isolates, so compounding grief; the companionship of believers assuages sorrow by love, and moves us to seek out and take pleasure in the divine solace. More especially, the common life of believers can be an instrument of cognitive and emotional advance. Disordered sorrow is exacerbated by existing in hurtful emotional regimes or cultures which block apprehension of spiritual goods, and so stimulate or reinforce the misperception and misperformance of our nature. Fitting emotions are learned in part by participation in the community of the saints which has been taught *how* to rejoice, *how* to weep; and such participation also enables discernment of fitting occasions for emotions: *when* to rejoice, *when* to weep. Further, sorrow may find fitting expression in the common life of the saints. Private, unexpressed sorrow causes secret damage, and may come to destructive expression as inarticulate, uncommunicative rage which further isolates the one who sorrows. Taking part in the common life, one can learn to express sorrow in a way which is not simply an isolating cry of pain but an act of *communication,* part of life in conjunction with others who have spiritual goods in common, and in conjunction with God who is present and attentive. The expression of sorrow is then no longer a howl of anguish but a *lament,* directed not to a void but to God and the company gathered around God, and, because so directed, already holding out the prospect of some refreshment and ease. 'Hurtful things hurt still more if they are pent up within us, for the soul is then more concentrated upon them; but if they are released, the soul's energies are turned to things outside itself and interior pain is lessened. This is why sorrow is assuaged by outwardly expressing it in tears or sobs or even words.'[54]

Last: the soul that sorrows is embodied, and *remedia corporalia* are not to be despised. Take a bath, get some sleep, Aquinas counsels, for they afford pleasure, restore the body's vital motions, and so impede and relieve the smarting of the soul.[55]

VI

The Christian gospel is instruction in human happiness, vouchsafed to us by revelation and reconciliation: by revelation, because it is first spoken to us not by a fellow creature but by God through the mouth of Christ; by reconciliation, because only as wickedness, pride, and resentment are pardoned and friend-

54. Aquinas, *Summa theologiae* IaIIae 38.3 resp.
55. Aquinas, *Summa theologiae* IaIIae 38.5.

ship with God is renewed can we attend to the divine word concerning our restoration to happiness. Included in the restoration is the repair of the emotions, and of sorrow among the emotions. Restored to fellowship with God, we are summoned, not to the eradication of sorrow but to its disciplined, well-instructed cultivation and enactment in accordance with our new nature, and within the setting of the history of the redemption of the saints. Even in our restored condition, the penal consequences of the fall linger, one of which is the sheer hard work, which an emotion like sorrow requires of us. Yet the one who has borne our sorrows once for all continues to bear them, and will do so until we attain the final happiness for which God destines us, when mourning, crying, and pain will be no more because the former things will have passed away.

Know Thyself! The Return of Self-Love

Oliver O'Donovan

To the affectionate attention that has been shown to me in this collection of essays I am forbidden, by editorial decree, to respond in detail, and it would, I think, be a poor return for the intelligence the contributors have lavished on their work to lapse into the ramblings of autobiographical reminiscence. So I take up, as a challenge the essays have presented me with, the counsel of the ancient Greeks, "Know thyself!" With it I have an opportunity to revisit and reconsider some reflections I first pursued in my earliest published book about Augustine and self-love.[1]

Those who first framed this advice meant it as a mundane practical caution. Μηδὲν ἄγαν, ἔγγυα παρὰ δ' ἄτη, γνῶθι σεαυτόν, read the Delphic inscription: "Nought in excess! Give surety, and ruin's next! Know thyself!" There is much that we are not, much that we cannot be; overreaching is an ever-present danger. Prompted by Socrates and Plato, philosophy learned to read the third element in a more positive but less worldly sense, as an intimation of affinity between the contemplative soul and the divine. When Christian theologians took it up, they did so in a way that built a bridge between the two poles, combining an element of ontological reflection with a practical content. God's summons that we should know ourselves calls us to live and act as his children within a world he has created and redeemed. Knowing ourselves is a matter of

---

1. *The Problem of Self-Love in St. Augustine* (New Haven, CT: Yale University Press, 1979; Eugene, OR: Wipf & Stock, 2006[2]). In this work I made some suggestions about the chronology of the development of Augustine's idea of self-love which were fortunate enough to win the favour of the late R. A. Markus.

hearing, and of accepting responsibility before God for what we hear. It involves belief, but not in ourselves; we must believe in one who is not ourselves, without whom we cannot be ourselves. Self-knowledge accompanies obedience at every stage of practical reason, beginning at the beginning with the discovery of faith that we are given to be competent agents, called by God's word to live and act within the frame of world and time. "Behold the handmaid of the Lord; let it be to me according to your word!" (Luke 1:38); the Virgin's answer to the angelic commission has been taken as the paradigm of agency on the threshold of existence, embracing the calling that God had given her. It might seem that we could know almost anything *about* ourselves, but that we could not know ourselves. We could recount our histories, our circumstances, our fears and intentions, but how might our attention be drawn inwards through these concentric circles of experience to the personal centre they revolve around? How can the knower become the object of knowledge? That was the question Augustine faced when, concluding his great autobiographical narrative, he proposed to move on from "what I have been" to "what I now am." "What I am" is precisely what I can never get a final purchase on.[2] The extraordinary tenth book of the *Confessions,* unparalleled even in the author's own output, following the clue established earlier that "I am a great question to myself," ventured into what Philip Cary has called "the self as inner space."[3]

One certainty about himself Augustine had to start from: he had an *apriori* certainty of his love for God — whatever God might be, whatever he himself

2. On this Jean-Yves Lacoste has always been eloquent. Cf. *Être en Danger* (Paris: Cerf, 2011), pp. 295f: "We do not possess ourselves. We are not ourselves in totality. . . . The self always escapes us in part. It escapes us for the very good reason that we have only penultimate propositions to get a hold on it with."

3. *Confessions,* 10.3.4; 4.4.9. Cf. Philip Cary, *Augustine's Invention of the Inner Self: The Legacy of a Christian Platonist* (Oxford: Oxford University Press, 2000). Did Augustine "invent" this idea of the self? There was always a complex and dialectical character about "the heart" in Hebrew Scriptures, "elusive above all things," as Jeremiah observes, "and fainting, so that who can comprehend it?" (17:9). Jesus' own teaching constantly reverted to the heart as the source of action, and to the importance of solitude in prayer. And if it is true that the counsel to turn inward and explore the soul owed much to the inspiration of Plotinus, that inspiration had already led Ambrose to find in the Psalms an encouragement "to wander around in our heart as in an expansive house, and converse with it as with a good companion" (*De officiis* 3.1.1). Nor was the Eastern Christian tradition without its ways of entering this territory, as Maximus Confessor's teaching on *philautia* reveals. Nevertheless, Augustine pursued the thought of inner space with a complexity and philosophical inquisitiveness that forms a landmark in Western philosophy. The feature that stands out as innovatory is the concentration of the self within a magnetic field set up between God's inner summons and the objective order of the world.

might be. Unarguable, unfathomable, and simply *there*, love was the gateway to an introspective journey in which both God and self receded as he pursued them, opening his gaze to the extraordinary psychological spaces within him, himself and yet not himself, the "caverns" of his memory. The "spatiality" of the Augustinian self is induced by the believer's need to distinguish himself from what is not himself, and so to achieve the objectivity that agency demands. In pursuit of God and self, he finds the variety and complexity of world and time reflected in his mind, and seeks to place their elements in due order. Much care is given to that order: earth and its contents (including the physical self), the "force" that ties the soul to the body, the "force" that commands the senses in common with the beasts, the memory, involving both "images" and the contents of an "inner memory" — categories of reason, laws of mathematics, and the awareness of temporal distance — and finally the self itself, for though transcending its experiences, the self is still the object of its own remembering, and therefore not immutable, not to be confused with God. The capacity to hold oneself before one's own eyes is the central core of memory, the point furthest removed from the empirical images which are its acquired content. The inner ascent through memory displays the power of self-objectification, the climax of which is the discovery that self is not God, but "under" God, a thing within the world. How, then, can God be seen, or known, or loved? He is the memory's categorical presupposition, the undefined "happiness" that makes sense of active life. Divine transcendence is seen through memory as an object of striving — always within it, yet beyond it, never held in the focus of its eye.

The second section of the book turns from the speculative to the practical, following another route of ascent, that of moral discipline or "continence," according to the anthropological structure of body, soul, and spirit. At its climax Augustine introduces the idea of justice, and with it the neighbour, whose entry is powerful because long delayed. It would have been possible, Augustine thought, to try to get to neighbour-love too quickly, taking too much for granted, assuming we knew what the neighbour was and what he needed. In a sermon contemporary with the *Confessions* he wondered why it was not enough to say, "You shall love your neighbour', and replied that if we did not know how to love ourselves rightly, we should go wrong in loving our neighbour, too. "So the Lord resolved to give you a form for your love of yourself through the love of God; and only then did he entrust you with your neighbour, to love him as yourself."[4] Without a developed self-love shaped to

---

4. Augustine, *Sermo* Mainz 40.12. Cf. *Sermo* 128.3.5: "First see whether you have learned

the love of God, we are not equipped to care for our neighbour's welfare. The discovery of the self in God is the precondition for ranging the self alongside the neighbour in a just equality. But the neighbour, when he arrives, comes accompanied by God. Indeed, the neighbour *par excellence* is God himself in Christ. So the God who lay *behind* Augustine's memory can now be seen to walk *with* him: "You have always walked beside me, truth that instructs me!"[5] What has been unfolded as the exertion of the self towards its own innermost realisation, has proved to be at the same time a taking hostage of the self by God for the realisation of the truth of his ordering of things.

Christian moral theory has been intrigued by Augustine's paradox about the foundational love of self realised in the love of God and its polar, also "self-love," which entrenches us at the centre of our own universe. The first self-love paves the way for genuine engagement with not-self, the second precludes any relation to not-self apart from "concupiscence." The relation to the self is un-repeatable; no other can be a self to us, nor the equivalent of a self. Unique, coming first in the order of moral responsibility, "every man is nearest to himself." Yet we are human beings like others, and our unique centre of per-ception confers no privileged moral status. When we speak of self-love in the subjective sense, we are not speaking of the self as a concrete object of love which we prefer before other objects, but of the presupposition of all love in the glad acceptance of the self's status as agent, conferred by God and exercised under God. The self makes no claim on material or spiritual goods in which it does not concede priority (of material) or equality (of spiritual goods) to the neighbour who is "as" self. And as subjective self-love is a condition of being, there is a perverse subjectivity that distorts and destroys being. Augustine's joyful explorations of this paradox never stoop to entertain the pusillanimous calculation that the interests of self and neighbour may be judiciously weighed and apportioned. *All* must be self-love — for "human beings must also be told how to love, that is, how to love themselves so as to do themselves good" — while at the same time *nothing* must be self-love, for "when it says 'all your heart, all your soul, all your mind', it leaves no part of our life free from this obligation, no part free as it were to back out and enjoy some other thing; any other object of love that enters the mind should be swept towards the same goal as that to which the whole flood of our love is directed."[6]

---

to love yourself; then I will trust you with your neighbour to love as yourself. If you have not learned how to love yourself, I am afraid you will cheat your neighbour as yourself!"

5. Augustine, *Confessions* 10.40.

6. Augustine, *De doctrina Christiana* 1.25, 22.

To think of the self as a claimant among other claimants, self-love as an interest in competition with other interests, is to leave Augustine's paradox behind and enter the world of the modern rights-possessing self. When the debate over self-love re-surfaced in the seventeenth and eighteenth centuries, this was the concept that dominated it. Joseph Butler's musing wonderment "not that men have so great regard to their own good or interest . . . for they have not enough," may appear to bring the Augustinian paradox back before us, but a moment's further reading shows that everything has changed: ". . . but that they have so little to the good of others," he goes on, making a difference between an interest in our own good and an interest in others' good which Augustine could never have countenanced. Self-love, for Butler, is distinct from other impulses of action, a "cool" affection, as he liked to call it. He thinks it only a "strange affectation" to represent "the whole of life as nothing but one continued exercise of self-love."[7] On his terms that "affectation" could mean only one thing, Epicureanism. Those who could not share Butler's confidence, on the other hand, that Epicureanism could be evaded by maintaining a proper balance of interests between self and other, had no refuge but the extravagant thesis that one might attain indifference to one's own good, even to one's salvation or damnation.[8] What earth-tremor had disturbed the grammar of self-love to throw the Augustinian paradox out of kilter?

The first shifting of the ground had occurred in the scholastic age, when Aristotle's dictum that everything seeks to prolong its own existence drew down good self-love into the magnetic field of self-preservation. At that point, of course, there was no reductionism implied in that. The essential coinherence of material and spiritual existence as the scholastics understood it was a safeguard against such a thing. By conceiving that spiritual being depended for existence on communion with a holy God, it erected a bulwark against a purely worldly notion of self-preservation, whether sensual, emotional, or intellectual. However, as the key anthropological premises fell away beneath the feet of a tottering Christendom, and the pursuits and aversions of human nature began to be thought of as instinctive animal impulses, things began to look very different. Combine a version of the scholastic proposition, "Reason postulates that each should love himself and . . . endeavour to preserve his being," with the materialist premise that "the knowledge of good or evil is nothing else than the consciousness of pleasure or pain," and it is evident that the

---

7. Butler, *Sermons* (1726; London: SPCK, 1970), Preface §29-34.

8. Thus Fénélon, of whom I have written briefly in *The Ways of Judgment* (Grand Rapids: Eerdmans, 2005), pp. 301f.

conclusion will consecrate material self-interest — not necessarily sensual, but quite definitely the welfare of the unit as opposed to the universal. "No virtue can be conceived prior to the virtue of self-preservation" — so wrote Spinoza on behalf of the "new moral science" of the mid-seventeenth century.[9] The results, garnered up by Adam Smith in his well-known theory of providence, survive like mammoth-tusks fossilised in the rock-strata of our contemporary moral landscape.

A certain clarity is brought to the paradox of self-love if we understand the elementary forms of self-love, negative and positive, as faith and faithlessness. Believing that we are loved precedes our loving. The self is held before our mind because we have learned that we are ourselves the objects of God's demanding and perfecting love. No love for any object we could imagine could be grounded other than on that love, in which we are (from our own point of view, at least) the first beloved. We cannot overlook where we stand; love of God and neighbour is not absent-minded, but self-aware. But precisely because God's love is the ground of our active self, it presents itself to us as a call; it demands of us the effort of existence, and does not allow us to remain where we are.[10] The challenge to responsibility is always heard within it. That is why faith, in the Reformers' view, is necessarily both passive and active.

It is therefore no adequate response to the paradox of self-love to take the gift of self for granted, forget it, and focus our whole attention on the world, as was urged by those advocates of "self-forgetfulness" who thronged the literature a century ago.[11] The only meaning we could assign to this proposal would be to wrap the gift of agency in a napkin and bury it rather than venture upon the exchange of life. Augustine's elaboration of the paradox of the reflexive self was prompted precisely by the need to underpin the moral imperatives at the root of his conversion. To assume a commanding point of view from which all else in the universe appeared to us, but we ourselves did not appear, that would indeed be the false self-love that presumed on its own ontological security, denying its call to engage actively in world and time.[12]

9. Benedict de Spinoza, *Ethica ordine geometrico demonstrata* 4.8, 18, 22.

10. Cf. Karol Wojtyła, *Person and Community* (New York: Peter Lang, 1993), p. 198: "Action is what most fully and profoundly reveals the human being as an I — indeed, as a person, for that which we express in categories of being by the concept 'person' is given in experience precisely as a self, as an I."

11. For example, Kenneth Kirk, *The Vision of God* (London: Longmans Green, 1931).

12. As John Milbank expressed it, discussing Kant: "the 'I' is essentially a pure *noumenon*. . . . We may not see angels, but out of the corner of our eye we glimpse our own angelic outline" (*The Future of Love: Essays in Political Theology* [London: S.C.M. Press, 2009],

OLIVER O'DONOVAN

Freedom

Modernity generated two rival myths-of-origin about the individual and society, both constructivist. According to the one the individual constructed society, according to the other society constructed the individual. Each took one pole of the dialectic for granted and problematised the other. What we call "individualism" is thus a theory of how *society* is generated; "social behaviourism," on the other hand, is an account of *individual self-consciousness*. Contractarians interest themselves in politics, social behaviourists in psychology. A Christian belief which understands the self as summoned forth in active faith by the deeds and words of God can settle with neither myth, for it takes neither of the two poles for granted. Agency conferred by God cannot withdraw into the status of a presupposition. Arising from God's gift and call, it is a focus of questioning; no questions can be begged about it, not even whether it is singular or plural. It is always to be sought after, prayed for, appropriated with new thanksgivings for deliverance, both in its individual form, as "person," and in its communitarian form, as "church."

The two myths display their constructivist character in the difficulty either has in locating or describing freedom. It was the tragedy of that late-twentieth-century reassertion of the individual, commonly called "neoliberalism," that it hoped to save freedom by locating it at the beginning of everything, only to find that this denied it any way of describing and elaborating the conditions of freedom. Its rhetoric reduced freedom to a geometrical point, a private energy lying behind all social forms, an undifferentiated impulse with no lived dimensions. If talk of freedom is to have substance, it has to imagine how it can be exercised in a sustainable social order. It cannot realise freedom through declarations of a protological kind, any more than Marxism could through declarations of an eschatological kind. Neoliberalism, indeed, ended up with a curious looking-glass version of the Marxist Utopia: instead of the state withering away to leave society, society withered away to leave the state, which now, however, rested on nothing more solid than an aggregation of supposed individual preferences. Our contemporary difficulty in shoring up the authority of governments to resist the voracious appetite of a consumer-electorate springs from the neoliberal legacy, which cut solid social ground from under governments' feet.

---

p. 191). He continues: "We may not commune with angels, but to act ethically is to act with other human spirits in an angelic kingdom of ends, where we need not take account of goals and consequences — not out of a kind of moral priggishness . . . but because here there are no ends and consequences."

It was never a sufficient objection to individualism that there was no point being free unless one were "free for" something. For that did not put to rest the anxiety that freedom may be hi-jacked in service of some alienating social goal: "freedom for" can always veil totalitarian aims. When rival claims pursue rival goals, the defence of freedom means securing social conditions in which the ground of each claim may be made apparent. The exercise of freedom requires understanding. So the right way to put the objection is that freedom cannot be secured except as *evoked by a comprehensible good*. Freedom requires its goals, its material social content, and also its vocation. Freedom needs to find fulfilment *in and through* the fulfilling of social goals. To be "free for" anything is to be "satisfied in" that thing, which implies a measuring of the agent-self against its goals, but that cannot be derived circularly from the goals themselves. Only if cooperation is a comprehensible good as such, can we find satisfaction in cooperating with those whose social goals are not our own. Something stands behind freedom, some destining of every agent that calls it to be true to itself in community with other agencies. Freedom shrinks as we lose the capacity to imagine ourselves within the wider common agency.

The acting self, then, needs a depth and dimension, a reflexivity to see itself in a social context, carrying within its knowledge of itself a knowledge of the world beyond. Everything turns on what the self, in its "inner space," contains. The pin-point self, *homo oeconomicus* reduced to a single impulse, is simply not equipped for the exercise of freedom. The free self must be richly related, capable of satisfaction in its undertakings and so reflective, an agency that can "appropriate" itself. This is what the Reformers' thesis of the priority of faith intended in denying that any agency can please God which has not been received from God by faith as a gift of grace. The content of the self which gives agency its purchase on the world is the call of God that summons the self out into existence, responsive to the multiple gifts and purposes of God for his world.

In the opposite myth, that of the socially constructed self, it appears that such an elaborated and receptive self is on offer. But the appearance is deceptive. The interest, as we have said, is to account for the individual self, and in the service of that interest society is viewed not as an agent-self in its own right but as an "organism" *out of which* agency and selfhood are spun. Agency is therefore a product; but this reduces it to a function, allowing no accommodation for the agent's own conception of his or her agency. In representing thought as a subjective experience accompanying social processes, the myth cannot avoid making redundant whatever it is we *think* we are doing when we act. The supposed social rationality of thought never meets up with its intentional content. The way the mind frames the world it looks out on is an irrelevance. But that means that freedom has no place in action, for we certainly have no freedom if we do not know what is up with us when we think we act.

The thesis of the social construction of the self is most persuasively read as a thesis about how the individual self becomes morally mature through the interplay of self and society. From the classic text of Mead we can learn some useful if pedestrian lessons of this sort: that socialisation is not only a question of adapting ourselves to society but of finding ways to adapt society to ourselves, that being in touch with social reality need not suppress our originality, and that we may laugh when someone falls over but should be sympathetic if he has really hurt himself.[13] From one angle and another freedom takes form as a capacity to act within an exchange of symbolic communication. But whose is this freedom? To what can we ascribe the capacity to act? Mead answers the problem in terms of his well-known distinction between the "I" and the "Me": the I responds to stimuli, the Me belongs within the field of stimuli; the I is subjective, the Me objectified, and so on.[14] But since with the passage of time the I passes into the Me, and not *vice versa,* and since it is the Me, not the I, that absorbs the attitudes of others into the self, it appears that the I is simply an aspect of the self which got forgotten in the original thesis that the self was socially constructed. The I appears as a *deus ex machina* lowered onto the stage of the social self precisely to supply what it lacked, which is to say, freedom.

As we have complained, then, of the state-positivism of the individualist construct, so we must complain of the self-positivism of the social construct. What is lacking from it is a We — not an Us, an *object* of engagement, a social aspect of the objectified Me, but a genuine subject-We which is an *accompanying condition* of the freedom of an I. To be free is not merely to *have* an agent's point of view on the world, but to *share* one. Such a point of view, indeed, can only be had as it is shared. The active self is plural as well as singular, and is so from its very inception. It cannot think of itself without a neighbour except by reducing itself to become a passive receptor of impressions; as soon as it recalls its agency, it participates in shared perspectives. Agency is operative within the field of common meanings and purposes, of communication and participation. This is summed up by saying that God's gift of other people is not "society," an objective whole of which we can take a view, but "community," in which we can only participate. Community is communication: not a

13. G. H. Mead, *Mind, Self and Society* (Chicago: University of Chicago Press, 1934), p. 206.

14. Mead, *Mind, Self and Society,* pp. 196-200.

container, but a field of shared space and context. The active self, from its first calling forth, must participate in that field, and therefore must take the measure of it in love and understanding.

The Neighboured Self

Here there is a second stage in the self's objectification of itself and love of itself. If the elementary motions of self-love are best characterised as faith and faithlessness, the world of the self's observation and understanding now reflects the self back to itself as an object of love alongside other objects of love. In my first naive wonder at the world I fail to notice that the pair of eyes through which I see it are themselves a part of the world I see. I see cities, mountains, books and people, questions and answers, problems and triumphs, but I do not see my eyes. But as I interrogate each thing about its connexions to other things, I come across myself among the things that are in the world. I find I am a factor in the world's events. I trace the connexions back to the eyes through which I look: — How are my eyes like other eyes? What is it that eyes generally show us and fail to show us? What difference do eyes make to what they see? How did they get where they are, and where, precisely, is that? And so I come to understand that my observation is also a thing observed, and as such cannot be excluded from the judgment pronounced by God upon all that he has made that it is very good. My gaze rests on myself with what tradition has called *amor complacentiae,* "love of complacence," but this is no longer myself as agent, but as a thing among other things within the good world that God has made. "Love what in you God has made," as Augustine repeatedly tells us. And as I locate myself within God's world, I observe others like me. For to understand a thing — any thing — is to see it as one of a kind, and to understand oneself is to observe a kind to which one belongs. Self-love as ordered by knowledge of an ordered world is love of a kind — not a "species" in the reductive biological sense defined solely by animal characteristics, but a kind constituted through self-awareness and agency. And so there emerges into view as the object of loving knowledge the self's inevitable companion, the neighbour, the other member of the kind, always and from the beginning "as yourself." The self finds itself alongside other selves, beside them in a situation of fundamental equality and reciprocity, the object of their gaze as they are the object of its. That moment of reflexive self-discovery in the gaze of others is a disconcerting one, characteristically accompanied by blushing. For whom, or what, do we blush? For ourselves, certainly, but for ourselves as others see us, ourselves as we have only now learned to see ourselves. We blush because we find we have lost sight of ourselves when we were mere things-in-the-world, mortal creatures, other people's other people. At that moment of discovery there opens up a possibility of loving ourselves with what the tradition calls *amor benevolentiae*, "love of benevolence." "Have mercy on your own soul," Augustine liked to quote the Vulgate of Sirach 30:24, "pleasing God."

Of this moment of self-awareness, overcoming the temptations of solipsism, much has been said. One thing which might seem unnecessary to say, but is not, is that it must be self-conscious. We cannot arrive at ourselves by default. "Only be yourself!" the enthusers tell us, as though the whole trick of living were to give less attention and less study than we are used to bringing to the tasks of life! But to see ourself *alongside* the neighbour, to see the neighbour *as* ourself, this is no spontaneous observation, but requires care and consideration. When Jesus warned, "everyone who exalts himself will be humbled, and he who humbles himself will be exalted" (Luke 14:11), he spoke apparently of two alternative mistakes and not only one, a false self-promotion and a false self-humiliation, both to be corrected. The reality that exposes all false pretensions catches up with us, not only to throw us down from heights of importance we have arrogated to ourselves, but to dig us up from bunkers of insignificance we have hollowed out for ourselves. Hiding like Saul among the baggage, we shall be dragged uncomfortably before those who expect something of us. Perhaps, after all, there is truth in the suggestion that the two faults meet up behind the curtain, that modest invisibility is not all that different from boastful self-promotion. Whether publicising oneself or shrinking from publicity, one hopes to avoid the candid gaze that sees through one's self-image. What is required of us is that we know ourselves as we are known. To refuse self-knowledge is to refuse to find ourselves within the world God loves and to love ourselves for the sake of God's love for us.

This moment of self-awareness has often been taken to be the decisive moment for morality, the threshold of moral awareness.[15] Over this claim we may hesitate. What kind of threshold must it be, if it is to have such weight? Not only a threshold in the way we see *ourself,* but in the way we see *the world* as a result of seeing ourselves within it. There is here, it is suggested, a total shift from subjective perception to objective perception, from an "inside" point of view to an "outside" point of view. As Thomas Nagel describes it, the "objective" is the viewpoint in which we "raise our understanding to a new level (as) we

15. Cf. Robert Spaemann, *Persons,* trans. Oliver O'Donovan (Oxford: Oxford University Press, 2006), p. 184.

examine that relation between the world and ourselves which is responsible for our prior understanding, and form a new conception that includes a more detached understanding of ourselves, of the world, and of the interaction between them."[16] Three proposals stand out from this summary, which are taken to belong together: (i) a distinction between two ways of learning, "accumulating information" and "raising our understanding to a new level"; (ii) a reflective moment in which we take our own viewpoint into the field of knowledge; (iii) the description of this moment as "detachment." Accepting the first proposal, that there is indeed a threshold between the acquisition of knowledge and understanding, we have to ask whether the second proposal accounts for it and whether the third proposal accounts for the second.

"The natural place to begin," Nagel tells us, "is with our own position in the world," a sentence whose awkward construction betrays the problem with its apparent self-evidence: "begin with," or "begin from"?[17] It is not at all "natural" (in the sense of "unreflective" or "untutored") to begin *with* our own position in the world. That we even have an "own position" is not something that a naive knowledge will recognise; it is discovered through reflection. What we begin "with" is the world itself, presenting itself to our wondering and uncritical gaze, and what is "natural" is to take it at face value. To question the face value, we need some interrogative skills. Nagel might better have said, "begin from . . . ," which would have been guilty of nothing worse than ironic understatement, for it is not only "natural," but quite inevitable, that our initial point of view is our own point of view. But this, too, is misleading in that it suggests the idea of "moving away from," or leaving "the personal or merely human perspective further and further behind."[18] Here there is a confusion of human *perspectives* with human *realities*. It is easy to move away from thinking of personal or human realities, less easy to move away from personal or human perspectives of thought. If in order to grasp the sheer contingency of human existence I concentrate my mind on galaxies exploding in pre-historic space, I imagine those non-human and non-personal events from the perspective of a human scientist and in a way shaped, no doubt, by human experiences of watching special effects on video-screens.

Behind this programme we detect the notorious confrontation in political philosophy between liberalism with its objective view of justice — "the perspective of eternity," as Rawls described it — and the "situated" viewpoint of commu-

---

16. Thomas Nagel, *The View from Nowhere* (Oxford: Oxford University Press, 1986), p. 5.
17. Nagel, *The View from Nowhere*, p. 13.
18. Nagel, *The View from Nowhere*, p. 6.

nitarianism. This opposition gave voice to deep-seated antinomies of thought: "subjective-objective," "inside-outside." These antinomies are difficult to elude, and yet they generate self-refuting paradoxes. If the liberal really takes an objective view of the point of view he occupies, he must actually occupy it, and not stand outside it. If the communitarian declares all points of view "situated," he seems to assume a universal point of view in doing so. What underlies these self-refutations is the common assumption that there is no "particular point of view" on the world that can ever allow us to view the world as a whole. It is not difficult to suspect that this assumption has fallen victim to its spatial metaphors.

Let us propose instead that *every* particular point of view affords a view of the whole, or, to be more modest, the promise of such a view. All perspectives are windows, and reality is to be seen and studied through them. There is no "departure," "distance," "detachment" from the point of view in which consciousness is born, which is, after all, the point of view of our bodies, which we are not free to step outside. What there may be, however, is persistent attention to what lies beyond the immediate presentations of the world, which brings more and more to light. We discover that the world is not merely a surface or a series of images; there is an "in and behind," also visible from our point of view though not immediate to it. The "objective" viewpoint, then, can only be occupied by one who still occupies the subjective viewpoint. Its form is, "I realise that I have a particular point of view on this question and recognise other factors that may weigh more heavily with other people, but it still seems to me impossible to ignore. . . . etc. etc." The only way to reach objectivity is to take note of *more,* not to take note of *less* nor to take *less note* of what one noted at first. Objectivity may, in the storms of experience, too easily be simulated by the simple expedient of changing one's mind: "I used to think that justice was worth striving for, but since I lost my court case, I have realised that justice is merely the interest of the stronger!" It is almost perilously easy to alter one's perspective; the difficult thing is to enlarge it.

The observing self can never renounce itself as a centre, which would be to renounce its observation. It can observe beyond itself, embarking on wider and more comprehensive exploration, which makes it more, not less, a "centre." Does this claim for knowledge have the character of an imperial conquest, referring realities on the periphery back to a centre which controls and dominates? Once again, the problem lies with the spatial analogies. "Centre" is a misleading notion if we think of just one centre of one universe. The discovery of the world is precisely the discovery of other "centres," other viewpoints that are irreducibly plural. Other centres do not mean no centres, nor that this centre which is mine is capable of being exchanged for another. The paradox in the idea of seeing myself as others see me, an object among other objects and my neighbour's neighbour, is that I feel myself at the same time as agent and object. My proposition is not the straightforward one, "Here is another member of the species *homo sapiens*," but the more interesting and complex one, "This member of the species *homo sapiens* is, as it happens, identical with the self that I am." From that proposition we may derive the genuinely important inference, "It is not similarity of others to myself that is in view, but the same incomparable uniqueness."[19] Or, as C. S. Lewis nicely put it: not "I'm no more special than anyone else," but "everyone is as special as me."[20]

Rejecting the notion of "detachment" from Nagel's thesis, then, we are left with the question whether the qualitative threshold of thought, which makes the difference between accumulated knowledge and understanding, is attained simply by the reflective turn to the self, taking one's own point of view into the field of vision. To which we must reply that, if we have broken with the idea that self-awareness is a kind of prison we must break out from, there is no reason any longer to focus on this element in the complex knowledge of the world and its relationships. The threshold is not attained by knowing just one thing, but as we conceive and explore the relations of things, setting our minds to seek wisdom. This is a theme we must leave for another occasion. But a preliminary conclusion may be offered: it is a prerogative of Christian moral wisdom, perhaps, not to be hung up by the self and the obsessive potential of self-consciousness, whether negative or positive, but to teach us to "think judiciously . . ." of ourselves (Rom. 12:3), which is the very opposite of thinking discontently and anxiously.

Homo, cognosce te ipsum!

Self-knowledge and self-love must be purely formal apart from the order of creation that gives substance to the likeness and "alongsideness" of self and neighbour. "As myself" must be *in some respect,* and it is of decisive importance what that respect is. Christian understanding, speaking with the voice of a humanism made possible by monotheism, has said that my neighbour is my equal *as man.*[21]

"Anthropocentrism" is something to disapprove of these days. After a long

19. Spaemann, *Persons,* p. 185.
20. *Letters of C. S. Lewis,* ed. W. H. Lewis (London: Bles, 1966), p. 242.
21. Every English speaker is aware of the embarrassment of lacking a concrete noun equivalent to the Latin *homo* or the German *Mensch.* I trust readers not to blame me personally for this well-known linguistic deficit, and not to ask me to confuse what should be clear by adopting one of the inadequate expedients commonly used to compensate for it.

period in when the moral high-ground was occupied by a nihilism that called itself "humanism," a swing of philosophical fashion brought about a general loss of nerve concerning the human race. The sin of "speciesism" has been added to the indefinitely expanding catalogue of unjust discriminations. But a concept of practical reason must be anthropocentric in one sense of the word, at least, for the human agent thinking into the world as a sphere of action necessarily takes him- or herself as the baseline. An objective non-participational point of view on the universe of goods is not accessible — not, at any rate, to us. We see ourselves situated "in the middle" of the cosmic order, as in the eighth Psalm, with the angels above us and the animals below us, a bridge between spiritual and material worlds. That is the point of view that opens up before us as we engage with the world practically. Reflective enough to understand that there could in principle be other points of view, we must also be reflective enough to understand why no such point of view could ever be our own. The imagination of a universe where man is not in the centre is the speculation of a "post-humanism" which begins by repudiating human self-knowledge and human experience. Nothing is achieved for other kinds of creature by doubting man's conception of his position in the scheme of things, for such doubt is not prompted by attention to other creatures, but by uneasy self-preoccupation with man's capacity to change himself. Post-humanism is anti-humanism, and anti-humanism is a variety of anthropocentrism. There are better varieties of anthropocentrism, which allow more scope for humility before the complex wonder of non-human creation and for responsibility for how we treat it.[22] There is the Book of Job, for example, which explores the animal kingdom's independence of mankind precisely by calling Job to answer before his, and its, creator.

If we refuse to speak of a human kind, we shall certainly not be able to speak to any purpose of equality. Without a "kind" in which all human beings participate the sense of the neighbour as moral equal has no purchase. Equality, as we have learned it in the Western moral tradition, is co-humanity. Yet since that tradition understands human nature in a many-layered way, as physical, sensitive, animal, rational, and so on, the question has easily been put whether equality between any two members of the human species is due to their membership of a common biological kind or to something else that they may possibly share with other kinds — a "rational nature," perhaps, as Kant speculated, or (a more popular alternative with those who believe they have overcome "the essence of man") sensitivity to pain, since "the same things as cause me to suffer

22. There are important insights about the question of anthropocentrism at the hymnic climax of C. S. Lewis's novel, *Perelandra* (London: Bodley Head, 1943).

cause him to suffer."[23] In fact, as Spaemann has well insisted, it is not regard for some common competence that elicits recognition of equality, but fellow-membership of a community. As love ordered by knowledge is due to itself, so it is due to the community where ordered love is conceived and communicated, and due to it from itself. Ordered love is due not in respect of a feature which we recognise and admire separately in each instance — due to her because she has it, due to me because I have it, due to porpoises if, and to the extent that, they have it. Ordered love is not so distributed. It is what we, as a community, communicate. We owe equal love to each other because we communicate with each other in something we either share together equally or do not have at all.

If the idea of human equality is cut off from that of co-humanity, then, two consequences follow for our moral thinking. First, a jungle of new and unsuspected duties springs up to bar our path. Mainly new duties to animals, in the first instance: there is an organisation, we are told, that campaigns for "fair trials for dogs." But that is simple want of imagination, since there is no good reason left to take the likenesses between human and animal species with greater seriousness than those between humans and non-animals. Hume's sarcastic illustration of the sapling that "murders" its parent tree thus returns as a genuine moral difficulty: why should arboreal parricide be less weighty a crime than human parricide, or arboricide than zoocide? Let us be quite clear: there are certainly duties in respect of animals, and (why not?) of plants, too. We can know enough about the way in which different living species flourish and suffer harm to know what kinds of use will foster their well-being and what treatment of them is consistent with care for the world God made. When we read of dolphins killed in drag-nets, of battery hens denied the possibility of walking on two legs, or of ancient oaks felled to make motorways, we feel a justified guilt on behalf of our race. But these are not relations of *equality,* for they are not relations of reciprocity. We cannot without lunacy demand that equal respect be paid to us by trees. Our responsibility for them is unilateral.

In the same way there could be no relations of equality with superior beings such as angels. But what if we imagine a species wholly different from us biologically (and so inaccessible for intermarriage) yet possessing more or less comparable powers of reason, with which we could communicate fully and at will by speech? There is nothing intrinsically impossible in this imagination, which has been widely explored in fiction.[24] Are we not told

---

23. R. M. Hare, *Freedom and Reason* (Oxford: Clarendon Press, 1963), p. 222.

24. For instance, and with serious philosophical intent, by C. S. Lewis in *Out of the Silent Planet* (London: Bodley Head, 1938).

these days that evolution proceeds by distant species developing the same traits independently? As far as we know, of course, it is counter-factual, and so does nothing to undermine the assertion that duties of equality and reciprocity are owing to all members, and only to members, of our human kind. But if it were one day to prove factual, we should simply conclude that the "kind" that laid claim on us was constituted not by one biological species alone but by the intercommunicating *ensemble* of two or more species. A kind it would still be, but one in which we participated on equal terms with members of our own and members of the other participating species. We might call it, in C. S. Lewis's invented term *hnau*, or with Kant, "rational being" — but the point either way would be that *community* of the kinds founded duties of equality, not the regard we felt for rational powers as such or for speech as such.[25]

The other and more immediately threatening consequence is that the idea of equality no longer supports duties we know we owe to other human beings. This is true especially of duties of "attributive justice" (to use Grotius's term), obligations to treat people in certain ways on the basis of special aptitudes or needs: scholarships for able students, jobs for competent applicants, milk for growing babies, materials and tools for willing workers, medical care for the sick and elderly, and so on. There are still those who believe (and expect to be admired for it!) that no child should be educated beyond a level to which every child can aspire to. This type of egalitarianism is an utter confusion, failing to grasp human equality as a matter of being equally human, which of itself demands a diversity of kinds of engagement. Human participants, variously endowed, are equal before death, before social communication, and before judgment. Their lives, their capacity to occupy a place in society, their responsibility for what they do is of equal weight and makes equal demands on others in the face of all variants.[26] But precisely these foundational equalities allow variants to develop without subjugating some human beings to others. Practical respect for them allows attributive justice to respond to variations with differences of treatment consistent with equality but not derived from it. Differentiation is a principle underlying all cultural growth and enrichment, for persons and for societies. On this matter, too, we had better come to know ourselves.

---

25. On this, cf. Spaemann, *Persons*, pp. 236-248, and especially p. 248: "Yet if there exist within the universe other natural species of living beings possessing an inner life of sentience, whose adult members usually command rationality and self-awareness, we would have to acknowledge *not only those instances but all instances* of that species to be persons."

26. On this, see my remarks in *The Ways of Judgment*, pp. 31-51.

Publications by Oliver O'Donovan

BOOKS

The Problem of Self-Love in Saint Augustine (New Haven, CT: Yale University Press, 1980; reprint: Eugene, OR: Wipf & Stock, 2006).

Begotten or Made? (Oxford: Oxford University Press, 1984, 2002).

Resurrection and Moral Order: An Outline for Evangelical Ethics (Grand Rapids: Eerdmans, and Leicester, UK: IVP-Apollos, 1986, 1994); French translation: *Resurrection et l'Expérience Morale*, tr. J. Y. Lacoste (Paris: Presses Universitaires de France, 1992).

On the Thirty-Nine Articles: A Conversation with Tudor Christianity (Exeter and Carlisle, UK: Paternoster Press, 1986, 1993; London, SCM, 2011).

Peace and Certainty: A Theological Essay on Deterrence (Oxford: Oxford University Press, and Grand Rapids: Eerdmans, 1989).

The Desire of the Nations: Rediscovering the Roots of Political Theology (Cambridge: Cambridge University Press, 1996).

From Irenaeus to Grotius: A Sourcebook in Christian Political Thought (Grand Rapids: Eerdmans, 1999), ed. with Joan Lockwood O'Donovan.

Common Objects of Love: Moral Reflection and the Shaping of Community (Grand Rapids: Eerdmans, 2002).

The Just War Revisited (Cambridge: Cambridge University Press, 2003).

Bonds of Imperfection: Christian Politics Past and Present (Grand Rapids: Eerdmans, 2004), with Joan Lockwood O'Donovan.

The Ways of Judgment (Grand Rapids: Eerdmans, 2005).

Church in Crisis: The Gay Controversy and the Anglican Communion (Eugene, OR: Cascade Books, 2008).

A Conversation Waiting to Begin: The Gay Controversy and the Anglican Communion (London: SCM, 2009).

The Word in Small Boats: Sermons from Oxford (Grand Rapids: Eerdmans, 2010).
Self, World, and Time. Vol. 1 of *Ethics as Theology* (Grand Rapids: Eerdmans 2013).

BOOKLETS

The Christian and the Unborn Child (Nottingham, UK: Grove Books, 1972).
In Pursuit of a Christian View of War (Nottingham, UK: Grove Books, 1977).
Measure for Measure: Justice in Punishment and the Sentence of Death (Nottingham, UK: Grove Books, 1977).
Marriage and Permanence (Nottingham, UK: Grove Books, 1978).
Transsexualism and Christian Marriage (Nottingham, UK: Grove Books, 1982); 2nd ed., entitled *Transsexualism: Issues and Argument* (Cambridge: Grove Books, 2007).
Principles in the Public Realm (Oxford: Oxford University Press, 1983).
Peace and War: A Debate about Pacifism (Nottingham, UK: Grove Books, 1985), with Ronald Sider.
Liturgy & Ethics (Nottingham, UK: Grove Books, 1993).

CONTRIBUTIONS TO COLLECTIONS

"Marriage and the Family." In *Obeying Christ in a Changing World,* Vol. 3: *The Changing World,* ed. Bruce Kaye (Glasgow: Fountain, 1977), pp. 94-114.
"The Natural Ethic." In *Essays in Evangelical Social Ethics,* ed. D. F. Wright (Exeter, UK: Paternoster, 1979), pp. 19-35.
"Again: Who Is a Person?" In *Abortion and the Sanctity of Human Life,* ed. J. H. Channer (Exeter, UK: Paternoster, 1985), pp. 125-137.
"The Reasonable Man." In *The Rationality of Religious Belief: Essays in Honour of Basil Mitchell,* ed. W. J. Abraham and S. W. Holzer (Oxford: Oxford University Press, 1987), pp. 1-15.
"Discussing Homosexuality with St. Paul: A Theological and Pastoral Approach." In *A Crisis of Understanding: Homosexuality and the Canadian Church,* ed. Denyse O'Leary (Burlington, ON: Welch, 1988), pp. 51-61.
"Begotten or Made?" In *The Ethics of Reproductive Technology,* ed. Kenneth D. Alpern (Oxford: Oxford University Press, 1992), pp. 195-202.
"Evangelicalism and the Foundations of Ethics." In *Evangelical Anglicans,* ed. R. T. France and A. E. McGrath (London: SPCK, 1993), pp. 96-107.
"A Summons to Reality." In *Understanding "Veritatis Splendor,"* ed. J. Wilkins (London: SPCK, 1994), pp. 41-45.
"Reading the Saint Andrew's Day Statement." In *Anglican Life and Witness: A Reader for the Lambeth Conference of Anglican Bishops 1998,* ed. Chris Sugden and Vinay Samuel (London: SPCK, 1997), pp. 38-51.
"Homosexuality in the Church: Can There Be a Fruitful Theological Debate?" In *The*

Way Forward? Christian Voices on Homosexuality and the Church, ed. Timothy Bradshaw (London: Hodder & Stoughton, 1997, 2003), pp. 20-36.

"The Death-Penalty in 'Evangelium Vitae.'" In *Ecumenical Ventures in Ethics: Protestants Engage Pope John Paul II's Moral Encyclical,* ed. Reinhard Hütter and Theodor Dieter (Grand Rapids: Eerdmans, 1998), pp. 216-236.

"War by Other Means." In *Some Corner of a Foreign Field: Intervention and World Order,* ed. Roger Williamson (London: Macmillan, 1998), pp. 87-98.

"Keeping Body and Soul Together." In *On Moral Medicine,* ed. Stephen E. Lammers and Allen Verhey, 2nd ed. (Grand Rapids: Eerdmans, 1998), pp. 223-238.

"Again, Who Is a Person?" In *On Moral Medicine,* ed. Stephen E. Lammers and Allen Verhey, 2nd ed. (Grand Rapids: Eerdmans, 1998), pp. 380-386.

"In a Glass Darkly." In *On Moral Medicine,* ed. Stephen E. Lammers and Allen Verhey, 2nd ed. (Grand Rapids: Eerdmans, 1998), pp. 496-504.

"Political Theology, Tradition and Modernity." In *The Cambridge Companion to Liberation Theology,* ed. Christopher Rowland (Cambridge: Cambridge University Press, 1999), pp. 235-247.

"Het evangelie en christelijke ethiek." In *Christelijke Ethiek: Een inleiding met sleutelteksten,* ed. G. G. de Kruijf (Zoetermeer: Meinema, 1999), pp. 80-95.

"Publicity." In *Dumbing Down: Culture, Politics and the Mass Media,* ed. Ivo Mosley Thorverton (Imprint Academic, 2000), pp. 181-198.

"Freedom and Reality." In *Theology after Liberalism: A Reader,* ed. John Webster and George P. Schner (Oxford: Blackwell, 2000), pp. 132-151.

"Where Were You?" In *The Care of Creation,* ed. R. J. Berry (Leicester, UK: Inter-Varsity Press, 2000), pp. 90-94.

"John Finnis on Moral Absolutes." In *The Revival of Natural Law: Philosophical, Theological, and Ethical Responses to the Finnis-Grisez School,* ed. Nigel Biggar and Rufus Black (Aldershot, UK: Ashgate, 2001), pp. 111-128.

"Homosexuality in the Church: Can There Be a Fruitful Theological Debate?" In *Theology and Sexuality: Classic and Contemporary Readings,* ed. Eugene F. Rogers, Jr. (Oxford: Blackwell, 2002), pp. 373-386.

"Die Geschichte des Texts der Geschichte: Ethik, Geschichte und Politk in der Lektüre des Deuteronomiums," trans. Bernd Wannenwetsch. In *Kirche-Ethik-Öffentlichkeit: Christliche Ethik in der Herausforderung,* ed. Wolfgang Schoberth and Ingrid Schoberth, Ethik im Theologischen Diskurs 5 (Münster: LIT-Verlag, 2002), pp. 216-232.

Response to Walter Moberly, Response to Gordon McConville, Response to Craig Bartholomew, Response to Daniel Carroll R., Response to Andrew Lincoln, Response to N. T. Wright, Response to Bernd Wannenwetsch, Response to Gerrit de Kruijf, Response to Christopher Rowland, Response to Jonathan Chaplin, Response to Colin Greene, Response to Peter Scott, Response to Joan Lockwood O'Donovan, Response to James W. Skillen. In *A Royal Priesthood? The Use of the Bible Ethically and Politically — A Dialogue with Oliver O'Donovan,* ed. Craig Bartholomew, Jonathan Chaplin, Robert Song, and Al Wolters

(Carlisle, UK: Paternoster, and Grand Rapids: Zondervan, 2002), pp. 65-68, 89-90, 113-115, 144-146, 170-172, 194-195, 221-224, 238-240, 255-258, 309-313, 341-343, 374-376, 395-397, 418-420.

"Keeping Body and Soul Together." In *Covenants of Life*, ed. Kenneth L. Vaux, Sarah Vaux, and Mark Stenberg (Dordrecht: Kluwer, 2002), pp. 35-56.

"Christianity and Territorial Right." In *States, Nations, and Borders: The Ethics of Making Boundaries*, ed. Allen Buchanan and Margaret Moore (Cambridge: Cambridge University Press, 2003), pp. 127-139.

"'Establishment': State-Church Relations in England." In *Religionsfreiheit als Leitbild: Staatskirchenrecht in Deutschland und Europa im Prozess der Reform*, ed. Hartmut Kreß (Münster: LIT-Verlag, 2004), pp. 275-292.

"Law, Moderation and Forgiveness." In *Church as Politeia: The Political Self-Understanding of Christianity*, ed. Christoph Stumpf and Holger Zaborowski (Berlin: de Gruyter, 2004), pp. 1-11.

"Political Theology." In *God's Advocates: Christian Thinkers in Conversation*, by Rupert Shortt (London: Darton, Longman & Todd, 2005), pp. 248-272 (with Joan Lockwood O'Donovan and Rupert Shortt).

"All Authority Is from God" and "Fellow-Citizens with the Saints." In *Pilgrims and Citizens: Christian Social Engagement in East Asia Today*, ed. Michael Nai-Chiu Poon (Wayville, South Australia, Australia: ATF Press, 2006), pp. 81-91, 193-196.

"What Can Ethics Know about God?" In *The Doctrine of God and Theological Ethics*, ed. Alan J. Torrance and Michael Banner (London: T&T Clark, 2006), pp. 33-46.

"Une communauté morale?" and "Contrainte sur les croyances morales dans l'Etat constitutionel." In *Sujet moral et communauté*, ed. Denis Müller, Michael Sherwin, OP, Nathalie Maillard, and Craig Steven Titus (Fribourg: Academic Press, 2007), pp. 99-110, 260-273.

Foreword to *On Rowan Williams: Critical Essays*, ed. Matheson Russell (Eugene, OR: Wipf & Stock, 2009).

"Bonhoeffer's 'Past.'" In *Who Am I? Bonhoeffer's Theology through His Poetry*, ed. Bernd Wannenwetsch (London: T&T Clark, 2009), pp. 31-45.

"Deliberation, Reflection and Responsibility." In *The Grandeur of Reason*, ed. Peter Candler and Conor Cunningham (London: S.C.M., 2010).

"How Can We Frame the Right Questions?" In *Human Sexuality and the Nuptial Mystery*, ed. Roy R. Jeal (Eugene, OR: Wipf & Stock, 2010).

"Interpreting the Theological Criteria of Moral Thinking." In *What Am I Doing When I Do Moral Theology?* International Colloquium, Studia Moralia Supplemento 5, xlix, 1 (Rome: Editiones Academiae Alfonsianae, 2011), pp. 73-97.

"Lesen und Gehorsam." In *Wie kommt die Bible in die Ethik? Beiträge zu einer Grundfrage theologischer Ethik*, ed. Marco Hofheinz, Frank Mathwig, and Matthias Zeindler (Zürich: Theologischer Verlag, 2011), pp. 229-242.

Journal Articles

"Christian Morals and Pagan Society." *Christian Graduate* 25, no. 4 (1972): 99-104.

"Style and Genre in Ephesians." *TSF Bulletin* 64 (1972): 12-16.

"The Possibility of a Biblical Ethic." *TSF Bulletin* 67 (1973): 15-23.

"The Old Testament and Moral Change." *Tyndale Bulletin* 25 (1974).

"Wealth." *New Fire* 4 (1976): 73-77.

"Towards an Interpretation of Biblical Ethics." *Tyndale Bulletin* 27 (1976): 54-78.

"*Usus* and *Fruitio* in Augustine, *De doctrina Christiana* I." *Journal of Theological Studies* 33 (1982): 361-397.

"Transsexualism and Christian Marriage." *Journal of Religious Ethics* 11 (1983): 135-162.

"Chastity." *The Furrow* 36 (1986): 727-735.

"The Political Thought of the Book of Revelation." *Tyndale Bulletin* 37 (1986): 61-94.

"A nouveau: Qui est une personne?" (trans. J.-Y. Lacoste). *Revue Catholique Internationale Communio* 11, no. 3 (1986): 104-117.

"Augustine's *City of God* XIX and Western Political Thought." *Dionysius* 11 (1987): 89-110.

"Moral Disagreement as an Ecumenical Issue." *Studies in Christian Ethics* 1 (1988): 5-19.

"Obituary: Paul Ramsey (1913-88)." *Studies in Christian Ethics* 1 (1988): 82-90.

"The Loss of a Sense of Place." *Irish Theological Quarterly* 55 (1989): 39-58.

"How Can Theology Be Moral?" *Journal of Religious Ethics* 17, no. 2 (1989): 81-94.

"Karl Barth and Ramsey's 'Uses of Power.'" *Journal of Religious Ethics* 19, no. 2 (1991): 1-30.

"John Finnis on Moral Absolutes." *Studies in Christian Ethics* 6, no. 2 (1993): 50-66.

"Pour une éthique évangélique" (trans. F. Mathieu). *Revue Catholique Internationale Communio* 18, no. 5 (1993): 12-22.

"Ne pas séparer l'âme du corps" (trans. M. B. Mesnet). *Éthique* 11 (1994): 64-89.

"Gerechtigkeit und Urteil," trans. Bernd Wannenwetsch. *Neue Zeitschrift für Systematische Theologie und Religionsphilosophie* 40, no. 1 (1998): 1-16.

"Response to Respondents: Behold the Lamb!" *Studies in Christian Ethics* 11, no. 2 (1998): 91-110.

"Government as Judgment." *First Things* 92 (1999): 36-44.

"The Concept of Publicity." *Studies in Christian Ethics* 13, no. 1 (2000): 18-32.

"Payback: Thinking about Retribution." *Books & Culture* (July-August 2000): 16-21.

"Deliberation, History and Reading: A Response to Schweiker and Wolterstorff." *Scottish Journal of Theology* 54, no. 1 (2001): 127-144.

"Law, Moderation and Forgiveness." *Gregorianum* 82, no. 4 (2001): 625-636.

"The Conjoined Twins." *Medicine, Science and the Law* 42, no. 4 (2002): 280-284.

"Wer ist eine Person?" (trans. Holger Zaborowski). *Internationale Katholische Zeitschrift Communio* 32 (2003): 201-214.

"J. S. Bachs musikalische Darstellung der Taufe Jesu" (trans. Holger Zaborowski). *Internationale Katholische Zeitschrift Communio* 34 (2005): 68-75; English: "Bach's Musical Treatment of Jesus' Baptism." *Communio: International Catholic Review* 32, no. 1 (2005): 119-127 (with Matthew O'Donovan).

"Scripture and Christian Ethics." *Theologia Reformata* 48, no. 2 (2005): 121-129.

"What Kind of Community is the Church? Hooker Lectures 2005." *Ecclesiology* 3, no. 2 (2007): 171-193.

"The Object of Theological Ethics." *Studies in Christian Ethics* 20 (2007): 203-214.

"Judgment, Tradition and Reason: A Response." *Political Theology* 9, no. 3 (2008): 391-409.

"Reflections on Pluralism." *Princeton Seminary Bulletin* 29 (2008): 54-66. Reprinted: *Kuyper Center Review* 1 (2010): 1-13.

"A Response." *Ecclesiology* 5 (2009): 93-94.

"The Language of Rights and Conceptual History." *Journal of Religious Ethics* 37, no. 2 (2009): 193-208.

"Prayer and Morality in the Sermon on the Mount." *Studies in Christian Ethics* 22 (2009): 21-33.

"The Path." *American Journal of Jurisprudence* 61 (2011): 1-16.

"Providence and Prudence." *Journal of Law, Philosophy and Culture* 6, no. 1 (2011): 1-16.

"The Future of Theological Ethics." *Studies in Christian Ethics* 25, no. 2 (2012): 186-98.

MAGAZINE ARTICLES

"Is It a Natural Alternative?" *Insight* (Wycliffe College, Toronto, Canada) 4 (1978): 6-7.

"New Trends in Christian Initiation — Solution or Problem?" *Insight* (Wycliffe College, Toronto, Canada) (1979): 4-5.

"Wycliffe College Graduation Dinner." *Insight* (Wycliffe College, Toronto, Canada) 12 (1982): 8-9.

"Remembrance Sunday." *Third Way* 6, no. 10 (November 1983): 6-7.

"Hope for a MAD World." *Third Way* 9, no. 8 (August 1986): 10-13; 9, no. 9 (September 1986): 22-24.

"War or Peace? A Delicate Moral Choice." *The Tablet*, 7 December 1990.

"Were We Right to Fight?" *The Tablet*, 15 June 1991, pp. 733-734.

"A Summons to Reality." *The Tablet*, 27 November 1993, pp. 1550-1552.

"Life in Christ." *The Tablet*, 2 July 1994, pp. 826-828.

"Anointing of the Sick." *Linkup* (Dublin), December 1995, p. 19.

"More Gospel, Please." *The Tablet*, 2 November 1996, p. 1439.

"Community Repentance?" *Transformation* 14, no. 4 (1997): 12-13.

"Perfect Hatred." *The Anglican* 29, no. 2 (April 2000): 21-24.

"Archbishop Rowan Williams." *Pro Ecclesia* 12 (2003): 5-9.

"Forgetting What Lies Behind, and Straining Forward to What Lies Ahead." *The Anglican* 33, no. 3 (July 2004): 24-26.

"An Act of Judgment?" *The Living Church,* 5 June 2011, pp. 20-22.

"Public Illusionists." *The Living Church,* 11 September 2011, pp. 28-31.